Sustainability in Transitio

Sustainability in Transition: Principles for Developing Solutions offers the first in-depth education-focused treatment of how to address sustainability in a comprehensive manner. The textbook is structured as a learning-centered approach to walk students through the process of linking sustainable behavior and decision-making to green innovation systems and triple-bottom-line economic development practices, in order to achieve sustainable change in incremental to transformational ways.

All chapters combine theory and practice with the help of global case study and research study examples to illustrate barriers and best practices. Each chapter begins with learning objectives and ends with a 'check on learning' section that ties the main points back to the core themes of the book. Chapters include a section focused on measuring progress and a box comparing international research or case studies to the North American focus of the chapter. A list of additional academic sources for students that complement each chapter is included.

Building sustainability tools, techniques, and competencies cumulatively with the help of problem- and project-based learning modules, *Sustainability in Transition: Principles for Developing Solutions* is a comprehensive resource for learning sustainability theory and doing sustainability practice. It will be essential reading for advanced undergraduate and graduate level students who have already completed introductory sustainability classes.

Travis Gliedt is an Assistant Professor of Geography and Environmental Sustainability at the University of Oklahoma, USA.

Kelli Larson is an Associate Professor in the School of Sustainability and the School of Geographical Sciences and Urban Planning at Arizona State University, USA.

"... ... *... y in Transition* offers a comprehensive and thorough examination of how multi-level sustainability transitions work, why they are so difficult to achieve, and what skills and strategies are needed to advance sustainable solutions. Clearly written – while not sacrificing sophistication for simplicity – this book will be accessible to a broad range of readers. The discussion of sustainability competencies – combined with the clearly articulated learning objectives and 'checks on learning'– will be helpful pedagogical resources for instructors at all levels. I highly recommend this book to anyone interested in developing a deep and nuanced understanding of sustainability or seeking to become an effective sustainability champion."

—*Jennifer H. Allen, Associate Professor,*
Mark O. Hatfield School of Government, Senior Fellow,
Institute for Sustainable Solutions, Portland
State University, USA

Sustainability in Transition

Principles for Developing Solutions

Travis Gliedt and Kelli Larson

Routledge
Taylor & Francis Group

LONDON AND NEW YORK

First published 2018
by Routledge
2 Park Square, Milton Park, Abingdon, Oxon OX14 4RN

and by Routledge
711 Third Avenue, New York, NY 10017

Routledge is an imprint of the Taylor & Francis Group, an informa business

© 2018 Travis Gliedt and Kelli Larson

British Library Cataloguing-in-Publication Data
A catalogue record for this book is available from the British Library

Library of Congress Cataloging-in-Publication Data
Names: Gliedt, Travis, author. | Larson, Kelli, author.
Title: Sustainability in transition : principles for developing solutions /
    Travis Gliedt and Kelli Larson.
Description: Abingdon, Oxon ; New York, NY : Routledge, 2018. |
    Includes bibliographical references and index.
Identifiers: LCCN 2018002774 (print) | LCCN 2018018779 (ebook) |
    ISBN 9781315537139 (eBook) | ISBN 9781138690097 (hbk) |
    ISBN 9781138690134 (pbk) | ISBN 9781315537139 (ebk)
Subjects: LCSH: Sustainability. | Economic development.
Classification: LCC HC79.E5 (ebook) | LCC HC79.E5 G5872018
    (print) | DDC 338.9/27—dc23
LC record available at https://lccn.loc.gov/2018002774

ISBN: 978-1-138-69009-7 (hbk)
ISBN: 978-1-138-69013-4 (pbk)
ISBN: 978-1-315-53713-9 (ebk)

Typeset in Bembo
by Swales & Willis Ltd, Exeter, Devon, UK
Printed by CPI Group (UK) Ltd, Croydon CR0 4YY

Visit the companion website: www.routledge.com/cw/gliedt

Contents

Tables

Figures

Acknowledgements

We are grateful for the constructive feedback on an earlier draft by Ashlee Tziganuk, Madeleine Wiens, Jesus Zubillaga, Sali Mahdy, Kaitlyn Holland, Claude Beurger, Becca Castleberry, Tyler Larson, Daniel Moses, and Kelsey Warren-Bryant. Thank you to Paul Parker, Jean Andrey, Emanuel Carvalho, Clarence Woudsma, Dawn Parker, Christina Hoicka, Jeffrey Widener, Jack Friedman, and Fred Shelley for inspiring different portions of this book through your teaching, mentoring, and collaboration. A special recognition goes to Nathan Jackson who provided detailed editing and content suggestions on the final version of the manuscript.

Glossary of terms

Accelerator centers help provide low-cost or free resources and expertise to start-ups that have graduated from incubators and are ready to scale rapidly. Often associated with or funded by universities.

Active protective space intentionally creating a supportive environment to protect niche experiments, an example being incubator centers.

Adaptive capacity resources and capabilities that allow a system to adjust to shocks and pressures including through innovation.

Adaptive co-management formal or informal collaborative governance arrangements that help in "responding to and managing feedbacks from ecosystems, instead of blocking them out . . . to avoid ecological thresholds at scales that threaten the existence of social and economic activities" (Berkes et al., 2000, p. 1260).

Agent of change individuals, organizations, partnerships, or social movements that work to create change in communities or in the regime subsystems.

Agglomeration economies financial (economies of scale), social (division of labor), and structural benefits (network benefits) that accrue to organizations because they are located in a cluster or place with many similar organizations including networks of suppliers/competitors and supportive institutional actors including universities.

Anthropocene "the time when human impacts are widespread on earth" (Barnosky et al., 2014, p. 78), including climate change, species extinctions, loss of ecosystem diversity, air, water and land pollution, and human population and material consumption levels.

Base of pyramid sustainable development strategies by organizations in developed countries focused on technology transfer, environmental remediation, or poverty reduction in developing countries.

Behavioral intention "the motivational factors that influence a behavior . . . indicators of how hard people are willing to try, of how much of an effort they are planning to exert, in order to perform the behavior" (Ajzen, 1991, p. 181).

Biophysical limits the biocapacity of land area or the carrying capacity of materials and energy throughput necessary to sustain socio-economic system functions and activities.

Boomerang effect if presented with information about how their personal consumption compares to that of their neighbors, a boomerang effect may occur whereby residents discover that their energy use levels are lower than their neighbors and consequently use more energy (Schultz et al., 2008).

Bottlenecks path dependence and lock-in characteristics of regime subsystems that slow down institutional, infrastructure, or technology change in socio-technical systems.

Boundary chains   partnerships or networks that translate and present climate science for practical consumption in municipal departments (Kalafatis et al., 2015) or in society more broadly.

Boundary object   a model, scenarios, or other tools that are used by boundary spanners to communicate science to decision-makers and other actors.

Boundary organizations   overlap the intersection of science and politics; linking agents and translators of scientific information to decision-makers.

Boundary spanners   individuals or organizations that link science to policy, or that link an organization to other actors in its external operating environment.

Business attraction strategies   triple-bottom-line economic development agents can use outreach, marketing, and engagement efforts to identify green businesses in other jurisdictions and build relationships with them as a means of convincing them to relocate. Strategies can include offering financial incentives, cheap land or buildings, prime locations next to transportation corridors or universities with high-skilled labor pools, or the opportunity to be part of a cluster that will offer the business agglomeration and reputation benefits.

Business expansion strategies   triple-bottom-line economic development agents can identify green businesses or sectors that are performing well in the community and provide support to help them grow faster. Support can include resources and capabilities and tax incentives.

Business retention strategies   triple-bottom-line economic development agents can use the same strategies as above but to focus on keeping green businesses in the community.

Cascading effects   a chain of events as a result of an act in the system.

Championing intermediaries   use their personal values as a driver of their actions. This can include supporting the learning and networking activities of the non-championing intermediaries.

Circular economy perspective   aims to reduce resource and energy use while taking waste outputs from the traditional linear economy and using them as inputs to additional production processes. It focuses on designing products and infrastructure from a lifecycle perspective and on orienting value cycles towards achieving triple-bottom-line objectives (Moreau et al., 2017).

Clean technology   new technologies and infrastructures that have lower pollution and/or higher efficiency performance than existing technologies.

Climate protection networks   international networks of cities collaborate to share information, experiences, and strategies and instruments for improving sustainability including mitigating and adapting to climate change and building resilience.

Cluster   "geographically proximate groups of interlinked individuals and organizations . . . that generate knowledge spillovers and agglomeration economies" (Catini et al., 2015, p. 1749).

Cluster champions   individuals or organizations within clusters that work to mobilize support for the cluster from external sources of knowledge and resources.

Collective action dilemma   some individuals/stakeholders within open systems consume more resources or create more pollution in the short-term to increase personal economic gains. If all individuals in a system consume at that rate, the system may collapse. Collaborative solutions may help manage resource use rates within sustainable limits.

Comfort effect homeowners do not reduce energy use even when presented with data on a real time visual display energy monitor showing high use times or potential savings because they are accustomed to a certain level of comfort-related benefits from the energy services (Hargreaves et al., 2013).

Common but differentiated responsibilities principle all countries are responsible for mitigating climate change but they have different responsibilities given the different historical contributions to greenhouse gas (GHG) emissions.

Community-based social marketing a structured process for encouraging sustainable behavior using strategies that focus on commitment, social norms, social diffusion, prompts, communication, incentives, and convenience.

Competitive advantage strategies, resources, structures, capabilities, or other factors that are hard to imitate and give an organization power or leverage over competition.

Complex adaptive cycle ongoing phases of growth, stagnation, collapse, and renewal that are found in ecological systems and socio-technical systems.

Complexity stems from the interactions and feedbacks within coupled human natural systems or socio-technical systems, which are complicated and difficult to solve and often involve tradeoffs.

Conflict stems from the numerous actors that have different views on whether to keep the system the same or to change the system through various means.

Co-production of knowledge "the process of producing useable, or actionable, science through collaboration between scientists and those who use science to make policy and management decisions" (Meadow et al., 2015, p. 179).

Creation of legitimacy function support from policy entrepreneurs, lobbyists, advocacy coalitions, or industry associations to help new technologies break into the regime subsystems while gaining momentum towards infrastructure or institutional changes.

Decoupling economic growth from GHG emissions given the historical coupling of energy and economic growth, strategies and instruments can aim to allow average incomes to increase while slowing the growth in GHG emissions through fuel substitution, efficiency gains, and behavioral conservation.

Deliberative public participation citizens can solve problems from the bottom-up.

Descriptive normative messages describe what others are doing in order to influence sustainable behavior from those who are performing worse than the norm.

Direct jobs jobs created by a new primary company or organization coming to the region or an expansion of an existing company or organization.

Disturbance ranges from minor turbulence to major shocks that threaten system collapse.

Dynamic capabilities the organizational "ability to integrate, build, and reconfigure internal and external competences to address rapidly changing environments" (Teece et al., 1997, p. 516 in Hartman et al., 2017).

Ecological economics a branch of economics that combines elements of natural resource economics, which examines questions related to resource supply, with elements of environmental economics, which examines questions related to pollution outputs. This interdisciplinary approach combines energy (laws of thermodynamics) with economic (monetary) flows to understand and prioritize a sustainable level of materials and energy throughput, then a socially just distribution of the benefits and costs of resource development, and finally after those criteria are met, an efficient allocation of resources.

Ecological footprint   a "measure of the land required for population activities taking place on the biosphere within a given year while considering the prevailing technology and resource management" (Fang et al., 2014, p. 510). It is composed of six components: cropland, grazing land, forest products, fishing grounds, built-up land, and carbon (Isman et al., 2018). The ecological footprint is expressed in global hectares (gha), which is the flow of resources produced by a hectare of average land area. An ecological footprint value below 1.7 global hectares per person suggests that a country, state/province, or city has a sustainable level of resource use rates that is supported by the level of biocapacity available (Global Footprint Network, 2017). An ecological footprint above 1.7 gha per person suggests that the jurisdiction is exceeding the level of resource replenishment rates that are considered sustainable.

Ecological modernization theory   views solving environmental problems as an opportunity for economic development based on technology and infrastructure changes.

Ecological resiliency   the capacity of natural systems to recover from shocks and absorb threats while continuing to function.

Economic efficiency   optimize resource use and minimize waste.

Economies of scale   increasing the scale of operations by for example volume or bulk purchasing discounts on supplies to reduce per unit costs of production.

Economies of scope   diversifying by for example creating multiple versions of a technology, product, or service using the same production line or innovation process.

Eco-prosumption   framed as a societal responsibility to reduce risks posed by global and local threats. It focuses on mitigation efforts (including reducing social risks) and co-producing economic and environmental value through reorganizing modes of consumption, production, and value creation (Eizenberg and Jabareen, 2017).

Energiewende   German energy transition in technology, institutions, and infrastructure.

Energy efficiency gap   the gap between economically beneficial energy investments and actual behavior.

Energy network constraints   when new renewable energy supply is added in areas with abundant solar or wind resources before the transmission grid has been expanded or upgraded to get the new supply to markets.

Energy-return-on-energy-investment (EROEI)   the amount of energy output that is gained from a given amount of energy input associated with mining, extraction, and transformation.

Energy Star   voluntary labelling program that shows consumers the energy use and costs associated with purchasing different appliances and buildings.

Entrepreneurial function   turning ideas and knowledge into products, technologies, or infrastructure experiments that can be adopted by the market.

Entrepreneurship strategies   turning ideas into products, services, or technologies with the help of experiments.

Environmental champions   individuals within organizations or communities who work to improve the sustainability performance of the organization or the community in line with their personal sustainability values.

Environmental stewardship   responsible use of land and natural resources based on ethical or moral responsibilities.

Evolutionary institutionalism   how institutions adapt and change over time as a result of "habits, conventions, attitudes or simply the routines that define institutions" (Hayter, 2008, p. 834).

Extended producer responsibility   producers are responsible for the sustainability impacts of their products and technologies after the sale and until the end of its lifecycle.

Factor 4 theory   to achieve sustainability of materials and energy use, a 75 percent cut in resource and energy use while doubling wealth creation is required (von Weizsäcker et al., 1998).

Factor 10 theory   to achieve sustainability of materials and energy use, a massive decrease in energy use and material flows (by a factor of 10) in addition to a massive increase in efficiency (by a factor of 10) is required (Schmidt-Bleek, 2008).

Feedback loops   outputs of a system are returned to the system as inputs.

Feed-in tariff   a program where the government pays individual homeowners or organizations a set price per kilowatt hour to generate renewable energy (often from solar or wind) on their property and sell it back through the grid. This can include 20-year contracts to provide a stable income for the distributed producers. These programs help create new supply without having to build costly centralized generation options like nuclear or natural gas plants.

First movers and early adopters   entrepreneurs and organizations that create or adopt new technologies, capabilities, or strategies before the mainstream. See also consumers that are the innovators and early adopters in Rogers' (2010) diffusion of innovations theory.

Food hubs   "urban facilities that engage in aggregation (which can include growing), preparation, distribution, and marketing of food" (Martin et al., 2016, p. 13).

Free riders   the stakeholders/individuals that benefit when other stakeholders/individuals take actions to reduce environmental pollution.

Greenhouse gas emissions   anthropogenic GHG emissions include carbon dioxide (CO_2), methane, nitrous oxide, chlorofluorocarbons, and hydrofluorocarbons that are emitted by human activities like fossil fuel combustion and land-use changes. GHG emissions lead to concentrations in the atmosphere that absorb and trap radiant energy and heat, which regulates changes to global average temperatures. Other important greenhouse gases are water vapor and ozone. Although methane has a higher global warming potential than CO_2, CO_2 is emitted in much greater quantities due to human activities and therefore is a core focus for sustainability professionals.

Green new urbanism   an integrated set of principles to guide sustainable urban development.

Green state theory   government and governance frameworks focused on strong sustainability and the non-substitutability of natural capital and ecosystem services.

Governance systems   formal or informal arrangements of actors working towards managing or guiding systems inclusive of government and non-governmental actions as well as institutions and policies.

Guidance of the search function   activities that frame the needs and expectations of organizational actors concerning new technology or infrastructure innovations.

Human Development Index (HDI)   a composite index that combines income, health, and education, and is calculated every year for countries (UNDP, 2017).

Incremental   minor or slow improvements to technology, infrastructure, or institutions that can directly or indirectly lead to sustainability value.

Incubators   they provide low-cost or free services and resources to help entrepreneurs turn ideas into innovations and then into businesses. They are often associated with or funded by municipalities or universities.

Indirect jobs   jobs that are created by secondary companies or organizations that supply parts or services to the primary company or organization.

Induced jobs   jobs that are created by tertiary companies or organizations that support and provide services to employees of the primary or secondary companies.

Industrial ecology systems   managing material and energy flows within industrial production systems.

Industry associations   many firms or organizations in the same industry collaborate and share resources to form a common front as a means of gaining political power.

Inertia   an object at rest tends to stay at rest, and an object in motion tends to stay in motion.

Injunctive normative messages   highlight behaviors that others approve or disapprove of.

Innovation intermediaries   organizations that support entrepreneurs and small organizations that are creating new technologies, products, or services.

Innovation strategies   supply chain management, operations management, research and development, and marketing initiatives focused on creating new technology or process changes that can generate sustainability value.

Institutional economics   considers the role of institutions in shaping economic behavior.

Institutional gatekeepers   institutional actors like governments and governance organizations that promote the transfer of knowledge within and between clusters.

Institutional thickness   collection of countercultural institutions, networks, groups, and practices that characterizes places including green clusters (Longhurst, 2015).

Institutions   formal and informal rules, norms, and guiding principles.

Instruments   see *strategies and instruments*.

Intermediary subsystem   a new subsystem of the regime that includes organizations and actors specifically focused on learning and networking between niche and regime actors.

Internet of things   the internet is connected to devices and appliances using a network of sensors that can send and receive information automatically. It can be used for smart homes, smart grids, building automation, and self-driving vehicles.

Intervention points   key moments/points on unsustainable pathways where strategies and instruments can help to change course towards more sustainable pathways.

Intra–organizational boundary shaking   champions or intrapreneurs attempt to gain support for an initiative from others within the organization thereby altering the status quo (Smink et al., 2015).

ISO certification systems   criteria and certification systems for total quality management in an organization. Helps organizations minimize costs and reduce environmental impacts.

Job creation multiplier effects   the number of indirect and induced jobs that result from each new direct job created by triple–bottom–line economic development strategies and instruments.

KAYA Identity   a method for measuring progress towards sustainability–oriented socio–technical system transitions where growth in CO_2 emissions = population growth rate + economic development growth rate (gross domestic product [GDP]/population) + rate of change in energy efficiency (energy/GDP) + rate of change in carbon intensity (CO_2/energy). The implication is that reducing emissions will require improvements in the energy intensity and carbon intensity rates by more than the percentage increase in population and economic development. This method therefore relates progress directly to technology and infrastructure change.

Knowledge development function   research and development and other formal and informal types of learning.

Knowledge diffusion function   using networks, partnerships, and organizational structures to share knowledge and learning about entrepreneurial experiments with other key actors who could help scale those experiments through the market.

Laboratories of democracy   experiments in sustainability or climate change legislation creation and implementation between states and cities as a formal or informal competition to improve efficiency and effectiveness.

Laboratories of innovation   experiments in sustainability or climate change mitigation technology creation and implementation between states and cities as a formal or informal competition to improve efficiency and effectiveness.

Laboratories of opposition   state governments, leaders, and institutional regimes using policies to slow down transitions to more sustainable energy systems.

Landscape   in the multi-level perspective, the landscape is the external pressures that influence or drive changes in the regime. They are often considered beyond the direct control of regime actors, and can include oil price shocks, natural disasters, wars, and global recessions.

Landscape awareness   a capability of transition actors to identify and capitalize on external pressures during windows of opportunity.

LEED   a labeling system to guide builders, architects, and engineers in making more environmentally sustainable buildings. It can also encourage consumers to purchase more environmentally sustainable buildings.

Legitimacy   the acceptance of a government or governance arrangement to make changes and influence outcomes in socio-technical systems.

Lifecycle analysis   an assessment of the full environmental impacts of a product, infrastructure, or program including material and energy inputs and waste and pollution outputs.

Lifecycle sustainability assessment   used to evaluate the cradle-to-cradle economic, social, and environmental impacts of a product, technology, or infrastructure.

Market formation function   niche protection functions that protect and allow new technologies to develop.

Micro-grids   distributed energy systems that combine renewable energy, supply options, and automation.

Model legislation   sample bills written by lobbyists from the fossil fuel industry that are provided to politicians and passed into law. It is a means of pressuring lawmakers to support bills in line with the existing regime.

Multi-level perspective (MLP)   a framework to understand changes to socio-technical systems as driven by changes in the niche, regime, and landscape levels. These are not governance levels, but rather, functional levels that increase in the structure and stability as you move from niche to landscape. The speed of change that can occur decreases as you move from niche to regime to landscape. See Loorbach et al. (2017) for a detailed review of the MLP and its components and functions.

Natural resource curse   "the paradox that countries endowed with natural resources such as oil, natural gas, minerals etc. tend to have lower economic growth and worse development outcomes than countries with fewer natural resources" (Badeeb et al., 2017, p. 124).

Negative externality pollution created as a result of economic activity within a socio-economic system that is not accounted for in prices but has negative impacts on stakeholders, natural capital, or human-made capital. The interdependence between one actor's actions and its impacts on another actor.

Neoclassical economics this is the conventional approach to economics that focuses on supply and demand relationships as an invisible hand that guides the economy, where rational actors including consumers and producers respond to price fluctuations in free and open markets.

Niche in the multi-level perspective, niches are composed of, protect, and scale-up new technologies and solutions to societal problems. There are many niches within a single regime.

Niche actors organizations or individuals working to create new technologies, products, services through experiments as part of entrepreneurship processes.

Niche creation the process of developing a supportive environment for creating technologies and solutions.

Niche empowerment strategies that aim to support niche experiments either in the context of the existing regime or with the help of regime changes (Smith and Raven, 2012).

Niche experiments processes that help create new technologies and solutions to societal problems that can also generate revenue and/or profit.

Niche nurturing processes social learning, social networks, and institutional factors that support and accelerate technology and solution expansion.

Niche protection functions that can support and enable new technologies and organizations to scale-up while being protected from market forces.

Niche shielding the financial and resource support that can protect innovations from market forces by reducing transaction costs in the early stages of development (Huijben et al., 2016).

Niche-to-regime interactions that occur when research and development investments made by an organization lead to green technologies/solutions that can influence environmental performance changes in the industry and society in general.

NIMBY Not In My Back Yard. The theory that people are willing to accept changes in society as long as they do not directly impact them in an actual or perceived negative way.

Non-championing intermediaries facilitate learning through education, advice, knowledge sharing, and creating spaces for new ideas, while using networking skills to mobilize resources and connect different project actors. They do not use their personal values as a driver of their actions.

Non-intermediary champions use their personal values as a driver of their actions, but do not carry out learning or networking activities.

Non-linearity outputs or outcomes of processes within coupled human-natural systems or socio-technical systems may be difficult to predict based on the quantity or nature of inputs to the system.

Panarchy a nested set of complex adaptive cycles that attempts to explain change and resilience in a multi-level system. It is different than but combines elements of hierarchy (structured change) and anarchy (unstructured change).

Participatory action research researchers work with community members, business leaders, and government actors to examine the process of solving problems while solving the problems.

Participatory integrated assessments   including stakeholders in the entire process of a project from design to implementation and assessment.

Passive protective space   pre-existing conditions that were not intentionally created but can serve to protect a niche experiment from market forces, an example being creating a renewable energy and storage system in a remote off-grid community as an alternative to expensive diesel fuel imports.

Perceived behavioral control   the level of difficulty of executing the behavior based on past experiences and various barriers (Ajzen, 1991).

Personal responsibility   individuals feel they have a duty to care for the environment and make sustainable decisions.

Political influence strategies   focus on shaping or influencing changes to policies that will align with the organizations innovation and business strategies.

Political opportunity structure   the policy and institutional subsystems of the regime that can enable or constrain sustainability strategies and instruments by organizations.

Policy entrepreneurs   government or governance actors who "try to effect change" to policies or institutions and who "use their agency to do so" by "using the resources and strategies available to them to achieve their desired outcome" (Green, 2017, p. 1473).

Policy mixes   collections of complimentary policies designed to simultaneously encourage niche experiments and regime destruction to accelerate a sustainability transition.

Polycentric organizations   no central authority or hierarchy, but rather, many organizations of different sizes and relatively similar power dynamics.

Post-materialism   a theory that individuals, groups, or societies may emphasize or value quality of life improvements over economic and material gains.

Proactive environmental management   taking sustainability actions within an organization voluntarily without being coerced by regulations.

Problem- and project-based learning   "students investigate a real-world problem and work on solution options to this problem by engaging in small-group work (ideally in an interdisciplinary team) to which instructors contribute as coaches for the teams" (Brundiers and Wiek, 2013, p. 1727).

Product service systems   frameworks for viewing the product lifecycle as a circular economy where producers and consumers are engaged in the process of "reworking the ways products and services are calibrated to meet human needs" (Hobson, 2016, p. 97).

Product stewardship   managing the sustainability implications during each stage of production where suppliers voluntarily take ownership of the environmental and social impacts throughout the product lifecycle.

Property Assessed Clean Energy (PACE)   commercial or residential owners can pay for renewable energy or energy efficiency upgrades over time as part of an increase in their property value and resulting taxes. See http://pacenation.us/ for more details.

Prosumption   a process where citizens (consumers) and organizations (producers) aim to co-create value (Hobson, 2016).

Radical   major or rapid improvements to technology, infrastructure, or institutions that can directly lead to sustainability value.

Rapid assessment processes   uses teams to conduct field work and carry out triangulation techniques to examine situations and inform policy.

Rebound effects   monetary savings that result from energy efficiency investments are spent on further energy using technologies. Behavior changes can also erode the energy savings and in some cases, can lead to an increase in energy relative to the pre-retrofit levels.

Reconfiguration approach attempts to combine elements of the reformist and revolutionary approaches to simultaneously reshape production and consumption behavior in the direction of sustainability.

Reflexivity circular relationships where the direction of cause and effect is not clear or may change over time.

Reformist approach aims to accelerate innovation through interventions at the supply and demand side based on rational economic principles.

Regime in the multi-level perspective, the regime is the combination of economic, political, policy, institutional, social, cultural, technology, industry, and science subsystems that represent the dominant and locked-in socio-technical system. There are many regimes within a single landscape.

Regime actors organizations or individuals working to create change in the subsystems including culture, institutions, policy, politics, economics, industry, science, which could support niche actors in creating technologies and pairing them with ongoing institutional and infrastructure changes.

Regime change altering the regime subsystems to the point where they are no longer recognizable and moved from an unsustainable pathway to a sustainable pathway.

Regime destruction processes aiming to weaken or alter the regime subsystems to increase the likelihood that niche experiments can break through and change the institutions and infrastructure of the socio-technical system.

Regime stability results from the "active resistance by incumbent actors" (Geels, 2014, p. 23) reflecting the role of power dynamics between actors. It contributes to the lock-in and path dependence of regime subsystems.

Regime-to-niche interactions that occur when institutional pressures and industry factors influence organizations to undertake sustainability innovation.

Regional open innovation road mapping a process to plan a regional innovation strategy from entrepreneurship to business development and technology diffusion.

Regulationist approach governance and institutions can help guide the direction of technological innovation and development with enabling policies based on a normative sustainability goal or a strategic vision.

Renewable portfolio standard requires energy system actors such as utilities to produce a set percentage of their electricity from renewable sources, which may include wind, solar, wave, tidal, or biofuels. The renewable portfolio standard is a regulation that can be strengthened over time to encourage innovation.

Reserves the amount of a natural resource that is believed to be economically recoverable with current technology levels.

Reserve-to-production ratio the number of years that reserves will last at current production rates.

Resilience the ability of a system to absorb and respond to shocks while returning to its original structure or function.

Resource mobilization function niche expansion functions that help attract public or private investment and resources to scale-up the technology or infrastructure innovation.

Resources the amount of a natural resource that is in the ground.

Resource systems the physical systems that support the stocks and flows of resource units, which include food, energy, and water systems.

Resource units characteristics of natural resources including physical and energy units and economic value.

Resource users social and economic characteristics of actors within governance systems.

Revolutionary approach considers the need for alternative political-economic systems to capitalism that may be based on frugality, sufficiency, and localism principles. Uses ethical, spiritual, social, and eco-centric arguments to suggest that the scale of the current system of production and consumption needs to be reduced to become sustainable.

R-value a measure of the resistance to heat flow of insulation for attics, walls, foundations; higher values are more resistant to heat flow and can therefore reduce heat loss and lower energy bills during heating season, while keeping cool air inside the home during cooling season. R-values do have a point of diminishing returns beyond which adding a new unit of insulation will provide a decreasing energy and cost savings. A professional energy audit can help determine the amount of insulation that will provide the greatest economic benefit.

Social enterprise non-profit organizations that operate like a business with plans and strategies and may deliver services for fees, but do not take a profit, rather, reinvest revenues into program or service delivery.

Social sufficiency meeting needs based on normative goals or non-economic criteria for success.

Socio-political environment includes policy makers, civil society, activists, advocacy coalitions, and grassroots movements.

Social movement theory attempts to explain why and how social mobilization occurs in society.

Social practices views decisions as habits that are ingrained and shaped by people's abilities and understanding, the physical world (e.g., infrastructure, technology), and social context (e.g., culture, norms, institutions) (Leray et al., 2016).

Socio-cultural strategies include public relations and advertising campaigns used by organizations to respond to pressures from the socio-political environment.

Socio-technical system a framework for studying the integrated and coupled nature of changes to institutions, technologies, infrastructures, and social practices as part of niches, regimes, and landscapes.

Socio-technical solutions strategies or instruments influence changes to practices, technologies, infrastructures, and institutions that solve sustainability problems.

Strategic learning "the organization's capacity to retool rapidly to create and execute new strategy through learning at the individual and system levels in response to changes and uncertainties in complex environments" (Moon and Lee, 2015, p. 630).

Strategic niche management is a structured and planned approach involving multiple phases to identify opportunities and build teams of actors interested in niche creation as a means of initiating or supporting a sustainability transition and to guide the process of creating and scaling-up new technologies/solutions.

Strategic sustainability integrating sustainability into organizational strategy to address sustainability issues or solve sustainability problems as an opportunity to improve organizational performance and gain a competitive advantage.

Strategies and instruments interventions by organizations, governments, or governance arrangements designed to encourage, support, or enable sustainability transitions. Strategies can be created by businesses and non-profits to pursue strong sustainability, while instruments can be created by governments to guide and encourage changes by actors within society to pursue strong sustainability.

Strong sustainability   for sustainability to be achieved, the stocks of human and social capital, human-made capital, *and* ecological capital must each be maintained or increase over time in a particular region.

Subjective norms   the degree to which an individual perceives that important people in their life would either approve or disapprove of the behavior.

Substantive actions   actual investments of resources into technologies or processes (Penna and Geels, 2015).

Subsystems of the regime   include cultural (e.g., customs and collective social behavior), scientific (e.g., science and education), political (e.g., political parties and actors), governance (e.g., municipal and regional administration), industrial (e.g., business competition or cooperation), intermediaries (e.g., labor unions, chambers of commerce, network connectors), financial (e.g., funding, venture capital, banks), and civil society (e.g., non-governmental organizations, mobilized citizens) processes composed of structures and actors (Mattes et al., 2015).

Sustainability competencies   combinations of skills, experiences, and knowledge that can be developed and applied to understand and encourage sustainability.

Sustainability indicators   individual measures of progress towards one or more components of socio-technical system change.

Sustainability jobs   generate sustainability value either directly or indirectly by providing capacity for other people or communities to do so.

Sustainability metrics   an integrated system of measurement combining multiple indicators that can be tracked to understand progress towards sustainability.

Sustainability professionals   individuals or collections of people who work to advance sustainability principles and encourage transitions to strong sustainability pathways in organizations, communities, and countries.

Sustainability science   a transdisciplinary field working to understand interactions between coupled human natural systems in order to encourage sustainability transitions in socio-technical systems.

Sustainability sector   composed of technology manufacturing or service jobs that directly or indirectly generate sustainability value.

Sustainability value   in line with the strong sustainability definition, sustainability value is created only if economic, social, and environmental value are each enhanced or maintained.

Sustainable behavior   new or alternative behaviors that lead to integrated economic, social, and environmental benefits.

Sustainable development   development that meets the needs of the present generation without compromising the ability of future generations to meet their needs.

Sustainable innovations orientation   the sustainability-oriented research and development intensity, which can be measured by the sustainability-related research and development expenditures made by the business divided by sales revenue per year (Varadarajan, 2017).

Sustainable niche experiments   the process of creating technologies and solutions that generate sustainability value.

Sustainable product innovation   "a firm's introduction of a new product or modification of an existing product whose environmental impact during the lifecycle of the product, spanning resource extraction, production, distribution, use, and post-use disposal, is significantly lower than existing products for which it is a substitute" (Varadarajan, 2017, p. 17).

Symbolic changes use communication, marketing, and lobbying to frame climate change or other sustainability issues in a light favorable to the organization. Technology development can also be used for symbolic purposes to enhance public reputation or to pre-empt and avoid regulations (Penna and Geels, 2015).

Techno-economic paradigm "articulated through the use of the new technologies as they diffuse, that multiplies their impact across the economy and eventually also modifies the way socio-institutional structures are organized" (Perez, 2010, p. 194).

Technological innovation systems framework views innovation as a process based on seven interrelated functions: entrepreneurship, knowledge development and research and development, knowledge diffusion, guidance of the search, market formation and development, resource mobilization including incubating and accelerating innovations, and the creation of legitimacy achieved in part due to the innovation influencing changes to institutions and infrastructures (Markard and Truffer, 2008).

Tradeoffs some strategies or instruments that increase human capital and human-made capital could accelerate the rate of depletion of natural capital.

Traditional ecological knowledge (TEK) a collective and cumulative "body of knowledge, practices and beliefs about the relationships among living things (including humans), the physical environment, and a society's culture" (Falkowski et al., 2015, p. 40).

Transaction costs market and non-market costs associated with buying and selling goods and services.

Transformative capacity the extent that a new technology has the potential to alter the subsystems of the regime and encourage new connections between niche and regime actors (Augenstein, 2015).

Transition arena formal or informal organizations or networks of actors interested in creating or supporting sustainability-oriented changes to socio-technical systems.

Transition management a formal approach to changing socio-technical systems that integrates top-down or bottom-up approaches, learning from experiments, and develops adaptive capacity for adjusting to shocks and pressures (Foxon et al., 2009).

Transitions changes to socio-technical systems that alter institutions and infrastructures in the direction of sustainability principles.

Transition towns grassroots environmental movements in response to landscape pressures of climate change and peak oil.

Transparency openness and accountability of policy making or governance processes by allowing the public and other stakeholders to view or participate in the process.

Triple-bottom-line economic development "programs, policies, or activities designed to create or retain jobs and wealth in ways that contribute to environmental, social, and economic well-being over time" (Hammer and Pivo, 2017, p. 3). To be consistent with strong sustainability, economic, social, and environmental well-being must be maintained or enhanced.

Turbulence bumps or shocks that test system resilience.

Uncertainty stems from the challenge of understanding complex interactions and associated future outcomes.

Upcycling the process of transforming what was considered waste into useful materials or technologies (McDonough and Braungart, 2013).

Value chains a series of steps from raw material extraction and processing to transportation and manufacturing and then to delivery and use by consumers. Each step is an opportunity for businesses to add economic value to increase returns.

Each step is also an opportunity to increase sustainability value by reducing materials, energy, and water consumption.

Value cycles value chains can be extended into value cycles that encourage reuse and recycling waste into inputs as part of closed-loop industrial ecology systems.

Voluntary-to-mandatory escalator mechanisms can be incorporated into international agreements or national laws. The idea is to encourage countries to strengthen voluntary agreements over time by adding penalties or incentives after a certain number of years or mandating that sustainability outcomes are achieved by the inclusion of additional strategies and instruments after a given date.

Water rights water laws that determine the amount of water that users including property owners can draw from rivers, streams, or aquifers.

Water rights stacking some jurisdictions allow water users to stack multiple water uses (e.g., for environmental use like fishing and recreation, or diversion for uses like irrigation) for the same water right to allow flexibility for how the water is used in a given year.

Weak sustainability frameworks allow for natural capital to be depleted if it is compensated for by increases in human or human-made capital.

Window of opportunity a moment when change to the regime subsystems is more likely or when accelerating sustainability transitions is possible due to external pressures from the landscape aligning with the creation of new technologies from the niche level.

References

Ajzen, I. (1991). The theory of planned behavior. *Organization Behavior and Human Decision Processes*, 50, 179–211.

Augenstein, K. (2015). Analysing the potential for sustainable e-mobility: The case of Germany. *Environmental Innovation and Societal Transitions*, 14, 101–115.

Badeeb, R. A., Lean, H. H., & Clark, J. (2017). The evolution of the natural resource curse thesis: A critical literature survey. *Resources Policy*, 51, 123–134.

Barnosky, A. D., Brown, J. H., Daily, G. C., Dirzo, R., Ehrlich, A. H., Ehrlich, P. R., . . . & Wake, M. H. (2014). Introducing the scientific consensus on maintaining humanity's life support systems in the 21st century: Information for policy makers. *The Anthropocene Review*, 1(1), 78–109.

Berkes, F., Colding, J., & Folke, C. (2000). Rediscovery of traditional ecological knowledge as adaptive management. *Ecological Applications*, 10(5), 1251–1262.

Brundiers, K., & Wiek, A. (2013). Do we teach what we preach? An international comparison of problem-and project-based learning courses in sustainability. *Sustainability*, 5(4), 1725–1746.

Catini, R., Karamshuk, D., Penner, O., & Riccaboni, M. (2015). Identifying geographic clusters: A network analytic approach. *Research Policy*, 44(9), 1749–1762.

Eizenberg, E., & Jabareen, Y. (2017). Social sustainability: A new conceptual framework. *Sustainability*, 9(1), 68.

Falkowski, T. B., Martinez-Bautista, I., & Diemont, S. A. (2015). How valuable could traditional ecological knowledge education be for a resource-limited future? An energy evaluation in two Mexican villages. *Ecological Modelling*, 300, 40–49.

Fang, K., Heijungs, R., & de Snoo, G. R. (2014). Theoretical exploration for the combination of the ecological, energy, carbon, and water footprints: Overview of a footprint family. *Ecological Indicators*, 36, 508–518.

Foxon, T. J., Reed, M. S., & Stringer, L. C. (2009). Governing long-term social–ecological change: What can the adaptive management and transition management approaches learn from each other? *Environmental Policy and Governance*, 19(1), 3–20.

Geels, F. (2014). Regime resistance against low-carbon energy transitions: Introducing politics and power into the multi-level perspective. *Theory, Culture, and Society*, 31(5), 21–40.

Global Footprint Network. (2017). What is your ecological footprint? *Personal Footprint Calculator.* Available at: www.footprintcalculator.org/

Green, J. F. (2017). Policy entrepreneurship in climate governance: Toward a comparative approach. *Environment and Planning C: Politics and Space*, 35(8), 1471–1482.

Hammer, J., & Pivo, G. (2017). The triple bottom line and sustainable economic development theory and practice. *Economic Development Quarterly*, 31(1), 25–36.

Hargreaves, T., Nye, M., & Burgess, J. (2013). Keeping energy visible? Exploring how householders interact with feedback from smart energy monitors in the longer term. *Energy Policy*, 52, 126–134.

Hartman, P., Gliedt. T., Widener, J., & Loraamm, R. (2017). Dynamic capabilities for water system transitions in Oklahoma. *Environmental Innovation and Societal Transitions*, 25, 64–81.

Hayter, R. (2008). Environmental economic geography. *Geography Compass*, 2(3), 831–850.

Hobson, K. (2016). Closing the loop or squaring the circle? Locating generative spaces for the circular economy. *Progress in Human Geography*, 40(1), 88–104.

Huijben, J. C. C. M., Verbong, G. P. J., & Podoynitsyna, K. S. (2016). Mainstreaming solar: Stretching the regulatory regime through business model innovation. *Environmental Innovation and Societal Transitions*, 20, 1–15.

Isman, M., Archambault, M., Konga, C. N., Lin, D., Iha, K., & Ouellet-Plamondon, C. (2018). Ecological Footprint assessment for targeting climate change mitigation in cities: A case study of 15 Canadian cities according to census metropolitan areas (CMA). *Journal of Cleaner Production*, 174, 1032–1043.

Kalafatis, S. E., Grace, A., & Gibbons, E. (2015). Making climate science accessible in Toledo: The linked boundary chain approach. *Climate Risk Management*, 9, 30–40.

Loorbach, D., Frantzeskaki, N., & Avelino, F. (2017). Sustainability transitions research: Transforming science and practice for societal change. *Annual Review of Environment and Resources*, 42(1), 599–626.

Longhurst, N. (2015). Towards an 'alternative' geography of innovation: Alternative milieu, socio-cognitive protection and sustainability experimentation. *Environmental Innovation and Societal Transitions*, 17, 183–198.

Markard, J., & Truffer, B. (2008). Technological innovation systems and the multi-level perspective: Towards an integrated framework. *Research Policy*, 37(4), 596–615.

Martin, G., Clift, R., & Christie, I. (2016). Urban cultivation and its contributions to sustainability: Nibbles of food but oodles of social capital. *Sustainability*, 8(5), 409.

Mattes, J., Huber, A., & Koehrsen, J. (2015). Energy transitions in small-scale regions: What we can learn from a regional innovation systems perspective. *Energy Policy*, 78, 255–264.

McDonough, W., & Braungart, M. (2013). *The Upcycle: Beyond Sustainability: Designing for Abundance*. North Point Press, New York, NY.

Meadow, A. M., Ferguson, D. B., Guido, Z., Horangic, A., Owen, G., & Wall, T. (2015). Moving toward the deliberate coproduction of climate science knowledge. *Weather, Climate, and Society*, 7(2), 179–191.

Moon, H., & Lee, C. (2015). Strategic learning capability: Through the lens of environmental jolts. *European Journal of Training and Development*, 39(7), 628–640.

Moreau, V., Sahakian, M., Griethuysen, P., & Vuille, F. (2017). Coming full circle: Why social and institutional dimensions matter for the circular economy. *Journal of Industrial Ecology*, 21(3), 498–506.

Penna, C. C., & Geels, F. W. (2015). Climate change and the slow reorientation of the American car industry (1979–2012): An application and extension of the Dialectic Issue LifeCycle (DILC) model. *Research Policy*, 44(5), 1029–1048.

Perez, C. (2010). Technological revolutions and techno-economic paradigms. *Cambridge Journal of Economics*, 34(1), 185–202.

Rogers, E. M. (2010). *Diffusion of Innovations*. 4th Edition. Simon and Schuster, The Free Press, New York, NY.

Schmidt-Bleek, F. (2008). Factor 10: The future of stuff. *Sustainability: Science, Practice & Policy,* 4(1), 1–4.

Schultz, W. P., Khazian, A. M., & Zaleski, A. C. (2008). Using normative social influence to promote conservation among hotel guests. *Social Influence,* 3(1), 4–23.

Smink, M., Negro, S. O., Niesten, E., & Hekkert, M. P. (2015). How mismatching institutional logics hinder niche–regime interaction and how boundary spanners intervene. *Technological Forecasting and Social Change,* 100, 225–237.

Smith, A., & Raven, R. (2012). What is protective space? Reconsidering niches in transitions to sustainability. *Research Policy,* 41(6), 1025–1036.

Teece, D.J., Pisano, G., Shuen, A. (1997). Dynamic capabilities and strategic management. *Strategic Management Journal,* 18(7), 509–533.

UNDP. (2017). Human Rights Reports. Public Data Explorer. *Human Development Index Public Data Tool.* Available at: http://hdr.undp.org/en/data-explorer

Varadarajan, R. (2017). Innovating for sustainability: A framework for sustainable innovations and a model of sustainable innovations orientation. *Journal of the Academy of Marketing Science,* 45(1), 14–36.

von Weizsäcker, E. U., Lovins, A. B., & Lovins, L. H. (1998). *Factor Four: Doubling Wealth-Halving Resource Use: The New Report to the Club of Rome.* Earthscan, New York, NY.

1 Strong sustainability principles and competencies

Learning objectives

- Outline a set of principles that provide a more comprehensive understanding of sustainability than the three pillars perspective
- Describe sub-principles of sustainability that are measurable at the level of energy or water systems
- Discuss competencies of sustainability that form the core of sustainability science
- Build a framework for solutions-oriented sustainability transitions
- Compare strong sustainability pathways containing different sets of strategies and instruments
- Define problem- and project-based learning as a means of achieving sustainability solutions

Origins of sustainability

Humans have always been interested in the environment that surrounds us. From the dawn of time to the end of great civilizations, humans and the natural environment have and will always be coupled. Researchers across a broad spectrum of fields have dedicated their careers to studying these relationships between society and physical systems. In fact, many university departments and government funding institutions around the world now focus their energies on questions related to socio-ecological system functions, and transitions. Yet despite growing academic knowledge and continually accumulating practical experiences of governments, businesses, and civil society, it is abundantly clear that society and the various actors focused on sustainability have failed to formulate and solve a sustainability equation. Reasons for this failure include the inability to agree on what sustainability means and how we should get there, the lack of strategies and instruments necessary to achieve sustainability, and the unwillingness to prioritize sustainability over other societal challenges.

Defining the concept of sustainability has become a politically charged and often futile endeavor. Debate persists as to whether sustainability is a single discipline or an interdisciplinary field or is rather a collection of efforts from multiple disciplines with little coordination between approaches and methods. Sustainability has become a buzzword used by many actors because of its broad appeal, and yet few examples exist to demonstrate multi-level sustainability transitions of coupled physical and human systems that are based on an integrated set of sustainability principles. Rather than making radical system changes, interventions more often focus on politically feasible and cost-effective incremental changes that represent business-as-usual pathways known as *weak sustainability*. These weak sustainability pathways allow tradeoffs between the economic, social, and environmental components of sustainability. Policies may lead to job creation, business attraction, or public safety improvements that enhance economic and/or social criteria by for example increasing the gross domestic product (GDP) or reducing the number of vehicle deaths. The side effect of these policies is that the performance of environmental criteria may decline by, for example, the destruction of natural capital or an increase in pollution levels associated with producing more human-made capital infrastructure and technologies.

Another major challenge that limits sustainability progress is the gap between the use of systems theory and modelling approaches by physical scientists and the attempts by social scientists and decision-makers to understand and in some cases support governance changes. Closing this gap is necessary to achieve a transition towards sustainability. What types of processes are needed to link science, technology, engineering, and math (STEM) frameworks to social sciences, humanities, anthropology, and political economy (SHAPE) frameworks in order to adjust our place within the world regarding sustainability? Finding a way to balance the *positive dimensions* (e.g., what the data and models tell us is occurring) with the *normative dimensions* (e.g., what we believe should occur) of sustainability science is critical to ensuring that the interconnections between systems and how to manage them become clear. Doing so may require a new type of *sustainability professional*, but what would a sustainability professional look like? What are the necessary skills and competencies that schools of all levels should be teaching? If business leaders seek a competitive advantage from sustainability, what employee characteristics do they look for? If government leaders are interested in the sustainability of their communities and jurisdictions, what decision-making tools and skills would help achieve their goals?

Alternative concepts to sustainability may be easier to measure or more straightforward to achieve, but most give preference to economic or social criteria relative to environmental imperatives. Even when global ecological footprint analyses tell us that we are overshooting our capacity to sustain ourselves, we continue to do so because it is what our systems are designed to do. Science tells us that we are in trouble, and social science attempts to tell us how to get out of trouble. And yet, even our best experts on human behavior and organizational theory are only beginning to establish approaches to help mitigate the challenges of climate change and biodiversity loss, let alone water shortages and food insecurity. One goal for sustainability professionals is to find new ways to convince citizens to solve challenges that are partly of their own making without shaming and blaming them.

Humans are both complex and yet incredibly simple creatures. The simplicity comes from our common desire for things that make us safe, productive, and successful. We know what these things are (e.g., homes, employment, roads, and other infrastructure) and have become effective producers of them. The complexity stems from disagreement on the definition of, and order of preference for, the necessary capabilities to make these things (e.g., human capital, social capital, institutional capital, natural capital). How did we get to a point where tradeoffs are made and accepted between capabilities that can improve safety, productivity, and success? We know now better than at any point in human history how systems function, as well as the impacts of destroying the functions and services provided by systems. However, we still do it, undermining our capabilities to continue to be able to produce things that make us safe, productive, and successful. Addressing this conundrum is the fundamental challenge of sustainability and the focus of this book.

In order to approach solving this puzzle, we must first build a definition and a framework for sustainability. Many countries and their leaders have played key roles in shaping the field of sustainability. From Gro Harlem Brundtland of Norway helping to define sustainable development as *development that meets the needs of the present without compromising the ability of future generations to meet their needs*, to Angela Merkel of Germany presiding over a sustainability transition based on green innovation, to the various researchers and academics who have worked hand-in-hand with societal actors to define *sustainability transition theory through practice* in the Netherlands, there is no shortage of sustainability champions in just about every country on earth. While early conceptions of sustainability focused on resource use and depletion, which was often related to population growth or the impact of technology on resource use rates, more recent integrated conceptions center on linking physical systems science and social systems science to recognize constraints (e.g., bio-physical and socio-political) while focusing on solutions (e.g., technology and policy innovation).

Figure 1.1 shows four common frameworks for understanding sustainability. The first (A) is a stool to represent sustainability as *balancing* economic, social, and environmental interests. This would imply that if one leg of the stool is underperforming, the entire stool may collapse. The second (B) is a pyramid, which suggests that economic and social systems rely on environmental systems for *stability*. The third (C) is the often-used Venn diagram, which implies that sustainability is achieved by focusing on the central overlapping section. Weak sustainability could be achieved by focusing on the overlap between two of the circles, for example, socio-economic, socio-environmental, or eco-environmental.

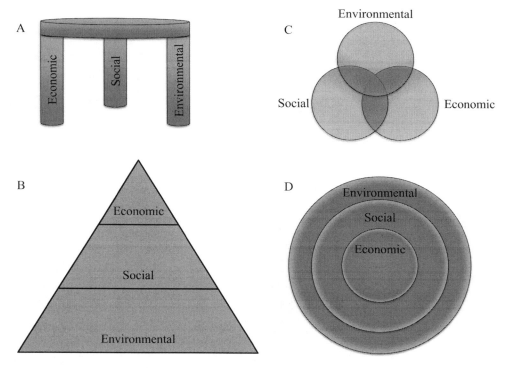

Figure 1.1 Frameworks for sustainability

Source: Authors' rendition.

A drawback of (A) and (C) is that they emphasize *tradeoffs* between the three pillars. For example, increases in human capital (the social circle) and human-made capital (the economic circle) could accelerate the rate of depletion of natural capital (the environmental circle). While accepting tradeoffs is often necessary to gain agreement from actors including business leaders and politicians who aim to maximize social and economic benefits in the short-term, it implies that each pillar is equal in importance. In contrast, the fourth framework (D) is frequently alluded to by ecological economists and Anthropocene researchers to highlight that economic development is dependent upon the social system, and furthermore, that the socio-economic system is limited by the natural capital and ecosystem services provided by the environment. Framework (D) implies that the environment/natural system is fundamental to the social and economic systems, which most closely aligns with the strong sustainability principles described below.

The challenge for sustainability professionals is to match interventions in the form of *strategies and instruments* to the goals and targets set by stakeholders in relation to the choice of sustainability framework. How would these frameworks be applied in your town, city, or country? What are some limitations of using these frameworks when trying to explain sustainability to business leaders, politicians, or primary school students? How do changes in global energy or climate systems relate to these frameworks?

Energy system changes: challenges and opportunities for sustainability

Centralized electricity systems have helped facilitate rapid improvements to income and quality of life. Increasing energy demands from industry, the commercial sector, and residential expansion has led to an increase in global electricity production since 1980 by nearly a factor of three (Figure 1.2). North America produced the most annual electricity from 1980 until 2004, at which time economic and population growth in China and India

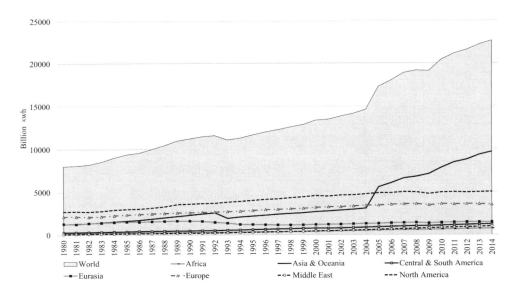

Figure 1.2 Total annual electricity production by region

Source: EIA (2017).

led to rapid increases in the annual production of electricity. Electricity production rates in Europe leveled off between 2006 and 2014 partly due to slowing population growth and an increase in sustainability-oriented policies aimed at energy efficiency and conservation. Electricity production rates in Eurasia declined from 1990 to 1998 partly due to declining economic growth rates in Russia. Central and South America, Africa, and the Middle East are all experiencing slow but steady growth in annual electricity production rates driven by increasing economic and population growth. The impact of the 2008 recession is also evidenced by slight declines in electricity production in North America and Europe, followed by another increase from 2009 to 2014.

When comparing electricity production by fuel type, several trends are evident. First, fossil fuels have continuously dominated the electricity supply mix, and their growth rate has remained steady through the late 1990s and early 2000s (Figure 1.3). This is due in part to increasing demand for coal power in Asia, as well as a switch from coal to natural gas plants in North America, which has reduced the emissions intensity of the supply mix. Hydropower has increased in share slightly, while nuclear has remained about the same after the Fukushima nuclear disaster in Japan in 2011 forced countries to rethink their nuclear energy strategies. Non-hydroelectric renewables including wind and solar production have increased between 2008 and 2014, while tide, wave, and fuel cell remain a minor portion of the global supply mix. Global wind electricity production increased exponentially between 2000 and 2014 (Figure 1.4). This was driven by rapid increases in annual production rates first in Europe (2000), then in North America (2006), and finally in Asia (2008).

Global petroleum consumption has increased from 1984 to 2014 (Figure 1.5). Rapid annual growth rates in Asia have largely driven this trend, while annual petroleum consumption rates have leveled off in North America and declined in Europe and Eurasia. Petroleum consumption has increased steadily in the Middle East and Central and South America. Due to technology changes and innovation in horizontal drilling and fracking, the United States has regained its position as the largest annual producer of petroleum

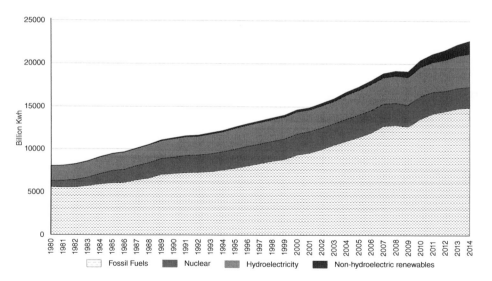

Figure 1.3 Total annual world electricity production by fuel type

Source: EIA (2017).

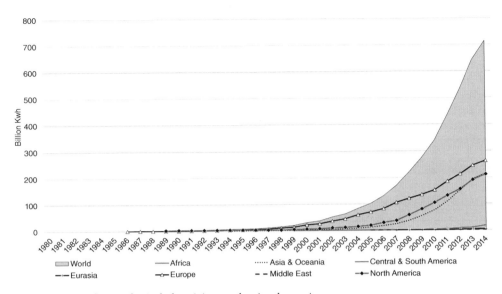

Figure 1.4 Total annual wind electricity production by region
Source: EIA (2017).

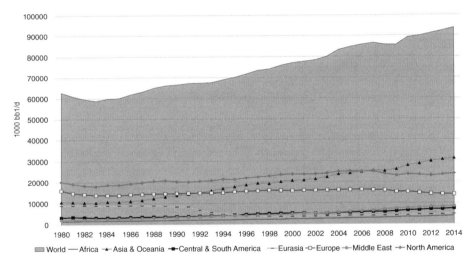

Figure 1.5 Total annual petroleum consumption by region
Source: EIA (2017).

overtaking Saudi Arabia. Russia became a major player on the global petroleum production market in the early 1990s and has increased production rates through 2016. Other major producers include China, Canada, and Iraq.

The aforementioned trends in electricity and petroleum use can help explain changes in annual CO_2 emissions from energy consumption (Figure 1.6). The United States was the

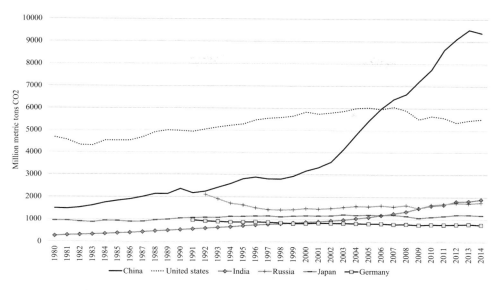

Figure 1.6 Highest emitting countries by annual CO_2 emissions from energy consumption

Source: EIA (2017).

world's leading contributor to CO_2 emissions from 1980 until being overtaken by China in 2006. China's rapid economic growth and industrialization have led to an exponential growth rate in CO_2 emissions from 1998 to 2014. CO_2 emissions in India have also risen rapidly, overtaking Russia as the world's third largest emitter. CO_2 emissions from Japan have remained relatively stable, while Germany has reduced emissions between 1991 and 2014 as part of the Germany Energy Transition, *Energiewende*, while increasing economic growth per capita. CO_2 emissions from the United States energy consumption have also declined from 2007 to 2014, in part due to the 2008 recession but also due to policy changes described in Chapter 8.

Sustainability professionals can learn from the examples of countries including Sweden, Denmark, and Germany that have successfully reduced CO_2 emissions while increasing living standards, life expectancy, and per capita incomes. Sustainability science can help sustainability professionals understand the connections between human and natural systems, and between technology, infrastructure, and institutional systems, so that interventions may be created and implemented for a strong sustainability pathway.

Germany vs. Denmark: who will achieve strong sustainability first?

Germany and Denmark are leaders in sustainability policy, technology, and education. In particular, both countries have achieved significant greenhouse gas (GHG) emission reductions in excess of 24 percent from 1990 levels (European Environment Agency, 2016) and have set ambitious targets to guide further reductions. Germany

(continued)

(continued)

has committed to reduce GHG emissions 80 to 95 percent by 2050 relative to 1990 levels with specific targets for energy, buildings, transport, industry, and agriculture sectors (Fransen and Levin, 2016). The German plan includes a focus on adaptive governance based on technological and economic changes, as well as allowing for flexibility between sectors (Fransen and Levin, 2016). Many cities in Germany are also leading the way with innovative municipal laws to encourage sustainability (Purvis, 2008). Germany is one of the world leaders in solar installation capacity (Zheng and Kammen, 2014) and has developed innovative integrated wind-hydro systems to increase energy system resilience and sustainability. Germany expects to meet 80 percent of its electricity needs with renewable energy by 2050 due to a policy mix including the Renewable Energy Sources Act and a *feed-in tariff* (Mundo-Hernández et al., 2014). Local examples of *niche experiments* that were instigated by the German *Energiewende* as well as changes that occurred in the *subsystems of the regime* (Mattes et al., 2015) are described throughout this book to highlight the processes, strategies, and instruments involved in a sustainability transition.

Denmark was one of the first countries to create renewable energy innovation clusters, which now employ 60,000 workers in over 400 companies in addition to 46 universities or colleges focused on environmental technology research (Cooke, 2015). Denmark adopted wind energy as part of an environmental movement in the 1970s led by citizen protests and a resulting government strategy to change from nuclear to renewable energy (Cooke, 2015). Denmark has consistently met 40 percent of its energy demand with renewables and on windy days can meet over 100 percent of its electricity demand from wind; the surplus is then exported to Norway, Germany, and Sweden (Neslen, 2015). The Danish wind industry is growing at 18 percent per year, which means that further and more consistent electricity exports will serve as a revenue source to meet growing demands from other northern European countries. Renewable energy exports represent an energy-based economic development opportunity for Denmark by surpassing their own electricity demand due to the tremendous wind resource available within their borders. This opportunity is also spurring competition from other countries in the region, as a new proposal from the Netherlands would build multiple giant offshore wind-farms and a centralized power transfer island in the middle of the North Sea to supply electricity via high-efficiency cables to the United Kingdom, Belgium, the Netherlands, Germany, and Denmark (Vaughan, 2017).

Despite their accomplishments, has Germany or Denmark achieved strong sustainability? What types of integrated metrics would sustainability professionals use to assess progress towards strong sustainability? How could sustainability science help other countries follow the lead of Germany and Denmark?

Sustainability science

Sustainability science is "a field defined by the problems it addresses rather than by the disciplines it employs" (Clark, 2007, p. 1737). The core focus of sustainability science is understanding "the complex dynamics that arise from interactions between human and environmental systems" (p. 1737). Sustainability science is a combination of practical research meant for applied purposes like solving problems, and basic research looking for fundamental knowledge and theory development (Clark, 2007). Given that its goal is to encourage a sustainability transition, sustainability researchers are simultaneously developing new theories and frameworks and learning from applications of those frameworks. But is sustainability science a discipline, or is it a transdisciplinary field? Moran and Lopez (2016) described transdisciplinary as "characterized by the tackling of *complexity, nonlinearity, reflexivity*, context-specific negotiation of knowledge, and a fusion of knowledge beyond disciplines" (p. 2). How are these characteristics aligned in order to address the challenges faced by sustainability professionals? Clark (2007, p. 1737) posed several questions for the field of sustainability science:

- How can the dynamic interactions between human and environmental systems be better incorporated into emerging models that integrate the Earth system, social development, and sustainability principles?
- How are long-term trends in environment and development reshaping nature–society interactions?
- What factors determine the limits of resilience and sources of vulnerability for such interactive systems?
- What systems of incentive structures can most effectively improve social capacity to guide interactions between nature and society towards more sustainable trajectories?
- How can science and technology be more effectively harnessed to address sustainability goals?

The next phase of sustainability science is to search for *socio-technical solutions* to the major human–environment problems including biological diversity loss, energy and water challenges, and global climate change (Miller et al., 2014). Environment and resource challenges (Mitchell, 2010), as well as sustainability problems more broadly, are fraught with complexity, uncertainty, and conflict (Miller et al., 2014). *Complexity* stems from systems' interactions, tradeoffs, and feedbacks, *uncertainty* stems from the challenge of understanding these complex interactions and associated future outcomes, and *conflict* stems from the numerous actors that have different views on whether to keep the system the same or to change the system through the use of strategies and instruments. Studying and building knowledge and understanding of coupled human-environmental systems will help to reduce uncertainty and handle the complexity challenges. Perhaps the biggest challenge and bottleneck to sustainability is conflict between countries, political parties, personal and social values, and decision/investment priorities.

As Miller et al. (2014) argued, "if the goal of sustainability science is to contribute to society's ability to operate along sustainable trajectories, then more scientific knowledge about coupled systems will not suffice" (p. 240). Miller et al. (2014) outlined four key areas for sustainability science research: (1) understanding and reflecting on sustainability values, (2) devising and seeking desirable futures, (3) discovering and bringing about socio-technical change, and (4) empowering social and institutional learning. These four areas draw heavily upon social science, and sustainability scientists working to address them will attempt to understand what values are most effective for supporting and encouraging sustainable outcomes, what future scenarios and the pathways to get there are needed to achieve sustainability, what *strategies* are effective at encouraging socio-technical system changes including behaviors and practices, and what *instruments* enable social and institutional learning that is needed to change policies and politics. Sustainability science research can itself be treated as "a social process operating at several scales, including . . . those of individual scientists and their communities as they set research agendas" (Miller and Neff, 2013, p. 308).

Sustainability science is the ultimate balancing act between *objective* facts and *subjective* values, where sustainability researchers and professionals want to find a solution that encourages change in part based on scientific principles (e.g., emission levels, coupled human–natural systems models and scenarios, materials and energy throughput levels, and the laws of thermodynamics) and in part based on societal values, norms, and priorities. Sustainability scientists are by their very nature seeking socio-technical solutions that maximize, optimize, or contribute to the public good by creating *sustainability value* for society.

Strong sustainability *is* sustainability

While conceptions of sustainability have changed over time and differ by region and scale, it is important to have a basic working definition to guide the creation of strategies and instruments. Strong sustainability is defined as the following: *for sustainability to be achieved, the stocks of human and social capital, human-made capital, and ecological capital must each be maintained or increase over time in a particular region.* This definition is in contrast with weak sustainability frameworks, which allow for natural capital to be depleted if it is compensated for or substituted by increases in human or human-made capital (Neumayer, 2013). While strong sustainability is supported by theory derived from ecological economists like Herman Daly and Joshua Farley (2010), it is difficult to achieve in practice because of the challenges faced when attempting to avoid tradeoffs between each form of capital. Allowing tradeoffs makes practical sense in the short term but violates the fundamental principle of sustainability as depicted in Figure 1.1D: *human systems depend on and are nested within ecological systems.* If we destroy or deplete ecological systems, at some point we will be limited in our ability to continually improve human systems. How, then, can sustainability be approached when many of the actions necessary to meet this definition are considered too radical or too costly by many business and government leaders?

Sustainability principles

Bob Gibson, a professor at the University of Waterloo in Canada, created a set of principles of sustainability for environmental impact assessments (Gibson, 2006; Gibson, 2017). The principles go beyond the three pillars (economic, social, and environmental) by incorporating transdisciplinary theory and integrated perspectives (Gibson, 2006, pp. 270–271):

- Socio-ecological system integrity

    o   Build human-ecological relations to establish and maintain the long-term integrity of socio-biophysical systems and protect the irreplaceable life support functions upon which human as well as ecological well-being depends.

- Livelihood sufficiency and opportunity

    o   Ensure that everyone and every community has enough for a decent life and that everyone has opportunities to seek improvements in ways that do not compromise future generations' possibilities for sufficiency and opportunity.

- Intra-generational equity

    o Ensure that sufficiency and effective choices for all are pursued in ways that reduce dangerous gaps in sufficiency and opportunity (and health, security, social recognition, political influence) between rich and poor.

- Inter-generational equity

    o Favor present options and actions that are most likely to preserve or enhance the opportunities and capabilities of future generations to live sustainably.

- Resource maintenance and efficiency

    o Provide a larger base for ensuring sustainable livelihoods for all while reducing threats to the long-term integrity of socio-ecological systems by reducing extractive damage, avoiding waste, and cutting overall material and energy use per unit of benefit.

- Civility and democratic governance

    o Build the capacity, motivation, and habitual inclination of individuals, communities, and other collective decision-making bodies to apply sustainability requirements through more open and better-informed deliberations, greater attention to fostering reciprocal awareness and collective responsibility, and more integrated use of administrative, market, customary, and personal decision-making practices.

- Precaution and adaptation

    o Respect uncertainty, avoid poorly understood risks of serious or irreversible damage to the foundations of sustainability, plan to learn, design for surprise, and manage for adaptation.

- Immediate and long-term interconnectivity from local to global scales

    o Apply all principles of sustainability at once, seeking mutually supportive benefits and multiple gains.
    o Integration of strategies and instruments from local to global and global to local.

These sustainability principles "are centered on the requirements for progress towards sustainability, and avoid any attempt to define sustainability" (Gibson, 2017, p. 12). Gibson (2017) argued that "sustainability is not an end point . . . in a complex and dynamic world, sustainability can only be an amorphous and ever-changing target" (p. 12). Furthermore, none of the principles fit into a single pillar of the economic, social, and environment model. Rather, they are integrative across the pillars to give sustainability professionals a guide to "what is required for progress towards sustainability" (p. 12). Finally, as Gibson proclaimed, "the really serious, rich, and fascinating work in sustainability assessment begins with bringing the criteria to the ground to be elaborated, re-phrased, and/or re-organized for application" (p. 13). To bring the global concept of sustainability down to the community level, studies have begun to adopt and critique these principles and turn them into measurable sub-principles of sustainability. This is useful for systems-level analysis, including environmental impact assessments, measuring energy system change, or planning sustainable water systems.

Building on Gibson's basic principles for sustainability broadly, Larson et al. (2013a, 2013b) and Wiek and Larson (2012, pp. 3163–3166) developed a set of principles and sub-principles for sustainable water governance and applied them to the case of metropolitan Phoenix, Arizona. For social-ecological system integrity, example sub-principles included maintaining or restoring minimum stream flows for wildlife and riparian areas, preserving or enhancing the quality of water through pollution prevention and mitigation, and recognizing and coordinating resource uses and impacts within watersheds and groundwater basins. Examples of sub-principles for resource efficiency and maintenance included reducing water use through technological and behavior change, recycling water by reusing gray water or treated wastewater, and eliminating water losses from leaky infrastructure or evaporation. For livelihood sufficiency and opportunity, sub-principles for water systems included meeting basic livelihood needs for drinking, eating, and sanitation, and meeting needs for economic activities that depend on water. For the civic engagement and democratic governance principle, sub-principles encompassed engaging diverse stakeholders through collaborative decision-making processes and encouraging social learning and the co-production of knowledge.

The intra-generational equity principle can be measured by sub-principles including guaranteeing that all residents have access to safe water for basic needs and ensuring a fair distribution of benefits and costs of water system change to all stakeholders. For inter-generational equity, sub-principles comprised providing a mechanism for representing future generations in policy making and ensuring that resource depletion rates and pollution absorption rates are maintained below sustainable material and energy throughput levels. The integration and interconnectivity principle included sub-principles like minimizing negative impacts on actors and activities even outside the immediate water system and planning across political jurisdictions that are connected within the same water systems. For precaution and adaptation, sub-principles focused on studying and understanding threats and possible impacts, lessening the stressors or effects of changes to the system, and creating capacity for making future strategies and instruments. These examples of sub-principles of sustainability allow sustainability professionals to measure progress towards the overarching Gibson principles of sustainability. They also enable national or global level systems to be changed by connecting state/province or local-level strategies and instruments to multi-level systems. Achieving progress in these principles and sub-principles of sustainability that connect many systems, levels, and actors is one of many complex problems facing sustainability professionals.

Complex problems and sustainability

One of the challenges facing sustainability professionals who aim to improve the principles and sub-principles of sustainability is that solving complex problems involving multiple sectors, levels, jurisdictions, and time periods requires a new set of skills and competencies. What makes a problem complex? What are some examples of complex problems? Sustainability problems are *complex* because they require integrating disciplines, connecting local to global scales, and drawing upon physical sciences and human sciences. Sustainability is often considered impossible to achieve because it requires a fundamental rethinking of how society operates and how we define success.

Take for example a recent report that calculates the global annual cost of all forms of pollution to be $4.6 trillion and nine million deaths (Lancet Report, 2017). That is more than twice as many annual deaths as can be attributed to obesity, alcohol, road accidents, and malnutrition. For some countries, pollution-related illnesses and deaths were found to reduce economic growth by 2 percent per year. Although annual pollution deaths represent approximately 5 percent of total deaths in the United States, for other countries like India it is more than 20 percent. Pollution is a complex problem because (1) the causes are often in different jurisdictions than the people who feel the impacts, (2) improvements to economic growth are often used as a justification to allow more pollution, and (3) technologies, infrastructure, and institutional changes needed to reduce pollution are often deemed to be politically infeasible.

The first step to solving complex problems is to understand them with better observations (e.g., data) and analytical methods. The Lancet Report (2017) helps address this need by providing a comprehensive global study that shows how the causes, consequences, and solutions to pollution are interconnected. Perhaps most importantly, the report finds that air pollution restrictions in the United States have generated a 30–1 return-on-investment from health and economic benefits to society since 1970. This implies that controlling pollution does not inhibit economic development but rather represents one of the best sustainability investments by generating economic, social, and environmental value to society.

The second step to solving complex problems is communicating the nature of problems and their importance in a meaningful and powerful manner to the niche and regime actors described in Chapter 7 as well as to the general public. Explaining climate science can be difficult because global models incorporate massive amounts of data and involve interactions and feedbacks between scales, sectors, and time periods. The complexity is made more difficult by downscaling these global models to regional, state/province, or even city levels. An effective example of communicating this type of information is a recent paper using downscaled climate models and scenarios (Garner et al., 2017). This study showed that climate change has already increased the frequency of severe floods in New York City from 500-year floods in preindustrial times to 25-year floods today. Of even more importance to sustainability professionals are projections for a further reduction to 5-year intervals between major floods within 30 years. The implication is that climate change is making severe storms more frequent and intense, and the impact will be that coastal cities need to adapt their institutions and infrastructure. Rather than highlighting global impacts (e.g., sea level rise or global average temperature increase), this study translated the findings into a powerful and meaningful scale to show direct impacts to a major city of economic and cultural importance. Cities can adapt institutions and infrastructures based on risk management regimes that change in response to observed and future scenarios focusing on *biophysical limits* and human needs (Solecki et al., 2017). Actors including city planners, infrastructure planners, and disaster risk management planners can act as *policy entrepreneurs* and *intermediaries* (Chapter 6) by helping to translate science into strategies and instruments.

Other problems may seem less complex on the surface, such as the California drought of 2015, but they are no less difficult to solve when you consider the range of actors involved and the short- and long-term physical processes that contribute to the water shortages. On January 6, 2015, 94 percent of California was in severe drought, and 78 percent was in extreme drought condition (U.S. Drought Monitor, 2015). A lack of precipitation and antiquated water management practices contributed to this situation, but a larger problem was the collective decision to expand agricultural practices in a place that is continually under threat for drought.

California implemented strict water policies designed to mandate conservation practices in 2015 and 2016, an example being Executive Order B-37-16 (Emergency Conservation Regulation, 2016). The process of water conservation itself represents a "complex sociotechnical system comprising interactions of political, sociodemographic, economic, and hydroclimatological factors" (Hornberger et al., 2015, p. 4635). Water utilities are a key part of this complex system, acting as *boundary organizations* (Chapter 6) at the intersection of science and politics (White et al., 2008). Water managers within utilities face scientific pressures from hydrologists, for example, who may argue that water supplies are insufficient for further development. They also must deal with political pressures from residential developers, agricultural producers, and industrial and commercial actors who seek infrastructure developments to meet their anticipated needs for an increase in water supply. These pressures are further amplified by climate change and its anticipated impacts on water systems. In particular, droughts in the southwest United States are projected to become longer and more severe over the next 50 years (Melillo et al., 2014). The California wildfires of 2017 are another indicator of a complex system being pushed to its limits as little precipitation and high winds have allowed fires to spread rapidly destroying buildings and infrastructure (Vercammen et al., 2017).

Attempting to change or manage a complex system, such as the water challenges facing California, requires understanding the system and its constituent parts and functions. Complex systems have multiple scales as well as interactions and feedbacks across those scales. A practical implication of complex systems thinking is the notion of *tradeoffs*, which implies that decision-making involves choosing one goal or outcome at the expense of others. For example, a strict water conservation mandate may have the effect of reducing water use rates, but it may also lead agricultural producers to switch production to other products that require less water. Making this switch also depends on consumer tastes and whether they are willing to pay higher prices to source the same commodities from elsewhere. Importing more of these commodities from other regions may intensify environmental pressures facing those regions. Solving complex problems involves multiple perspectives, theories, frameworks, and methods that require adjustments over time. Sustainability professionals need a set of tools and competencies that will allow for addressing complex problems of this nature.

Developing sustainability competencies

Wiek et al. (2011, p. 205) introduced an integrated framework for sustainability research and problem-solving based on four modules. The first module outlined how to analyze and understand the current state of the problems under investigation. The second focused on creating a set of sustainability visions that would represent pathways and objectives for solving the problems. The third module involved examining less desirable future scenarios that could occur absent strategies and instruments that alter the *subsystems of the regime* towards sustainability principles and sub-principles. The fourth focused on creating and implementing *strategies and instruments* to change course from undesirable pathways to more sustainable pathways at key moments called critical intervention points. To implement these modules, a set of *sustainability competencies* was introduced: systems thinking, anticipatory assessment, normative decisions, strategic action, and interpersonal relations (Wiek et al., 2011).

Systems thinking competence is "the ability to collectively analyze complex systems across different domains (society, environment, economy), and different scales from local to global" (Wiek et al., 2011, p. 207). Systems thinking competence requires an understanding of *cascading effects* (e.g., a chain of events as a result of an act in the system), *inertia* (e.g., an object at rest tends to stay at rest, and an object in motion tends to stay in motion), and *feedback loops* (e.g., outputs of a system are returned to the system as inputs). Systems thinking competence is important for creating governance strategies by "identifying intervention points, anticipating future trajectories and staging transition processes" (Wiek et al., 2011, p. 207). *Strategies and instruments* can focus on instigating cascading effects that will change multiple *subsystems of the regime* (e.g., the co-evolving subsystems of society). Regime lock-in and path dependence are *bottlenecks* (Chapter 9) that represent inertia by slowing attempts from strategies and instruments aimed at *niche creation* and *regime destruction*, which are processes described in Chapter 7. Interdisciplinary research, case studies, and modelling approaches including systems dynamics models (Abdelkafi and Täuscher, 2016; Inouye et al., 2017) are important for putting systems thinking competence into practice.

Anticipatory competence is defined as "the ability to collectively analyze, evaluate, and craft detailed 'pictures' of the future related to sustainability issues and sustainability problem-solving frameworks" (Wiek et al., 2011, p. 207). Sustainability professionals can use this competence to identify unintended consequences of strategies and instruments including implications for inter-generational equity. Anticipatory competence enables sustainability professionals to detect potential pitfalls if there is no intervention. Strategies and instruments aimed at fostering sustainable behavior (Chapter 2), supporting green organizational strategies (Chapter 3), encouraging green innovation (Chapter 4), or driving triple-bottom-line economic development (Chapter 5) all require anticipatory competence to be able to analyze the output and outcome permutations of the strategies and instruments before they are implemented. Environmental impact assessments (Gibson, 2017), cost–benefit analyses (Lajunen, 2014; Söderqvist et al., 2015; William et al., 2016), scenario analysis (Joshi et al., 2015), and visioning exercises (White et al., 2015) are methods used by sustainability professionals to put anticipatory competence into practice.

Normative competence is "the ability to collectively map, specify, apply, reconcile, and negotiate sustainability values, principles, goals, and targets" (Wiek et al., 2011, p. 209). Normative competence will help design strategies and instruments that take into account multiple values and viewpoints along with the intra- and inter-generational equity principles of sustainability. This competence can also help researchers and professionals think critically about sustainability transitions while continually learning and adjusting from initial interventions. Normative competence is critical to designing strategies and instruments aimed at fostering sustainable behavior and changes to social practices (Chapter 2). Conflict resolution and alternative dispute resolution techniques along with other approaches to participatory decision-making (Hornsby et al., 2017) can help sustainability professionals use normative competence.

Strategic competence is "the ability to collectively design and implement interventions, transitions, and transformative governance strategies toward sustainability" (Wiek et al., 2011, p. 210). This competence is about getting things done and includes social, policy, political, and other dimensions of creating change. Strategic competence provides a range of enabling skills that give sustainability professionals the ability to overcome barriers, draw upon alliances, break path dependencies, mobilize resources at key times, and understand how the system functions as well as the motivations and roles of the actors within the system. Environmental champions and policy entrepreneurs are two examples of actors who utilize strategic competence. Intermediary organizations (Chapter 6) can hire and train sustainability professionals to be experts in strategic competence in order to enable other organizations to develop and implement strategies and instruments. Policy making and planning, development, implementation, and evaluation of programs, as well as the creation and use of *policy mixes* (Chapter 8) that aim to use outputs of one portion of the system (e.g., governance experiments at the state level or corporate green strategies) as inputs back into the system (e.g., as part of triple-bottom-line economic development strategies) are all important for sustainability professionals to turn strategic competence into practice.

Interpersonal relations competence is "the ability to motivate, enable, and facilitate collaborative and participatory sustainability research and problem solving" (Wiek et al., 2011, p. 211). This competence provides the ability to comprehend and encourage diversity between social groups, communities, and individuals. It is therefore an underlying competence that can help enable all of the other competencies. Specific skills including leadership and empathy are important for fostering change within diverse multi-actor systems including during *adaptive co-management* (Chapter 3) and *transition arenas* (Chapter 7). Negotiation and collaboration are critical to working across boundaries, where sustainability professionals as *boundary spanners* or *policy entrepreneurs* (Chapter 6) can put interpersonal relations competence into practice.

An overarching **integrated sustainability research and problem-solving competence** involves "having the skills, competencies and knowledge to enact changes in economic, ecological and social behavior without such changes always being merely a reaction to pre-existing problems" (de Haan, 2006, p. 22, in Wiek et al., 2011, p. 205). This is a proactive competence that allows sustainability professionals to anticipate problems and adjust strategies and instruments over time. Governance actors involved in creating *policy mixes* (Chapter 8) and intermediaries involved in linking niche and regime actors in sustainability transitions (Chapter 6) can aim to hire sustainability professionals trained and experienced in this competence.

The goal of the Wiek et al. (2011) integrated framework is to help sustainability professionals use these key competencies to identify *intervention points* and implement strategies and instruments to be able to change the course of the system from an unsustainable or weak sustainability pathway, to a strong sustainability pathway. These *sustainability competencies* must be developed as a compliment to standard competencies including critical thinking. Wiek et al. (2011) cautioned that most sustainability professionals will only be able to master one or two of these competencies. Therefore, interpersonal relations competence is the linchpin required for organizing and coordinating individuals and organizations that have the collective expertise in systems thinking competence, anticipatory competence, normative competence, strategic thinking competence, and integrated sustainability research and problem-solving competence. Sustainability-oriented intermediary organizations (Chapter 6) can work to build coalitions of individuals and organizations that have complimentary expertise in all of these competencies.

Sustainability transition frameworks

One of the challenges facing sustainability professionals is that individual and organizational actions (e.g., sustainable behavior in Chapter 2; green strategies and investments by organizations in Chapter 3) are often encouraged by voluntary, non-regulatory, or unenforceable programs that suffer from *free rider* and *collective action dilemmas*. These dilemmas exist when some stakeholders/individuals take actions to reduce environmental pollution while all stakeholders/individuals benefit from those actions. The implication is that some stakeholders/individuals may calculate or decide that they are better off by not taking any actions and letting other stakeholders/individuals find and implement solutions. They can therefore avoid costs while continuing to benefit from creating pollution that is a *negative externality* within the socio-economic system. Addressing this challenge requires an analytical framework that combines strategies and instruments to accelerate a transition to sustainability and ensure that it is achieved.

A framework for sustainability transitions should enable an understanding of coupled human-natural systems when placed under the constraint of sustainability principles. This requires the inclusion of two elements: (1) strategies to encourage and amplify individual actions upward to affect system change and (2) policy instruments to structure and guarantee that the sustainability principles are achieved (Giddens, 2011). Sustainability professionals can draw upon different combinations of strategies and instruments as part of a toolbox for changing the *socio-technical system* in the context of complexity and uncertainty. A sustainability transition framework should also include a set of performance measures related to the sustainability principles and sub-principles.

One example framework combines resilience and sustainability based on objectives and metrics that act as a set of performance measures (Marchese et al., 2018). The overall sustainability objectives are environmental wellbeing, economic wellbeing, and social wellbeing, which are functions of performance improvements to a set of metrics including GHG emissions per capita, air quality, GDP per capita, poverty rate, literacy rate, and child mortality (Figure 1.7). Each metric can be improved by *strategies and instruments* for turning decisions into outcomes. However, each metric may also face shocks that could make it harder to improve or may even decrease performance. Marchese et al. (2018) suggested tracking the resilience of each metric so as to guide the use of strategies and instruments to not only improve performance of the sustainability metrics, but also to increase the adaptive capacity of institutions and infrastructure to shocks. This can be aided by organizational *dynamic capabilities* and collaborative governance frameworks including *adaptive co-management* and *co-production of knowledge*, which are described in later chapters.

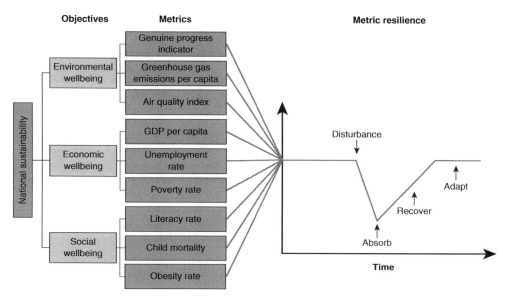

Figure 1.7 Resilient response of example sustainability metrics to a disturbance

Source: Marchese et al. (2018, p. 1279).

Similar to Figure 1.7, the Gibson (2006) principles of sustainability provide an alternative set of objectives, while the Larson et al. (2013a, 2013b) sub-principles provide a measurable set of sub-indicators as metrics, which can link individual and organizational decisions to higher scales. A set of strategies and instruments as part of a *policy mix* (Chapter 8) provides the mechanism for (1) ensuring that decisions become outcomes along the strong sustainability pathway, (2) shifting the weak sustainability pathway towards more rapid and radical changes of the strong sustainability pathway, and (3) enhancing resilience via adaptive capabilities. Each objective and sub-indicator can be measured against resilience criteria centered on developing adaptive capacity, which will support both incremental and radical changes to institutions and infrastructures.

The Gibson (2006) principles could help sustainability professionals understand the resilience of a socio-technical system given that they involve medium- and long-term objectives. The Larson et al. (2013a, 2013b) sub-principles could help understand the robustness of a socio-technical system, given that robustness "explicitly links the dynamics of systems to performance measures . . . it can be used to link resilience ideas about the nature of persistence and transformation in complex systems to performance measures and to operationalize the sustainability decision-making framework" (Anderies et al., 2013, p. 11). The Larson et al. (2013a, 2013b) sub-principles can therefore act as an intermediate step to evaluate the performance towards a sustainability transition with the ultimate goal of improving the performance of the Gibson (2006) principles.

When attempting to change a complex socio-technical system, it is important to know what types of interventions will lead to what types of changes. For example, Baird et al. (2017) argued that low and high levels of *disturbance* to a system support intermediate levels of diversity, which maximize the level of innovation. They also suggest that intermediate levels of disturbance lead to low levels of innovation. Their findings imply that systems are more likely to be highly innovative if they experience low or high levels of disturbance. They also explain that some systems display high levels of resilience and become stuck or resistant to change when they are exposed to intermediate levels of disturbance, including structural forms of disturbance that can lock-in and reinforce the system (e.g., the regime subsystems described in Chapter 7). Baird et al. (2017) cautioned that high levels of disturbance (e.g., fiscal shocks, natural disasters, political or policy shocks) should not be used as a strategy to encourage innovation but that low levels of disturbance (e.g., subversion, advocacy, protest, surprise, restoration, regulation) could be used as strategies to encourage innovation. Removing disturbance from the socio-technical system could also lead to undesirable outcomes by, for example, reducing the drive for innovation and creating stagnation in institutions and infrastructures.

How can sustainability professionals learn from systems theories and from concepts like resilience, robustness, and disturbance? Is it possible to guide change in a particular direction based on a set of principles prior to understanding the interactions and feedbacks within the system and before adding strategies and instruments as part of a policy mix? Sustainability professionals are faced with a decision: should they apply a resilience-driven *adaptive capacity* framework based on incremental change, responding to shocks, and maintaining the structure and subsystems of the regime? Or should they apply a change-driven *transition* framework based on radical actions led by actors aiming to create a new structure and subsystems of the regime (Redman, 2014)?

Benson and Garmestani (2011) explained that a "system's resilience is dependent upon the interactions between structure and dynamics at multiple scales" (p. 1421). Interactions between system structures and ongoing dynamics can be explained by a *panarchy*, which is defined as a nested set of complex adaptive cycles composed of "small, local, fast-responding systems; and large, global, slow-responding systems that affect one another through cross-scale feedback processes" (Evans, 2008, p. 39). The adaptive cycles go through a series of four stages from conservation and climax (**K**), to release and collapse (Ω), reorganization and renewal (α), and finally exploitation and consolidation (**r**). The lower and faster levels invent, create, experiment, test, and retest. They are the drivers within the multi-level system analogous to a collection of *niche experiments* (Chapter 7) that are continually creating change. The higher and slower levels hold onto the memories of previous experiments that were successful at changing the system. The higher levels provide the stability and resilience to the multi-level system (Gunderson et al., 2002). This could be positive for sustainability if it enables lower-level experiments via policy instruments and institutional pressures, or it could be negative for sustainability if it acts as path dependence and locks in existing unsustainable institutions and infrastructures. Figure 1.8 represents a panarchy that shows the connections between rapidly occurring energy system changes in local economies, like the coal producing regions of Australia, and slower moving changes in global energy markets and global climate systems. An additional level of complex adaptive cycles could be nested within the local economies to portray niche experiments as ongoing processes of technology creation as is outlined in Chapter 11.

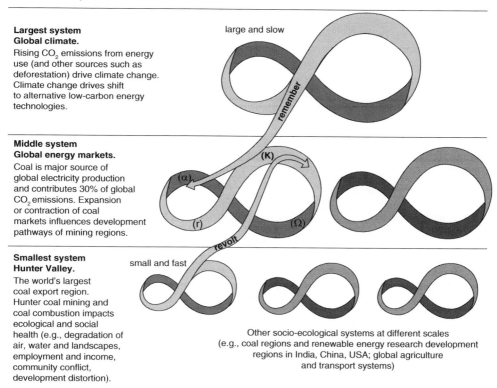

Three nested systems

Largest system Global climate.
Rising CO_2 emissions from energy use (and other sources such as deforestation) drive climate change. Climate change drives shift to alternative low-carbon energy technologies.

large and slow

Middle system Global energy markets.
Coal is major source of global electricity production and contributes 30% of global CO_2 emissions. Expansion or contraction of coal markets influences development pathways of mining regions.

Smallest system Hunter Valley.
The world's largest coal export region. Hunter coal mining and coal combustion impacts ecological and social health (e.g., degradation of air, water and landscapes, employment and income, community conflict, development distortion).

small and fast

Other socio-ecological systems at different scales (e.g., coal regions and renewable energy research development regions in India, China, USA; global agriculture and transport systems)

Figure 1.8 Panarchy for connecting local energy systems and global energy and climate systems

Source: Modified from Evans (2008).

The real test for sustainability professionals is to learn how to create change in complex socio-ecological systems. Bringing in the human element adds anticipation and creativity to the equation (Gunderson et al., 2002). Instead of simply waiting for natural phases to take their course, actors and institutions can alter the speed and timing of the phase transitions within lower-level adaptive cycles. This is critical because "patterns at the macro level emerge from interactions and selection processes at many lower levels of organization" (Moran and Lopez, 2016, p. 1), implying that sustainability professionals need to understand the lower-level creation processes as well as the cross-level interactions that enable them to be successful. Gunderson et al. (2002) suggested that the key roles played by organizations and social groups may change depending on the stage that the complex adaptive cycle above it (higher levels) is going through at that particular time. The roles may also change depending on the stage that the complex adaptive cycles within it (lower levels) are going through at that particular time.

Sustainability professionals as innovation intermediaries should focus on the *revolt and remember* cross-scale interactions (Gliedt et al., 2018) described in Chapters 6 and 7, which are critical for understanding the processes of creating change and adaptive capacity (Berkes and Ross, 2016). The *revolt interactions* take place when lower-level cycles break into higher levels and can even cascade up multiple levels. The *remember interactions* occur when higher-level cycles control, regulate, or influence the nature and rate of change in lower levels. Learning when a system is at a vulnerable phase provides an intervention point. Triple-bottom-line economic development strategies (Chapter 5) focused on instigating innovation for the purpose of job creation could target vulnerable infrastructure systems that are in the Ω release and collapse phase. Community sustainability leaders wishing to start green planning and energy management (Chapter 3) could introduce legislation to municipal council during periods of institutional change in the α reorganization and renewal phase within governance-level adaptive cycles. Although helpful for understanding change and resilience in a multi-level system, Berkes and Ross (2016) cautioned that the panarchy framework is incomplete when attempting to explain changes in coupled human-natural systems because "the view that one should focus mainly on the levels above and below the level of interest are contested by observations of direct vertical jumps from local to global, and also of horizontal processes within the same level" (p. 191). Additionally, using the panarchy as a sustainability transitions framework would require systems modelling and continually updated analytics to inform decision-making related to the choice of strategies and instruments.

Alternative and more broadly applicable frameworks are therefore needed to understand how to encourage sustainability transitions as a series of phases from system creation, to growth and interconnections, stagnation and lock-in, and finally to rejuvenation through incremental or radical changes to institutions and infrastructure (e.g., Bolton and Foxon, 2015). This framework outlined infrastructure lifecycles as long and slow, but susceptible to acceleration by technology innovation or institutional changes. Similar to the panarchy framework, change can be driven by rapid cycles (multiple niche experiments) from within the regime. Stability is provided by the current institutions and infrastructure that resist or enable rapid changes from the niche level. Policy innovation is necessary to weaken the regime subsystems and increase the chances for radical changes (revolts) to occur. Additional elements need to be considered for developing a solutions-oriented sustainability transitions framework, including the underlying processes and actions of actors who create and implement the strategies and instruments.

Solutions–oriented sustainability transitions framework

A framework outlining how green innovation (Chapter 4) and triple-bottom-line economic development (Chapter 5) are accelerated by sustainability-oriented innovation intermediaries (Chapter 6) is introduced in Gliedt et al. (2018). This framework highlighted the connections between the niche-creation processes and the regime-weakening processes that enable subsystem changes to socio-technical systems. A modified version is presented here as a *solutions-oriented sustainability transitions framework* (Figure 1.9), which is intended to act as a guide for sustainability professionals aiming to understand how to make changes to socio-technical systems consistent with strong sustainability. Each stage walks sustainability professionals along a pathway from identifying a set of guiding sustainability principles to actually doing problem- and project-based learning that helps create sustainability solutions. This practical roadmap for understanding change and resilience in socio-technical systems reflects the functions and structure of a panarchy by recognizing the interconnections between the slow-moving cycles that characterize the regime subsystems, which provide system resilience and guide the direction of change pathways, and the rapidly moving niche cycles, which create and drive change experiments that have the potential to breakthrough and change the regime subsystems.

Pathways to strong sustainability

There are three general pathways to achieving strong sustainability that are described and compared throughout this book: (1) Proactive, (2) Pragmatic, and (3) Reactive.

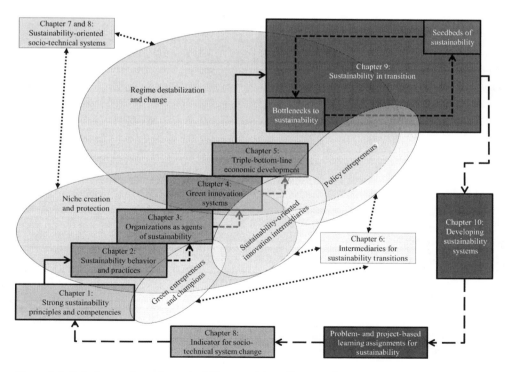

Figure 1.9 Solutions–oriented sustainability transitions framework

Source: Modified from Gliedt et al. (2017).

Each pathway has the potential to achieve strong sustainability, but the latter two will take longer and face additional ecological uncertainties due to the tendency to favor incremental over of radical interventions (Figure 1.10). The Proactive pathway is based on system- and subsystem-changing strategies and instruments that have the highest potential to eliminate tradeoffs and create *sustainability value* but faces the highest political uncertainties due to the radical nature of the interventions. Sustainability value implies creating and amplifying economic, social, *and* environmental value in line with the definition of strong sustainability described earlier. The Pragmatic pathway aims to create socio-economic value while developing solutions to problems through, for example, job creation strategies that align with environmental goals. The Reactive pathway has essentially become business-as-usual for many corporations and governments wishing to take easy and cheap low-hanging fruit environmental actions as a means of creating economic value.

The Gibson sustainability principles guide each of the pathways towards strong sustainability by encouraging different combinations of strategies and instruments, which range in focus from individuals, organizations, and technologies, to infrastructures, institutions, and political-economic systems. Acceleration Points are represented by the horizontal dotted arrows on Figure 1.10, which have the potential to speed up or scale-up a transition by shifting a pathway further to the left on the figure. This shift represents an increasing priority on ecological imperatives (relative to social and economic imperatives), encouraging more radical interventions, and focusing on simultaneously changing multiple systems towards strong sustainability. Throughout the remainder of the book, anytime an Acceleration Point appears, this signifies a tip for sustainability professionals to jump-start a shift from weak to strong sustainability pathways. These tips can help sustainability professionals identify the appropriate timing when subsystems of the regime are susceptible to interventions, or to amplify the impact of strategies and instruments aimed at strong sustainability solutions. The subsystems, which are described throughout the book, include *cultural* (e.g., customs and collective social behavior), *scientific* (e.g., science and education), *political* (e.g., political parties and actors), *governance* (e.g., municipal and regional administration), *industrial* (e.g., business competition or cooperation), *intermediaries* (e.g., labor unions, chambers of commerce, network connectors), *financial* (e.g., funding, venture capital, banks), and *civil society* (e.g., non-governmental organizations (NGOs), mobilized citizens) (Grin et al., 2010; Mattes et al., 2015).

Achieving strong sustainability can be driven in three ways: (1) by instigating changes to social practices and niche experiments that are designed to break into the regime and change the subsystems (Chapters 2, 3, 4), (2) by changing the subsystems directly through interventions at the regime level (Chapter 5), or by integrated strategies and instruments that combine both niche and regime solutions (Chapters 6, 7, 8). Chapters 2, 3, and 4 outline a range of individual, organizational, and technological innovation systems' strategies that can guide solutions along the Reactive, Pragmatic, and Proactive pathways to strong sustainability. Chapters 5 and 6 discuss economic development processes and intermediaries as key to the Pragmatic and Proactive pathways to strong sustainability. Chapters 7–10 describe and critique integrated perspectives to niche and regime solutions that have the potential to Proactively contribute to *sustainability value creation*. These solutions can change multiple subsystems of the regime simultaneously and link individual decisions to multi-level system change.

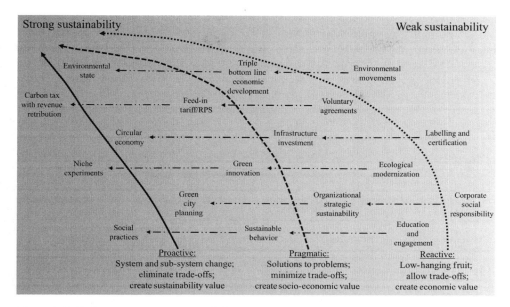

Figure 1.10 Pathways to strong sustainability: strategies, instruments, and Acceleration Points

Source: Authors' rendition.

Problem- and project-based learning for sustainability solutions

Making progress towards strong sustainability requires action-based solutions that draw on the *sustainability competencies*. Throughout this book, you will develop and apply the Wiek et al. (2011) competencies on route to becoming sustainability professionals by doing *problem- and project-based learning* assignments (Lippuner et al., 2015). Hands on learning, problem- and project-based learning, relational learning, and cooperative learning are all well-known ways to get you out of the classroom as part of creating change agents (Tziganuk and Gliedt, 2017). Problem- and project-based learning allows you to conduct applied research as part of assignments (Wiek et al., 2014). Assignments outlined on the textbook website relate directly to the theory, research, and case studies in each chapter and serve both as a review and an extension of the materials to real world applications. The goal is to have you experience all stages involved in creating a sustainability transition. The collection of assignments represents a solutions-based approach for learning and doing sustainability from a transdisciplinary perspective.

Problem- and project-based learning occurs when "students investigate a real-world problem and work on solution options to this problem by engaging in small-group work (ideally in an interdisciplinary team) to which instructors contribute as coaches for the teams" (Brundiers and Wiek, 2013, p. 1727). The goal is to replicate as closely as possible a real-world professional environment where you are sustainability professionals who work with community stakeholders, citizens, business leaders, or government agencies. Problem- and project-based learning focuses on conducting research rather than simply working for stakeholders or doing internships (Brundiers and Wiek, 2013). Instructors work with community stakeholders to pre-structure the assignments (Figure 1.11). Students work in teams to research and devise solutions to the problem and implement those solutions with the help of the stakeholders and the instructors. The responsibility for solving the problem rests with the student groups. As an introduction to the assignments, read the following articles focusing on problem- and project-based learning methods (Rosenberg Daneri et al., 2015; McGibbon and Van Belle, 2015; Wiek et al., 2014, 2015; Wiek and Kay, 2015; Wooltorton et al., 2015).

Check on learning

- Sustainability science is a relatively new field of research and practice driven by the desire to solve complex problems that must be understood and approached from multi-faceted, transdisciplinary perspectives. Given this definition, describe a few important skills and competencies that sustainability professionals should have. How would you teach these skills and competencies to your friends who are not taking sustainability classes or programs?
- Do some research about one country other than your own and write one page to answer each of the following questions:

    1   How has the country been able to make progress towards a sustainability transition?
    2   Why has the country not achieved strong sustainability?

- Name and describe the eight Gibson sustainability principles.

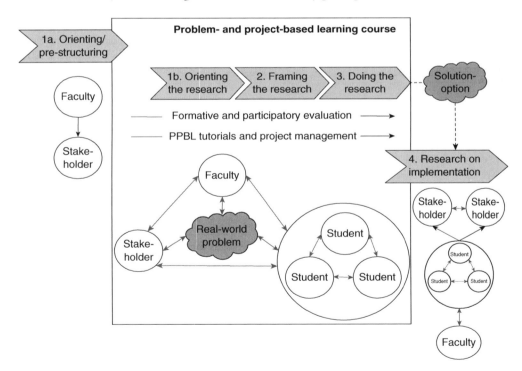

Figure 1.11 Problem- and project-based learning process model

Source: Brundiers and Wiek (2013, p. 1731).

- What are some interventions (strategies and instruments) that are on the Proactive pathway to strong sustainability? What other types of strategies and instruments do you think should be included on the Proactive pathway?
- Critical thinking exercise: For each of the Gibson principles, create a set of sub-principles to measure the progress of community energy planning initiatives in your city or town towards strong sustainability. How would each sub-principle be measured? What strategies and instruments would be needed to improve each sub-principle?
- Critical thinking exercise: Recall the California drought case described in this chapter. Do some research to examine why the pattern of expanding agricultural practices in sub-optimal growing environments has continued despite more frequent and intense droughts. What types of strategies and instruments could be used to address this complex problem? What actors should be involved in the solution making process?

Assignments

- Developing a collaborative problem- and project-based learning systematic review

References

Abdelkafi, N., & Täuscher, K. (2016). Business models for sustainability from a system dynamics perspective. *Organization & Environment*, 29(1), 74–96.

Anderies, J. M., Folke, C., Walker, B., & Ostrom, E. (2013). Aligning key concepts for global change policy: Robustness, resilience, and sustainability. *Ecology and Society*, 18(2): 8.

Baird, T. D., Chaffin, B. C., & Wrathall, D. J. (2017). A disturbance innovation hypothesis: Perspectives from human and physical geography. *The Geographical Journal*, 183(2), 201–208.

Benson, M. H., & Garmestani, A. S. (2011). Embracing panarchy, building resilience and integrating adaptive management through a rebirth of the National Environmental Policy Act. *Journal of Environmental Management*, 92(5), 1420–1427.

Berkes, F., Colding, J., & Folke, C. (2000). Rediscovery of traditional ecological knowledge as adaptive management. *Ecological Applications*, 10(5), 1251–1262.

Berkes, F., & Ross, H. (2016). Panarchy and community resilience: Sustainability science and policy implications. *Environmental Science & Policy*, 61, 185–193.

Bolton, R., & Foxon, T. J. (2015). Infrastructure transformation as a socio-technical process: Implications for the governance of energy distribution networks in the UK. *Technological Forecasting and Social Change*, 90, 538–550.

Brundiers, K., & Wiek, A. (2013). Do we teach what we preach? An international comparison of problem- and project-based learning courses in sustainability. *Sustainability*, 5(4), 1725–1746.

Clark, W.C. (2007). Sustainability science: A room of its own. *Proceedings of the National Academy of Sciences*, 104(6), 1737.

Cooke, P. (2015). Green governance and green clusters: Regional & national policies for the climate change challenge of Central & Eastern Europe. *Journal of Open Innovation: Technology, Market, and Complexity*, 1(1), 1–17.

Daly, H. E., & Farley, J. (2010). *Ecological Economics: Principles and Applications*. 2nd Edition. Island Press. Washington, DC.

De Haan, G. (2006). The BLK '21'programme in Germany: A 'Gestaltungskompetenz'-based model for Education for Sustainable Development. *Environmental Education Research*, 12(1), 19–32.

EIA. (2017). International energy statistics. U.S. Energy Information Administration. Available at: www.eia.gov/beta/international/data/browser/#/?pa=000000200000000000000000g2&c=ruvvvvvfvtvnvv1urvvvvfvvvvvvfvvvou20evvvvvvvvvvnvvuvs&ct=0&tl_id=2-A&vs=INTL.2-2-AFG-BKWH.A&cy=2014&vo=0&v=H&end=2015

Emergency Conservation Regulation. (2016). Water conservation portal. California Environmental Protection Agency. State Water Resources Control Board. Available at: www.waterboards. ca.gov/water_issues/programs/conservation_portal/emergency_regulation.shtml

European Environment Agency. (2016). Mitigating climate change – greenhouse gas emissions. Percentage change in total GHG emissions in EEA countries (1990–2012). Available at: www. eea.europa.eu/soer-2015/countries-comparison/climate-change-mitigation

Evans, G. (2008). Transformation from "Carbon Valley" to a "Post-Carbon Society" in a climate change hot spot: The coalfields of the Hunter Valley, New South Wales, Australia. *Ecology and Society*, 13(1), 39.

Fransen, T., and Levin, K. (2016). Germany becomes first country to release a 2050 emissions-reduction plan. World Resources Institute. Available at: www.wri.org/blog/2016/11/ germany-becomes-first-country-release-2050-emissions-reduction-plan

Garner, A. J., Mann, M. E., Emanuel, K. A., Kopp, R. E., Lin, N., Alley, R. B., . . . & Pollard, D. (2017). Impact of climate change on New York City's coastal flood hazard: Increasing flood heights from the preindustrial to 2300 CE. *Proceedings of the National Academy of Sciences*, 114(45), 11861–11866.

Gibson, R. (2006). Beyond the pillars: Sustainability assessment as a framework for effective integration of social, economic and ecological considerations in significant decision-making. *Journal of Environmental Assessment and Policy Management*, 8(3), 259–280.

Gibson, R. (2017). Foundations: Sustainability and the requirements for getting there. In Gibson, R. (Ed.). *Sustainability Assessment: Applications and Opportunities*. pp. 1–15. Routledge. New York, NY.

Giddens, A. (2011). *The Politics of Climate Change*. Polity Press. Cambridge, UK.

Gliedt, T., Hoicka, C. E., & Jackson, N. (2018). Innovation intermediaries accelerating environmental sustainability transitions. *Journal of Cleaner Production*, 174, 1247–1261.

Grin, J., Rotmans, J., & Schot, J. (2010). *Transitions to Sustainable Development: New Directions in the Study of Long Term Transformative Change*. Routledge. New York, NY.

Gunderson, L. H., Holling, C. S., & Peterson, G. D. (2002). Surprises and sustainability: Cycles of renewal in the Everglades. In: Gunderson, L. H., & Holling, C. S. (Eds). *Panarchy. Understanding Transformations in Human and Natural Systems*. pp. 315–332. Island Press. Washington, DC.

Hornberger, G. M., Hess, D. J., & Gilligan, J. (2015). Water conservation and hydrological transitions in cities in the United States. *Water Resources Research*, 51(6), 4635–4649.

Hornsby, C., Ripa, M., Vassillo, C., & Ulgiati, S. (2017). A roadmap towards integrated assessment and participatory strategies in support of decision-making processes. The case of urban waste management. *Journal of Cleaner Production*, 142, 157–172.

Inouye, A. M., Lach, D. H., Stevenson, J. R., Bolte, J. P., & Koch, J. (2017). Participatory modeling to assess climate impacts on water resources in the Big Wood Basin, Idaho. In S. Gray, M. Paolisso, R. Jordan, & S. Gray (Eds). *Environmental Modeling with Stakeholders*. pp. 289–306. Springer International Publishing, Cham, Switzerland.

Joshi, D. K., Hughes, B. B., & Sisk, T. D. (2015). Improving governance for the Post-2015 sustainable development goals: Scenario forecasting the next 50 years. *World Development*, 70, 286–302.

Lajunen, A. (2014). Energy consumption and cost-benefit analysis of hybrid and electric city buses. *Transportation Research Part C: Emerging Technologies*, 38, 1–15.

Lancet Report, The. (2017). The Lancet Commission on Pollution and Health. Global Alliance on Health and Pollution. Available at: http://gahp.net/the-lancet-report-2/

Larson, K. L., Wiek, A., & Keeler, L. W. (2013a). A comprehensive sustainability appraisal of water governance in Phoenix, AZ. *Journal of Environmental Management*, 116, 58–71.

Larson, K. L., Polsky, C., Gober, P., Chang, H., & Shandas, V. (2013b). Vulnerability of water systems to the effects of climate change and urbanization: A comparison of Phoenix, Arizona and Portland, Oregon (USA). *Environmental Management*, 52(1), 179–195.

Lippuner, C., Pearce, B. J., & Bratrich, C. (2015). The ETH Sustainability Summer School Programme: An incubator to support change agents for sustainability. *Current Opinion in Environmental Sustainability*, 16, 37–43.

Marchese, D., Reynolds, E., Bates, M. E., Morgan, H., Clark, S. S., & Linkov, I. (2018). Resilience and sustainability: Similarities and differences in environmental management applications. *Science of the Total Environment*, 613, 1275–1283.

Mattes, J., Huber, A., & Koehrsen, J. (2015). Energy transitions in small-scale regions: What we can learn from a regional innovation systems perspective. *Energy Policy*, 78, 255–264.

McGibbon, C., & Van Belle, J. P. (2015). Integrating environmental sustainability issues into the curriculum through problem-based and project-based learning: A case study at the University of Cape Town. *Current Opinion in Environmental Sustainability*, 16, 81–88.

Melillo, J. M., Terese (T.C.) Richmond, & Yohe, G W. (Eds) (2014). *Climate Change Impacts in the United States: The Third National Climate Assessment.* U.S. Global Change Research Program, doi:10.7930/J0Z31WJ2.

Miller, T. R., & Neff, M. W. (2013). De-facto science policy in the making: how scientists shape science policy and why it matters (or, why STS and STP scholars should socialize). *Minerva*, 51(3), 295–315.

Miller, T. R., Wiek, A., Sarewitz, D., Robinson, J., Olsson, L., Kriebel, D., & Loorbach, D. (2014). The future of sustainability science: A solutions-oriented research agenda. *Sustainability Science*, 9(2), 239–246.

Mitchell, B. (2010). *Resource and Environmental Management in Canada. Addressing Conflict and Uncertainty.* 4th Edition. Oxford University Press. Oxford, UK.

Moran, E. F., & Lopez, M. C. (2016). Future directions in human-environment research. *Environmental Research*, 144, 1–7.

Mundo-Hernández, J., de Celis Alonso, B., Hernández-Álvarez, J., & de Celis-Carrillo, B. (2014). An overview of solar photovoltaic energy in Mexico and Germany. *Renewable and Sustainable Energy Reviews*, 31, 639–649.

Neslen, A. (2015). Wind power generates 140% of Denmark's electricity demand. *The Guardian*. Available at: www.theguardian.com/environment/2015/jul/10/denmark-wind-windfarm-power-exceed-electricity-demand

Neumayer, E. (2013). *Weak Versus Strong Sustainability: Exploring the Limits of Two Opposing Paradigms.* 4th Edition. Edward Elgar Publishing, Northampton, MA.

Purvis, A. (2008). Is this the greenest city in the world? *The Guardian*. Available at: www.theguardian.com/environment/2008/mar/23/freiburg.germany.greenest.city

Redman, C. L. (2014). Should sustainability and resilience be combined or remain distinct pursuits? *Ecology and Society*, 19(2): 37.

Rosenberg Daneri, D. R., Trencher, G., & Petersen, J. (2015). Students as change agents in a town-wide sustainability transformation: The Oberlin Project at Oberlin College. *Current Opinion in Environmental Sustainability*, 16, 14–21.

Söderqvist, T., Brinkhoff, P., Norberg, T., Rosén, L., Back, P. E., & Norrman, J. (2015). Cost-benefit analysis as a part of sustainability assessment of remediation alternatives for contaminated land. *Journal of Environmental Management*, 157, 267–278.

Solecki, W., Pelling, M., & Garschagen, M. (2017). Transitions between risk management regimes in cities. *Ecology and Society*, 22(2), 38.

Tziganuk, A., and Gliedt, T. (2017). Comparing faculty perceptions of sustainability teaching at two US universities. *International Journal of Sustainability in Higher Education*, 18(7), 1191–1211.

U.S. Drought Monitor. (2015). U.S. Drought Monitor for California January 6, 2015. U.S. Department of Agriculture and the National Oceanic and Atmospheric Administration. Available at: http://droughtmonitor.unl.edu/

Vaughan, A. (2017). Is this the future? Dutch plan vast windfarm island in North Sea. *The Guardian*. Available at: www.theguardian.com/environment/2017/dec/29/is-this-the-future-dutch-plan-vast-windfarm-island-in-north-sea

Vercammen, P., Cullinane, S., & Simon, D. (2017). California wildfires have destroyed 1000 structures . . . and counting. CNN. Available at: www.cnn.com/2017/12/12/us/california-fires/index.html

White, D. D., Corley, E., & White, M. S. (2008). Water managers' perceptions of the science-policy interface in Phoenix, Arizona: Implications for an emerging boundary organization. *Society & Natural Resources*, 21(3), 230–243.

White, D. D., Withycombe Keeler, L., Wiek, A., & Larson, K. L. (2015). Envisioning the future of water governance: A survey of central Arizona water decision makers. *Environmental Practice*, 17(01), 25–35.

Wiek, A., & Larson, K. L. (2012). Water, people, and sustainability: A systems framework for analyzing and assessing water governance regimes. *Water Resources Management*, 26(11), 3153–3171.

Wiek, A., Withycombe, L., & Redman, C. (2011). Key competencies in sustainability: A reference framework for academic program development. *Sustainability Science*, 6, 203–218.

Wiek, A., Xiong, A., Brundiers, K., & van der Leeuw, S. (2014). Integrating problem-and project-based learning into sustainability programs: A case study on the School of Sustainability at Arizona State University. *International Journal of Sustainability in Higher Education*, 15(4), 431–449.

Wiek, A., Harlow, J., Melnick, R., van der Leeuw, S., Fukushi, K., Takeuchi, K., . . . & Kutter, R. (2015). Sustainability science in action: a review of the state of the field through case studies on disaster recovery, bioenergy, and precautionary purchasing. *Sustainability Science*, 10(1), 17–31.

William, R., Goodwell, A., Richardson, M., Le, P. V., Kumar, P., & Stillwell, A. S. (2016). An environmental cost-benefit analysis of alternative green roofing strategies. *Ecological Engineering*, 95, 1–9.

Wooltorton, S., Wilkinson, A., Horwitz, P., Bahn, S., Redmond, J., & Dooley, J. (2015). Sustainability and action research in universities: Towards knowledge for organizational transformation. *International Journal of Sustainability in Higher Education*, 16(4), 424–439.

Zheng, C., & Kammen, D. M. (2014). An innovation-focused roadmap for a sustainable global photovoltaic industry. *Energy Policy*, 67, 159–169.

2   Sustainable behavior and practices

Learning objectives

- Understand and critique key theories that attempt to explain sustainable behavior
- Contrast social practices with previous psychology and sociology understandings of behavior change
- Illustrate case studies of behavior change related to sustainability
- Outline methods for measuring progress towards sustainable behavior

Theories of sustainable behavior and practices

Achieving sustainability goals at the societal level begins with changing behavior at the individual level. *Sustainable behavior* is defined in this chapter as decisions by individuals that reduce environmental harms or enhance natural capital. *Strategies and instruments* to create or encourage sustainable behavior can be grouped into three categories as described by Strengers and Maller (2015, p. 2):

(1) changing individual behavior and social norms,
(2) using market prices to encourage 'rational' responses from consumers, and
(3) using smart or automated technologies to guide human behaviors.

The following sections describe frameworks and approaches that help understand how to change behavior in a manner consistent with one or more of the aforementioned categories.

Changing individual behavior and social norms

Environmental psychology and sociology theories tend to examine ways that *interventions* can encourage sustainable behavior. These interventions include messaging and communication strategies, which can be tailored to an individual's values, beliefs, or attitudes about what they believe about their own actions as well as those of others. Considering what other people may think of a particular behavior and associated outcomes is also a critical part of understanding the normative pressures to act – or not – in certain ways.

The theory of planned behavior

The theory of planned behavior (Ajzen, 1991; Armitage and Conner, 2001; Chao, 2012; Cordano and Frieze, 2000; Niaura, 2013; Trumbo and O'Keefe, 2001) suggests that sustainable behavior is influenced by *behavioral intention,* which Ajzen (1991) defined as "the motivational factors that influence a behavior . . . indicators of how hard people are willing to try, of how much of an effort they are planning to exert, in order to perform the behavior" (p. 181). This suggests that if a person is highly motivated and willing to invest a lot of time and effort, they are more likely to adopt an alternative behavior. The behavioral intention is further influenced or shaped by additional factors. The first factor is a person's *attitude* about the behavior. If an individual has a positive view of a behavior, they are more likely to put forth a strong effort to change. The second factor is *subjective norms,* or the degree to which an individual perceives that important people in their life would either approve or disapprove of the behavior. In this case, if an individual believes that their friends, family, mentors, neighbors, etc. would approve of the behavior, then they are more likely to invest a strong effort to change. The third factor is the *perceived behavioral control,* which is the level of difficulty of executing the behavior based on past experiences and various barriers (Ajzen, 1991). For example, if a person tries to take public transit for the first time and ends up missing their bus and having to walk 40 minutes to work, they may be less likely to invest a strong effort to change their transportation behavior again in the near future because of this bad experience. They may now perceive the new behavior to be difficult or unpleasant, which acts as a barrier to even attempting further behavior changes.

Many studies have tested the theory of planned behavior and have also added additional factors to the model. Chao (2012) compared the theory of planned behavior to the Hines et al. (1987) model of responsible environmental behavior. Chao (2012) found that the theory of planned behavior explained more of the variance in the behavioral intention than did the model of responsible environmental behavior, but that behavioral intention was critical to predicting environmental behavior in both models. An interesting finding was that the perceived behavioral control factor both directly influenced environmental behavior as well as indirectly influenced environmental behavior by first influencing behavioral intention. Acceleration Point: Sustainability professionals can develop strategies to target both the perceived behavioral control factor and the behavioral intention factor as a means of accelerating or reinforcing sustainable behavior change.

Norm-based models of behavior

Norm activation theory (Schwartz, 1973; Turaga et al., 2010) suggests that an individual's moral norms can be used to influence sustainable behavior. In order for this to occur, individuals must be aware of the consequences of their decision on other people and they must feel a sense of personal responsibility for making an alternative decision. This is accentuated by the values–belief–norms model (Stern et al., 1999). This model implies that individuals will make sustainable decisions if they believe their actions will have positive consequences on things they value, which includes themselves or other humans (anthropocentric values) as well as the natural environment, wildlife, and ecosystems (biocentric values) (Stern et al., 1999). Individuals who are aware of the consequences and acknowledge a sense of responsibility to mitigate negative consequences are more likely to change their behavior.

The consequences and personal responsibility beliefs are shaped by an underlying set of universal beliefs about the relationship between humans and ecosystems (Turaga et al., 2010). An individual's personality and belief systems influence their views on human–environment interactions (Turaga et al., 2010), and this may range from ethical and moral considerations that support the collective importance of preserving nature, to economic considerations that support the individual importance of using nature to further personal or societal well-being. These underlying environmental beliefs can influence the extent that people are motivated by their perception of the consequences of an alternative behavior and their sense of personal responsibility for making a behavior change. Taken together, these individual and collective beliefs help people evaluate the consequences of their actions on the things they value, which can guide sustainable behavior (Turaga et al., 2010).

Sustainability professionals can design behavior change programs with the help of normative messages. A *descriptive normative message* can be used to outline what others in your neighborhood are doing (e.g., energy or water use behavior) or what others in your office are doing (e.g., reusing hand towels or turning off computers and lights) in order to influence sustainable behavior from those who are performing worse than the norm (e.g., using more energy/water than the average household, not reusing the towels, or not turning off computers/lights) (Schultz et al., 2007). However, for individuals who are performing better than the norm, a *boomerang effect* could occur because they are now aware that they are performing better than their neighbors and thus may reduce their sustainable behavior (intensity or frequency of the action) because they do not see or value the benefits of continuing to perform better than others (Schultz et al., 2007). Adding *injunctive normative messages* that highlight what others approve or disapprove of was able to reduce the boomerang effect (Schultz et al., 2008). This suggests that individuals who are already performing a sustainable behavior at an intensity or frequency above the norm may be encouraged by the injunctive normative messages to continue performing at that level. In some cases, they may even increase their performance based on messages and engagement strategies that emphasize high sustainability performance as valued and approved of by others in their community or organization.

One limitation of behavior theories that focus on values, beliefs, attitudes, and norms is that they sometimes fail to consider structural factors that often constrain what people can do. Contextual and place-based factors are also often ignored. In response to these critiques, Douglas McKenzie-Mohr and colleagues developed the community-based social marketing (CBSM) approach, which is a targeted strategy for identifying the context-specific reasons for undertaking status quo behaviors, and alternative sustainable behaviors. Once identified, a variety of tools and interventions can then be applied to increase the benefits of sustainable behaviors while decreasing the barriers to them.

Community-based social marketing

Community-based social marketing is a social psychology process for encouraging sustainable behavior (McKenzie-Mohr, 2000; McKenzie-Mohr and Smith, 2011; McKenzie-Mohr and Schultz, 2014). The process is based on selecting behaviors, identifying barriers and benefits, developing strategies to overcome barriers and emphasize benefits, leading an experimental study, and scaling up implementation (CBSM, 2017). Community-based social marketing goes beyond traditional marketing techniques to actively engage people in behavior change at the level of *social practices*, which is the intersection between behavior and the broader context. Social practices help sustainability professionals understand how to move beyond examining individual behavior as the main objective to viewing choices as "moments in practice" (Strengers and Maller, 2015, p. 2), which are influenced by individual preferences as well as social structures and technological options.

This is important because as Heberlein (2012) argued, *environmental attitudes* are just one part of explaining sustainable behavior and must be considered in connection with the *context*, such as social influences (e.g., being part of networks), and the skills, opportunities, and resources available to individuals. Attitudes also change over time as individuals gain experience with a sustainable behavior. Many community-level sustainability programs use this to their advantage by involving citizens directly in activities like tours of eco-houses or drinking reused water that has been filtered from sewage because those experiences help shape their behavior and ingrain habits and routines into their daily lives. They also build confidence and a sense of accomplishment that can help influence those individuals to become *environmental champions* and further spread the behavior.

The following steps of the community-based social marketing process are available at CBSM (2017), along with a database of academic articles focusing on examples of behavior change related to recycling, water and energy conservation, transit, and other sustainable behaviors.

The first step is to select a specific behavior or set of behaviors that are essential for achieving a particular sustainability goal (e.g., energy conservation). An example outlined in CBSM (2017) is attic insulation where homeowners have an option to either install fiberglass batt insulation themselves or hire a contractor to blow in cellulose insulation. Blowing in cellulose insulation requires additional equipment and training and thus has additional barriers to the decision for individuals. However, some individuals will find that installing batt insulation themselves results in a series of physical and technical barriers that they may wish to avoid by simply paying a professional to do the work for them. Each insulation process includes a series of decisions that must be taken into account when designing interventions to encourage sustainable behavior. The choice of which process to follow acts as an overarching focal point decision, which can itself represent a barrier. Different strategies and instruments may be required throughout the behavior change process, with information at the focal point decision, financial incentives at the point of purchase, and prompts at the point of installing the insulation. Acceleration Point: Sustainability professionals can target this focal point as a means of accelerating the sustainable behavior by helping homeowners make this initial decision.

The second step is to identify the barriers and benefits to the sustainable behavior as well as the competing, status quo behavior. This can be done via literature review, observing people doing the behavior, conducting focus groups to explore people's attitudes and behaviors, or surveying people to compare differences in the behavior and its underlying attributes. The goal is to understand the barriers and benefits of the desired behavior, as well as the competing behavior that sustainability professionals want to switch people away from. A set of strategies will then be employed to emphasize the benefits of the sustainable behavior while deemphasizing the benefits of the status quo behavior, as well as deemphasizing the barriers of the sustainable behavior and emphasizing the barriers of the status quo behavior. Strategies can incorporate and combine the use of tools that focus on commitment, social norms, social diffusion, prompts, communication, incentives, and convenience (CBSM, 2017).

Commitment involves getting people to make a small agreement to do a future request (CBSM, 2017). Signing a form that says you agree to volunteer at an environmental non-profit organization increases the chances that the person will follow through and actually complete the volunteer hours when they are called upon at a later date. Making a public commitment is also important, such as posting on social media your intentions to support a green initiative, or having your name listed on a website of water users in the community who agreed to cut back on their consumption. Not requiring a commitment makes it easier for individuals to forget or ignore what can often be considered straight-forward sustainable behaviors.

Social norms can be used to influence sustainable behavior, and CBSM (2017) outlined many strategies including using injunctive and descriptive normative messaging as defined above. Two key approaches to instill and reinforce norms for behavior change include visual notifications and modeling of behaviors. For example, notes may include descriptive statements to normalize behaviors (e.g., 'I compost' stickers or signs) that may otherwise seem odd or undesirable. Modeling actions (e.g., picking up litter) can be important for people to see a behavior in action and replicate it themselves.

Social diffusion is the process of influencing sustainable behavior through conversations with people who we trust. CBSM (2017) discussed studies of solar panels in California neighborhoods and xeriscaping in the Pacific Northwest, both of which seem to cluster due to the social networks of homeowners who communicate the benefits of installing such systems. Social diffusion occurs due to trusting relationships built through social networks rather than through geographical proximity alone. Sustainability professionals can organize community events and workshops as a means of providing information, skills, and experiences that can then be spread through social diffusion to amplify sustainable behavior.

Prompts are defined as a:

> visual or auditory aid which reminds us to carry out an activity we might otherwise forget . . . the purpose of a prompt is not to change attitudes or increase motivation, but simply to remind us to engage in an action that we are already predisposed to do.
> (CBSM, 2017)

To be successful, the prompt should be noticeable, clear, and close to the place and time where the behavior is to occur (e.g., the seat belt warning chimes when you put your vehicle into drive). Prompts can help reinforce or build unconscious habits and are therefore critical tools for sustainability professionals working to ingrain sustainable practices.

Communication can help change behaviors when combined with other strategies and tools including prompts, commitment, and incentives (CBSM, 2017). To enhance the effectiveness of such communications, vivid information, direct personal contact, and providing feedback on how people are doing are key to behavior change, as is using credible sources such as influential community leaders. Sustainability professionals can use their **interpersonal relations competence** to amplify the impact of other CBSM tools including social diffusion and social norms for spreading sustainable behavior throughout a community.

Incentives for encouraging (or disincentives for discouraging) sustainable behavior can take many forms, from charging homeowners for extra garbage bags at the curbside pick-up, to paying a fee for bottles or paint stewardship programs to encourage the return of the bottle or unused paint, to government contracted payments per kilowatt hour of electricity generated by homeowners who installed solar panels as part of a feed-in-tariff. Although dis/incentives are often monetary in nature, recognition and awards are also tools that could be used, especially in the face of limited financial resources. One key consideration with incentives is that if they cannot be sustained to encourage desirable practices, then behaviors might fall back to the status quo.

Making the behavior as *convenient* as possible will increase the chances of success. One example described by CBSM (2017) was the free giveaway and delivery of composters to residents who agreed to accept them. This increased the composting rate dramatically by removing the barrier of inconvenience to acquire a unit. Another example is adding a paper recycling bin to each individual office cubical, which can increase recycling rates by 70 percent (CBSM, 2017). Providing infrastructure is often an important element for making behaviors convenient. Reducing the time and costs associated with sustainable behaviors is also critical.

Important lessons from the community-based social marketing process are that changing behavior depends on the context and that different combinations of strategies and tools work most effectively when paired together (CBSM, 2017). If the barrier is a lack of motivation, then effective tools include commitment, norms, and incentives. If the barrier is forgetting to act, then an effective tool is prompts. In cases where there is a lack of social pressure, normative messaging can be effective. For a lack of knowledge, communication and social diffusion techniques can be the desired tools. And for structural barriers, the key is to make the desired behavior as convenient as possible (CBSM, 2017).

Community-based social marketing has proven to be effective at encouraging sustainable behavior in many contexts. Education and engagement approaches require further examination, however, for the specific types and combinations of knowledge that may be important in sustainable behavior change. Community-based social marketing and education-based strategies can complement monetary interventions that aim to shape demand based on altered market prices.

Educational approaches for changing food and waste behaviors

Changing food and waste behaviors requires more than traditional educational approaches focusing on *declarative knowledge*. Redman (2013) integrated educational pedagogy and behavior change techniques with the Wiek et al. (2011) *sustainability competencies* (Chapter 1) in a problem- and project-based approach to change food and waste behaviors among students. The year-long study examined the impact of an increase in two types of *technical knowledge* (declarative and procedural) and two types of *subjective knowledge* (effectiveness and social) on sustainable waste and food behaviors.

- *Declarative knowledge* refers to "traditional social/ecological information . . . information about how ecosystems function and how people interact with and impact the environment through their actions and decisions" (Redman, 2013, p. 3).
- *Procedural knowledge* refers to "'how-to' information that builds an individual's capacity for action and correlates closely with situational and structural factors that may facilitate or constrain individual action" (Redman, 2013, p. 3).
- *Effectiveness knowledge* refers to "perceptions about desirability and the capacity to participate in various behaviors" (Redman, 2013, p. 3).
- *Social knowledge* refers to "what is commonly done (e.g., motives and intentions of others) and judgments of the behavior in a given social or cultural environment (e.g., perceived desirability of particular actions)" (Redman, 2013, p. 3).

Redman (2013) found that an increase in declarative knowledge in a particular domain did not necessarily lead to changes in behavior. For example, waste behavior changed more than food behavior despite a lower level of declarative knowledge for waste behavior. Waste behavior changes were maintained more successfully than food behavior over time due to social and cultural influences. In combination with declarative knowledge, *procedural, effectiveness, and social* knowledge may be critical to encourage changes to food and waste behavior (Redman and Redman, 2014). The theory is that if a program can increase these types of knowledge in individuals, especially knowledge that goes beyond the traditional focus on declarative knowledge, their sustainable behaviors will increase. Sustainability professionals can use different combinations of strategies and tools to develop and reinforce multiple types of knowledge to build and maintain sustainable behavior.

Economic approaches to sustainable behavior change

The aforementioned social science theories that explain sustainable behavior are context specific and provide a partial understanding of what motivates sustainability-oriented decisions (Kollmuss and Agyeman, 2002). In cases where consumers switch to greener products based on messages that target their personal values, beliefs, and attitudes, information and engagement strategies consistent with the community-based social marketing process are effective. But not all individuals respond to influence campaigns and social pressures in the same way. Sustainability professionals can look to economics for tools and techniques that can influence another segment of society to adopt sustainable behaviors.

Green product options are now available in most market segments including clothing, food, electronics, vehicles, and energy supply. Pickett-Baker and Ozaki (2008) discovered that consumers with sustainability-oriented beliefs were more likely to have confidence in the performance of green products. Strategies can incorporate community-based social marketing tools to improve the understanding of the green benefits and therefore increase the chances that consumers will want to voluntarily pay a premium price for those goods. Even in cases where environmental/social benefits and economic benefits of the sustainable behavior or decision are communicated effectively, many consumers still do not make behavior changes (Pickett-Baker and Ozaki, 2008) because of gaps between knowledge and actions or between values and actions (Frederiks et al., 2015). In other words, some sustainable behaviors are economically beneficial based on return-on-investment criteria and yet are still not undertaken. Behaviors that can be changed or maintained for a variety of reasons beyond or in addition to economic criteria may be characterized as (Frederiks et al., 2015, p. 1386):

- retaining the status quo,
- achieving a satisfactory rather than optimal result,
- being loss averse by weighing losses (e.g., risks, financial costs, safety, healthy, social pressure and criticism, environmental impacts, time) more heavily than equivalent gains,
- employing the sunk cost effect wherein a consumer who outlays time, effort, and money to purchase an electrical appliance (e.g., air conditioner, second fridge) may tend to use it more, even when it is not necessarily required,
- preferring smaller rewards immediately over larger future rewards, avoiding actions that are costly in the short-term (buying an appliance) despite offering long-term benefits (reduced electricity bills),
- making social comparisons and conforming to social norms,

- being motivated by rewards and incentives, both intrinsic (e.g., achieving social equity, acting altruistically) and extrinsic (e.g., saving money),
- taking less actions if they will gain the same benefits due to other's actions without having to pay for them (free-rider effect),
- taking actions or not based on the trustworthiness of the source of information,
- drawing on readily available information that is easily accessible in memory (e.g., personal anecdotes of family/friends, customers, recent, frequent, vivid, salient).

Many sustainable behaviors correspond with one or more of the aforementioned characteristics and are therefore motivated by things other than minimizing costs or maximizing financial returns. This suggests that sustainable behavior is more complex than neoclassical economic models based on traditional conceptions of rationalizing portray. Other potentially more important aspects of well-being need to be included such as happiness and sufficiency. The key questions for sustainability professionals are (1) how to use strategies and instruments to encourage sustainable behavior by taking into account both economic and non-economic factors and (2) how to use strategies and instruments to scale-up sustainable behavior. While prices do play an important role, consumers may respond to prices in rational or irrational ways. Consumers may be willing to pay higher prices for green products/services, but how sensitive is demand to increases in price due to the addition of green attributes? Can premium-priced green goods garner support because consumers are willing and able to pay for the green benefits in addition to the standard benefits provided by the product (Clark et al., 2003; Gliedt and Parker, 2010; Whitmarsh and O'Neill, 2010)? Another way of asking this is, can premium priced green goods maintain demand because consumers are willing and able to pay for public benefits in addition to private benefits?

The field of *ecological economics* can help provide answers to these questions by integrating the study of resource allocations (resource economics) with the pollution side of the equation (environmental economics) (Daly and Farley, 2010). Illge and Schwarze (2009) compared ecological economics to environmental economics and found several key differences, including how human behavior and ecosystem services are examined, how the relationship between sustainable development and growth is conceptualized, as well as the inclusion of social and distributional (intra-generational equity) considerations in ecological economics. Ecological economics is an interdisciplinary approach because it combines energy (the laws of thermodynamics) with economic (monetary) flows to understand and prioritize a sustainable level of materials and energy throughput, then a socially just distribution of the benefits and costs of development, and finally after those criteria are met, an efficient allocation of resources. Ecological economists study environmental and resource problems from a macro or micro perspective looking at human behavior, organizational strategies, and institutional changes as important to sustainable development. Ecological economics can help sustainability professionals understand *negative externalities* or the interdependence between one actor's actions and its impacts on another actor. Green innovation can be incentivized by internalizing pollution and health impacts into prices with the help of green taxes and tradable permits (Smith et al., 2010). These types of policy instruments can offer flexibility to producers while encouraging sustainable behavior from consumers by making greener products relatively more affordable. One limitation of using green taxes is that the level of taxes necessary to change behavior may be too high to be politically feasible in some jurisdictions (Smith et al., 2010). Therefore, price signals are "necessary, yet insufficient to assure innovative responses on the supply-side of the market" (p. 438).

Smith et al. (2010) argued for incorporating additional factors to influence green innovation on the supply-side including changes to the institutional, policy, politics, and culture regime subsystems. *Institutional economics* can help sustainability professionals understand these regime subsystems by examining how transaction costs can be positive or negative when it comes to the impacts on resources and the environment. *Transaction costs* are defined as the costs of using a particular market to buyers and sellers, including administrative expenses, travel time, risks associated with incomplete information, and uncertainties (Hayter and Patchell, 2011). Sustainability professionals can help manage the transaction costs associated with environmental governance, which include costs for collecting information, making decisions, and formulating, monitoring, and enforcing rules (Paavola and Adger, 2005), as a means of reducing barriers to sustainable behavior by organizations. In summary, both internal individual factors (e.g., personality traits, value systems, knowledge, attitudes) and external influences (e.g., infrastructure, political, social and cultural, economic) can help sustainability professionals design and implement strategies and instruments to overcome barriers to sustainable behavior (Kollmuss and Agyeman, 2002).

Political ecological approaches to behavior

Another way to study the connections between sustainable behavior and broader societal levels including technology, institutions, and infrastructure systems is political ecology. This approach is focused on structural and cultural factors, as opposed to the emphasis on values, beliefs, norms, and attitudes in the psychological realm and market-based mechanisms in the political realm. As Lawhon and Murphy (2012) stated, "understanding these (technological) artifacts and changing behavior patterns requires significant consideration of the social context wherein they developed" (p. 360). Political ecology can help sustainability professionals examine and shape the social context that underlies changes to economic and environmental systems by incorporating power and cultural dynamics between actors (Offen, 2004).

Reshaping social expectations regarding sustainability problems and solutions may take a long time and can be slowed by political barriers and a lack of broad acceptance (Lawhon and Murphy, 2012). Lawhon and Murphy (2012) suggested using co-production of knowledge options between natural and social scientists, citizens, and industrial/political leaders (described in Chapter 3) to address concerns about democratic decision-making while improving the likelihood of success. The goal is to find a balance between efficiency (e.g., time, financial resources, political cycles) and fairness (e.g., including stakeholders in the process). Empowering additional stakeholders in the transition process can have benefits for creating sustainability solutions. Rather than a transition arena composed of elites, Lawhon and Murphy (2012) recommended focusing on relationships to enhance decision-making across scales to connect niche and regime experiments.

Political ecology could compliment sustainability transitions theory in a number of ways including by identifying connections between problems and competing solutions; by recognizing a wider range of actors and incorporating their unique knowledge; by studying the impact of power relations on human–environmental interactions; and by better explaining socio-technical systems' outcomes and impacts (Lawhon and Murphy, 2012). Political ecology addresses critiques of sustainability transitions and the multi-level perspective (MLP) (Chapter 7) including that the MLP focuses on the national scale and does not explain how institutional and socio-economic processes at local scales could be incorporated (Lawhon and Murphy, 2012). This ignores place-based differences in the process and outcomes of sustainability transitions within countries. The challenge is to make sure that the benefits of sustainability strategies and instruments reach local communities including those with less political power.

Political ecology, social norms, and other theories that take into account the broader context that shapes sustainable behavior remind sustainability professionals that seemingly obvious technological solutions can fail to achieve sustainability impacts due to cross-scale political, cultural, or social dynamics. To address the oversimplification of sustainable behavior processes, Pisano and Lubell (2017) developed a multi-level framework for understanding the cross-level interactions between individual sustainable behavior and regime-level indicators of economic development, education, and environmental performance, as well as from the regime level to the individual-level public (e.g., working for environmental non-profit organizations) and private (e.g., energy or water conservation decisions) sustainable behavior.

Using data from a large sample international survey to build a multi-level statistical model, Pisano and Lubell (2017) found that wealthier countries with higher levels of *post-materialism* were more likely to have large proportions of citizens involved in sustainable behavior. Countries with a higher density of environmental non-profit organizations and a higher level of education of the population had more individuals highly engaged in public sustainable behaviors (e.g., activism). Pisano and Lubell (2017) concluded that strategies to encourage sustainable behavior (e.g., education, community-based social marketing techniques) may be unsuccessful unless paired with instruments at the societal level (e.g., regulations, taxes). This supports the idea of *policy mixes* (Kivimaa and Kern, 2016), which are designed to simultaneously encourage niche experiments and regime change and destruction to accelerate a sustainability transition (Chapter 8). Policy mixes must also ensure that individuals and other stakeholders are incorporated and empowered as part of sustainability transition processes.

Public participation in energy transitions

Chilvers and Longhurst (2016) reviewed four cases of energy transitions in the United Kingdom to compare different forms of public participation (deliberative public participation, social movement theory, practice theory, grassroots innovation) as methods of scaling sustainable behavior to multi-level system change. In all four cases, innovative technologies were important for managing, organizing, and coordinating interactions between actors in order to encourage individual or collective behavior changes. External actors or pressures were identified in each case that acted as threats to the program. The two models that were centralized or top-down (Energy 2050 Pathways Public Dialogue and the Visible Energy Trial) tended to constrain the range of decisions to certain technology solutions, while the bottom-up models (Camp for Climate Action and the Dyfi Eco Valley Partnership Solar Club) produced a more active engagement from citizens that allowed for broader socio-political solutions. The four cases are summarized from Chilvers and Longhurst (2016).

Energy 2050 Pathways Public Dialogue was a centralized program controlled by a few powerful actors from the energy regime. It used *deliberative public participation* to help the public, politicians, business, and non-profit leaders understand the difficulty of achieving an 80 percent reduction in greenhouse gas (GHG) emissions below 1990 levels that was legally required by the United Kingdom Climate Change Act of 2008. Workshops were used to walk participants through a range of scenarios to show them the tradeoffs that would occur if their preferred technological solutions were implemented.

Camp for Climate Action was a decentralized program led by experienced environmental activists but organized in a decentralized, bottom–up manner through regional networks. It used *social movement theory* to create an environmental movement with protests, education, and engagement for climate change mitigation solutions. In contrast to the Energy 2050 Pathways framing of sustainability actions around technology narratives, Camp for Climate Action framed the need for climate change actions as a moral issue that was being slowed down by resistance strategies from fossil fuel regime actors.

Visible Energy Trial used a centralized recruitment process to encourage the public to participate in a program to reduce their carbon footprint. It used *social practice theory* to engage residents to change their energy use practices through interactions with a smart meter and visual display technology. The results did not lead to substantial energy behavior changes partly because homeowners felt that the residential sector was being unfairly targeted and partly because information via visualization technology alone was not effective at encouraging sustainable behavior.

Dyfi Eco Valley Partnership Solar Club was led by a program officer and included a professional energy trainer and local engineers to conduct energy assessments. It used a *grassroots innovation model for participation* to organize public meetings while aiming to help reduce the costs to install solar water systems by negotiating bulk discounts and encouraging self-installation. Regime actors including the Department of Trade and Industry and the International Solar Energy Association were worried about liability for product failures and health and safety concerns due to self-installations. Although the program used social norms to encourage grassroots solar installations, it was framed as an economic development strategy based on renewable and distributed energy systems. This approach became less effective over time as new market competition from companies offering more affordable solar systems undermined the competitive advantage of the solar club model.

In all four cases, there was some question as to the outputs and outcomes that were actually achieved beyond the importance of the participatory processes themselves (Chilvers and Longhurst, 2016). Nevertheless, similar types of community and partnership programs for the development and diffusion of energy services have shown a measured ability to reduce GHG emissions (Hoicka et al., 2014). The following section outlines examples of sustainable behavior that have the potential to expand impacts from the individual to the community and social scales.

Practice of sustainable behavior change

Sustainability professionals are concerned with making changes and solving problems. Not all changes will have equal outcomes or impacts on the Gibson principles of sustainability. Technology focused solutions for example may suffer from limitations that make it more difficult to enhance the sustainability principles of livelihood sufficiency and opportunity, civility and democratic governance, and immediate and long-term integration if directed by a top-down approach controlled by powerful actors in the regime that does not incorporate citizens and other local stakeholders into the process. One means by which citizens and local stakeholders can be incorporated in sustainability within developing countries is through the use of traditional ecological knowledge.

Traditional ecological knowledge

Traditional ecological knowledge (TEK) is important for sustainability because local people who live and work within communities that are facing resource or environmental challenges have critical experience that can help devise solutions. TEK combines knowledge of environmental resources and processes, beliefs about how humans relate to the environment, and practices of resource use (Berkes et al., 2000). Culture and history are important because they can guide choices and inform strategies for sustainability. Within rural communities, sustainable behavior is the norm rather than the exception because local people live within the carrying capacity of nature based on applying their TEK.

Unlike sustainable behavior theories focusing on individuals, TEK is a collective and cumulative "body of knowledge, practices and beliefs about the relationships among living things (including humans), the physical environment, and a society's culture" (Falkowski et al., 2015, p. 40). TEK is an example of a collective intra- and inter-generational *social practice* because it is passed from family to family and from generation to generation. TEK can be transmitted through geographic diffusion, cross-scale interactions, community assessments, regulations, social and religious norms, rituals, ceremonies, cultural frameworks, and collective environmental ethics and cultural values (Berkes et al., 2000). The collective social practices at the family level can inform the development of *adaptive management* practices at the governance levels (Berkes et al., 2000) to help scale-up sustainable practices from the community to the broader region.

Sustainability professionals within communities can act as intermediaries (Chapter 6) between traditional farmers and ranchers on the one hand, and governance and industry actors on the other hand, to mobilize TEK as a means of guiding a sustainability transition. Sustainability transitions based on TEK can include technological solutions that are culturally appropriate if created by the local people. Niche experiments (Chapter 7) range from water pumps powered by humans via modified bicycles to distributed solar systems powering schools and hospitals. Sustainability professionals can change governance regimes (Chapter 7) rapidly by altering the structure and dynamics of institutions, or slowly by influencing changes to culture and worldviews. Sustainability professionals can help manage the *turbulence* from introducing new technologies into societies while reducing the environmental degradation that results from increasing incomes per capita due to economic development. While families provide effective levels for sustainability transitions in developing countries, households are also an important focal point for sustainable behavior in developed countries.

Households as nexus for sustainable behavior change

Households act as a functional unit that connects individual behavior to organizational and community levels through employment and social networks. Examples of energy programs that link individual to organizational and community levels (Hoicka et al., 2014; Hoicka and Parker, 2011) demonstrate that education, engagement, and incentives can influence changes to household energy use behavior. Social networks and community-based social marketing initiatives that rely on normative pressures and other tools are used to scale-up sustainable behavior via neighbor-to-neighbor interactions. A set of prioritized recommendations for energy investments is provided to homeowners by a third party, non-profit energy advisor who conducts an energy audit and produces a detailed report. The list of potential energy changes is based on the modelled energy and economic returns. Information, trust, framing, incentives, and timing are all important in helping homeowners make sustainable decisions (Hoicka et al., 2014; Parker et al., 2003, 2005). Sustainability professionals who are part of non-profit organizations delivering sustainability services (Gliedt and Parker, 2014) can help homeowners understand the sustainability impacts of these integrated technology investments.

Linking real-time energy use information to pricing schemes can provide an integrated energy-economic prompt at the point where the behavior occurs within households. Koksal et al. (2015) analyzed appliance-level electricity use data from a sample of households in Ontario, Canada. They found that the highest household usage, cost, and CO_2 emissions occurred in the summer between 3pm and 7pm. This was largely due to air conditioning load and time-of-use pricing schemes. With real-time energy use information, homeowners can try to manage end uses by avoiding non-essential appliance use during peak times, turning up the air conditioner thermostat, and switching to more efficient appliances. Circuit-level monitoring was conducted to provide energy use patterns for each individual appliance and energy service in the home, which allows for strategies to tailor behavior change to areas that have the largest potential energy and monetary savings (Rowlands et al., 2013). Utilities respond to residential energy preferences by creating time-of-use pricing and education campaigns to shift demand, while offering incentives to purchase more efficient appliances. Government agencies can increase appliance rating standards, for example, by raising the minimum Seasonal Energy Efficiency Ratio of air conditioners to reflect technology improvements that have brought down the price of these systems. The United States Energy Star program maintains a publicly available database of the most energy efficient appliances each year including operating costs and energy savings data (Energy Star, 2017). Homeowners, wholesalers, and builders can follow this database to make their own return-on-investment calculations for each appliance category.

Financial frameworks for household energy investment decisions including return-on-investment and net-present-value models do not allow homeowners to defer investment decisions or to make staged investments over time (Gahrooei et al., 2016). Gahrooei et al. (2016) attempted to overcome these limitations by developing a modified decision-making framework to generate scenarios for timing residential solar PV investments. This is important for two reasons: (1) the costs of solar PV decline over time, and (2) modular solar systems could allow for staged investment as technology and installation costs decline, conventional electricity prices increase, or energy demand within the household fluctuates. The framework allows for delayed investment decisions under uncertainty regarding the size of the system. Gahrooei et al. (2016) concluded that the size of the solar PV system depends on the growth rate of the electricity price and the sellback ratio, defined as the "ratio of the rate at which electricity is sold back to the grid to the rate at which the electricity is bought from the grid" (p. 114).

The extent that delaying investment could help increase returns depends on the rate of changes in electricity prices and installation costs of solar systems (Gahrooei et al., 2016). In a stable market for prices and costs, homeowners should either invest immediately or never invest. If changes to prices or costs are anticipated, then the homeowner is better to wait. Investment in solar PV in phases can increase the total return-on-investment and this is particularly important when the solar market is stable. Although Gahrooei et al. (2016) did not incorporate future uncertainty in battery storage technology, this would certainly be important in the sizing and timing of solar investments. Take for example the Tesla Powerwall 2, which can power an average sized home for an entire day (Tesla, 2017).

This could drastically reduce the size of solar PV system and depending on the climate would provide a more resilient home energy system even if sellback options are not available.

Sustainability professionals can work with homeowners and community programs to find ways of ingraining sustainable household behavior as habits and routines that become unconscious practices as part of everyday life. A promising area that integrates elements of psychology, sociology, and structural/contextual theories and applications to understand and encourage sustainable behavior is social practices.

Social practices and interventions

Social practices theory views habits, people, and things as having agency in contrast to only people having agency (Strengers, 2012). Social practices are routines within which people participate and through which individuals, structures, and technologies co-evolve (Shove et al., 2012). This implies that "the focus shifts from individuals as autonomous agents. . .onto assemblages of common understandings, material infrastructures, practical knowledge and rules, which are reproduced through daily routines" (Strengers, 2012, p. 229). Leray et al. (2016) suggested that social practices theory goes beyond microeconomic models that assume consumers make rational decisions and instead views social practices as a combination of people (e.g., abilities, understanding), the physical world (e.g., infrastructure, technology), and social context (e.g., culture, norms, institutions).

Social practices theories can help sustainability professionals scale-up household sustainable behavior to the community level. Naus and van der Horst (2016) outlined a study from the Netherlands that links social practices of energy use behavior in households to broader strategies involving technologies and community interactions. They found that the strategies that were most successful were ones that were easily integrated into pre-existing daily routines. Energy information designed to encourage sustainable behavior needs to be directly relevant to homeowners' interests (e.g., interest in solar energy or in new technologies). Information was transferred and used in energy decisions via three types of practices:

- *Household practices*
  - comfort settings, energy use patterns, and preferences
    - (e.g., how, why, and when are appliances used)

- *Monitoring practices*
  - use of smart meters and online applications
    - (e.g., pathways for change where users interact with a technology and feedback system)

- *Community interaction practices*
  - participants interact at workshops, events, and demonstrations
    - (e.g., grassroots innovation)

Naus and van der Horst (2016) argued that "information sometimes travelled between practices, and in other instances information remained relevant only within the context of the practice in which it was accomplished" (p. 14). They concluded that participation in community energy initiatives, including hands on energy demonstrations as well as social networks, encouraged people to take actions within their homes. This suggests that cross-level connections between different types of practices are important for sustainable behavior. Acceleration Point: Sustainability professionals can use strategies to develop social practices at the community level as a means of influencing sustainable behavior at the household level. Sustainability professionals can also develop programs that highlight energy use practices at the household level as an education and engagement mechanism to spread energy use practices to other homeowners.

Strengers (2012) used social practice theory to study peak electricity demand shifting and shedding as strategies to increase resilience to blackouts during summer peak demand spikes on the system. From a social practice perspective, energy consumers become co-managers by linking supply and demand with the help of technologies like on-site solar and storage, automated demand management systems, and variable pricing schemes. This involves homeowners creating an intentional disruption in response to peaking prices by changing practices in the house and effectively creating an artificial but temporary black-out of some energy services (e.g., air conditioning, lighting, washer and dryer) in accord-ance with their expectations and needs. It is the expectations and needs that structure energy demand and can therefore have a large impact on sustainable behavior outcomes (Strengers, 2012). Acceleration Point: Reframing energy into a practices model allows sustainability professionals to focus on understanding and reshaping consumer expecta-tions and needs rather than on helping consumers save resources and money. This can help homeowners see the *sustainability value* from energy behavior rather than just the economic costs.

Another example of social practices is the set of interconnected decisions involved in paying a bill. If viewed from a social practices perspective, paying a bill involves a series of interconnected decisions that require different combinations of abilities to perform the practice. This includes not just the decision of whether to pay the bill at a bank or online, but rather, a comparison of options for taking the bus or train, riding a bike, or driving a car to the bank. Alternatively, choosing to pay the bill online requires learning a new app or website. It also requires trusting that the technology and its organizational support system will protect your privacy and security. Each of these options involves technolo-gies and different sets of abilities that must be learned in order to carry out the practice of paying a bill.

Viewing paying a bill as a practice also gives the opportunity for sustainability profes-sionals to identify previously unknown barriers to technology adoption. For example, one reason why some individuals may be resistant to using a bike share system to travel to the bank and pay a bill is that they are unsure of the practice of using the machines and the card system that must be swiped in order to rent the bikes. To overcome this uncertainty, a community engagement program could invite individuals to participate in a training session, and a social network approach could be used to spread the practice (e.g., walk people step by step through how to find bike sharing systems and use them) rather than just spreading information about where bike sharing systems are located. This connection between the individual and the organizational or community levels can itself be a form of encouraging changes in people's lives and building commitment to sustainable behavior (Naus and van der Horst, 2016). Furthermore, sustainability professionals can partner with banks to promote e-banking as a greener option by reducing paper and transportation to and from the bank. In this case, the practice of paying a bill becomes ingrained in people's routines by prompts from the app or email system, and rewards for switching from paper billing to e-billing. Sustainability professionals could help organizations design bill pay programs to reduce barriers to each stage of the practice and to recommend a bill pay process that minimizes environmental impacts from a lifecycle perspective.

Geels et al. (2015) compared three approaches to understanding sustainable behavior. The first is the *reformist approach*, which is based on organizations investing in sustainability innovations and consumers switching to greener products. This approach aims to accelerate innovation through interventions at the supply and demand side based on rational economic principles. The second is the *revolutionary approach*, which considers the need for alternative political-economic systems to capitalism that may be based on frugality, sufficiency, and localism principles. This approach uses ethical, spiritual, social, and eco-centric arguments to suggest that the scale of the current system of production and consumption needs to be reduced to become sustainable. The third is the *reconfiguration approach*, which is based on the sustainability transitions MLP framework in combination with changes to social practices. This approach combines elements of the reformist and revolutionary approaches to simultaneously reshape production and consumption behavior in the direction of sustainability. The reconfiguration approach requires further research to develop models for understanding the connections between niche and regime processes in the socio-technical system and social practices at the individual level. One way for sustainability professionals to integrate social practices into the sustainability transitions MLP framework is by adding a capabilities approach.

Social practices and capabilities approach to sustainability

The key to linking sustainable behavior to system change is *sustain-ability* – or the *ability to sustain*. It is the specific abilities (of individuals) or capabilities (of organizations) that are critical for moving society closer to achieving strong sustainability. Teaching and learning these (cap) abilities is important to developing and training sustainability professionals. Abilities identified as key *sustainability competencies* (Chapter 1) are linked to higher levels through social practices (Strengers and Maller, 2015) and sustainability assessment metrics (Rauschmayer et al., 2015). In this case, individuals make decisions not simply based on self-interest or the influence of institutional and normative pressures, but rather, because of ingrained routines that are both created and enabled by individuals and the systems they are part of.

A framework that combines sustainability transitions and social practices is introduced by Rauschmayer et al. (2015). They suggested that *transition management* (Chapter 7) does not focus enough on how agents can change their practices as part of the broader sustainability transition. In response, Rauschmayer et al. (2015) linked the societal level regime subsystems (Chapter 7) and the individual-level behavior changes by adding a capability approach related to human well-being. Capabilities for sustainability combine elements of human capital (including knowledge) and social capital (including networks) as well as the specific *sustainability competencies* in Chapter 1. The goal is use those capabilities to shift individuals from unsustainable status-quo practices (the left side of Figure 2.1) to sustainable practices (the right side of Figure 2.1). Niches provide areas for sustainability professionals to apply strategies and instruments to encourage changes to locked-in unsustainable social practices. Sustainability assessments can be used to guide the direction of change towards the Gibson sustainability principles (Chapter 1). Sustainability professionals can then focus on scaling-up and amplifying successful changes to social practices into broader community change programs for sustainable behavior.

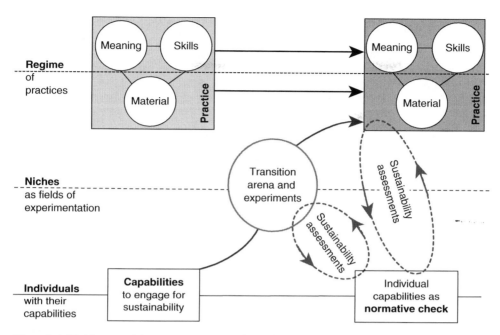

Figure 2.1 Linking transition management and social practices
Source: Rauschmayer et al. (2015, p. 218).

Social practices theories can help sustainability professionals understand how to change institutions and infrastructures by first changing individual and organizational behavior. These theories show how integration can occur across levels and can be used by change agents as a flexible mechanism to encourage the scaling-up of sustainable behavior. But how do sustainability professionals measure the contribution of sustainable behavior to transitions across levels in society? The following section outlines methods of measuring progress towards sustainability that focus on understanding sustainable behavior.

Methods for understanding progress towards sustainable behavior

Surveys of consumers' perceptions and attitudes prior to changing a behavior can be used to anticipate changes in sustainability-oriented behavior. Mah et al. (2012) surveyed residential consumers of electricity in Hong Kong and found that they expressed support for the development of a smart and sustainable grid, including pricing changes as well as switching to renewable energy and energy efficiency. A majority of respondents were willing to accept peaking prices to encourage efficiency and supported propositions for large energy users to pay more for their electricity. Interestingly, when asked what would motivate them individually to reduce electricity use, the top three answers were the environmental benefits, energy performance labels, and money savings. The least important was because everyone else is doing it, which suggests that some consumers may not believe that social norms are important in their electricity decisions in Hong Kong, or that norms are not as influential there as in other contexts.

Rhodes et al. (2015) conducted a nationally representative survey of Canadians to evaluate citizen awareness of and support for British Columbia's low-carbon fuel standard. A low-carbon fuel standard is a performance-based policy that aims to reduce average GHG emission intensities (GHG/unit of energy) in transportation fuels. They found that few respondents from British Columbia even knew about the low-carbon fuel standard, but once they were informed of how it works, 90 percent approved of it. They also found that political acceptability for the introduction of a low-carbon fuel standard was high in other provinces as well. This type of national survey can help sustainability professionals understand when a *window of opportunity* may open for introducing a new sustainability policy.

Egbue and Long (2012) analyzed consumer attitudes and perceptions of barriers to the adoption of electric vehicles. They electronically surveyed faculty and students at a university who were considered likely electric vehicle adopters. The results suggested that likely adopters place more value on the vehicle cost and performance (e.g., reducing the use of petroleum; less maintenance) than sustainability in the form of reduced GHG emissions. However, nearly 80 percent of the sample said that sustainability has some degree of influence on a vehicle purchase. Those with a higher level of education and over the age of 24 were more familiar with sustainability. It is interesting to note that a third of respondents defined sustainability as relating to product and/or resource longevity, as opposed to resource conservation or protecting the environment, which combined for 40 percent. These differences in understanding of sustainability may pose barriers to building collaborative support for a single strategy or instrument, but they could serve as opportunities for tailoring different types of strategies and instruments to individuals who are motivated by different dimensions of sustainability.

Using a collection of surveys of individuals in the United Kingdom, Gatersleben et al. (2018) categorized four consumer identities as motives for sustainable behavior: frugal, moral, wasteful, and thrifty. Respondents most frequently considered themselves as thrifty consumers, followed by frugal, moral, and wasteful consumers. Frugal and moral consumer identities were most strongly related to sustainable behavior. Frugal identities were related to sustainable behaviors that achieved waste reduction in particular (e.g., physical waste or money). Energy saving behaviors were positively associated with moral or frugal consumer identities. Interestingly, frugal consumer identities were not related to moral consumer identities, suggesting that either identity can influence sustainable energy behavior independent of the other. Acceleration Point: Sustainability professionals designing strategies focusing on behavior change should distinguish and then tailor messaging and incentives to different consumer identities.

Schmitt et al. (2018) used two large sample surveys, one in Canada and the other in the United States, to examine the impact of performing sustainable behavior on life satisfaction. Even after controlling for demographic differences and the ecological beliefs of respondents, they discovered that an increase in the frequency of performing sustainable behavior positively influenced life satisfaction for 37 of the 39 sustainable behaviors examined. Certain types of sustainable behavior had a bigger impact on life satisfaction including those that involved higher levels of social interaction, were publicly visible, or involved saving money, time, or effort. Sustainability professionals can design strategies and instruments that involve social and community interactions, which can serve to couple the new behavior to life satisfaction thereby reinforcing the sustainable behavior.

Interviews offer a means of understanding the why and how something is happening in addition to the what and when provided by surveys (Gubrium, 2012). While surveys can help identify and compare important factors, interviews provide insight into decision-making processes involved in organizational strategies. Process-level research is critical for linking individual and organizational decisions to broader social changes as part of green innovation and triple-bottom-line economic development strategies. Sustainability professionals can use interviews to investigate perceptions held by water managers about challenges facing their systems, which are outlined in Chapter 4. Interviews can also help examine social practices that involve complex connections between technology and infrastructures, institutions and norms, and individuals and organizations across multiple levels of socio-technical systems.

Focus groups and other collaborative and interactive forums can help sustainability scientists to co-produce knowledge with the help of stakeholders (Stewart and Shamdasani, 2014). Co-producing knowledge through *adaptive co-management* approaches can scale-up sustainable behavior of individuals and organizations. Transdisciplinary learning and adaptive governance can incorporate changing priorities of stakeholders vis-à-vis their demands of sustainability scientists (Moran and Lopez, 2016). Collaborative and interactive studies look at ways of fostering learning processes whereby individuals can influence change within organizations or communities, which are discussed in Chapter 3. Problem- and project-based learning can help improve knowledge levels and can encourage an understanding of sustainable behaviors as social practices. One way of looking at individual behavior and practices as part of a socio-technical system is through the ecological footprint calculation.

Ecological footprint calculation

The ecological footprint is a "measure of the land required for population activities taking place on the biosphere within a given year while considering the prevailing technology and resource management" (Fang et al., 2014, p. 510). It encompasses six components: cropland, grazing land, forest products, fishing grounds, built-up land, and carbon (Isman et al., 2018). The ecological footprint is expressed in global hectares (gha), which is the flow of resources produced by a hectare of average land area. An ecological footprint value below 1.7 gha per person suggests that a country, state/province, or city has a sustainable level of resource use rates that is supported by the level of biocapacity available (Global Footprint Network, 2017). An ecological footprint above 1.7 gha per person suggests that the jurisdiction is exceeding the level of resource replenishment rates (*carrying capacity*) that are considered sustainable. The ecological footprint can therefore be considered as a measure of sustainability that can link individual behavior to global scale impacts.

Isman et al. (2018) conducted an ecological footprint analysis for Canadian cities and found that Calgary had the highest footprint as measured by gha per capita. The main reason was the carbon component (Figure 2.2a), which was largely due to energy demand from housing (Figure 2.2b). Toronto and Vancouver had ecological footprints of less than half per capita that of Calgary and Edmonton due to a significantly smaller contribution from carbon and housing. No city included in the analysis was at or below 1.7 gha per capita, although Ottawa was the closest due to a low food component.

(continued)

(continued)

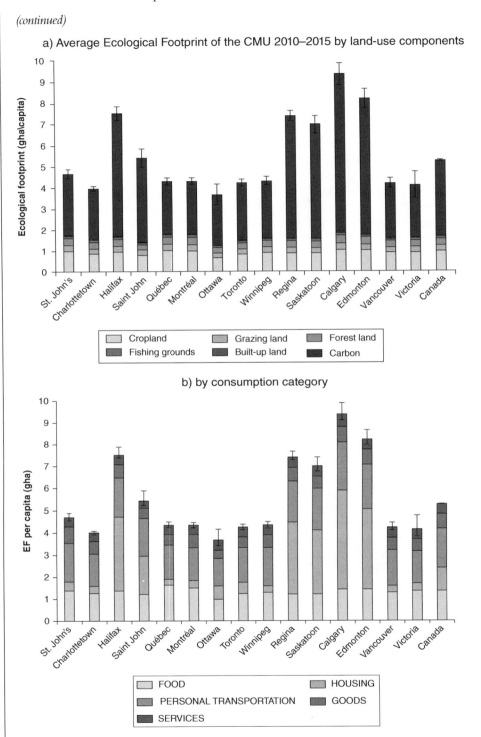

a) Average Ecological Footprint of the CMU 2010–2015 by land-use components

b) by consumption category

Figure 2.2 Ecological footprint for Canadian cities

Source: Isman et al. (2018, p. 1037).

Take the personal ecological footprint calculator quiz at the Global Footprint Network (www.footprintcalculator.org/) and determine how many earths we would need if everyone lived like you. After taking the quiz, what are the specific sustainable behaviors you could adopt to reduce your ecological footprint? What social practices would you have to change to reduce your beef consumption, car travel, or home energy consumption? Furthermore, the calculator identifies your personal earth overshoot day, which is the day of the year that your personal activities will exceed the earths' biocapacity to support those activities. How does your result compare to your friends and family members?

Check on learning

- Read one of the following studies testing the values-beliefs-norms model for recycling in Spain (Aguilar-Luzón et al., 2012), consumer decisions about green hotels (Choi et al., 2015), energy conservation behavior (Ibtissem, 2010), or environmental attitudes and behaviors among youth (Wray-Lake et al., 2010). Write two paragraphs summarizing the model as outlined in the context of sustainability transitions. Then select three principles of sustainability from Chapter 1 and describe how the sustainable behavior strategy from the article could be adopted in your country and/or city/town to help achieve those principles.
- When considering strong sustainability and the Gibson principles, what combination of technologies should a homeowner invest in? What size of furnace, how much insulation, what size of solar PV system, and how many batteries should a homeowner install to maximize their economic, social, and environmental benefits? Some homeowners undertake significant energy efficiency and conservation actions while other similar homeowners do not. Why are simple and cost-effective options not always taken despite homeowners claiming to have a high level of knowledge and a high level of intention to do so? And more importantly, what can sustainability professionals do to help increase the level of sustainable behavior from household programs?
- Find a recent academic journal article that focuses on social practices and sustainability. What research methods were used in the study? What strategies or instruments were used to try and guide or shift social practices? How would you design a campaign to get working professionals to purchase an electric car from a social practices perspective?
- Think about how food, waste, energy, and water behaviors are connected at the residential level. Choosing one combination of either food and waste, or energy and water, follow the steps of the community-based social marketing approach (CBSM, 2017) to design a campaign to encourage sustainable behavior from homeowners. The goal is to emphasize the benefits of an alternative sustainable behavior, de-emphasize the benefits of the status-quo unsustainable behavior, de-emphasize the barriers to the alternative sustainable behavior, and emphasize the barriers to the status-quo unsustainable behavior.

Assignments

- Devising an engagement strategy to minimize xeriscaping tradeoffs at the household level
- Creating a community-based social marketing plan and feasibility study to change public perceptions about storm water management at the community level

References

Aguilar-Luzón, M. D. C., García-Martínez, J. M. Á., Calvo-Salguero, A., & Salinas, J. M. (2012). Comparative study between the theory of planned behavior and the value–belief–norm model regarding the environment, on Spanish housewives' recycling behavior. *Journal of Applied Social Psychology*, 42(11), 2797–2833.

Ajzen, I. (1991). The theory of planned behavior. *Organization Behavior and Human Decision Processes*, 50, 179–211.

Armitage C J., & Conner, M. (2001). Efficacy of the theory of planned behavior: A meta-analytic review. *British Journal of Social Psychology*, 40, 471–499.

Berkes, F., Colding, J., & Folke, C. (2000). Rediscovery of traditional ecological knowledge as adaptive management. *Ecological Applications*, 10(5), 1251–1262.

CBSM. (2017). Fostering sustainable behavior: Community base social marketing. Created by McKenzie-Mohr, D. Available at: www.cbsm.com/pages/guide/preface/

Chao, Y. L. (2012). Predicting people's environmental behavior: Theory of planned behavior and model of responsible environmental behavior. *Environmental Education Research*, 18(4), 437–461.

Chilvers, J., & Longhurst, N. (2016). Participation in transition(s): Reconceiving public engagements in energy transitions as co-produced, emergent and diverse. *Journal of Environmental Policy & Planning*, 18(5), 585–607.

Choi, H., Jang, J., & Kandampully, J. (2015). Application of the extended VBN theory to understand consumers' decisions about green hotels. *International Journal of Hospitality Management*, 51, 87–95.

Clark, C. F., Kotchen, M. J., & Moore, M. R. (2003). Internal and external influences on pro-environmental behavior: Participation in a green electricity program. *Journal of Environmental Psychology*, 23(3), 237–246.

Cordano, M., & Frieze, I. H. (2000). Pollution reduction preferences of U.S. environmental managers: Applying Ajzen's Theory of Planned Behavior. *Academy of Management Journal*, 43(4), 627–641.

Daly, H. E., & Farley, J. (2010). *Ecological Economics: Principles and Applications*. 2nd Edition. Island Press, Washington, DC.

Egbue, O., & Long, S. (2012). Barriers to widespread adoption of electric vehicles: An analysis of consumer attitudes and perceptions. *Energy Policy*, 48(1), 717–729.

Energy Star. (2017). >Energy Star most efficiency 2017. Available at: www.energystar.gov/products/most_efficient

Falkowski, T. B., Martinez-Bautista, I., & Diemont, S. A. (2015). How valuable could traditional ecological knowledge education be for a resource-limited future? An energy evaluation in two Mexican villages. *Ecological Modelling*, 300, 40–49.

Fang, K., Heijungs, R., & de Snoo, G. R. (2014). Theoretical exploration for the combination of the ecological, energy, carbon, and water footprints: Overview of a footprint family. *Ecological Indicators*, 36, 508–518.

Frederiks, E. R., Stenner, K., & Hobman, E. V. (2015). Household energy use: Applying behavioural economics to understand consumer decision-making and behaviour. *Renewable and Sustainable Energy Reviews*, 41, 1385–1394.

Gahrooei, M. R., Zhang, Y., Ashuri, B., & Augenbroe, G. (2016). Timing residential photovoltaic investments in the presence of demand uncertainties. *Sustainable Cities and Society*, 20, 109–123.

Gatersleben, B., Murtagh, N., Cherry, M., & Watkins, M. (2018). Moral, wasteful, frugal, or thrifty? Identifying consumer identities to understand and manage pro-environmental behavior. *Environment and Behavior*. Available at: http://journals.sagepub.com/doi/abs/10.1177/0013916517733782

Geels, F. W., McMeekin, A., Mylan, J., & Southerton, D. (2015). A critical appraisal of Sustainable Consumption and Production research: The reformist, revolutionary and reconfiguration positions. *Global Environmental Change*, 34, 1–12.

Gliedt, T., & Parker, P. (2010). Dynamic capabilities for strategic green advantage: Green electricity purchasing in North American firms, SMEs, NGOs and agencies. *Global Business and Economics Review*, 12(3), 171–195.

Gliedt, T., & Parker, P. (2014). Green community entrepreneurship 2.0: Collective response or individual adaptation strategy to funding cuts in Canada (2006–2012). *International Journal of Social Economics*, 41(7), 609–625.

Global Footprint Network. (2017). What is your ecological footprint? Personal Footprint Calculator. Available at: www.footprintcalculator.org/

Gubrium, J. F. (Ed.). (2012). *The Sage Handbook of Interview Research: The Complexity of the Craft.* 2nd Edition. Sage Publications, Los Angeles, CA.

Hayter, R., & Patchell, J. (2011). *Economic Geography: An Institutional Approach.* Oxford University Press, Oxford, UK.

Heberlein, T. A. (2012). *Navigating Environmental Attitudes.* Oxford University Press, Oxford, UK.

Hines, J. M., Hungerford, H. R., & Tomera, A. N. (1987). Analysis and synthesis of research on responsible environmental behavior: A meta-analysis. *The Journal of Environmental Education*, 18(2), 1–8.

Hoicka, C. E., & Parker, P. (2011). Residential energy efficiency programs, retrofit choices and greenhouse gas emissions savings: a decade of energy efficiency improvements in Waterloo Region, Canada. *International Journal of Energy Research*, 35(15), 1312–1324.

Hoicka, C. E., Parker, P., & Andrey, J. (2014). Residential energy efficiency retrofits: How program design affects participation and outcomes. *Energy Policy*, 65, 594–607.

Ibtissem, M. H. (2010). Application of value beliefs norms theory to the energy conservation behaviour. *Journal of Sustainable Development*, 3(2), 129–139.

Illge, L., & Schwarze, R. (2009). A matter of opinion: How ecological and neoclassical environmental economists and think about sustainability and economics. *Ecological Economics*, 68(3), 594–604.

Isman, M., Archambault, M., Konga, C. N., Lin, D., Iha, K., & Ouellet-Plamondon, C. (2018). Ecological Footprint assessment for targeting climate change mitigation in cities: A case study of 15 Canadian cities according to census metropolitan areas (CMA). *Journal of Cleaner Production*, 174, 1032–1043.

Kivimaa, P., & Kern, F. (2016). Creative destruction or mere niche support? Innovation policy mixes for sustainability transitions. *Research Policy*, 45(1), 205–217.

Koksal, M. A., Rowlands, I. H., & Parker, P. (2015). Energy, cost, and emission end-use profiles of homes: An Ontario (Canada) case study. *Applied Energy*, 142, 303–316.

Kollmuss, A., & Agyeman, J. (2002). Mind the gap: Why do people act environmentally and what are the barriers to pro-environmental behavior? *Environmental Education Research*, 8(3), 239–260.

Lawhon, M., & Murphy, J. T. (2012). Socio-technical regimes and sustainability transitions: Insights from political ecology. *Progress in Human Geography*, 36(3), 354–378.

Leray, L., Sahakian, M., & Erkman, S. (2016). Understanding household food metabolism: Relating micro-level material flow analysis to consumption practices. *Journal of Cleaner Production*, 125, 44–55.

Mah, D. N. Y., van der Vleuten, J. M., Hills, P., & Tao, J. (2012). Consumer perceptions of smart grid development: Results of a Hong Kong survey and policy implications. *Energy Policy*, 49, 204–216.

McKenzie-Mohr, D. (2000). Promoting sustainable behavior: An introduction to community-based social marketing. *Journal of Social Issues*, 56(3), 543–554.

McKenzie-Mohr, D., & Schultz, P. W. (2014). Choosing effective behavior change tools. *Social Marketing Quarterly*, 20(1), 35–46.

McKenzie-Mohr, D., & Smith, W. (2011). *Fostering Sustainable Behavior.* New Society, Gabriola Island, BC.

Moran, E. F., & Lopez, M. C. (2016). Future directions in human-environment research. *Environmental Research*, 144, 1–7.

Naus, J., & van der Horst, H. M. (2016). Accomplishing information and change in a smart grid pilot: Linking domestic practices with policy interventions. *Environment and Planning C: Government and Policy*, 35(3), 379–396.

Niaura, A. (2013). Using the Theory of Planned Behavior to investigate the determinants of environmental behavior among youth. *Environmental Research, Engineering and Management*, 63(1), 74–81.

Offen, K. H. (2004). Historical political ecology: An introduction. *Historical Geography, 32*, 19–42.

Parker, P., Rowlands, I. H., & Scott, D. (2003). Innovations to reduce residential energy use and carbon emissions: An integrated approach. *The Canadian Geographer/Le Géographe Canadien*, 47(2), 169–184.

Parker, P., Rowlands, I. H., & Scott, D. (2005). Who changes consumption following residential energy evaluations? Local programs need all income groups to achieve Kyoto targets. *Local Environment*, 10(2), 173–187.

Paavola, J., & Adger, W. N. (2005). Institutional ecological economics. *Ecological Economics*, 53(3), 353–368.

Pickett-Baker, J., & Ozaki, R. (2008). Pro-environmental products: marketing influence on consumer purchase decision. *Journal of Consumer Marketing*, 25(5), 281–293.

Pisano, I., & Lubell, M. (2017). Environmental behavior in cross-national perspective: A multilevel analysis of 30 countries. *Environment and Behavior*, 49(1), 31–58.

Rauschmayer, F., Bauler, T., & Schäpke, N. (2015). Towards a thick understanding of sustainability transitions: Linking transition management, capabilities and social practices. *Ecological Economics*, 109, 211–221.

Redman, E. (2013). Advancing educational pedagogy for sustainability: Developing and implementing programs to transform behaviors. *International Journal of Environmental and Science Education*, 8(1), 1–34.

Redman, E., & Redman, A. (2014). Transforming sustainable food and waste behaviors by realigning domains of knowledge in our education system. *Journal of Cleaner Production*, 64, 147–157.

Rhodes, E., Axsen, J., & Jaccard, M. (2015). Gauging citizen support for a low carbon fuel standard. *Energy Policy*, 79, 104–114.

Rowlands, I. H., Mallia, E., Shulist, J., Parker, P. (2013). Developing smart tools for households: Making the smart grid work. *Municipal World*, 123, 5–9.

Schmitt, M. T., Aknin, L. B., Axsen, J., & Shwom, R. L. (2018). Unpacking the relationships between pro-environmental behavior, life satisfaction, and perceived ecological threat. *Ecological Economics*, 143, 130–140.

Schultz, W. P., Nolan, J. M., Cialdini, R. B., Goldstein, N. J., Griskevicius, V. (2007). The constsructive, destructive, and reconstructive power of social norms. *Psychological Science*, 18(5), 429–434.

Schultz, W. P., Khazian, A. M., & Zaleski, A. C. (2008). Using normative social influence to promote conservation among hotel guests. *Social Influence*, 3(1), 4–23.

Schwartz, S. H. (1973). Normative explanations of helping behavior: A critique, proposal, and empirical test. *J. Exp. Soc. Psychol.*, 9, 349–364.

Shove, E., Pantzar, M., & Watson, M. (2012). *The Dynamics of Social Practice: Everyday Life and How it Changes*. Sage, London, UK.

Smith, A., Voß, J. P., & Grin, J. (2010). Innovation studies and sustainability transitions: The allure of the multi-level perspective and its challenges. *Research Policy*, 39(4), 435–448.

Stern, P. C., Dietz, T., Abel, T. D., Guagnano, G. A., & Kalof, L. (1999). A value-belief-norm theory of support for social movements: The case of environmentalism. *Human Ecology Review*, 6(2), 81–97.

Stewart, D. W., & Shamdasani, P. N. (2014). *Focus Groups: Theory and Practice*. 3rd Edition. Sage Publications, Los Angeles, CA.

Strengers, Y. (2012). Peak electricity demand and social practice theories: Reframing the role of change agents in the energy sector. *Energy Policy*, 44, 226–234.

Strengers, Y., & Maller, C. (Eds.). (2015). *Social Practices, Intervention and Sustainability: Beyond Behaviour Change*. Routledge, New York, NY.

Tesla. (2017). Powerwall 2. Available at: www.tesla.com/powerwall

Trumbo, C. W., & O'Keefe, G. J. (2001). Intention to conserve water: Environmental values, planned behavior, and information effects: A comparison of three communities sharing a watershed. *Society and Natural Resources*, 14, 889–899.

Turaga, R. M. R., Howarth, R. B., & Borsuk, M. E. (2010). Pro-environmental behavior. *Annals of the New York Academy of Sciences*, 1185(1), 211–224.

Whitmarsh, L., & O'Neill, S. (2010). Green identity, green living? The role of pro-environmental self-identity in determining consistency across diverse pro-environmental behaviours. *Journal of Environmental Psychology*, 30(3), 305–314.

Wiek, A., Withycombe, L., & Redman, C. (2011). Key competencies in sustainability: A reference framework for academic program development. *Sustainability Science*, 6, 203–218.

Wray-Lake, L., Flanagan, C A., & Osgood, D W. (2010). Examining trends in adolescent environmental attitudes, beliefs, and behaviors across three decades. *Environment and Behavior*, 42(1), 61–85.

3 Organizations as agents of sustainability

Learning objectives

- Critically review theories of organizational change in the context of sustainability
- Understand the role of organizations in a multi-level sustainability transitions framework
- Examine various case studies that highlight the contributions of governments, non-profits, and businesses to sustainability
- Identify metrics for measuring progress of organizations towards sustainability

Theories of organizations as sustainability agents

Organizations are effective change agents in various aspects of society. For example, businesses create new products and technologies, non-profits deliver new services and programs, and governments mobilize support and resources for new policies, programs, and infrastructure. In the case of sustainability, organizations can play important roles in changing the subsystems of the regime (Chapter 7), or in creating the right conditions for successful niche experiments that develop technological or social innovations (Chapter 4). Various frameworks and models show how organizations are important to sustainability transitions, while case studies illustrate the practice of organizations that have demonstrated effective sustainability solutions.

Organizational adaptability for sustainable competitive advantage

Successful organizations are constantly responding to changes in their environment while drawing on internal capabilities to gain a *competitive advantage*. But can organizations develop and leverage specific capabilities that can give them a competitive advantage based on sustainability? Organizations can gain competitive advantages and create innovations through *strategic learning* (Senge, 2006), defined as "the organization's capacity to retool rapidly to create and execute new strategy through learning at the individual and system levels in response to changes and uncertainties in complex environments" (Moon and Lee, 2015, p. 630). Arguably, organizations engaged in strategic learning would be more resilient in facing the complex problems known to sustainability professionals. Hart and Dowell (2011) suggested that managers and other employees frame sustainability issues and the interactions between organizational strategy and the natural environment as either an opportunity or a threat. Viewing sustainability as a threat can lead to reactive and low-hanging fruit strategies to manage or minimize risks to the organization from sustainability problems. Viewing sustainability as an opportunity can lead to proactive or pragmatic strategies to develop new capabilities, programs, products, and services that can enable innovation and create competitive advantages. As Hart and Dowell (2011) concluded, "proactive companies see the management of their interactions with the natural environment as requiring organizational capabilities that include stakeholder integration, higher order learning, and continuous innovation" (p. 1469). Acceleration Point: Sustainability professionals can help organizational leadership view sustainability as an opportunity as a first step for scaling-up actions and strategies for resolving complex problems.

Sustainability strategies

Some organizations operate in ways that minimize impacts on the environment while others follow the status quo and continue with business-as-usual strategies. The wide range of organizational strategies related to sustainability occurs because of the existence (or not) of different combinations of drivers to influence change such as regulations, public pressure, internal leadership, or previous green organizational strategies. Many studies have looked at these motivating factors both using empirical data collection (Banerjee, 2001, 2002; Bansal and Roth, 2000; Clemens and Douglas, 2006; Cordano et al., 2010; Delmas et al., 2011; Delmas and Toffel, 2004; Hahn et al., 2010; Hart and Milstein, 2003) and reviews of the literature (Montiel, 2008; Orlitzky et al., 2011). The challenge for sustainability professionals is to understand the combinations of factors that are most effective at encouraging organizations in their community, state/province, or country to embrace strategies that can create *sustainability value*.

Indicators for measuring sustainability performance of organizations (Joung et al., 2012) highlight the connections between sustainability and organizational strategies while informing adjustments to strategies over time. Performance management and technological advancement are identified as overarching groups of indicators that directly relate to firm strategy (Joung et al., 2012). Performance management can include financial, human relations, and environmental flows. Technological advancement can include investments in research and development and new technologies that make processes more efficient or provide a competitive advantage. Sub-indicators within each of these groups track improvements to social well-being (e.g., employee, customer, and community factors), economic development (e.g., costs, profits, investments), and environmental stewardship (e.g., emissions, pollution, resource consumption).

The resource consumption sub-indicator, for example, is measured by changes to the use of water, materials, energy, and land (Joung et al., 2012). Influencing improvements to resource consumption is achieved by following a sustainability decision-making process. This process involves a) setting a sustainability objective, b) selecting indicators, c) specifying performance targets, d) choosing measurement procedures, e) analyzing data, f) reporting and making managerial decisions, and g) evaluating impacts (Joung et al., 2012). It is important to consider the nuances and limits of indicator-based approaches. For example, not all metrics are equally meaningful, and a quantitative focus on metrics sometimes ignores important considerations that are not readily measured. This is discussed further in Chapter 8.

One theory that attempts to explain linkages between environmental strategy and corporate financial performance is the natural resource-based view of the firm (Hart, 1995). Hart and Dowell (2011) revisited the propositions of Hart (1995) and suggest that empirical and theoretical developments have allowed them to expand the original framework to four categories: pollution prevention, product stewardship, clean technology, and base of pyramid, the last of which is described as sustainable development focused on poverty reduction. Pollution prevention and *product stewardship* strategies aim to achieve *incremental* and short-term improvements to current products and processes, while *clean technology* and *base of pyramid* strategies focus more on *radical* and future technology and market development as integrated strategies for sustainability. These strategies can be used by sustainability professionals working within firms to identify resources and capabilities to develop and implement green technology into production processes as well as for commercialization purposes. This includes individual skills and abilities as well as organizational capabilities to operationalize sustainability strategies. The goal is to combine strategies of today with strategies for tomorrow to generate internal and external sustainability value for the organization, which can generate a competitive advantage (Figure 3.1). Sustainability value is created by integrating economic, social, and environmental value creation strategies within each of these categories.

Developing a pollution prevention strategic capability will help minimize waste and create a competitive advantage based on minimizing operational costs (Hart and Dowell, 2011). Companies that innovate, invest in total quality management programs, and implement more efficient processes are able to reduce the materials and energy required to produce their products or services. If these changes are difficult to imitate, they provide a competitive advantage. Companies that reduce emissions can leverage this into a competitive advantage through a risk reduction strategy by marketing the environmental performance to stakeholders and by preemptively negating the need for government regulations. Developing a *product stewardship* strategic capability will help minimize triple-bottom-line costs by turning the product *value chain* into a *value cycle*. This requires reducing materials and energy at each stage in the value chain, as well as closing the loop by creating valuable inputs to new production processes from what was once considered waste outputs. The result is an improved firm reputation and an increase in public

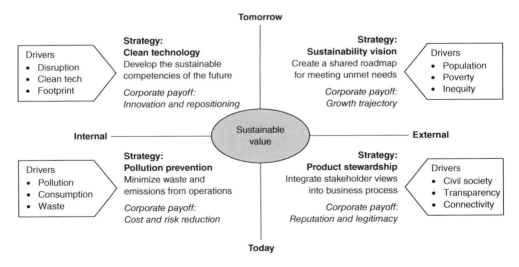

Figure 3.1 Sustainability value creation framework

Source: Hart and Milstein (2003, p. 60).

legitimacy as a competitive advantage. Developing a clean technology strategic capability will help create hard to imitate technology improvements to gain a competitive advantage through innovation. It can also generate a long-term competitive advantage by repositioning product lines around the new technologies and shifting into new markets that demand refined or more efficient processes. Developing a base of pyramid sustainability vision strategic capability will enhance company reputation through corporate social responsibility in the short term and could create a pathway for growth in emerging markets as a long-term competitive advantage.

Sustainability professionals can help companies follow these strategies to enhance competitive advantages by lowering costs, building a positive public reputation, solidifying a future position by upgrading technology, and fostering long-term integration into emerging markets. The key is to look for strategies that produce complementarities between the four strategic capabilities. For example, technology innovation strategies could also contribute to pollution prevention and product stewardship if the new technologies are implemented in the production process of the firm and its suppliers throughout the value chain. A base of pyramid sustainability vision strategy could also contribute to product stewardship if new partnerships are developed with suppliers in developing countries to not only transfer more efficient technologies and enhanced capabilities but also develop new practices that can create sustainability value in both countries. Acceleration Point: Strategies that encourage integration between all four strategic capabilities will have the potential to create sustainability value for the organization and its surrounding community.

Dyllick and Muff (2016) argued that sustainability challenges should be viewed as business opportunities. They introduced a typology for business sustainability based on three categories that represent a shift away from a strictly economic focus toward the triple-bottom-line and problem solving more broadly. The first category aims to create economic value from opportunities and managing risks related to sustainability challenges. The second focuses on managing the triple-bottom-line by creating sustainability value. The third suggests that businesses can help solve major societal challenges. This typology requires sustainability professionals to shift the perspective of business leadership from an inside-out profit focus (under the assumption that profit-driven strategies lead to environmental and social benefits) to an outside-in focus (environmental and social opportunities lead to economic profits). Solving societal problems has traditionally fallen within the scope of governments and non-profit organizations, but many businesses are increasingly seeing opportunities to fill in the gap left by governments that are cutting environmental budgets and moving away from welfare state models. Acceleration Point: Firms wishing to gain a competitive advantage from triple-bottom-line value creation strategies can develop new capabilities to capitalize on sustainability opportunities that include solving environmental problems.

Is there evidence that sustainability strategies actually do create triple-bottom-line value for organizations? Trumpp and Guenther (2017) examined corporate financial performance relative to carbon performance of a large sample of international service sector and manufacturing businesses. Corporate financial performance was measured by the return-on-assets (net income divided by beginning of year total assets). Carbon performance was measured by greenhouse gas (GHG) emissions divided by sales. Trumpp and Guenther (2017) found that corporate financial performance first decreased with increasing carbon performance but then increased, displaying a U-shaped relationship. Stock market performance – as measured by total shareholder return (annual change in stock price plus dividends) – also decreased and then increased with increasing carbon performance for manufacturing businesses. The U-shaped relationship suggests that the cost of initial investments in new technologies to reduce emissions had a negative effect on the financial bottom line until a certain level when savings from more efficient technologies and green reputation benefits from reducing CO_2 emissions led to an increase in financial performance.

While a relationship was not found between stock market performance and carbon performance for service sector businesses, Trumpp and Guenther (2017) explained that this may be due to higher levels of stakeholder interest and knowledge of carbon performance of manufacturing firms, which are more carbon intensive than the service sector. Furthermore, the relationship between financial performance and environmental performance was negative for firms with low environmental performance but positive for firms with high environmental performance. Based on their statistical results, Trumpp and Guenther (2017) concluded that "it pays to be green after exceeding a minimum level of corporate environmental performance" (p. 64). The implication is that companies should move from reactive strategies to proactive strategies to increase the chances of having a positive relationship between environmental performance and financial performance. Acceleration Point: The advice for sustainability professionals is to shift from reactive (low-hanging fruit solutions that create economic value) to proactive (system and subsystem change solutions that create sustainability value) strategies and not to simply calculate a minimum level of corporate environmental performance.

The Corporate Sustainability Index: Sao Paulo

Orsato et al. (2015) reviewed studies focusing on the Corporate Sustainability Index in Sao Paulo, Brazil and concluded that most showed similar financial performance of the sustainability index to the regular Sao Paulo Stock Exchange Index. They discovered little evidence of correlations between market performance (financial value) and corporate sustainability performance (economic, social, and environmental value). One interesting finding from Orsato et al. (2015) is that once companies join the Corporate Sustainability Index, there is a collective pressure to improve social and environmental performance because if they do not improve performance and/or leave the index, investors will perceive that sustainability performance has declined. This is important because it will encourage firms to improve over time. Leadership believed their firms were listed on the Corporate Sustainability Index because they had successfully integrated social and environmental strategies with business strategy-making processes. Firms listed on the Corporate Sustainability Index had higher levels of sustainability performance if they had a larger return-on-equity, were larger in size, had lower ownership concentration, and were more likely to be listed in international financial markets (Lourenço and Branco, 2013). Larger firms and those with larger return-on-equity being the higher performing sustainability firms supports a similar study in the United States (Artiach et al., 2010). Firms in emerging markets can improve their sustainability performance by accessing finances from international markets (Lourenço and Branco, 2013). This suggests that sustainability professionals can look to sustainability indexes in other countries to identify firms that may be candidates for cross-border investment as part sustainability value creation strategies.

Sustainability indexes help encourage sustainable behavior of organizations by using social norms (publicly displaying sustainability performance), prompts (continually updated with frequent reports), and incentives (financial investments and stock performance). Sustainability indexes also act as a structure to guide the decisions of organizations in the direction of sustainability by comparing to competitors and well-known firms with high sustainability performance from other sectors.

Strategy-as-practice framework

How can sustainability professionals help organizations develop sustainability value creation strategies? Egels-Zandén and Rosen (2015) introduced a strategy-as-practice framework that treats sustainability strategy as a process that links individual employees and organizational leadership to specific activities at key times. Based on studying a Swedish manufacturing company, Egels-Zandén and Rosen (2015, p. 145) described four interrelated types of activities that are important for creating and implementing sustainability strategies:

1   *Visionary activities*:

    a   these activities inform the goals guiding the strategy;
    b   they are created from within the top levels of the organization;
    c   leadership or strategic teams develop sustainability visions.

2   *Prescribed activities*:

    a   these activities help implement the strategy;
    b   they work from the top-down;
    c   plans are developed, the strategy is communicated, and its importance is emphasized to lower-level managers/employees, guiding them towards a preferred understanding of the strategy.

3   *Autonomous activities*:

    a   activities that are constantly occurring and may identify the need for a sustainability strategy, or they may help improve the effectiveness of a sustainability strategy through learning processes;
    b   they occur at the base of the organization, e.g., line workers;
    c   these emergent activities include design reviews, simulation exercises, and testing product performance.

4   *Evaluative activities*:

    a   they assess, advise, and respond to the strategy;
    b   they occur at the intermediate levels of the organization;
    c   these activities are conducted by sustainability staff and change intermediaries;
    d   activities of change intermediaries included redefining practices and reformulating strategies.

Sustainability strategies are created and implemented by a combination of top leadership, middle management, and operations level workers. Evaluative activities carried out by change intermediaries helped to connect top-down vision and prescribed activities with the bottom-up and emergent activities to create a coordinated sustainability strategy for the organization (Egels-Zandén and Rosen, 2015). This represents a type of sustainability-oriented intermediary (Chapter 6) who can work within an organization to create or accelerate changes towards sustainability outcomes. Intermediaries can also work between organizations within a multi-level network to encourage changes and coordinate actions.

Multi-level organizations and social-ecological systems

Sustainability challenges and climate change in particular require multi-level governance solutions. Multi-level governance could be hierarchical, where cities and higher-level governments coordinate their actions to more effectively address the cross-boundary and time scale effects of climate change (Bulkeley and Betsill, 2005, 2013). Multi-level governance could also take the form of collaboration between *polycentric organizations*, where there is no central authority but rather many organizations of different sizes and relatively similar power dynamics (Ostrom, 2009). Polycentric organizations are considered one option for overcoming the *collective action dilemmas* of open pool resources including water systems (Ostrom, 2012), which are discussed in the next section as an example of the practice of organizations as sustainability agents. Governance can occur within or as a result of *institutions*, which are formal and informal rules that constrain or guide decision-making within social-ecological systems by actors including polycentric organizations.

A social-ecological system differs from the socio-technical system outlined in Chapter 7 in that the social-ecological system explicitly examines natural resource stocks and flows. Both systems are similar in that highlight the roles of actors within multi-level systems at creating change in the direction of sustainability principles. While the social-ecological system model focuses on collaborative governance as a solution to managing sustainability problems, the socio-technical system model emphasizes innovation and disrupting the existing governance regime in order to create sustainability solutions. The subsystems of the social-ecological system are *resource units* (e.g., growth or replacement rate, economic value), *resource systems* (e.g., water, forests, fish, energy), *governance systems* (e.g., government and non-government organizations, property-rights, constitutional rules, policies), and *resource users* (e.g., socioeconomic attributes of users, history of use, leadership and entrepreneurship, norms and social capital, technology used) (Figure 3.2). Interactions between the subsystems (e.g., resource harvesting levels of users, information sharing, deliberation processes, conflicts among users, investment activities, lobbying activities, networking) lead to outcomes related to sustainability principles (e.g., social performance measures such as efficiency, equity, accountability; ecological performance measures such as resilience and biodiversity). Changes in one social-ecological system are also influenced by external factors including climate change, pollution patterns, and materials and energy flows into and out of the social-ecological system (Ostrom, 2009). Acceleration Point: Sustainability professionals should focus on understanding the interactions between the subsystems prior to designing strategies and instruments to encourage change because the interactions are what leads to sustainability outcomes. This lesson is also important for socio-technical systems because it is the interactions between niche and regime levels (Chapters 6 and 7) that lead to *strong sustainability*.

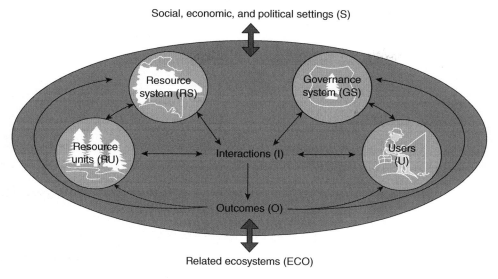

Figure 3.2 The core subsystems framework for analyzing social-ecological systems
Source: Ostrom (2009, p. 420).

Integrated model of sustainability and organizations

Chang et al. (2017) outlined a model for understanding the economic, social, and environmental components of sustainability in relation to organizations (Figure 3.3). This model highlights interdisciplinary and systems approaches that focus on how to achieve sustainability including the *multi-level perspective* (MLP) and *transition management*. The implication is that organizations can follow the triple-bottom-line to generate sustainability value by responding to stakeholder demands, policy changes, and pressures from the institutional environment or as an internal strategy to gain a competitive advantage through innovation, product stewardship, or efficiency improvements (Hart and Dowell, 2011). This model recognizes the integrated role of organizations within *socio-technical systems* as both creators of change (e.g., technology, industry, infrastructure) (Chapters 7 and 8) and as bottlenecks to change in regime subsystems (Chapter 9).

Sustainability professionals can help organizations understand how to respond to changes in the policy environment, the stakeholder environment, and the strategic environment as a means of solving problems and creating *sustainability value* (Figure 3.3). Guided by **normative competence**, sustainability professionals can use their **systems thinking** and **anticipatory competence** to create organizational sustainability strategies that capitalize on changes or opportunities in the different subsystems of the policy environment including institutions, infrastructure, education and labor, natural capital, and innovation and industry. Sustainability professionals draw upon **interpersonal relations competence** to encourage collaboration and in some cases competition between the different actor groups that compose the stakeholder environment, including employees, local communities, social pressure groups, governments, competitors, shareholders, customers, media,

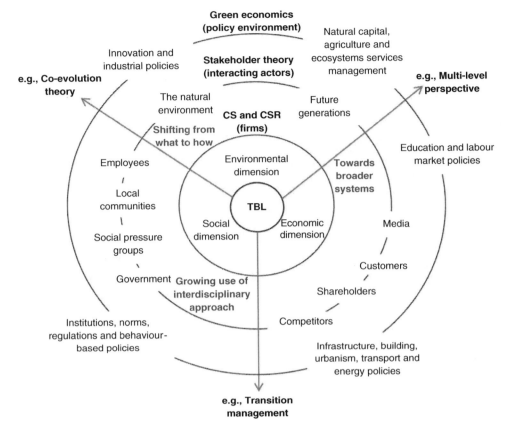

Figure 3.3 A landscape for examining sustainability in organizations

Source: Chang et al. (2017, p. 53).

and future generations. The natural environment is included as an additional stakeholder group to highlight the importance of protecting natural capital as the basis of sustainability value creation. Sustainability professionals navigate the strategic environment, which encompasses interactions between the internal and external organizational environment. They apply their **strategic competence** to integrate the stakeholder and policy environments into organizational sustainability strategies centered on the triple-bottom-line. Acceleration Point: Sustainability professionals can use their **integrated sustainability research and problem-solving competence** to understand and combine internal and external organizational capabilities as a means of supporting product, process, or service solutions that can generate sustainability value. The following cases illustrate examples of organizations that have worked to create sustainability value.

Practice of organizations as sustainability agents

Sustainability-oriented organizations can be non-profits, government agencies, or businesses, as well as various forms of partnerships and networks. Each type of organization has strengths when it comes to sustainability transitions. For example, businesses are able to influence change throughout global value chains. Non-profits are able to build trust with communities to encourage sustainable behavior. Government agencies have regulatory powers to encourage sustainability and mobilize resources for innovation systems.

Environmental non-profit organizations:Entrepreneurship, engagement, and advocacy

Gliedt and Parker (2007, 2014) identified a process of green community entrepreneurship centered on the service creation abilities of environmental non-profit organizations (Figure 3.4). These organizations used human capital, social capital, and strategic partnerships to develop new energy services that help citizens reduce their environmental impacts. These services focused on information provision, communication techniques, education and engagement processes, and technology change programs. The services were partially funded by federal, state, and local governments and increasingly by client service fees. Environmental non-profit organizations demonstrated resilience to government funding cuts by adjusting their operations and by developing and offering new services to appeal to broader markets. Unlike businesses, these organizations do not generate profits, but rather, are sometimes run like a *social enterprise* that aims to generate revenues that are reinvested back into the organization to fund further

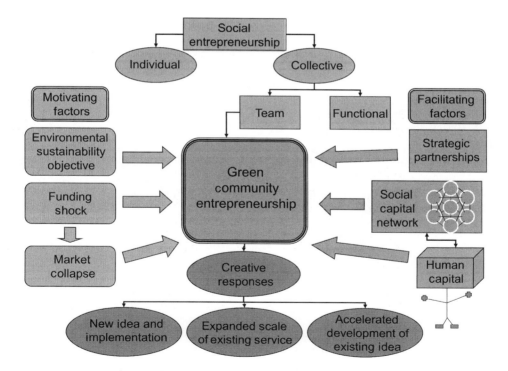

Figure 3.4 Green community entrepreneurship

Source: Gliedt and Parker (2007, p. 549).

service creation and delivery capabilities. Some leaders of environmental non-profits are uneasy about delivering services for a fee because they see their mission to provide public goods that address externalities ignored by the public and private sectors (Gliedt and Parker, 2007).

One major challenge for environmental non-profit organizations is scaling-up sustainability value creation (Lyakhov et al., 2016). Critical questions include: Once services have been created, do organizations continue to expand them? Do they diversify into new service offerings? And how do organizations increase the sustainability impacts beyond just delivering a service to a small population within a community? Environmental non-profit organizations must overcome a number of barriers related to financial capital (how to access and sustain sources over time), human capital (how to retain highly skilled employees for low wages), and social capital (how to develop and draw on networks with businesses, government agencies, and other non-profits to leverage additional resources). Acceleration Point: Organizations can use social capital networks to co-produce knowledge and outcomes with other actors that helps improve the sustainability principles.

Partnerships can be developed to formalize these relationships (Lyakhov and Gliedt, 2017), but sometimes entrepreneurship and service delivery are not enough to scale-up sustainability impacts beyond the local region or market. In this case, environmental non-profits can use engagement and advocacy techniques to influence changes in the political arena including funding, policies, and public sentiment towards sustainability actions and services. Greenpeace, the Sierra Club, and the Nature Conservancy, among others, use these techniques to encourage sustainable behavior and changes to the regime subsystems. How effective these engagement and advocacy techniques are at weakening the regime subsystems may depend on timing, including whether there are pressures from the *landscape* that can be aligned with *niche experiments* that are ready to be scaled-up. The niche, regime, and landscape levels that make up the MLP are described in Chapter 7.

Water conservation: the southwestern United States

Water systems face many challenges in the southwestern United States including increasing population and economic growth pressures on water demand, changing precipitation patterns, and aging infrastructure (Hartman et al., 2017). These challenges can be addressed through technological and institutional innovation (Chapter 4), which often occurs in response to pursuit of one or more of the Gibson sustainability principles (Widener et al., 2017). *Participatory action research* approaches can act as *transition arenas* (Chapter 7) to develop collaborative technical and social solutions through the *co-production of knowledge*. Meadow et al. (2015) defined co-production of knowledge as "the process of producing useable, or actionable, science through collaboration between scientists and those who use science to make policy and management decisions" (p. 179). Co-produced knowledge is popular among decision-makers partly due to higher *transparency* and *legitimacy* of the final output but also because it complements pre-existing organizational decision-making structures. Examples of co-production techniques include *action research, rapid assessment processes, participatory integrated assessments*, and *boundary organizations* (Meadow et al., 2015). The following case studies illustrate ongoing efforts in the southwestern United States to change regime subsystems and create niche experiments aiming to improve the sustainability of water systems.

Truckee-Carson River system Nevada, U.S.

Singletary and Sterle (2017) used participatory research approaches that linked scientists with water managers to build a collaborative model for drought resiliency based on the co-production of knowledge in Nevada's Truckee-Carson River system. Water managers worked to accelerate water system changes by increasing flexibility in water management through various strategies and instruments designed to change water leasing programs and encourage *water rights stacking* on productive agricultural lands while fallowing marginal lands (Singletary and Sterle, 2017). Other strategies and instruments aimed to encourage water conservation practices and to support business attraction (Chapter 5) to bring low water intensity firms to the region. Most water managers said that their organization/utility had already implemented adaptation strategies to droughts (Singletary and Sterle, 2017). These strategies included communication and coordination between water users, data collection and monitoring, and drought planning. The researchers created two climate scenarios with the help of a stakeholder affiliate group (this included city departments, tribes, environmental non-profit organizations, state water agencies, and federal environmental agencies) as a means of co-producing knowledge among scientists (government and university), local water managers, and the stakeholders themselves. Acceleration Point: Co-producing knowledge is one tool for sustainability professionals to incorporate the ideas, values, and preferences of all stakeholders into the strategies and instruments created during the research process. This can help improve performance of the civility and democratic governance principle of sustainability (Chapter 1).

Lessons from California water system changes

Escriva-Bou et al. (2015) built an integrated water-energy-emissions-costs model for residential conservation decisions in California. They examined ten cities and found an average 3 percent water savings due to a combination of water conservation actions such as technology changes (e.g., toilet, shower, dishwasher, or clothes washer retrofits; substitution of artificial turf, xeriscaping, or smart irrigation) and behavioral changes (e.g., using the toilet, shower, laundry, or bath less frequently; taking shorter showers, fixing leaks, or using drought tolerant plants). When excluding outdoor water use, indoor water savings were 24 percent, and water-related energy savings were 30 percent. This equated to a 53 percent GHG emissions reduction. The highest potential for external water conservation improvements was from smart irrigation and drought-tolerant plants, while efficient toilets resulted in significant indoor water savings and changes to showering behavior led to significant energy savings. The implication of the modelling exercise is that consumers may make different water related decisions if the energy savings are also included as part of an integrated analysis, which could lead to additional sustainability benefits.

Maggioni (2015) discovered that mandates to reduce outdoor water usage in Southern California had a significant impact on residential water use, while rebates for efficient technologies, and changes to water use rates did not. Rebates suffered from encouraging low-yield technologies or options that lead to marginal water use changes. Although water rate changes alone were not as effective because they were limited by political factors (e.g., fear of voter reprisals; mandates to increase prices only to recover construction or maintenance costs) (Maggioni, 2015), combining mandatory restrictions with a price increase may in some cases lead to even greater water savings (Mini et al., 2015). Income is also an important driver of water demand since higher incomes lead to larger houses with technology and landscape features that increase water use (e.g., hot tub, pool, irrigation of lawns and gardens) (Gonzales and Ajami, 2017). Higher income households can overcome increases to water prices since they have the resources to pay for higher rates of consumption.

Gonzales and Ajami (2017) developed an integrated regional resilience framework for urban water transitions in San Francisco, California. This study highlighted the fragmentation challenges in water systems as evidenced by an overarching regional water agency coordinating and representing 26 urban water utilities. These utilities operate independently but are linked to a single common pool resource: imported water supplies from snow melt in the Sierra Nevada mountains. The framework includes an assessment of *adaptive capacity*, which is calculated as a combination of conservation capacity and augmentation capacity. In this context, adaptive capacity is limited by technical and financial factors and the willingness of managers to invest in innovations. *Conservation capacity* is defined as "projections of the potential savings achievable through conservation and water use efficiency measures, computed as a fraction of total demand" (Gonzales and Ajami, 2017, p. 132). *Augmentation capacity* is defined as the "fraction of total demand that may be satisfied by feasible alternative supplies" (p. 132). The framework is important because it provides a lens through which to assess the integrated supply and demand capacity for water transitions as a measure of the resilience of water systems.

The framework also includes metrics for supply stress and supply diversity, water use per capita, and demand diversity. *Supply stress* is defined as the "fraction of allocations from the San Francisco Regional Water System currently being used" (Gonzales and Ajami, 2017, p. 132). This means that a utility may be drawing anywhere from 1–100 percent of its allocations at any given time, and the higher the fraction the more supply stress a utility is under. *Supply diversity* is defined as "the capacity to shift between supply sources if a particular source becomes compromised" (p. 130). This implies that a utility has one or more alternative options and/or the ability to quickly develop alternative supply options if needed. *Demand diversity* is defined as "flexibility in terms of the capacity of a system to incorporate tailored water supplies to meet the different water quality needs of different users, reducing stress on existing high-quality sources" (p. 130). This is reflective of a system that can use higher quality water for residential and commercial uses, while using lower quality and/or reused or recycled water for industrial or agricultural uses. During times of high stress, lower quality water options may become more important to substitute for higher quality options in all but potable water needs.

Many smaller utilities in California are dependent on a single water source that comfortably exceeds their current and projected demands. The smaller utilities have therefore not felt the same pressure to diversify as larger utilities have. Many utilities scored high on the demand diversity metric, which represents flexibility in that different qualities of water can be used for different water users (e.g., drinking water needs to be high quality to be safely potable; industrial uses only need lower quality/reused water options). Most utilities had high adaptation capacity, and thus, the potential to further develop water conservation initiatives. Gonzales and Ajami (2017) found that small utilities in the San Francisco region may lack adaptive capacity relative to larger utilities, and thus, could benefit from regional-scale water projects that could be collectively funded and managed. They also found that utilities increased their resilience metrics from the 2010–11 year prior to the drought, to the 2014–15 year after the fourth straight year of drought. These resilience improvements were due to efficiency and conservation changes rather than supply options, which were not added during this time.

Mobilizing support for infrastructure and institutional innovations is difficult due to fragmented water governance arrangements that cross government scales and extend throughout water basins made up of different sizes and types of water users and supply options (Gonzales and Ajami, 2017). Multi-level governance can benefit overall water system resilience by distributing resources to where they are most needed for enhancing capacity and flexibility of the water system. Both the Gonzales and Ajami (2017) and Hartman et al. (2017) studies called for increased collaboration between utilities to help achieve water management goals as part of an integrated water sustainability framework (Figure 3.5). The challenge of using an integrated water sustainability framework is exemplified by the case of the Colorado River and its delta in Mexico. Countless water users in two countries and many states depend on the river. While market-based or adaptive co-management arrangements can be used to manage the water system, new pressures from climate-induced droughts as well as population and agricultural demands make it difficult to see how this water source could be available to future generations. The question is, can the Gibson sustainability principles be used to create a more sustainable management scheme that protects the ecosystem functions and services provided by the river while accounting for economic and social impacts from not having as much water available in the future? And how could the principles be turned into strategies and instruments to achieve radical institutional and infrastructure changes? Similar questions face the Red River of the South Water Basin.

Red River of the South Water Basin-level management for sustainability

Understanding how major rivers are managed from end-to-end is a critical challenge. The Red River of the South cuts through four states, eight different climate regions, and impacts or is impacted by over 1,100 towns and cities. While the quantity of water that flows between each of the four states (Texas, Oklahoma, Arkansas, and Louisiana) is set by interstate compacts, these agreements reflect a time when the demand for water was lower and the stressors on the Red River were far less than they are today. Rapid urban growth in Texas and Oklahoma, increased agricultural demand for water, worsening impacts of run-off from agriculture, and the looming risks associated with precipitation variability due to climate change have combined to push the Red River Basin to the breaking point.

Sustainability professionals can encourage more sustainable water decisions by understanding how the fragmentation of major river basins comes from a confluence of social and physical factors including the interaction of differing management/governance priorities, land-use/land cover changes, and climatic conditions (e.g., the dramatic climate gradient from the semi-arid Texas Panhandle to the subtropics of Louisiana's Mississippi Alluvial Plains). Basin-level governance was identified as a critical regional conservation priority in Article 1 of the Red River Compact (1978) but is increasingly challenging in practice given the impact of precipitation variability on water manager's capabilities to meet diverse and changing economic efficiency, social sufficiency, and ecological resiliency demands. In addition to the increased demands placed on the water in the Red River Basin, recent downscaled climate data (Qiao et al., 2017) indicate that by the middle of the 21st century, the western regions of the basin will face increased risk of drought while the eastern/southern regions will face increased risk of severe high-precipitation events (McCorkle et al. 2016) that can lead to extreme and flash flooding.

While many water studies focus on one sector (e.g., municipal water planning), it is important to examine the connections between a multitude of sectors in order to understand the linkages between water decisions and actors throughout the Red River Basin. Sustainability professionals can help water managers understand how local decisions can also impact resources and decisions in other parts of the basin. Important research questions for sustainability professionals examining basin-level management include:

(1) Are water managers more focused on water quantity or water quality? Which water management goals are prioritized, and why?
(2) When comparing water management across the basin, what explains the choice of different strategies and instruments (e.g., cultural factors related to drought and flooding experiences, or economic and political factors)?
(3) How do water management decisions relate to the type of state-level governance in place (e.g., individual *water rights* or interstate systems emerging from the Red River Compact agreement)?

   (3a) How do water management decisions differ in cases where formal government utilities or informal water governance arrangements are more prevalent?
   (3b) What is the role of *boundary spanners* (Chapter 6) in linking science to policy, local to state/regional governance, and economic, social, and environmental criteria to outcomes?
   (3c) How do water managers value/understand impacts beyond their jurisdiction?

(4) How do water management decisions differ throughout the basin in their level of focus on technology, institutional/policy, or social/education/engagement solutions, and what are the implications for sustainability transitions?

It is important to focus on both (1) water management practices of actors in the region whose decisions have a significant impact throughout the basin (e.g., tribal, large water users in the agriculture, ranching, recreation, energy, and non-governmental organization sectors); and (2) municipal utility water management strategies and instruments. This includes actors and utilities that directly impact the Red River, and those distant from the River whose behavior and practices shape and are shaped by the dynamics between the River, climate conditions, and broad systems of governance and economic factors. Acceleration Point: Sustainability professionals can contribute to a co-production of knowledge that will inform more sustainable management at the basin level, which is important for ensuring water quantity and water quality demands for both human and ecological uses.

Arizona water decision-making

White et al. (2010, 2015a) identified best practices for integrating scientific knowledge about the natural environment with political decision-making, including framing the issue, having high-quality linkages between knowledge and action, and the importance of boundary spanners between science and policy spheres. How did the stakeholders involved in the co-production of knowledge view the credibility (trustworthiness), salience (usefulness), and legitimacy (validity) of the process (Cash et al., 2003; Guston, 2001, as cited in White et al., 2010)? White et al. (2010) examined a WaterSim simulation model in the Decision Center for a Desert City viewing arena at Arizona State University. The model generated scenarios for water supply and demand under the influence of changes to climate, land-use population, and water policies. The Decision Center is itself a *boundary organization* (Chapter 6), overlapping the science generation and the policy decision-making spheres to "establish and maintain the productive tension between science and policy" (p. 221).

White et al. (2010) found that many policy makers and decision analysts who participated in the study felt that the process of communicating scientific findings through the WaterSim scenarios and Decision Theatre (boundary organization) lacked credibility, salience, and legitimacy. One reason that some respondents questioned the credibility was that the scientists who made the model were not present during the Decision Theatre. This poses interesting questions about the role of boundary organizations as linking agents and translators of scientific information to decision-makers. Decision-makers need to be able to trust the data and the modelling process if they are to believe in the scenarios. Decision-makers believed that the *boundary object* (the WaterSim model and scenarios) needed to be modified to increase its salience to them by incorporating geographic scale, institutional contextual differences, and scenario development flexibility. The model did allow for adjusting of key parameters (e.g., drought, population growth, water shortages policies) via policy levers, and the policy makers found this to be an effective way to build legitimacy. A critique of the legitimacy of the model was that it did not appropriate a portion of water supply to demands from ecosystem services, instead focusing all of the water supply to meet direct human demands. One way that the boundary organization attempted to increase legitimacy of the model and scenarios was by garnering feedback and input from additional stakeholders via focus groups.

White et al. (2015b) described a scenario-building exercise based on survey research with water experts for informing sustainable management of Central Arizona water systems. The exercise revealed two visions for water in central Arizona: "one in which water experts and policy makers pursue supply augmentation to serve metropolitan development, and another in which broadened public engagement is used in conjunction with policy tools to reduce water consumption, restore ecosystem services, and limit metropolitan expansion" (p 25). Scenarios helped managers overcome the limitations of linear projections of water demand by incorporating a range of economic, social, environmental, and scientific uncertainties. In particular, scenarios can take into account the competing demands from multiple water users and the complex impacts of climate change on temperature and precipitation patterns. Even when water managers understand the general impacts of climate change, the information they receive from scientists often does not match with the time and spatial scales of water planning horizons. This complicates the decision-making process for policies and the investment decisions for new technologies and infrastructure. Scenarios allow for the creation of multiple plausible futures, which takes into account a range of uncertainties and thus allows for adaptive planning (White et al., 2015b).

The co-production of knowledge (Meadow et al., 2015) is outlined as part of an integrated water sustainability framework (Figure 3.5) that can generate scenarios to change water systems. The framework uses a *transition arena* (viewed here as an action arena) to facilitate continual adjustments based on the incorporation of new research and modelling studies that are guided by the principles and sub-principles of sustainability (Chapter 1). The result is *adaptive co-management* (Plummer and Armitage, 2007), which is actualized by multi-level and collaborative research and practice that is adjusted through continual learning mechanisms. While frameworks such as this are effective for encouraging sustainability in certain sectors such as water or energy, broader approaches are needed when considering transitioning entire cities towards strong sustainability.

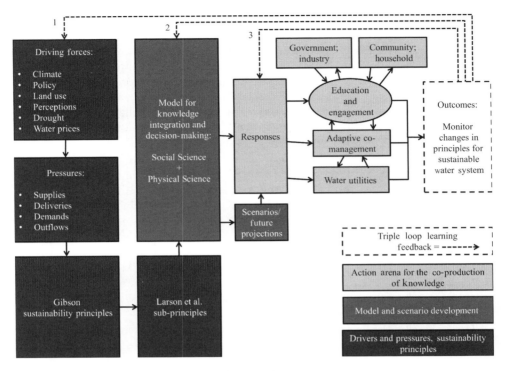

Figure 3.5 Integrated water sustainability framework

Source: Authors' rendition.

Sustainable city planning

One of the challenges for municipal decision-makers is to design long-term plans that are consistent with sustainability principles but also with short-term political cycles of two to four years. Sustainability professionals can help bridge this dichotomy by fusing green planning with triple-bottom-line economic development strategies (Chapter 5), for example, by following a set of integrated green new urbanism principles centered on energy and materials, water and biodiversity, and urban planning and transport (Lehmann, 2010). This type of integration between economic development and planning can increase the likelihood that sustainability-oriented policies and plans endure changes to policy regimes because it spreads the risk and responsibility for success broadly among stakeholders from the business, government, and non-profit spheres. The following are examples of integrated sustainability approaches from cities that are undergoing sustainability transitions.

New York City and urban sustainability

City planning can impact urban sustainability performance. Planners are now trained in a variety of disciplines and methods, including economic development, land-use planning, neighborhood improvement, resilience, sustainability, data analysis, and decision-making

(NYC, 2017). This includes, in the case of New York City, an explicit focus on mitigating and adapting to climate change, with a municipal goal to reduce GHG emissions by 80 percent by 2050. Many initiatives driven by the Department of City Planning are coordinated to achieve this target, including organizing population growth around urban transit corridors, designing walkable neighborhoods, bike sharing programs, and urban tree planting initiatives, and encouraging more energy and water efficient buildings. Sustainable urban planning in New York City also focuses on climate change adaptation and increasing the resilience of buildings (retail, industry), infrastructure (energy, transportation), and neighborhoods to more frequent and intense flooding events.

New York City council adopted a Green Zone amendment to eliminate red tape for constructing and retrofitting green buildings (Green Zone, 2012). One proposal is to remove restrictions for adding exterior insulation to buildings and to exempt them from floor area calculations. This would allow for significantly higher *R-values* (resistance to heat flow) for insulation without having to disrupt the interior of the building and interrupt building occupants. Another proposal is to change zoning to allow horizontal and vertical sun control devices to be added to existing buildings, which are often prohibited by open area requirements. These devices offer a cost-effective way to reduce air conditioning loads. The zoning changes will also permit solar panels on flat roofs to exceed building height requirements, allowing for larger systems on commercial buildings that had previously been restricted.

Austin and livability

Austin, Texas aims to make the city the most livable in the United States. A number of plans and initiatives were created, including Imagine Austin, a 30-year plan to grow more sustainably (Imagine Austin, 2017). This plan focuses on the creative economy, compact and connected communities, water and environmental integration in urban spaces, affordability for living and skill development for the workforce, and improving the health of communities and citizens. One specific initiative is CodeNEXT, an attempt to revise the land development code to improve housing affordability, access to healthy lifestyles, and to reduce the use of natural resources (CodeNEXT, 2017).

Vancouver and sustainability principles

Vancouver, British Columbia has long been known for its sustainable city planning. This has led to the term 'Vancouverism' to represent a set of principles for sustainable city living based on the initiatives taken in Vancouver. These principles include (Vancouver Urban Planning, 2017):

- having a deep respect for nature with enthusiasm for busy, engaging, active streets and dynamic urban life;
- having tall slim towers for density, widely separated by low-rise buildings, for light, air, and views;
- having many parks, walkable streets, and public spaces, combined with an emphasis on sustainable forms of transit;
- using carefully crafted development policies, guidelines, and bylaws;
- extensively consulting with residents, businesses, and experts;
- continuously reevaluating where we are as a city and where we would like to go.

Vancouver's green zoning policy aims to increase the number of LEED (Leadership in Energy and Environmental Design) certified buildings, increase consumer choices and knowledge of sustainable buildings, and use a process to work with industry to rezone their properties (Vancouver Urban Planning, 2017). The City has a set of sustainable development guidelines, including strict environmental standards, passive building design guidelines, electric vehicle recharging requirements, and guidelines for designing landscapes to use less water. As part of the Winter Olympics 2010 development plan, Vancouver built Canada's first multi-unit net-zero residential building that generates as much energy as it uses (Vancouver Urban Planning, 2017). Each suite has its own energy meter to encourage behavioral actions that can help reduce energy and water use beyond the technology improvements. Two large solar arrays, high insulation levels, natural ventilation, triple-glazed windows, and a heat recovery system are used to bring heat from the neighboring grocery store to the residences. Many of the suites are now used for affordable housing.

Swedish cities in transition

The world's first city to set a goal of becoming fossil-fuel independent (by 2030) was Växjö, Sweden, in 1991. Since then, the city has reduced its CO_2 emissions per capita by 48 percent to 2.4 tonnes, while achieving a rise in gross domestic product (GDP) per capita of 90 percent (Slavin, 2015). Another Swedish transition project, the Hammarby Sjöstad development in Stockholm, has successfully implemented a master plan to transition its infrastructure, housing, and lifestyles towards sustainability (Fraker, 2013; Iverot and Brandt, 2011). District heating and cooling systems, neighborhood scale closed-loop waste-to-energy systems, solar plants and distributed building integrated solar systems, and bus and tram systems have been critical to improving the sustainability of Swedish cities.

Underlying these structural changes are four key reasons why Swedish cities are able to make rapid technology and infrastructure changes. First, income tax revenues go to municipal councils that have the authority to decide how the money is spent. Second, the eight political parties in Sweden generally all agree on the importance of green transitions, which has led to a high level of collaboration and consensus (Slavin, 2015). Third, many building projects were managed as experiments, involving up to 40 contractors in design and implementation, which led to competition to produce the most sustainable and innovative designs (Future Communities, 2017). Fourth, sustainable behavior is achieved mostly by structural design changes (75 percent) and less so by individual changes of citizens via incentives and education (25 percent). This suggests that encouraging sustainability-oriented decisions is more easily accomplished if structural changes are made first in order to guide, enable, or make clear the most sustainable behaviors (Future Communities, 2017).

German energy towns

In Germany, towns are developing around solar energy systems. Freiburg for example is adding solar systems to passive homes that already used little to no energy (Purvis, 2008). The solar systems generate and sell energy back to the grid as a source of annual income guaranteed for 20 years. Many residents of this solar town do not own or drive a car (Purvis, 2008), and large-scale stormwater management systems, combined heat and power at the community scale, and mixed land-use and transportation planning are all undertaken as part of participatory planning and design processes (Coates, 2013). This type of integrated sustainability transition is possible when multiple regime subsystems are changed simultaneously (Chapter 7) including culture, policy, industry, and technology.

International networks for city sustainability

Cities are part of multi-level sustainability-oriented governance networks that connect energy, water, food, and transportation systems to improve the sustainability of the city. These networks including Local Agenda (Action) 21, the Local Governments for Sustainability Network (ICLEI, 2017), and the Resilient Cities Network (Resilient Cities, 2017), have been able to successfully scale-up actions and spread knowledge and techniques across political boundaries. While grassroots organizations may partially influence municipal decisions to participate in sustainability (Berry and Portney, 2017; Yi et al., 2017), multi-level networks can help cities create capacity for addressing complex environmental challenges like climate change (Bulkeley and Newell, 2015; Sovacool and Brown, 2009). Some cities may choose to frame these initiatives as job creation, economic development, or infrastructure upgrades in order to avoid political debates centered on the term sustainability (Berry and Portney, 2017).

International networks can help cities integrate sustainability principles into municipal strategies and instruments. For example, cities are focusing on adaptation as part of the 100 Resilient Cities program (Resilient Cities, 2017). Stormwater management, infrastructure upgrades (e.g., aging infrastructure, infrastructure failures), preparation for natural disasters (e.g., earthquakes, floods, landslides), economic challenges (e.g., lack of economic diversification, economic transitions), environmental challenges (e.g., pollution, heat waves, drought, disease outbreaks), and social issues (e.g., social justice, social cohesion, inequality, affordable housing, crime and violence) are commonly included in the resilient city plans. Some goals are ambitious, for example, Rotterdam's target of being 100 percent climate-proof by 2025. This is largely driven by a land constraint (80 percent of the land area is below sea level), which makes the city vulnerable to catastrophic flooding. Other goals relate to economic transitions, like Pittsburgh, Pennsylvania, which is integrating resilience and sustainability into its city services, programs, and policies to improve its infrastructure, create green jobs, and transition the city from an industrial center to a modern economy driven by the tertiary (e.g., service) and quaternary (e.g., knowledge-based) sectors (Pittsburgh, 2017). Acceleration Point: Sustainability professionals can use their cities' participation in these international networks as leverage to encourage further municipal building code changes, green city planning, and green building programs.

Commercial property managers: beyond LEED and Energy Star programs

Commercial property owners play important roles as sustainability champions or intermediaries within organizations. Property owners and managers of buildings that achieved an *Energy Star* score of 75 or higher were able to overcome barriers by considering and selling energy upgrades as either financial or strategic investments, using knowledge and decision-making tools, and expanding funding options (Gliedt and Hoicka, 2015). Improving the energy performance of buildings as a financial investment suggests that property owners and managers reduced costs, increased revenues, and achieved a return-on-investment. Energy investments that were strategic (rather than rational economic) were conducted for environmental sustainability or corporate social responsibility reasons. This occurred when property owners and managers were confident that economic returns could be achieved by first improving sustainability metrics and second amplifying those improvements with marketing and outreach efforts. Many Energy Star property owners/managers increased their energy performance over time, achieving higher Energy Star scores after undertaking additional efficiency and automation measures. The findings from this study suggest that energy investment decision-making processes are complex; there are multiple complimentary motivations that depend on the property type. Furthermore, an *energy efficiency gap* was identified because less than half of the respondents invested in insulation improvements to the building envelope despite viewing these options as a sound financial investment.

Energy Star certification is appealing because (1) it allows organizations to earn a score and a label, which can be leveraged through marketing to gain a strategic advantage, and (2) it is a performance system that is based on a third-party audit and verification. Many property owners/managers improved their energy performance over time (Gliedt and Hoicka, 2015), which is significant because the Energy Star score is calculated based on the current performance of the building stock. If you achieved an Energy Star score of 80, that means that your building was in the top 20 percent of energy performance for that building type. If the property owner/manager applies for another Energy Star score five years later, the performance of the building stock has improved, and therefore the building owner/manager has to do additional retrofits to achieve an 80. The Energy Star system did not include water, transportation, or building materials like paints and carpets, which are included in LEED certification.

LEED encourages improvements in water efficiency (maximum 10 points), energy and atmosphere (maximum 35 points), materials and resources (maximum 14 points), indoor environmental quality (maximum 15 points), and sustainable sites (maximum 26 points) (Gauthier and Wooldridge, 2012). If a building gains 80 points or more in the U.S. LEED system, it can attain the highest level of platinum certification. Building owners/developers have to pay to have the building officially certified, which is an additional barrier and therefore is often not completed despite taking actions that would lead to a certification. LEED has a set of advantages including that it focuses on energy and water, specific regional priorities (e.g., building waste management), building materials, and transportation credits from low- or zero-emission parking options and siting near public transit. However, LEED does not take into account behavior of building occupants and broader social and quality of life factors.

Other systems include additional factors. The National Australian Built Environment Rating System (NABERS) includes the focus on energy, water, waste, and indoor environmental characteristics, while adding user perceptions (NABERS, 2017). The Living Building Challenge includes all of the aforementioned characteristics, as well as aesthetics and social justice factors, and is focused on the regenerative potential of the building and the occupant experience (LBC, 2017). The Living Building Challenge also measures actual building performance over time, which takes into account occupant behavior and therefore potential *rebound effects*. Rebound effects can occur when building occupants or energy managers change their energy use behavior or settings to increase comfort (e.g., adjusting the thermostat) and improve the user experience (e.g., turning on lights), which can reduce the energy savings that were achieved by the technology improvements (Greening et al., 2000; Santarius and Soland, 2018).

Building design is always improving and designers and engineers are pushing technological innovation in building science towards sustainability principles. The SUNY College of Environmental Science and Forestry LEED Platinum building goes beyond reducing environmental impacts to also produce extra energy that can supply 60 percent of the entire campus's heat and 20 percent of its power (SUNY, 2014). The historic federal building and courthouse in Grand Junction, Colorado, was retrofitted to meet net-zero standards including the installation of a large solar array added to the roof, while preserving the historical features and look of the building (American Institute of Architects, 2017). The Drake Landing Solar Community in Okotoks, Alberta, is a neighborhood-scale integrated solar community that generates solar power and stores solar energy in a centralized system capable of distributing the energy back to the houses. This planned neighborhood has 52 super energy efficient houses that, when combined with the solar system, can reduce GHG emissions by 5 tonnes per home per year (Drake Landing, 2017). The Edge is a commercial building in Amsterdam that aims to move from net-zero to absolute-zero carbon. It includes solar systems and an Aquifer Thermal Energy Storage system that provides the heat and cooling for the building. This system makes the heating and cooling in the Edge six-times more efficient than a similar sized building (BREEAM, 2017). The Edith Green-Wendell Wyatt Federal Building in Portland, Oregon, was built in 1974 and retrofitted in 2013 with funding from the American Recovery and Reinvestment Act (American Institute of Architects, 2017). The renovations had to meet the energy and water conservation requirements of the Energy Independence and Security Act (Public Law 110-140) signed by President Bush in 2007 (EPA, 2017). Not only has the retrofitted building achieved a 45 percent energy savings, it is able to harvest over 600,000 gallons of water annually, reducing water use by 65 percent. While sustainability professionals can work within organizations to encourage sustainability improvements to new and existing buildings, they can also work within communities to encourage new types of organizations for generating renewable energy that can power those buildings.

Community solar farms: Colorado

Another form of organization working to encourage sustainability are community solar projects, which are gaining interest in the United States as a community solar garden subscription service (SunShare, 2017). In this case, homeowners do not need to have panels installed on their homes, but rather, subscribe to a community solar garden via payments to a company like SunShare in Colorado and Minnesota, which develops new solar capacity to meet the demands from its customers. In many cases, the homeowners can pay less for their electricity than they did before subscribing to the solar service. Solar gardens were first enabled in Colorado with the passage of HB 10-1342, known as the Community Solar Gardens Act (Levy et al., 2010). This bill allowed independent companies to generate energy from solar gardens, feed it into the grid, and bill homeowners and organizations for that green energy. State governments as part of the regime subsystems (Chapter 7) can have an instrumental role in either accelerating (seedbeds) or decelerating (bottlenecks) the transition to sustainability by either enabling or disabling organizations like community solar projects from making sustainable decisions (Chapter 9).

Measuring progress of organizations as sustainability change agents

Organizations can play various roles as change agents towards sustainability. But how do policy makers, environmental leaders, and academics know how successful organizations are at encouraging sustainability changes? How can sustainability professionals measure progress towards sustainability goals related to societal change? One way is through the development of metrics that can capture and track integrated economic, social, and environmental criteria. Many societal-scale metrics are discussed in later chapters, including the sustainable social net product and the ecological intensity of human well-being. It is more challenging to equate societal-level impacts to individual organizational decisions. Lifecycle analysis, Energy Star, LEED, and ISO certification systems can all be used to measure sustainability at the organizational scale. But these systems do not measure the strategy-making process, the innovation process, or the integration between the two with respect to the organizational capacity to generate *sustainability value* and instigate radical innovations that will have larger scale and transformational impacts on society.

The following set of output, integrated, and process metrics could be used to measure the impact of organizations as sustainability agents. Examples of **output metrics** include tracking the number of new green services or products developed each year or the number of new ideas for services/products that have not yet been developed to identify green innovation potential. Output metrics are relatively simple to calculate but do not measure the processes involved in changing organizational behavior, strategies, or mobilizing resources for implementing green innovation.

Many large organizations like Coca Cola track their GHG emissions and water use down to the department and even the building level, and this can be used as an **integrated metric** by comparing GHG emissions or water reduced per unit of product (Coca Cola, 2017). Alternatively, the amount of GHG emissions reduced per number of organizational green strategies or number of employees working in a sustainability-related department/committee can be tracked. For economically focused decision-makers, integrated metrics that may be appealing include the amount of annual revenue per dollar invested in green product/service creation processes, the revenue per green innovation partnership created, or the profit per number of employees working on environmental management.

Process metrics include the percentage of an organization's budget or revenue that was spent on green innovation annually, the percentage of sales from green services/products that were introduced during the previous year, or the number of external partnerships or capabilities that contributed to each new service/technology/product produced per year. Other process metrics could focus on the percentage of employees who have received training, certification, and/or tools for green innovation or environmental management. Organizations can track the number of new *sustainability competencies* (skills, knowledge, practices) that were created per budget dollar invested in green strategies, or the amount of GHG emissions reduced per new sustainability competencies created.

Improving performance against metrics requires resources that are often considered overhead that add to the costs of operating the organization. To justify investment in capabilities to improve sustainability performance, sustainability professionals can help turn environmental and social value creation (public benefits) into economic value creation (private benefits). This can be accomplished by viewing proactive sustainability strategies as *dynamic capabilities* that become the basis for green competitive advantage if they are measurable, complex, and difficult for other organizations to replicate (Hart and Dowell, 2011). Organizations can invest in dynamic capabilities to enable continual adjustments to changing economic, social, and environmental conditions (Hartman et al., 2017). These capabilities help organizations balance stakeholder demands for improved financial performance during tougher economic times with societal demands for improved social and environmental performance during good economic times. Organizations of all size and type can focus on sustainability value creation strategies to guide investments into sustainability competencies and dynamic capabilities that can improve the competitive position of the organization and increase the chances of generating sustainability solutions.

Check on learning

- Go to the Living Building Challenge website (LBC, 2017). Identify three principles that you believe will help guide architects and planners in designing more sustainable buildings and neighborhoods. How do these principles relate to or differ from the principles of sustainability in Chapter 1?
- Do some research on the website of a well-known corporation in your country. Find a sustainability plan/report that you believe effectively communicates the strategies and initiatives used by the business to improve sustainability performance. In your view, explain why this plan relates more closely to a reactive, pragmatic, or proactive sustainability pathway (Figure 1.10)?
- Review Figure 3.3: A Theory Landscape of Sustainability in Firms from Chang et al. (2017). In one or two paragraphs, explain how the societal-level sustainability theories have been integrated with theories of organizational change.
- Read Ostrom (2009 and 2012). In one or two pages, make an argument as to why polycentric governance arrangements are important for achieving sustainability. At what scales are these arrangements most and least effective? Can polycentric governance arrangements guarantee that sustainability principles are improved over time? Which principles of sustainability are more likely to be improved? Which are less likely to be improved?
- Where are the lines between being a traditional business, a social purpose business, or a non-profit organization? How much do profit and public goods motives overlap when it comes to organizational environmental strategy? Can improvements to environmental performance lead to improvements in financial performance? Explain in one or two paragraphs why or why not?
- Given that the priorities of water users, types of political and legal frameworks, and precipitation levels differ within a single water system, should water systems continue to be managed by centralized water utilities that focus on water supply? Describe in one or two paragraphs how multi-level governance arrangements could help foster solutions that increase the sustainability of water systems, including water recycling and reuse, stormwater management, desalination, and smart meters and demand response programs.
- In one or two pages, outline specific strategies and tools for sustainable behavior change (Chapter 2) that would help convince your city to incorporate the principles of 'Vancouverism'. What actors would be important for you to target, and how would you engage them in the process?

Assignments

- Service learning for local food systems
- Integrating technology and financing decisions to improve commercial building energy performance

References

American Institute of Architects. (2017). Wayne N. Aspinall Federal Building and U.S. Courthouse. Project Overview. Available at: http://aiatopten.org/node/367 and http://aiatopten.org/node/494

Artiach, T., Lee, D., Nelson, D., & Walker, J. (2010). The determinants of corporate sustainability performance. *Accounting & Finance*, 50(1), 31–51.

Banerjee, S. B. (2001). Managerial perceptions of corporate environmentalism: Interpretations form industry and strategic implications for organizations. *Journal of Management Studies*, 38(4), 489–513.

Banerjee, S. B. (2002). Corporate environmentalism: The construct and its measurement. *Journal of Business Research*, 55, 177–191.

Bansal, P., & Roth, K. (2000). Why companies go green: A model of ecological responsiveness. *Academy of Management Journal*, 43(4), 717–736.

Berry, J. M., & Portney, K. E. (2017). The Tea Party versus Agenda 21: Local groups and sustainability policies in US cities. *Environmental Politics*, 26(1), 118–137.

BREEAM. (2017). The Edge winner of the BREEAM Award for Offices New Construction in 2016. Available at: www.breeam.com/index.jsp?id=804

Bulkeley, H., & Betsill, M. (2005). Rethinking sustainable cities: Multilevel governance and the 'urban' politics of climate change. *Environmental Politics*, 14(1), 42–63.

Bulkeley, H., & Betsill, M. M. (2013). Revisiting the urban politics of climate change. *Environmental Politics*, 22(1), 136–154.

Bulkeley, H., & Newell, P. (2015). *Governing Climate Change*. Routledge, New York, NY.

Cash, D. W., Clark, W. C., Alcock, F., Dickson, N. M., Eckley, N., Guston, D. H., . . . & Mitchell, R. B. (2003). Knowledge systems for sustainable development. *Proceedings of the National Academy of Sciences*, 100(14), 8086–8091.

Chang, R. D., Zuo, J., Zhao, Z. Y., Zillante, G., Gan, X. L., & Soebarto, V. (2017). Evolving theories of sustainability and firms: History, future directions and implications for renewable energy research. *Renewable and Sustainable Energy Reviews*, 72, 48–56.

Clemens, B., & Douglas, T. J. (2006). Does coercion drive firms to adopt 'voluntary' green initiatives? Relationships among coercion, superior firm resources, and voluntary green initiatives. *Journal of Business Research*, 59, 483–491.

Coates, G. J. (2013). The sustainable urban district of Vauban in Freiburg, Germany. *International Journal of Design & Nature and Ecodynamics*, 8(4), 265–286.

Coca Cola. (2017). Coca Cola 2016 sustainability report. Available at: www.coca-colacompany.com/content/dam/journey/us/en/private/fileassets/pdf/2017/2016-sustainability-update/2016-Sustainability-Report-The-Coca-Cola-Company.pdf

CodeNEXT. (2017). CodeNEXT. Shaping the Austin we imagine. Draft LDC: Review and Comment. Available at: www.austintexas.gov/department/codenext

Cordano, M., Marshall, R. S., & Silverman, M. (2010). How do small and medium enterprises go 'green'? A study of environmental management programs in the U.S. wine industry. *Journal of Business Ethics*, 92, 463–478.

Delmas, M., Hoffmann, V. H., & Kuss, M. (2011). Under the tip of the iceberg: Absorptive capacity, environmental strategy, and competitive advantage. *Business & Society*, 50(1), 116–154.

Delmas, M., & Toffel, M. W. (2004). Stakeholders and environmental management practices: An institutional framework. *Business Strategy and the Environment*, 13, 209–222.

Drake Landing. (2017). Drake Landing solar community. Okotoks, Alberta, Canada. Available at: –www.dlsc.ca/

Dyllick, T., & Muff, K. (2016). Clarifying the meaning of sustainable business: Introducing a typology from business-as-usual to true business sustainability. *Organization & Environment*, 29(2), 156–174.

Egels-Zandén, N., & Rosén, M. (2015). Sustainable strategy formation at a Swedish industrial company: Bridging the strategy-as-practice and sustainability gap. *Journal of Cleaner Production*, 96, 139–147.

EPA. (2017). Summary of the Energy Independence and Security Act. Public Law 110–140 (2007). Environmental Protection Agency Laws and Regulations. Available at: www.epa.gov/laws-regulations/summary-energy-independence-and-security-act

Escriva-Bou, A., Lund, J. R., & Pulido-Velazquez, M. (2015). Optimal residential water conservation strategies considering related energy in California. *Water Resources Research*, 51, 4482–4498.

Fraker, H. (2013). Hammarby Sjöstad, Stockholm, Sweden. In H. Fraker. *The Hidden Potential of Sustainable Neighborhoods*. pp. 43–67. Island Press/Center for Resource Economics, Washington DC.

Future Communities. (2017). Hammarby Sjostad, Stockholm, Sweden, 1995 to 2015. Building a green city extension. Available at: http://futurecommunities.net/case-studies/hammarby-sjostad-stockholm-sweden-1995-2015

Gauthier, J., & Wooldridge, B. (2012). Influences on sustainable innovation adoption: Evidence from leadership in energy and environmental design. *Business Strategy and the Environment*, 21(2), 98–110.

Gliedt, T., & Hoicka, C. E. (2015). Energy upgrades as financial or strategic investment? Energy Star property owners and managers improving building energy performance. *Applied Energy*, 147, 430–443.

Gliedt, T., & Parker, P. (2007). Green community entrepreneurship: Creative destruction in the social economy. *International Journal of Social Economics*, 34(8), 538–553.

Gliedt, T., & Parker, P. (2014). Green community entrepreneurship 2.0: Collective response or individual adaptation strategy to funding cuts in Canada (2006-2012). *International Journal of Social Economics*, 41(7), 609–625.

Gonzales, P., & Ajami, N. K. (2017). An integrative regional resilience framework for the changing urban water paradigm. *Sustainable Cities and Society*, 30, 128–138.

Green Zone. (2012). Zone Green text amendment. New York City Planning. Available at: www1.nyc.gov/assets/planning/download/pdf/plans/zone-green/zone_green.pdf

Greening, L. A., Greene, D. L., & Difiglio, C. (2000). Energy efficiency and consumption – the rebound effect – a survey. *Energy policy*, 28(6), 389–401.

Guston, D. H. (2001). Boundary organizations in environmental policy and science: An introduction. *Science Technology and Human Values*, 26(4), 399–408.

Hahn, T., Figge, F., Pinkse, J., & Preuss, L. (2010). Trade-offs in corporate sustainability: You can't have your cake and eat it. *Business Strategy and the Environment*, 19(4), 217–229.

Hart, S. L. (1995). A natural-resource-based view of the firm. *Academy of Management Review*, 20, 986–1014.

Hart, S. L., & Dowell, G. (2011). A natural-resource-based view of the firm: Fifteen years after. *Journal of Management*, 37(5), 1464–1479.

Hart, S. L., & Milstein, M. B. (2003). Creating sustainable value. *The Academy of Management Executive*, 17(2), 56–67.

Hartman, P., Gliedt, T., Widener, J., & Loraamm, R. (2017). Dynamic capabilities for water system transitions in Oklahoma. *Environmental Innovation and Societal Transitions*, 25, 64–81.

ICLEI. (2017). Local Governments for Sustainability USA. Available at: http://icleiusa.org/

Imagine Austin. (2017). Imagine Austin. A vision for Austin's Future. Available at: www.austintexas.gov/department/imagine-austin

Iverot, S. P., & Brandt, N. (2011). The development of a sustainable urban district in Hammarby Sjöstad, Stockholm, Sweden? *Environment, Development and Sustainability*, 13(6), 1043–1064.

Joung, C. B., Carrell, J., Sarkar, P., & Feng, S C. (2012). Categorization of indicators for sustainable manufacturing, *Ecological Indicators*, 24, 148–157.

LBC. (2017). Living Building Challenge 3.0: A visionary path to a regenerative future. International Living Future Institute. Available at: http://living-future.org/lbc

Lehmann, S. (2010). Green urbanism: Formulating a series of holistic principles. *SAPI.EN.S. Surveys and Perspectives Integrating Environment and Society*, (3.2), 1–10. Available at: http://sapiens.revues.org/1057#tocto2n4

Levy,et al. (2010). HB 10–1342. The Community Solar Gardens Act, Colorado. Available at: http://tornado.state.co.us/gov_dir/leg_dir/olls/sl2010a/sl_344.pdf

Lourenço, I. C., & Branco, M. C. (2013). Determinants of corporate sustainability performance in emerging markets: The Brazilian case. *Journal of Cleaner Production*, 57, 134–141.

Lyakhov, A., & Gliedt, T. (2017). Understanding collaborative value creation by environmental nonprofit and renewable energy business partnerships. *VOLUNTAS: International Journal of Voluntary and Nonprofit Organizations*, 28(4), 1448–1472.

Lyakhov, A., Gliedt, T., & Jackson, N. (2016). Scaling sustainability value in sustainability purpose organizations: A non-profit and business comparison. *International Journal of Sustainable Entrepreneurship and Corporate Social Responsibility*, 1(1), 17–31.

Maggioni, E. (2015). Water demand management in times of drought: What matters for water conservation. *Water Resources Research*, 51(1), 125–139.

McCorkle, T. A., Williams, S. S., Pfeiffer, T. A., & Basara, J. B. (2016). Atmospheric contributors to heavy rainfall events in the Arkansas-Red River Basin. *Advances in Meteorology*. Available at: www.hindawi.com/journals/amete/2016/4597912/abs/

Meadow, A. M., Ferguson, D. B., Guido, Z., Horangic, A., Owen, G., & Wall, T. (2015). Moving toward the deliberate coproduction of climate science knowledge. *Weather, Climate, and Society*, 7(2), 179–191.

Mini, C., Hogue, T. S., & Pincetl, S. (2015). The effectiveness of water conservation measures on summer residential water use in Los Angeles, California. *Resources, Conservation and Recycling*, 94, 136–145.

Montiel, I. (2008). Corporate social responsibility and corporate sustainability. Separate pasts, common futures. *Organization and Environment*, 21(3), 245–269.

Moon, H., & Lee, C. (2015). Strategic learning capability: Through the lens of environmental jolts. *European Journal of Training and Development*, 39(7), 628–640.

NABERS. (2017). National Australian Built Environment rating system. Available at: www.nabers.gov.au/public/WebPages/Home.aspx

NYC. (2017). Strategic objectives. New York City Planning. Department of City Planning. Available at: www1.nyc.gov/site/planning/index.page

Qiao, L., Zou, C. B., Gaitán, C. F., Hong, Y., & McPherson, R. A. (2017). Analysis of precipitation projections over the climate gradient of the Arkansas-Red River Basin. *Journal of Applied Meteorology and Climatology*. 56(5), 1325–1336.

Orlitzky, M., Siegel, D. S., & Waldman, D. A. (2011). Strategic corporate social responsibility and environmental sustainability. *Business and Society*, 50(1), 6–27.

Orsato, R. J., Garcia, A., Mendes-Da-Silva, W., Simonetti, R., & Monzoni, M. (2015). Sustainability indexes: why join in? A study of the 'Corporate Sustainability Index (ISE)'in Brazil. *Journal of Cleaner Production*, 96, 161–170.

Ostrom, E. (2009). A general framework for analyzing sustainability of social-ecological systems. *Science*, 325(5939), 419–422.

Ostrom, E. (2012). Nested externalities and polycentric institutions: Must we wait for global solutions to climate change before taking actions at other scales? *Economic Theory*, 49(2), 353–369.

Pittsburgh. (2017). Sustainability & Resilience. Pittsburgh Climate Action Plan. Available at: http://pittsburghpa.gov/dcp/sustainability&resilience.html

Plummer, R., & Armitage, D. (2007). A resilience-based framework for evaluating adaptive co-management: Linking ecology, economics and society in a complex world. *Ecological Economics*, 61(1), 62–74.

Purvis, A. (2008). Is this the greenest city in the world? *The Guardian*. Available at: www.theguardian.com/environment/2008/mar/23/freiburg.germany.greenest.city

Red River Compact. (1978). Red River Compact Commission. Available at: www.owrb.ok.gov/rrccommission/rrccommission.html

Resilient Cities. (2017). 100 resilient cities. Available at: www.100resilientcities.org/cities#/-_/

Santarius, T., & Soland, M. (2018). How technological efficiency improvements change consumer preferences: Towards a psychological theory of rebound effects. *Ecological Economics*, 146, 414–424.

Senge, P. M. (2006). *The Fifth Discipline: The Art and Practice of the Learning Organization*. Broadway Business, New York, NY.

Singletary, L., & Sterle, K. (2017). Collaborative modeling to assess drought resiliency of snow-fed river dependent communities in the western United States: A case study in the Truckee-Carson river system. *Water*, 9(2), 99.

Slavin, T. (2015). What can the world learn from Växjö, Europe's self-styled greenest city? *The Guardian*. Available at: www.theguardian.com/cities/2015/nov/25/what-can-the-world-learn-from-vaxjo-europes-self-styled-greenest-city

Sovacool, B. K., & Brown, M. A. (2009). Scaling the policy response to climate change. *Policy and Society*, 27(4), 317–328.

SunShare. (2017). SunShare Community Solar. Colorado, USA. Available at: www.mysunshare.com/

SUNY. (2014). SUNY-ESF's Gateway Center earns LEED Platinum certification. Available at: www.esf.edu/communications/view.asp?newsID=2672

Trumpp, C., & Guenther, T. (2017). Too little or too much? Exploring U-shaped relationships between corporate environmental performance and corporate financial performance. *Business Strategy and the Environment*, 26, 49–68.

Vancouver Urban Planning. (2017). Urban planning, sustainable zoning, and development. Available at: http://vancouver.ca/home-property-development/planning-zoning-development.aspx

White, D. D., Wutich, A., Larson, K. L., Gober, P., Lant, T., & Senneville, C. (2010). Credibility, salience, and legitimacy of boundary objects: Water managers' assessment of a simulation model in an immersive decision theater. *Science and Public Policy*, 37(3), 219.

White, D. D., Wutich, A. Y., Larson, K. L., & Lant, T. (2015a). Water management decision makers' evaluations of uncertainty in a decision support system: The case of WaterSim in the Decision Theater. *Journal of Environmental Planning and Management*, 58(4), 616–630.

White, D. D., Withycombe Keeler, L., Wiek, A., & Larson, K. L. (2015b). Envisioning the future of water governance: A survey of central Arizona water decision makers. *Environmental Practice*, 17(01), 25–35.

Widener, J., Gliedt, T., & Hartman, P. (2017). Visualizing dynamic capabilities as adaptive capacity for municipal water governance. *Sustainability Science*, 12(2), 203–219.

Yi, H., Krause, R. M., & Feiock, R. C. (2017). Back-pedaling or continuing quietly? Assessing the impact of ICLEI membership termination on cities' sustainability actions. *Environmental Politics*, 26(1), 138–160.

4   Green innovation systems

Learning objectives

- Understand contemporary theories of green innovation and the role of various actors within green innovation systems
- Compare and contrast technological innovation systems theory with multi-level sustainability transitions theory
- Identify strategies and instruments designed to simultaneously encourage niche innovation processes and enable regime transitions
- Outline case studies of green innovation that highlight processes that have the potential to lead to radical innovations

Theories of green innovation

Green innovation is defined broadly as the creation and implementation of new or adapted institutional and technological changes that generate *sustainability value* and enhance social-ecological system integrity (Hartman et al., 2017). This definition views innovation as a process, from idea creation to implementation, and further, to the adjustments that take place upon feedback from niche and regime actors (Chapter 7) and technology users over time. Organizations (Chapter 3) and economic development processes (Chapter 5) help create and diffuse technologies for private (organizational) and public (societal) benefits, while governance researchers experiment with mixes of strategies and instruments to encourage public and private investment in organizational capabilities to create sustainability-oriented innovations (Chapter 8). The challenge for sustainability professionals is how to encourage and support green innovation that will lead to socio-technical system changes including infrastructure and policies that have substantial and wide-reaching impacts on the Gibson principles of sustainability (Chapter 1). Key contributions from the following interdisciplinary theories help understand how technological innovation systems including actors and institutions can enable green innovation.

Environmental economic geography

Environmental economic geographers study the integrated relationships between economic changes and environmental changes in relation to sustainability challenges and opportunities from a technological innovation perspective. This subfield of geography builds on *ecological modernization theory* by adding an additional *regulationist approach* (Gibbs, 2006), which implies that governance can help guide the direction of technological innovation and development with enabling policies (Chapter 8) based on a **normative** sustainability goal and a **strategic** vision (see the *sustainability competencies* in Chapter 1). One specific objective is to examine the role of environmental performance as a driver of innovation (Bridge, 2008). A critique of environmental economic geography is that it does not specifically focus on developing innovation processes, but rather describes the problems and characteristics of environmental–economic relationships that could lead to innovation. Given that both economic processes (e.g., investment, trade, research and development) and non-economic processes (e.g., institutional habits and norms) are important to innovation, sustainability professionals need to focus on how these processes can be coordinated, accelerated, and guided in the direction of *strong sustainability*.

Environmental economic geographers have argued that a green *techno-economic para-digm* is possible by viewing innovation as a driver of economic change (Hayter, 2008). Each of the previous techno-economic paradigms (the industrial revolution; steam and railways; steel, electricity, and heavy engineering; oil, the automobile, and mass produc-tion; information and communications) was characterized by a set of commonly accepted innovation principles that became universally adopted as *social practices* (Perez, 2010). For example, in the case of the information and communications paradigm, the commonly accepted innovation principles included rapid information exchanges, network struc-tures, knowledge as capital, adaptability of processes and technologies, diversity of market niches, economies of scope and economies of scale, globalization, and clusters for com-petition and collaboration (Perez, 2010). These innovation principles enabled changes to technologies and infrastructures, which co-evolved with changes to institutions. Hayter (2008) described *evolutionary institutionalism* as a driver of ecological modernization: "the analytical focus of evolutionary institutionalism is the habits, conventions, attitudes or simply the routines that define institutions – what routines are and why routines are cre-ated, maintained, destabilized and restructured" (p. 834). The extent that a new green techno-economic paradigm could occur is therefore related to changes in institutions, technologies, and infrastructures, and would become recognizable when a set of com-monly accepted innovation principles "become ingrained and act as inductors and filters for the pursuit of technical, organizational, and strategic innovations as well as for business and consumer decisions" (Perez, 2010, p. 195).

Patchell and Hayter (2013) argued that environmental economic geography would benefit from integrating with evolutionary economic geography, as both focus on inno-vation processes and societal change from a multi-level perspective. Three areas for research are identified as "extending place-based analysis of localized clusters; broadening the scope of global value chain analysis; and reengaging the analysis of core-periphery relations" (p. 1). Each of these areas relates to sustainability transitions in socio-technical systems in different ways. First, *clusters* are one of the key drivers of green innovation and are an important landscape for sustainability-oriented innovation intermediaries to oper-ate, which is described further in Chapter 6.

Second, *value chains* are inter- and intra-organizational networks that transform raw materials into finished products including the marketing and distribution to end users. Value chains can be extended into *value cycles* that encourage reuse and recycling waste into inputs as part of closed loop *industrial ecology systems*. Value cycles can help improve *job creation multiplier effects* for economies and reduce transaction costs for businesses (Patchell and Hayter, 2013). Value cycles offer opportunities for greening corporate performance that relate directly to all four strategies of the Hart and Dowell (2011) framework including pollution prevention, product stewardship, clean technology, and sustainable development (Chapter 3). Examining value cycles will also help address Truffer et al.'s (2015) call for research to "trace the ways in which innovations emerge in different places and then enter into contact with each other within and across different spatial scales" (p. 64).

Third, core–periphery dynamics are important for examining the relationships between resource rich/producer nations (e.g., Saudi Arabia, Canada) and resource poor/consumer nations (e.g., Japan, the United Kingdom). Core–periphery relations are also applicable within countries, for example, resource rich/producer states (e.g., Oklahoma, Texas, Alaska) and resource poor/consumer states (e.g., New York, California, Illinois). These relations offer an opportunity for intervention that could encourage both producer (e.g., carbon intensity improvements) and consumer (e.g., efficiency improvements) changes in the direction of sustainability. Producer states have an incentive to reduce the environmental impacts of their energy production in order to mitigate the social and political pressure from consuming states. Consuming states have an incentive to improve efficiency of domestic consumption systems to reduce demand and dependence on producer states.

Geographers and other researchers examining the space, place, and scale implications of green innovation can benefit from viewing innovation as a process composed of different stages and functions.

Technological innovation systems framework

The *technological innovation systems framework* views innovation as a process based on seven interrelated functions: entrepreneurship, knowledge development (R&D), knowledge and technology diffusion, guidance of the search, market formation and development, resource mobilization including incubating and accelerating innovations, and finally, the creation of legitimacy achieved in part due to the innovation influencing changes to institutions and infrastructures (Markard and Truffer, 2008). The advantage of viewing innovation as a process is that it allows for targeted interventions at different stages of the process that may require adjustment. If for example the commercialization of green innovation is progressing at higher rates than other innovations, but the entrepreneurship processes are turning ideas into patents at a slower rate than the broader economy, then strategies and instruments could target the earlier stages of the innovation process (Chapple et al., 2011). An important research question for sustainability professionals concerns the appropriate timing and complementarity between technology and policy innovations.

Markard and Truffer (2008) identified recommendations for integrating the technological innovation systems framework and the multi-level perspective (MLP) framework (Chapter 7) in order to help understand radical innovation processes. Technological innovation systems can focus on the national, regional, or sectoral level, and are composed of actors and institutions that compete/contradict or collaborate/complement each other. Niche actors, regime actors, and intermediaries all contribute different functions and sub-functions to the development of innovation systems. Functions aim to create and use new technologies, while sub-functions include the related activities such as entrepreneurship processes, the creation and use of knowledge, the development of new markets, the financing choices related to innovation processes, changes to institutions and other subsystems of the regime, and the mobilization of resources directed towards technology creation (Markard and Truffer, 2008). Each sub-function of innovation systems can be measured with indicators. For example, entrepreneurial processes can be measured by counting the number of new businesses or the number of new strategies of existing businesses focused on green innovation. Indicators for knowledge development can include the amount of investments in research and development and the number of green patents. Indicators for resource mobilization include the amount of venture capital and the number of workers devoted to green innovation functions. Sustainability professionals can identify and measure specific combinations of indicators to highlight a pathway for reorienting innovation systems towards sustainability experiments that have the potential to create radical technology innovations.

Technological innovation system for solar PV in Ethiopia

Kebede and Mitsufuji (2017) examined how the collection of technological innovation system functions important to the development and diffusion of Ethiopian solar PV systems changed over time. The functions were actualized by a series of key events detailed in Kebede and Mitsufuji (2017). The Ethiopian solar PV industry emerged in the 1980s and the technological innovation system functions at that time included entrepreneurial experimentation, knowledge development, and guidance of search. During the 2000–05 period, the number and diversity of events and functions expanded and by 2006–10, events had contributed to each of the seven functions. Key events included 1,100 solar home systems installed in a town called Rema, including on policy and administration offices, churches, and mosques in 2007 (entrepreneurial function); Bill Clinton went to the Rema solar village in 2008 (creation of legitimacy function); the Ministry of Finance and Economic Development lifted the import duty fees on PV modules and systems in 2009 (market formation function); training for Ethiopian microfinance providers, banks, and public authorities in 2010 (knowledge diffusion function); a master plan report of wind and solar energy in Ethiopia was conducted in 2011 by a Chinese corporation interested in solar energy in Ethiopia (knowledge development function); the government of Ethiopia developing a Climate Resilient Green Economy Strategy in 2011 (guidance of the search function); market development for renewable energy and energy efficient products fund was made available in 2012 (resource mobilization function); a national feasibility study in 2012 indicated that 50,000 jobs could be created in the solar sector (guidance of the search function); and the first solar PV modules assembly plant finished in 2012 was a joint venture of an Ethiopian government owned company and a United States company (entrepreneurial function). For more information about sustainable development in Ethiopia, read ECRGE (2011), Simane et al. (2012, 2014), and Simane and Zaitchik (2014). Acceleration Point: Sustainability professionals can work with intermediaries to focus on creating key events that highlight or improve performance of each of the functions of technological innovation systems and to orient them towards sustainability principles.

A critique of the technological innovation systems framework is that it does not incorporate user practices into the process of understanding and accelerating technological adoption rates. Sustainability professionals can use surveys, interviews, and focus groups

(Chapter 2) to address this limitation by examining to what extent technology producers are responding to societal demand for clean energy and sustainability solutions. Additionally, sustainability professionals can help understand which strategies or instruments would help accelerate consumer adoption of new, efficient, or exciting technologies. User practices change as prices, problems, and priorities are constantly shifting and new knowledge and experiences emerge. The combination of user practices and preferences, institutional regime characteristics, and organizational strategies can lead to different technology creation and commercialization environments.

Technology innovation and commercialization environments

Renewable energy and other green technology innovations can expand for two reasons: (1) market demand as a pull factor, and (2) the sophistication of the market for novel technologies as a push factor (Walsh, 2012). Walsh (2012) outlined four environments for renewable energy technology commercialization characterized by different combinations of innovation type, level of commercial risk, and commercialization strategies:

(1) **Innovation wasteland** is characterized by innovations that are higher risk to the entrepreneurs, and commercialization strategies include government incentives, external research and development contracts, and utility funding and support. Innovation wasteland would have little or no incentive for renewable energy innovation and is likely characterized by locked-in *subsystems of the regime* that are resistant to change. As a result, the funding and policy environment may be hostile to renewable energy innovation. Innovations that succeed in this environment must therefore disrupt the existing regime and gain broad support by offering significant value to society such as triple-bottom-line economic development benefits (Chapter 5). Example countries: China, India, Mexico, Russia, Turkey. It should be noted that innovation conditions in China and India are rapidly changing, and the growth in renewable energy is pulling this environment to be more favorable to innovation.

(2) **Innovation push** is characterized by innovations with moderate risk, and commercialization strategies include outsourcing and licensing. Innovation push environments have low but increasing growth in demand for renewable energy and supporting technologies and infrastructures. This is in part due to an effective and supportive enabling institutional environment including a highly sophisticated market for green technology. Example countries: Australia, Canada, Finland, France, Japan, Norway, South Korea, Sweden, Switzerland, United Kingdom, United States.

(3) **Innovation pull** is also characterized by innovations with moderate risk, but commercialization strategies tend to be joint ventures and strategic alliances. There is a low level of green technology market sophistication and a low level of institutional support for sustainability and triple-bottom-line economic development. Increasing growth in demand for renewable energy makes companies interested in future market investment. Sustainability professionals can help with instruments aiming to increase the availability of cost effective renewable energy technologies including to markets without access to cheap fossil fuel energy. Example countries: Brazil, Czech Republic, Greece, Hungary, Italy, Poland, Slovakia.

(4) **Innovation nirvana** is characterized by innovations with low risk, and strategies for commercialization include venture capital, equity financing, and acquisitions by large incumbent firms. Sequential innovation processes involve producers continually

improving technologies as a form of competitive advantage by staying ahead of the competition. Consumers in this environment are highly knowledgeable of the sustainability benefits of the new technologies. Companies are able to achieve impressive returns on their research and development investment, which encourages further investment in innovation. Example countries: Austria, Belgium, Denmark, Germany, Iceland, Ireland, Netherlands, New Zealand, Spain.

Green technology manufacturers follow different strategies based on the innovation and commercialization environment that exists at a particular time in different countries. The challenge is to match and adjust the strategy to ongoing changes in the environment. It is also important to think about connections between large and small businesses that play distinct yet complimentary roles in sustainability transitions.

Industry innovation for sustainability transitions

Hockerts and Wüstenhagen (2010) developed a typology to suggest that sustainability start-ups have a lower market share but a higher potential for radical innovations that could change the *socio-technical system* (Figure 4.1). Market incumbents have a large market share but a lower potential for radical innovations that could change the socio-technical system. However, given the large market share, market incumbents have a high potential for changing the sustainability of an entire industry through influencing incremental innovations through its *value chains*. Sustainability professionals can help coordinate the green innovation processes ongoing within large incumbents with the *niche experiments* created by start-ups to combine scale advantages in the first case with the rapid creativity and dynamic change processes in the latter. Clusters provide a supporting environment for small and large businesses that focus on green innovation to collaborate and compete, which can further drive innovation processes.

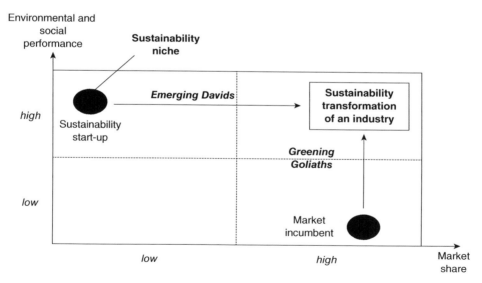

Figure 4.1 Co-evolution of sustainability start-ups and market incumbents towards the sustainability transition of an industry

Source: Hockerts and Wüstenhagen (2010, p. 488).

Clusters and green innovation

Clusters are defined as "geographically proximate groups of interlinked individuals and organizations. . .that generate knowledge spillovers and agglomeration economies" (Catini et al., 2015, p. 1749). Engel (2015, p. 37) defined clusters of innovation as:

> global economic 'hot spots' where new technologies germinate at an astounding rate and where pools of capital, expertise, and talent foster the development of new industries and new ways of doing business. They are vibrant, effervescent ecosystems composed of startups, businesses that support the startup process, and mature companies (many of whom evolved rapidly from a startup history). In these ecosystems, resources of people, capital, and know-how are fluidly mobile and the pace of transactions is driven by a relentless pursuit of opportunity, staged financing, and short business model cycles.

Evidence suggests that green businesses that are located in clusters grow faster than similar businesses that are not in clusters (Muro et al., 2011). Triple-bottom-line economic development (Chapter 5) can therefore be accelerated by clusters due to the interacting dynamics between institutional, economic, policy, culture, and resources/capabilities that continually evolve and act as seedbeds for new ideas, technologies, and businesses. Many clean technology clusters in the United States emerged due to supportive local governments that linked economic development strategies to climate change mitigation as part of the U.S. Conference of Mayor's Climate Protection Agreement and the C40 Cities Climate Leadership Group (Marra et al., 2015). Acceleration Point: Sustainability professionals can work with local economic development officers to help create the conditions (interacting dynamics) for clusters to occur in order to pull high-growth and innovative green businesses into the area as part of a business attraction strategy (Chapter 5).

Clusters that emerge around a central technology lead to many complimentary technology start-ups and business arrivals. A network analysis revealed that clean technology clusters in the United States focused on solar systems (solar PV, smart-grid applications, solar lighting, solar water purification systems, solar financing), wind systems (wind turbine technology, wind power forecasting, wind energy patents, energy storage, wind turbine raising systems, micro-grid technology), and interconnected clean web-based technologies (big data, software, information technology, mobile phone applications, storage, product stewardship) (Marra et al., 2015). Successful green clusters specialized in water technology (Milwaukee), fuel cells, energy services and wind (Albany), battery technology, green architecture and construction services (Atlanta), electric vehicle technology (Kansas City), energy efficient products, fuel cells, and solar PV (San Jose), air and water purification technology, and solar PV and solar thermal (Phoenix) (Muro et al., 2011). San Francisco alone has hundreds of clean technology companies as part of numerous, interconnected clean energy clusters focused on solar technologies, energy management, carbon trading market development (e.g., carbon offsets, renewable energy certificates, carbon sequestration, carbon balancing programs, carbon credits and emissions management software), and smart mobility (e.g., electric cars, green transportation, lithium-ion batteries) (Marra et al., 2015). The Austin Technology Incubator at the University of Texas includes a specific focus on clean energy and water filtration technology (Austin Technology Incubator, 2017). New York and Boston also have a high percentage of clean technology startups. Sustainability professionals could help identify clusters as they are emerging as well as mobilize the necessary knowledge creation resources (e.g., university research labs, incubators and accelerator centers) that will be needed to develop the cluster into an innovation growth engine (Gilbert, 2012).

Although geographic clusters are important for innovation, networks connecting multiple clusters in different places are also critical for providing a competitive advantage (Bathelt and Glückler, 2003, 2011). This can include open innovation systems (Kennedy et al., 2016; Schwerdtner et al., 2015) where champions act as boundary agents linking multiple clusters (McLennan et al., 2016). In this case, *cluster champions* are highly interconnected businesses to external sources of knowledge, *institutional gatekeepers* are governments, associations, or universities that promote the transfer of knowledge to established and start-up businesses in the cluster, and *innovation intermediaries* are central and enabling organizations that connect different clusters through networks while facilitating the transfer of knowledge and information (McLennan et al., 2016).

Clusters are a generator of new ideas and technology, but once established, they can also act to inhibit change because the concentration of similar firms gains political power and the ability to control or funnel resources to maintain the dominant technologies that they produce (Gilbert, 2012). This may decrease the likelihood of firms in the cluster developing or investing in radically new technologies. How can clusters both create radical technologies while expanding existing technologies? One approach is to use competitions and challenges as strategies through regional innovation and economic development programs focused on innovation.

Regional innovation strategies

The United States Economic Development Association Office of Innovation and Entrepreneurship funds an annual Regional Innovation Strategies Program. This program offered competitive grants for building regional capacity to translate innovations into jobs (EDA, 2017). The grants are designed to support proof-of-concept centers (Hayter and Link, 2015a) with commercialization assistance to entrepreneurs and operational support for organizations that provide early stage capital to entrepreneurs. A sub-competition was known as the i6 Challenge, which supported the creation of proof-of-concept centers to increase the rate of moving ideas to innovations, intellectual property, and eventually products and services, companies and organizations, and jobs in communities.

In 2011, the i6 program was used as a Green Challenge in partnership with the United States Departments of Energy and Agriculture, and the Environmental Protection Agency to award funds to six university research teams with innovative ideas to drive green energy and building technology innovation and commercialization through entrepreneurship (Energy.gov, 2011). The goal was to draw upon university capabilities to generate new knowledge, transform that knowledge into products and technologies, and expand those technologies throughout the economy (Hayter and Link, 2015b). Proof-of-concept centers help researchers commercialize their technologies by overcoming barriers such as a lack of access to services, networks, and other capabilities needed for scaling innovations. Federal or state/provincial regional innovation programs focused on green technologies contribute to triple-bottom-line economic development strategies aiming to create jobs, reduce disparities between regions, and increase sustainability value.

Technology road mapping and open innovation systems are another means of instigating green innovation (Schwerdtner et al., 2015). The regional open innovation road mapping framework is defined by Schwerdtner et al. (2015, p. 2304) as:

a strategic innovation planning process in which a roadmap for future innovation opportunities or a specific innovation is developed . . . the planning process described in advance of all phases of the entire innovation development chain, including R&D, prototype, implementation/mass production and market introduction in detail and usually in diagrammatic form.

The resulting regional development strategy includes a sustainability assessment to help select the innovations that will be developed and scaled in the region. This form of strategically planned approach is similar to a *transition arena* (Chapter 7), which could suffer from a lack of *legitimacy* or *transparency* due to power dynamics between actors. While the stakeholders involved viewed this framework positively, longer term research is needed to evaluate the effectiveness of innovation creation from road mapping in comparison to market-based or bottom-up approaches in other contexts.

Bottom–up movements and grassroots innovation for sustainability

Marsden and Farioli (2015) sketched out an alternative paradigm for sustainable development, which does not rely exclusively on technology and scientific progress as the driver of change. Rather, it is based on participatory, action-based, and other formats for integrating community stakeholders into the innovation process. This paradigm is centered on the agency and power of places rather than the reliance upon technological niches as the driver of triple-bottom-line economic development. Production and consumption patterns are constructed and guided by social and institutional forces in addition to market forces. Social and technological systems can co-evolve through bottom–up movements and grassroots innovation processes (Fressoli et al., 2014). Sustainability-oriented grassroots innovation processes can take many forms including using community currency for sustainable experiments (Seyfang and Longhurst, 2016), the ecovillage movement as a *niche-to-regime* function (Boyer, 2015), and social entrepreneurship for the creation of sustainability services (Gliedt and Parker, 2014; Muok and Kingiri, 2015).

Ecovillages combine niche practices with policy change at the regime level. Practices created in a niche can be adopted and turned into policies within the regime through a translation process, which occurs when niche actors and regime actors "internalize the values and design heuristics of the other" to a point where the lines between niche and regime begin to disappear (Boyer, 2015, p. 323). The ecovillage movement "has created a niche for alternative construction, social governance, and resource management practices that defy conventions of the urban development mainstream" (Boyer, 2015, p. 324). Ecovillages provide *niche protection* for sustainability experiments and act as an *intermediary* by combining elements of agency (e.g., individuals driven to make sustainability changes) and structures (e.g., guidelines, policies, best practices). Ecovillages as an actor within a socio-technical system can work with municipal governments to change laws, which allows for mainstreaming the use of sustainable building concepts for other residential developments in the town, city, or region. A grant from the United States Environmental Protection Agency helped diffuse ecovillage concepts into municipal zoning and housing development practices (Boyer, 2015). The grant, which was written by county planners, incorporated best practices from the ecovillage, created model building codes and policies based on the ecovillage principles, and instigated new demonstration projects to test these principles as experiments. To summarize, ecovillages can act as an actor and a structure for linking sustainability experiments to regime subsystem changes.

Jaeger-Erben et al. (2015) combined innovation and *social practices* to study social innovations that are able to drive sustainability transitions. Social actors are the "carriers of social practice, who are, on the one hand, pre-structured in their actions by prior social practices but, at the same time, are also able to change social practices" (Jaeger-Erben et al., 2015, p. 785). Jaeger-Erben et al. (2015) outlined different phases of practice innovation. The first phase occurs when current practices are no longer effective or desirable for solving problems. Change agents including *environmental champions* or other *sustainability professionals* can identify and frame this as a *window of opportunity* for new solutions to be created. The second phase identifies and selects alternative practices such as choosing to repair a product instead of replacing it, or purchasing more sustainable products. Experiments influence the selection of new practices through trial and error much like supply and demand selects winning companies and products in the market. The third phase aims to scale-up and expand the new practices by structuring them into the regime. When the new practices become institutionalized and less vulnerable to attack or disruption by existing regime actors, "they can persist without their former inventors or promoters" (Jaeger-Erben et al., 2015, p. 786). Sustainability professionals at the community and organizational levels can work to encourage and coordinate changes to social practices and technologies through community-based social marketing strategies (Chapter 2). Sustainability professionals at the government or governance levels can help instigate green technological innovation systems in practice through government research laboratories.

Practice of green innovation

National Renewable Energy Laboratory (Colorado)

The National Renewable Energy Laboratory (NREL) is one of 17 Department of Energy Laboratories focused on science and innovation in the United States. NREL in particular examines innovation in energy technology and infrastructure related to green energy supply and integrated energy systems. With nearly half a billion dollars in funding, NREL has the potential to accelerate a sustainability transition by conducting science and experiments in key areas including at the National Center for Photovoltaics and the National Wind Technology Center. The National Center for Photovoltaics focuses on a spectrum of areas that range from material creation, testing, design, and processing, to technology and market analysis, modelling and theory development, and manufacturing prototyping. Technology research areas include a focus on nanomaterials, thin-film, catalysts, fuel cells and batteries, organic PV, carbon nanotubes, and quantum dots as innovations to make green technologies more efficient or cost-effective (National Renewable Energy Laboratory, 2018). These innovative materials are becoming a reality because of the socio-technical systems approach taken by NREL in partnership with other government agencies and private actors to develop the technology, change the institutions and infrastructure to support the technology, and understand the market and user demand characteristics in order to accelerate mass production and diffusion.

NREL is also partnering with the Office of Energy Efficiency and Renewable Energy on a program to help cities make sustainable energy decisions. The Cities Leading through Energy Analysis and Planning program (Cities-LEAP) provides specific and local energy data to municipalities in order to influence green energy innovation and strategic planning related to sustainable infrastructure investments (Office of Energy Efficiency and Renewable Energy, 2017). Various tools that are related to the *sustainability competencies*

(Chapter 1) help cities develop climate or energy related goals, select energy strategies, model potential impacts of climate and energy interventions, learn from other cities best energy planning practices, access data, and inform city-level decision-making. For example, a database of city energy profiles allows sustainability professionals working for a municipal government to search for similar cities, compare GHG emissions and energy use by sector, analyze energy costs, and assess the capacity potential for solar PV on roofs. A local energy action toolbox provides sustainability professionals with a list of resources (e.g., case studies, guides, tools, databases) developed by NREL and the Department of Energy based on an analysis of 20 city-level sustainability and climate action plans in the United States. This database of resources can help cities make energy decisions that create sustainability value and change institutions and infrastructures in support of a sustainability transition. Acceleration Point: Sustainability professionals can help accelerate local government progress towards sustainability by generating and providing up-to-date data and decision-making tools by using their **normative**, **strategic**, and **anticipatory competences**.

Electrified charging lanes as a socio-technical innovation

A new technology called dynamic power charging is being created and tested in different countries simultaneously. This would allow lanes on roads and highways to act as wireless chargers for electric vehicles as they drive continuously without a need to stop. Electric charging lanes represent a socio-technical system innovation because infrastructure will have to be changed (e.g., new types of road construction connected to the energy grid), technology will require modifications (e.g., electric cars with new types of batteries that can be wirelessly charged while driving), institutional rules will need updating (e.g., insurance industry changes), and user behavior will have to adjust accordingly (e.g., consumers have to purchase a different type of car, consumers would not have to stop at gas stations anymore) (Oak Ridge National Laboratory, 2016). Electric charging lanes are being tested in China, the United Kingdom, and the United States and could someday become mainstream within *social practices* because they improve upon the current situation in two ways: enabling unlimited range and reducing charge time to zero. This means that the alternative technology can outperform the current technology. The challenge for electric charging lanes is that regime actors will work to slow these innovations because they fear the disruptive potential for the current regime including the demise of the internal combustion engine and supporting industries. Acceleration Point: Niche experiments are more likely to succeed and have bigger impacts on socio-technical systems if they improve upon the current technology and infrastructure and enhance the user experience.

Williams (2017) reviewed different types of electric charging lane technologies that are based on inductive charging using electromagnetic fields rather than direct current. The electricity grid is connected to a secondary sub-station next to the highway and then into a power transfer loop underneath the lane. This could work for cars, trucks, and buses. In fact, in South Korea, Utah, Germany, Italy, and the Netherlands, buses are already being charged wirelessly while parked on induction charging stations next to roads (Barry, 2013). The next step is to expand these systems so electric vehicles could charge while driving without having to stop.

Descriptions of the technology, diagrams of the proposed charging systems, and a full feasibility study are available at Highways England (2015). A further application is to combine charging lanes with integrated solar PV systems built into the road as a means of powering the highway, which is already being tested in Jinan City, China (Moneycontrol News, 2018). This can improve the sustainability of the system by substituting fossil fuel-powered grid electricity with on-site renewables. Acceleration Point: Sustainability professionals can use partnerships to coordinate technology entrepreneurs, government innovation research labs, public and private infrastructure development actors, and environmental non-profit organizations to help craft and deliver strategies and instruments to change behavior and practices related to this type of system.

Water system innovation in Oklahoma

The continued safe operation of water systems is threatened by the slow pace of institutional and infrastructure change, which characterizes not only rural but also urban regions. Funding pressures, especially budget cuts, have limited the ability of water managers to instigate incremental – let alone radical – changes that would improve the sustainability of water systems. The antiquated state of the water system infrastructure in the United States and Oklahoma (American Society of Civil Engineers, 2013) combined with a changing climate (Melillo et al., 2014) provides a window of opportunity for studying innovation in public water systems. Addressing the innovation deficit in water systems (Kiparsky et al., 2013) requires understanding how changes to institutions and infrastructures can be encouraged at multiple levels. A key question for sustainability professionals is how best to initiate and facilitate innovation processes, which lead to water system changes as part of transitions towards sustainability (Lieberherr and Truffer, 2015).

Oklahoma offers an intriguing case for examining water system innovation because of the creation of a statewide water policy, which was featured as a national example for water management and innovation at the White House Water Summit (OWRB, 2016). In 2012, the Oklahoma legislature passed House Bill 3055, more commonly referred to as the Water for 2060 Act. To accomplish the goals outlined in Water for 2060, Oklahoma's towns and cities must transition their water utilities to mitigate risks that threaten the availability of water resources for current and future generations. Significant changes are needed if Oklahoma is to meet its target of using no more fresh water in 2060 than it did in 2012. This equates to a 33 percent reduction in water use by 2060, something that will be even more challenging given that every region of Oklahoma is projected to see an increase in demand for water in the business-as-usual scenario (OWRB, 2012b). Water for 2060 is an important piece of legislation for two reasons.

First, it may help to coordinate water management plans and actions across the state. This is critical given the drastic geographic differences within Oklahoma with respect to income, population, quality of infrastructure, and precipitation patterns (Widener et al., 2017). For example, the variability of precipitation patterns is quite extreme, with the semi-arid panhandle and western regions of the state averaging only 43–68 centimeters of precipitation, while central and eastern Oklahoma receive 95–146 centimeters of precipitation annually. These disparities are further amplified by frequent droughts (OWRB, 2012a). In 2015, extreme rainfall events brought many of these previously drought stricken regions their annual precipitation totals in less than two months. Oklahoma went from a dry period that stressed its water and economic resources to a statewide flooding event that tested the resilience of crumbling water system infrastructure.

Second, Water for 2060 provides an enabling policy for innovation that can help guide the transition of municipal water infrastructure. The Act promotes municipal education programs and incentives to develop various water system innovations such as wastewater reuse and water conservation measures. Oklahoma's governor supported Water for 2060 by implementing a Drought Grant Program (OWRB, 2014b). By March 2015, public institutions had requested over US$18 million for water conservation projects (Allen, 2015). Of these, $1.5 million were awarded for water efficiency improvements in four rural communities in the panhandle and northwest regions of Oklahoma (Boise City, Fort Supply, Shattuck, and Butler), which were expected to collectively save over 22 million gallons of water annually (OWRB, 2015b). This is in addition to Oklahoma's Emergency Drought Commission and Relief Fund, which awarded $1.13 million to four municipal water utilities, three of which are in the southwest region of the state (Altus, Tipton, Hollis) and the fourth in the panhandle (Guymon) (OWRB, 2013). Oklahoma also has a Drinking Water State Revolving Fund, which provides loans to rural water districts for improving drinking water infrastructure (OWRB, 2015c). During the past 30 years, the Oklahoma Water Resources Board has approved more than $3 billion in loans and grants for water system upgrades in Oklahoma (OWRB, 2015c). Given the propensity of grant and loan programs, it is reasonable to expect that these financial mechanisms have been used to support water system innovation across the state, in spite of a recent finding that Oklahoma is one of the poorest performing states on water conservation (Hornberger et al., 2015).

Many water utilities undertook technological and institutional innovations including changes to water distribution systems, water treatment plants, water storage facilities, as well as incorporating smart meters and new water pricing systems (Hartman et al., 2017). Many water managers were motivated to do water system innovation by economic and social factors, but some also felt that environmental drivers were important (Widener et al., 2017). Two of the Gibson principles of sustainability (inter- and intra-generational equity) were particularly important to most water managers who were concerned for maintaining water supply for current water users as well as for their children's generation. Water utilities in drought stricken areas that experienced the largest annual decline in precipitation from the norm also created and implemented the most innovations per capita, suggesting that they were responding to actual climate changes when making water system changes (Gliedt et al., 2017). These utilities were efficient innovators because they had a high ratio of innovation (outputs) to dynamic capabilities (inputs). *Dynamic capabilities* allowed organizations to adjust strategies and processes and to develop innovations. Other water utilities in the south and eastern portion of the state where precipitation levels are consistently higher created fewer innovations relative to the level of dynamic capabilities identified. They were therefore categorized as having surplus *adaptive capacity*, which could be drawn upon in the future if water system changes are needed (Widener et al., 2017).

Utilities in Oklahoma that were experiencing water system stress from precipitation changes were able to successfully develop capabilities and innovations in part due to securing financial resources through grants from the state water agencies (Hartman et al., 2017). Few managers outside of the drought stricken western and panhandle regions had knowledge of the state-level enabling policy Water for 2060 (Hartman et al., 2017). This suggests that there is a need for sustainability professionals at the state level to increase their outreach and engagement mechanisms. This will help implement numerous innovations that water managers were planning for the future, including recycled water, stormwater reuse programs, greywater projects, and large-scale water transfers from other regions. Acceleration Point: Researchers can help sustainability professionals who are also water managers develop capacity for innovation by writing grant proposals for drought funding, partnering with other utilities to co-develop innovations including water transfer and storage systems, and supporting training and education of the managers especially in rural areas. While water utilities and other public organizations develop technology and service innovations, businesses focus on creating sustainable production innovations.

Sustainable product innovation

Varadarajan (2017, p. 17) defined *sustainable product innovation* as:

> a firm's introduction of a new product or modification of an existing product whose environmental impact during the lifecycle of the product, spanning resource extraction, production, distribution, use, and post-use disposal, is significantly lower than existing products for which it is a substitute.

What influences an organization to pursue sustainable product innovation? The conceptual model of sustainable innovations orientation in Figure 4.2 outlines a set of institutional, industry, and firm-level factors that may influence a business to focus on sustainable innovation. The *sustainable innovations orientation* is the sustainability-oriented research and development intensity, which is measured by the sustainability-related research and development expenditures divided by sales revenue per year (Varadarajan, 2017). Increases in the sustainable innovations orientation may enhance the sustainable process and product innovation performance, which in turn can directly influence environmental performance (e.g., reduction in CO_2 emissions) and marketing performance (e.g., customer loyalty), and indirectly influence financial performance (e.g., return-on-investment). This model outlines a multi-level perspective with cross-level interactions, including *regime-to-niche* (e.g., institutional pressures and industry factors influence organizations to undertake sustainability innovation) and *niche-to-regime* (e.g., research and development investments made by an organization leading to green technologies that can influence environmental performance changes in the industry and society).

Hallstedt et al. (2013) outlined a *strategic sustainability* model for organizational product innovation based on four elements: (1) organization, (2) processes, (3) roles, and (4) tools. These elements are related, for example, because the tools are used by people in the organization to carry out processes as part of their functional roles. The combination of processes, roles, and tools can be considered intra-organizational social practices. Additionally, processes are put in place by actors within the organization to guide the organizational strategy. Senior management can implement a *strategic sustainability* plan to guide the processes, roles, and tools for green innovation from the top-down. A strategic sustainability plan can include short- and long-term strategies to develop green technologies, as well as strategies to change processes to minimize lifecycle impacts from design to reuse. A strategic sustainability plan can include strategies and instruments to mobilize resources for increasing the sustainable innovation orientation of the business. Strategic sustainability can guide organizational leadership, champions, and intra-organizational

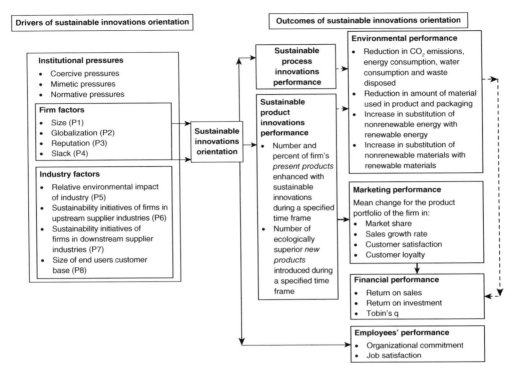

Figure 4.2 A conceptual model of sustainable innovations orientation
Source: Varadarajan (2017, p. 26).

social practices towards interventions at one or more processes of the product innovation and product lifecycle (Figure 4.3). The key is to incorporate recycling, remanufacturing, and reuse strategies to extend the product lifecycle to create sustainability value by reducing costs and environmental impacts and creating opportunities beyond the end use of a product. Sustainability professionals with expertise in lifecycle assessment can be critical to organizational strategic sustainability initiatives. Another way to encourage strategic sustainability processes for product innovation is to engage the purchasing department, as purchasing managers have connections with suppliers and can influence greener processes, or alternatively, switch suppliers to greener options in *value cycles* (Hallstedt et al., 2013).

Metz et al. (2016) identified best practices for increasing sustainability innovation in businesses. These practices include leadership helping to build a "sustainability mindset", mandating "high standards for sustainability performance", and consistently and purposefully scanning and researching for new "sustainability-based opportunities" (p. 50). One of the most important drivers of green innovation is the desire to attain a *competitive advantage* (Dangelico, 2015), but additional and related drivers include cost reduction, improved reputation, responding to current or anticipated regulations, higher productivity, and increasing exports to new markets. Factors that enable the successful development and diffusion of green product innovation include top management commitment, valuing environmental principles, having environmental champions, formalizing environmental

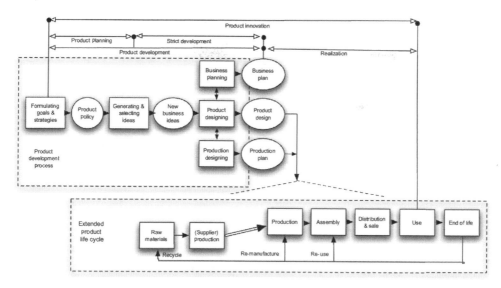

Figure 4.3 Strategic sustainability model for product innovation with extended product lifecycle
Source: Hallstedt et al. (2013, p. 280).

policies/targets, building networks and knowledge flows, increasing cross-functional integration, and developing resources and capabilities (Dangelico, 2015).

Sustainability-oriented innovation management requires aligning strategies, innovation processes, learning mechanisms, internal and external linkages, and innovation capabilities (Adams et al., 2016). Innovation capabilities include enabling structures, communications mechanisms, training and leadership development programs, as well as rewards and incentives. One way to align these factors for encouraging sustainability-oriented product innovation is total quality management including *ISO certification systems* (Cuerva et al., 2014). Policy makers can support green innovation by making it easier for businesses to participate in this type of certification program. Businesses proactively choose to participate in these programs because it can help reduce costs and increase reputation benefits. Dias Angelo et al. (2012) argued that the level of *proactive environmental management* in a company can influence the level of sustainability-oriented innovation. Sustainability professionals can help businesses design strategies to overcome the following barriers to green innovation (Dias Angelo et al., 2012, p. 119):

- inefficiencies in the internal communication process;
- lack of environmental training for companies' employees;
- managerial limitations to understanding the relevance of green issues;
- difficulties to build networks between partners and green teams;
- unskilled green team for research and development (R&D);
- poor economic perspective with low perception of green innovation gains;
- investments with long-term returns;
- difficulties in obtaining financial resources; and
- sluggish environmental regulatory system based on governmental inefficiencies.

Institutional innovation for biological diversity preservation:
The Yellowstone to Yukon Conservation Initiative

Habitat fragmentation is a major barrier to ecosystem functions and species survival. Cities, highways, and roads are expanding rapidly, creating barriers for species migration to find food and shelter, adapt to changing seasons, and adjust to a changing climate that is pushing plant and animal ranges further north. Infrastructure and urban development have created an island effect, where species are no longer able to adjust to these changes in their environment. To overcome this challenge, wildlife corridors including the Yellowstone to Yukon Conservation Initiative (Y2Y) have been created through institutional innovation that required collaboration between multiple states, provinces, and federal governments, as well as scientists and land-use planning (Y2Y Conservation Initiative, 2017). A network of protected lands (e.g., national, provincial, state parks) was created as a continental conservation corridor to facilitate biological diversity.

The Y2Y Initiative has fostered numerous partnerships between local conservation organizations to encourage better management practices, purchased hundreds of thousands of acers of private lands to protect wildlife pathways, established two new large national park reserves and a new wildlife management area, worked with the British Columbia government to ban oil and gas developments in a sensitive area of the Flathead River Valley, funded numerous education and engagement projects to help humans and animals coexist, and worked with planners to develop wildlife overpasses that have reduced wildlife-vehicle accidents by 80 percent (Y2Y Conservation Initiative, 2017). The Y2Y Initiative also influenced conservation policy instruments, for example, convincing Alberta to list the grizzly bear as threatened, and driving the creation of a new Alberta land-use plan that will guide wildlife friendly corridors. The Y2Y Initiative also provided millions of dollars in support for conservation researchers and scientists.

A partnership between the Y2Y Initiative and other conservation organizations facilitated the development of a technology innovation in the form of an app (Road Watch BC, 2017). The app allows citizens to use their smart phones to record wildlife sightings on highways in British Columbia. Alternatively, people can record wildlife sightings on a mapping tool available online and free to use by the public. Government researchers with the Canadian Ministry of Transportation and Infrastructure and the Ministry of Forest Land and Natural Resource Operations will use the database of information collected by the public to identify common wildlife crossings and inform strategies and interventions to facilitate safe wildlife movements over, under, or around infrastructure systems. This app represents a tool for incorporating citizens into science, and can act as a means of changing behavior through education and engagement. Social networks can help ingrain practices to encourage more participation and data collection. Sustainability professionals can develop programs using apps and interactive technologies to scale sustainable behavior to multi-level system changes. The information collected from a large number of individuals influences policy changes at the government level. As policies change, wildlife will adapt to new corridors. Ongoing feedback from citizen data collection allows for adjustments to policies and resulting strategies. A similar tool for incorporating citizens into science is called Rinkwatch, a website program that allows people to report ice conditions of their backyard or local hockey rink including uploading a photo of the rink (RinkWatch, 2017). Citizens then record each day they are able to skate on their rink. The researchers will take all of the data that is collected on an ongoing basis and use it to track climate changes in Canada. This can inform strategies and instruments that help adapt technologies (e.g., ice-making machines) and infrastructures (e.g., public rinks) to climate changes.

Measuring progress towards green innovation

The MLP framework focusing on socio-technical systems (Chapter 7) examines changes in technology development and adoption as related to changes in user practices and institutional structures (Markard et al., 2012). This includes behavior, regulatory, and cultural changes, as well as institutional and social innovations. The goal is to examine how the social and technological systems co-evolve (Markard et al., 2012). One way to measure sustainability changes that result from innovation is by comparing the gross expenditure on research and development (GERD) as a percentage of gross domestic product (GDP) versus CO_2 emissions per capita (Figure 4.4). GERD tells us something about the level of institutional support for innovation. Countries that are more innovative tend to have higher GERD, while countries with fast growing economies tend to increase GERD over time. As countries spend more on GERD, they also experience an increase in economic development and CO_2 emissions as evidenced by a weak association (R = 0.27) between GERD as a percentage of GDP and CO_2 emissions per capita. This trend may change over time, however, as the top eight countries for GERD as a percentage of GDP (South Korea, Israel, Japan, Finland, Sweden, Austria, Denmark, and Germany) average eight tonnes of CO_2 per capita, and only South Korea exceeds 10 tonnes. Many of these countries are using their high GERD to make significant changes to socio-technical systems in the direction of sustainability, including Finland, Sweden, Denmark, and Germany.

China's economy and CO_2 emissions per capita has grown rapidly at the same time as it has increased its GERD as a percentage of GDP by 179 percent between 1991 and 2014 (OECD, 2017). Although still ranking in the top ten, the United States only increased its GERD as a percentage of GDP during the same time period by 5 percent. As countries go through an economic transition from manufacturing to the service sector, CO_2 emissions begin to decrease after a certain level of income per capita is achieved (Chapter 5).

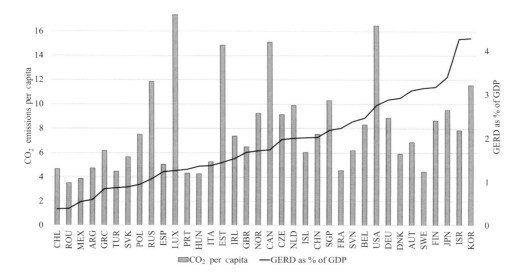

Figure 4.4 Gross expenditure on research and development (GERD) as a percent of GDP versus CO_2 emissions per capita, 2014

Source: GERD from OECD (2017); CO_2 emissions per capita from World Bank (2017). Note: abbreviations are from OECD (2017).

One reason for this may be that GERD continues to increase and new technologies and infrastructures are made possible by higher levels of spending on research and development as a percentage of GDP. Acceleration Point: Sustainability professionals should encourage and support strategies and instruments that focus on increasing GERD. In particular, investments in green GERD can be made through national research and innovation laboratories, regional innovation strategies, and public-private partnerships focused on integrated technology-infrastructure system changes like renewable energy generation, storage, and transmission systems.

Ecocities in Sweden and China

What types of technology and infrastructure innovations would be required to build an ecocity? How are multiple innovation processes coordinated at the city level? Yin et al. (2016) used a comparative case study approach to assess the process of developing ecocities in Sweden and China. They examined three institutional conditions that impact sustainability performance of cities: (1) level of political support, (2) knowledge and experience, and (3) organizational coordination. The four cases were Hammarby Sjostad, Stockholm and the Stockholm Royal Seaport in Sweden; and the Sino-Swedish Low-Carbon Eco-City in Wuxi and the Tangshan Bay Eco-City in Tangshan, both in China. The findings indicated the importance of clear and local political support and the role of individual politicians in Chinese sustainability planning. The critical role of practices and participation was evident in overcoming a lack of government knowledge and experience. Another key finding was the need for developing cross-sector organizations to reduce conflicts between sectors and foster collaborative and integrative decision-making. Sweden created organizations to act as *intermediaries* (Chapter 6) focusing on sustainability integration. China used regular organizations but added new units within them to manage cross-sector sustainability issues as a *boundary spanner* function (Chapter 6). The implication is that cross-level organizations are important to developing technology and infrastructure innovations in cities within different national contexts.

Check on learning

- Read Hayter (2008) and in two pages describe how a green techno-economic paradigm would differ from the current information and communications technology paradigm. What types of innovation principles would be required for a green techno-economic paradigm and how would they differ from the innovation principles of the previous techno-economic paradigms outlined by Perez (2010)? Would the technological innovation system functions described in this chapter need to be modified for a green techno-economic paradigm? Why or why not?
- Read Jaeger-Erben et al. (2015) and make a table to summarize the differences between the five types of social innovations. Which type of social innovation do you believe will have the biggest impact on changing the subsystems of the socio-technical regime? How do you see the relationship between social innovation and sustainability innovation?

- Read the full list of events and technological innovation system functions in Table A1 in Kebede and Mitsufuji (2017). As a sustainability professional, how would you create similar events to carry out the functions of green innovation systems in your country or region?
- Do some research and find a recent academic journal article that uses the technological innovation systems theory in relation to sustainability transitions. How are the functions of technological innovation systems oriented to incorporate sustainability principles? What types of technologies are described in the article, and how are those technologies related to supporting infrastructure or institutional changes?
- How can sustainability professionals help incorporate sustainability principles into value chains? What is the role of value cycles in connecting industry-level innovation systems with the product-level innovation processes within businesses?
- Read the feasibility study for wireless charging roads by Highways England (2015). Examine the diagrams that outline how the system would work. Thinking about your town or city, what actors would you as a sustainability professional need to engage with if you wanted to instigate this type of socio-technical systems innovation? What barriers would need to be overcome?
- Read Yin et al. (2016) and outline a set of best practices for developing an ecocity. How would you incorporate the Gibson sustainability principles into the process of creating an ecocity? How would you encourage the creation of green innovations and infrastructures?

Assignments

- Using a community energy management and financing model to create a city energy innovation plan

References

Adams, R., Jeanrenaud, S., Bessant, J., Denyer, D., & Overy, P. (2016). Sustainability-oriented innovation: A systematic review. *International Journal of Management Reviews*, 18, 180–205.

Allen, S. (2015). Western Oklahoma cities look to conserve water amid drought. Available at: http://newsok.com/western-oklahoma-cities-look-to-conserve-water-amid-drought/article/5399400

American Society of Civil Engineers. (2013). Infrastructure report card. 2013 report card for Oklahoma's infrastructure. Available at: www.infrastructurereportcard.org/oklahoma/oklahoma-overview/

Austin Technology Incubator. (2017). About the Austin Technology Incubator. University of Texas at Austin and the IC² Institute. Available at: http://ati.utexas.edu/about-us/

Barrie, K. (2013). In South Korea, wireless charging powers electric buses. *Wired*. Available at: www.wired.com/2013/08/induction-charged-buses/

Bathelt, H., & Glückler, J. (2003). Toward a relational economic geography. *Journal of Economic Geography*, 3(2), 117–144.

Bathelt, H., & Glückler, J. (2011). *The Relational Economy: Geographies of Knowing and Learning*. Oxford University Press, Oxford, UK.

Boyer, R. H. (2015). Grassroots innovation for urban sustainability: Comparing the diffusion pathways of three ecovillage projects. *Environment and Planning A*, 45, 320–337.

Bridge, G. (2008). Environmental economic geography: A sympathetic critique. *Geoforum*, 39(1), 76–81.

Catini, R., Karamshuk, D., Penner, O., & Riccaboni, M. (2015). Identifying geographic clusters: A network analytic approach. *Research Policy*, 44(9), 1749–1762.

Chapple, K., Kroll, C., Lester, T. W., & Montero, S. (2011). Innovation in the green economy: An extension of the regional innovation system model? *Economic Development Quarterly*, 25(1), 5–25.

Cuerva, M. C., Triguero-Cano, Á., & Córcoles, D. (2014). Drivers of green and non-green innovation: Empirical evidence in Low-Tech SMEs. *Journal of Cleaner Production*, 68, 104–113.

Dangelico, R. M. (2015). Green product innovation: Where we are and where we are going. *Business Strategy and the Environment*, 25(8), 560–576.

Dias Angelo, F., Jose Chiappetta Jabbour, C., & Vasconcellos Galina, S. (2012). Environmental innovation: In search of a meaning. *World Journal of Entrepreneurship, Management and Sustainable Development*, 8(2/3), 113–121.

ECRGE. (2011). Ethiopia's climate resilient green economy strategy. *Federal Democratic Republic of Ethiopia*. Available at: www.uncsd2012.org/content/documents/287CRGE%20Ethiopia%20Green%20Economy_Brochure.pdf

EDA. (2017). Regional Innovation Strategies Program. Office of Innovation and Entrepreneurship. U.S. *Economic Development Association*. Available at: https://eda.gov/oie/ris/

Engel, J. S. (2015). Global clusters of innovation: Lessons from Silicon Valley. *California Management Review*, 57(2), 36–65.

Energy.gov. (2011). Obama administration announced launch of i6 Green Challenge to promote clean energy innovation and economic growth. Available at: www.energy.gov/articles/obama-adminstration-announces-launch-i6-green-challenge-promote-clean-energy-innovation-and

Fressoli, M., Arond, E., Abrol, D., Smith, A., Ely, A., & Dias, R. (2014). When grassroots innovation movements encounter mainstream institutions: Implications for models of inclusive innovation. *Innovation and Development*, 4(2), 277–292.

Gibbs, D. (2006). Prospects for an environmental economic geography: Linking ecological modernization and regulationist approaches. *Economic Geography*, 82(2), 193–215.

Gilbert, B. A. (2012). Creative destruction: Identifying its geographic origins. *Research Policy*, 41(4), 734–742.

Gliedt, T., & Parker, P. (2014). Green community entrepreneurship 2.0: Collective response or individual adaptation strategy to funding cuts in Canada (2006–2012). *International Journal of Social Economics*, 41(7), 609–625.

Gliedt, T., Widener, J., & Hartman, P. (2017). Water system innovation in Oklahoma: Climate change adaptation strategy? *Southern Climate Monitor*, 7(4), 2–4.

Hallstedt, S. I., Thompson, A. W., & Lindahl, P. (2013). Key elements for implementing a strategic sustainability perspective in the product innovation process. *Journal of Cleaner Production*, 51, 277–288.

Hart, S. L., & Dowell, G. (2011). A natural-resource-based view of the firm: Fifteen years after. *Journal of Management*, 37(5), 1464–1479.

Hartman, P., Gliedt, T., Widener, J., & Loraamm, R. (2017). Dynamic capabilities for water system transitions in Oklahoma. *Environmental Innovation and Societal Transitions*, 25, 64–81.

Hayter, C. S., & Link, A. N. (2015a). On the economic impact of university proof of concept centers. *The Journal of Technology Transfer*, 40(1), 178–183.

Hayter, C. S., & Link, A. N. (2015b). University proof of concept centers. *Issues in Science and Technology*, 31(2), 32.

Hayter, R. (2008). Environmental economic geography. *Geography Compass*, 2(3), 831–850.

Highways England. (2015). Feasibility study: Powering electric vehicles on England's major roads. Available at: http://assets.highways.gov.uk/specialist-information/knowledge-compendium/2014-2015/Feasibility+study+Powering+electric+vehicles+on+Englands+major+roads.pdf

Hockerts, K., & Wüstenhagen, R. (2010). Greening Goliaths versus emerging Davids: Theorizing about the role of incumbents and new entrants in sustainable entrepreneurship. *Journal of Business Venturing*, 25(5), 481–492.

Hornberger, G. M., Hess, D. J., & Gilligan, J. (2015). Water conservation and hydrological transitions in cities in the United States. *Water Resources Research*, 51(6), 4635–4649.

Jaeger-Erben, M., Rückert-John, J., & Schäfer, M. (2015). Sustainable consumption through social innovation: a typology of innovations for sustainable consumption practices. *Journal of Cleaner Production*, 108(A), 784–798.

Kennedy, S., Whiteman, G., & van den Ende, J. (2016). Radical innovation for sustainability: The power of strategy and open innovation. *Long Range Planning*, 50 (6), 712–725.

Kebede, K. Y., & Mitsufuji, T. (2017). Technological innovation system building for diffusion of renewable energy technology: A case of solar PV systems in Ethiopia. *Technological Forecasting and Social Change*, 114, 242–253.

Kiparsky, M., Sedlak, D. L., Thompson Jr, B. H., & Truffer, B. (2013). The innovation deficit in urban water: The need for an integrated perspective on institutions, organizations, and technology. *Environmental Engineering Science*, 30(8), 395–408.

Lieberherr, E., & Truffer, B. (2015). The impact of privatization on sustainability transitions: A comparative analysis of dynamic capabilities in three water utilities. *Environmental Innovation and Societal Transitions*, 15, 101–122.

Markard, J., & Truffer, B. (2008). Technological innovation systems and the multi-level perspective: Towards an integrated framework. *Research Policy*, 37(4), 596–615.

Markard, J., Raven, R., & Truffer, B. (2012). Sustainability transitions: An emerging field of research and its prospects. *Research Policy*, 41(6), 955–967.

Marra, A., Antonelli, P., Dell'Anna, L., & Pozzi, C. (2015). A network analysis using metadata to investigate innovation in clean-tech–Implications for energy policy. *Energy Policy*, 86, 17–26.

Marsden, T., & Farioli, F. (2015). Natural powers: From the bio-economy to the eco-economy and sustainable place-making. *Sustainability Science*, 10(2), 331–344.

McLennan, C. J., Becken, S., & Watt, M. (2016). Learning through a cluster approach: Lessons from the implementation of six Australian tourism business sustainability programs. *Journal of Cleaner Production*, 111, 348–357.

Melillo, J. M., T.C. Richmond, & G. W. Yohe (Eds) (2014). *Climate Change Impacts in the United States: The Third National Climate Assessment*. U.S. Global Change Research Program, doi:10.7930/J0Z31WJ2.

Metz, P., Burek, S., Hultgren, T. R., Kogan, S., & Schwartz, L. (2016). The path to sustainability-driven innovation: Environmental sustainability can be the foundation for increasing competitive advantage and the basis for effective innovation. *Research-Technology Management*, 59(3), 50–61.

Moneycontrol News. (2018). China tests its first solar-powered highway that can charge electric cars. Moneycontrol.com. Available at: www.moneycontrol.com/news/technology/china-tests-its-first-solar-powered-highway-that-can-charge-electric-cars-2472605.html

Muok, B. O., & Kingiri, A. (2015). The role of civil society organizations in low-carbon innovation in Kenya. *Innovation and Development*, 5(2), 207–223.

Muro, M., Rothwell, J., & Saha, D. (2011). Sizing the clean economy: A national and regional jobs assessment. The Brookings Institution. Metropolitan Policy Program. *Battelle Technology Partnership Practice*. Available at: www.brookings.edu/wp-content/uploads/2016/06/0713_clean_economy.pdf

National Renewable Energy Laboratory. (2018). Researching energy systems and technologies. *United States Department of Energy*. Available at: www.nrel.gov/research/index.html

Oak Ridge National Laboratory. (2016). ORNL surges ahead with 20-kilowatt wireless charging for vehicles. *United States Department of Energy*. Available at: www.ornl.gov/news/ornl-surges-forward-20-kilowatt-wireless-charging-vehicles

OECD. (2017). Gross domestic spending on R&D. Available at: data.oecd.org/rd/gross-domestic-spending-on-r-d.htm

Office of Energy Efficiency and Renewable Energy. (2017). Cities leading through energy analysis and planning. Available at: https://energy.gov/eere/cities-leading-through-energy-analysis-and-planning

OWRB. (2012a). *Hydrologic drought of water year 2011: A historical context*. *Oklahoma Water Resources Board*. Available at: www.owrb.ok.gov/supply/drought/pdf_dro/DroughtFactSheet2011.pdf

OWRB. (2012b). Oklahoma comprehensive water plan: Central watershed planning region report. Available at: www.owrb.ok.gov/supply/ocwp/pdf_ocwp/WaterPlanUpdate/regionalreports/OCWP_Central_Region_Report.pdf

OWRB. (2013). Oklahoma Emergency Drought Commission and Relief Fund. *Oklahoma Water Resources Board.*

OWRB. (2014a). Water Resources Bulletin. *Oklahoma Water Resources Board.*

OWRB. (2014b). Water for 2060 drought grants: Financial assistance and project eligibility. Oklahoma Water Resources Board. Available at: www.owrb.ok.gov/financing/grant/droughtgrants.php.

OWRB. (2015a). Final Report of the Water for 2060 Advisory Council. *Oklahoma Water Resources Board.*

OWRB. (2015b). Water News: Tulsa Metropolitan Utility Authority receives $21,000,000 OWRB Loan Approval for Several Wastewater System Improvements. *Oklahoma Water Resources Board.*

OWRB. (2015c). Water News: Water for 2060 Grants Awarded. *Oklahoma Water Resources Board.*

OWRB. (2016). Oklahoma's Water for 2060 Initiative Featured at White House Water Summit. *Oklahoma Water Resources Board.*

Patchell, J., & Hayter, R. (2013). Environmental and evolutionary economic geography: A time for EEG? *Geografisca Annaler: Series B, Human Geography*, 95, 1–20.

Perez, C. (2010). Technological revolutions and techno-economic paradigms. *Cambridge Journal of Economics*, 34(1), 185–202.

RinkWatch. (2017). Welcome to RinkWatch, where skating meets environmental science! Available at: www.rinkwatch.org/

Road Watch BC. (2017). Road Watch BC App and database system. Available at: www.roadwatchbc.ca/about.php

Schwerdtner, W., Siebert, R., Busse, M., & Freisinger, U. B. (2015). Regional open innovation roadmapping: A new framework for innovation-based regional development. *Sustainability*, 7(3), 2301–2321.

Seyfang, G., & Longhurst, N. (2016). What influences the diffusion of grassroots innovations for sustainability? Investigating community currency niches. *Technology Analysis & Strategic Management*, 28(1), 1–23.

Simane, B., & Zaitchik, B. F. (2014). The sustainability of community-based adaptation projects in the Blue Nile Highlands of Ethiopia. *Sustainability*, 6(7), 4308–4325.

Simane, B., Zaitchik, B. F., & Mesfin, D. (2012). Building climate resilience in the Blue Nile/Abay Highlands: A framework for action. *International Journal of Environmental Research and Public Health*, 9(2), 610–631.

Simane, B., Zaitchik, B. F., & Foltz, J. D. (2014). Agroecosystem specific climate vulnerability analysis: application of the livelihood vulnerability index to a tropical highland region. *Mitigation and Adaptation Strategies for Global Change*, 21(1), 39–65.

Truffer, B., Murphy, J. T., & Raven, R. (2015). The geography of sustainability transitions contours of an emerging theme. *Environmental Innovation and Societal Transitions*, 17, 63–72.

Varadarajan, R. (2017). Innovating for sustainability: A framework for sustainable innovations and a model of sustainable innovations orientation. *Journal of the Academy of Marketing Science*, 45(1), 14–36.

Walsh, P. R. (2012). Innovation nirvana or innovation wasteland? Identifying commercialization strategies for small and medium renewable energy enterprises. *Technovation*, 32(1), 32–42.

Widener, J., Gliedt. T., & Hartman, P. (2017). Visualizing dynamic capabilities as adaptive capacity for municipal water governance. *Sustainability Science*, 12(2), 203–219.

Williams, J. (2017). Transport innovation of the week: Electric charging lanes. *Make Wealth History*. Available at: https://makewealthhistory.org/2017/01/23/transport-innovation-of-the-week-electric-charging-lanes/

World Bank. (2017). DataBank World Development Indicators. Available at: http://databank.worldbank.org/data/reports.aspx?source=world-development-indicators&preview=on#

Y2Y Conservation Initiative. (2017). Yellowstone to Yukon Conservation Initiative. Available at: http://y2y.net/

Yin, Y., Olsson, A. R., & Håkansson, M. (2016). The role of local governance and environmental policy integration in Swedish and Chinese eco-city development. *Journal of Cleaner Production*, 134, 78–86.

5 Triple-bottom-line economic development

Learning objectives

- Review and critique theories of the green economy
- Understand business creation, expansion, attraction, and entrepreneurship strategies in the context of sustainability
- Assess societal benefits from green job creation including multiplier effects and government revenues
- Examine case studies of successful triple-bottom-line economic development strategies and instruments

Theories of triple-bottom-line economic development

The green economy can be defined as institutions including markets that aim to foster economic development by decoupling economic benefits from environmental and social costs. Much of the debate about what is considered sustainable economic development relates to questions about quantitative (growth) versus qualitative (development) improvement, the invisible hand (*neoclassical economics*) versus the laws of thermodynamics (*ecological economics*), and strong versus weak sustainability pathways (Chapter 1). Economic growth as measured by the gross domestic product (GDP) or per capita income "refers to a change in the size of the economy" while economic development as commonly measured by the *Human Development Index* (HDI) "refers either to a change in the structure of the economy facilitative of economic growth or a qualitative improvement in societal conditions stemming from economic activity" (Hammer and Pivo, 2017, p. 2). Broadly defined, economic development aims to reduce disparities between regions, socio–economic groups, or urban–rural divides through the process of wealth and opportunity creation. Economic developers may work for governments (e.g., municipalities), non-profits (e.g., First Nations community development council), or business associations (e.g., Chamber of Commerce).

Bailey and Caprotti (2014, p. 1800) described four functional domains of the green economy:

1 Financial: green economy as global financial opportunity focused on opportunity and risk management

- e.g., clean technology sectors like solar, wind, electric vehicles, building automation

2 Institutional: green economy driven by transitional policies focused on regional regeneration and competition

- e.g., green service sectors like car sharing and microgrids

3 Regulatory: green economy guided by standards and rules focused on harnessing innovation via green patents

- e.g., international trade rules and protections for green intellectual property protection
- e.g., environmental labeling and certification programs
- e.g., public and private sector partnerships

4 Green cultural economy: new geographies of production and consumption driven by radical, transitional, and oppositional movements

- e.g., circular economy and efficiency improvements in production processes
- e.g., green economy branding like fair trade and organic products
- e.g., radical reductions in demand like tiny house movements and ecovillages

Taken together, these functional domains overlap sectors, integrate practices, and interact through networks to form a green economy composed of actors who critically examine local and global production and consumption to better satisfy the needs and wants of green consumers. There are many traditional and emerging sectors in the green economy ranging from industrial production to lifestyle and consumption changes, which are composed of actors from government (e.g., federal, state/provincial, municipal, as well as public universities), the social economy (e.g., non-profits), and businesses (e.g., manufacturing, service sector, utilities, unions, and trade associations) (Figure 5.1). Key sectors include clean technology research, development and manufacturing, sustainable agriculture systems, food processing and organic gardening, green financial services, investment and commercialization, sustainable energy, transportation and buildings, as well as green retail, repair and cleaning services.

Sustainability-related sectors represent growth areas for green job creation (Hess, 2012). In particular, energy efficiency services and renewable energy manufacturing and installation offer tremendous potential as green jobs that are projected to offset job losses in fossil fuel sectors (Wei et al., 2010). Elliott and Lindley (2017) used data from the United States Bureau of Labor Statistic's Green Goods and Services survey from 2010 and 2011 to analyze how green services and manufacturing affected the economy. They found that states that had a lot of green jobs in 2010 increased those employment concentrations in 2011. They also discovered that the green goods manufacturing sectors that increased the number of green jobs experienced a decrease in productivity, although no decrease in productivity was found for green service sectors. One explanation for the decrease in productivity is that the higher green job creators reduced expenditures on technology during the 2010–11 period. Interestingly, the same sectors that increased green jobs hired additional medium-educated workers (e.g., some college), while reducing the number of lower skilled workers that were hired (e.g., high school drop outs). This suggests that sustainability professionals wishing to get a green job may need higher levels of education, skills, and training to be competitive. It also signals a potential social and political bottleneck (Chapter 9) to building support for a sustainability transition because individuals who do not have higher levels of education may face barriers to attaining these new types

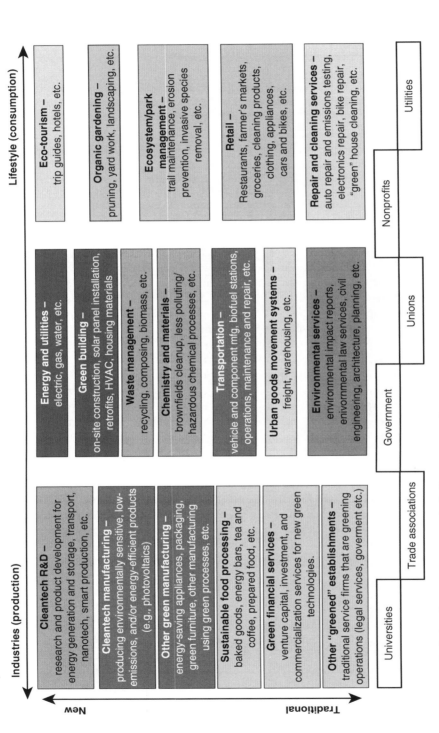

Figure 5.1 Defining the green economy including sectors and actors

Source: Chapple et al. (2011, p. 8).

of jobs, which they may not have faced in the past when attempting to attain employment in the fossil fuel industry. Sustainability professionals should address this bottleneck when working as economic developers to incorporate triple-bottom-line criteria into strategies and instruments designed to create jobs and sustainable value.

Triple-bottom-line economic development

Hammer and Pivo (2017) defined *triple-bottom-line economic development* as "programs, policies, or activities designed to create or retain jobs and wealth in ways that contribute to environmental, social, and economic well-being over time" (p. 3). The key difference from economic development is the imperative that "economic systems exist to serve human well-being, that human and economic well-being are inextricably linked to environmental well-being, and thus, that human, environmental, and economic well-being must be considered in the design and evaluation of economic development efforts" (p. 3). This definition follows a *strong sustainability* pathway (Figure 1.10) consistent with ecological economics, which prioritizes ecological scale and social justness over economic efficiency because the latter depends on the former. The challenge for triple-bottom-line economic development is to ensure that natural capital stocks are not depleted as a tradeoff for increasing the social and economic components, which would represent a weak sustainability pathway. Neoclassical economists and some industry leaders may prefer a weak sustainability pathway because it allows for maximizing profits in the short-term while excluding long-term impacts on the environment. Sustainability professionals must incessantly seek solutions that improve the economic bottom line in order to build broad political support.

Successful triple-bottom-line strategies included integrated and inclusive planning and partnerships, continuous learning processes, business incubators, infrastructure upgrades, having a clear vision and a long-term plan, a flexible and adaptable strategy to respond to new opportunities or threats, and the ability to link innovation with existing programs (Hammer and Pivo, 2017). Triple-bottom-line professionals emphasized the need for staff with *sustainability competencies* (e.g., **systems thinking**) including **interpersonal relations competencies** (e.g., network development, stakeholder engagement) (Hammer and Pivo, 2017). Sustainability professionals can help encourage economic development training, education, and accreditation programs to incorporate triple-bottom-line concepts (Hammer and Pivo, 2017) by influencing regime actors including politicians to change the criteria for project evaluation and rewards to reflect sustainability principles. Acceleration Point: Changing the criteria for evaluation and rewards can speed-up or scale-up sustainability transitions by incentivizing triple-bottom-line economic development and related technology and infrastructure investment strategies.

Ecological modernization theory

Ecological modernization theory (Bakari, 2014) is based on the assumption that economic development as measured by increasing GDP per capita will eventually solve sustainability problems. The logical result of this theory would be the Environmental Kuznets curve (Panayotou, 1997), which suggests that at some point society will reach a level of GDP per capita when it will either demand regulatory action from government or be able to afford to develop and purchase new technologies that will reduce pollution levels. Ecological modernization theory is focused on technology and scientific innovation as the drivers of both economic development and sustainability performance improvements. This implies an inherent focus on eco-efficiency and technology without providing an understanding of how socio-political processes could be changed aside from indirect pressure from environmental movements and non-profit organizations as part of a weak sustainability pathway. How can societies change in the direction of sustainability, and is it simply due to an increase in wealth?

According to Buttel (2000), ecological modernization theory considers that institutional changes (e.g., political practices) lead to economic changes, which influence organizations to make different technology choices. Buttel (2000, p. 59) summarized three phases of ecological modernization theory:

1   **Capitalist liberal democracy** has the institutional capacity to reform its impact on the natural environment . . . one can predict that the further development (modernization) of capitalist liberal democracy would tend to result in improvement in ecological outcomes;
2   **Sociopolitical processes** through which the further modernization of capitalist liberal democracies leads to (or blocks) beneficial ecological outcomes;
3   **Comparative perspectives** including but not limited to the ways in which globalization processes might catalyze ecological modernization processes in countries in the South.

The relationship between increasing levels of income per capita and increasing and then eventually declining levels of environmental impacts (known as the Environmental Kuznets Curve – EKC) has held for many pollutants including lead and sulphur dioxide (SO2) (Stern, 2004). Arrow et al. (1995, p. 520) advised that while

> economic growth may be associated with improvements in some environmental indicators, [these EKC theories] imply neither that economic growth is sufficient to induce environmental improvement in general, nor that the environmental effects of growth may be ignored, nor, indeed, that the Earth's resource base is capable of supporting indefinite economic growth.

They outlined four specific critiques:

1   The EKC has been shown for selected pollutants involving short-term costs (e.g., SO2), but not for long-term accumulating pollutants that are more dispersed (e.g., CO_2).
2   The EKC has been shown for emissions of pollutants but not for changes to resource stocks.
3   The EKC speaks to specific reductions in a single pollutant, but does not explain system-wide consequences (e.g., reducing a pollutant in one country but increasing pollutants in other countries, or switching from one fuel type and thus one pollutant to another).
4   The cause of the decline in the EKC curve may not be economic growth levels (e.g., GDP per capita), but rather, environmental regulations and incentives that are instigated in a particular jurisdiction to reduce short-term and direct environmental impacts. Longer term impacts (e.g., inter-generational equity) are often not incorporated into environmental legislation and therefore CO_2 levels continue to increase.

Recent evidence suggests that the United States has now decoupled economic development from CO_2 emissions (Obama, 2017). Figure 5.2 shows that CO_2 emissions were rising with increases to GDP per capita until approximately 2007, when they began to decline through the 2008–09 recession and then fluctuated until 2014. A polynomial relationship ($R^2 = 0.7616$) suggests that the EKC hypothesis may hold for CO_2 for the U.S.. Recent studies suggest that individual U.S. states may have also experienced the EKC for CO_2 (Apergis et al, 2017; Atasoy, 2017). Ontario, Canada has likely displayed the EKC due to policies that closed all coal power plants, which occurred concurrently to increasing levels of GDP per capita (Chapter 9).

Critiques of ecological modernization theory include that it can be used as a way to continue growing while gaining public support or credit for the perception that sustainability actions are being taken; justifying a focus on incremental changes while avoiding making the investments necessary to foster radical system changes (Bakari, 2014). A related critique is that ecological modernization theory does not incorporate sociological theories to advance our understanding of economic, social, and environmental interactions (Buttel, 2000). Hammer and Pivo (2017) cautioned that "correlation does not equal causation . . . some gains in well-being may be attributable to technological advances and policy agendas rather than economic growth" (p. 2). Arrow et al. (1995) similarly argued that institutions are critical to reducing environmental degradation while continuing to develop economically. Institutions must be designed to encourage and enable more efficient uses of resources and more creative solutions to pollution. York and Rosa (2003) concluded that ecological modernization theory needs to focus on mechanisms for ensuring sustainability performance outcomes are achieved rather than simply making changes to policy instruments or institutions.

The extent that a socio-technical system undergoes radical rather than incremental changes to technologies, institutions, and infrastructures may influence the point at which the EKC slows its upward trend and starts to decline. Two potential EKC curves are shown in Figure 5.3. The first slows its upward climb and begins to decline earlier as a result of radical changes to technologies, institutions, and infrastructures. This curve allows society to remain at or near a strong sustainability threshold that is consistent with

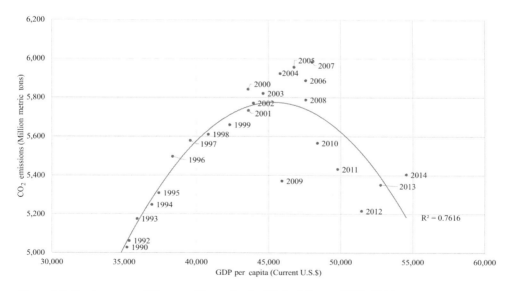

Figure 5.2 Environmental Kuznets Curve for the United States, 1990–2014

Source: CO_2 Emissions from EIA (2017b); GDP per capita data from the World Bank (2017). Calculations by the authors.

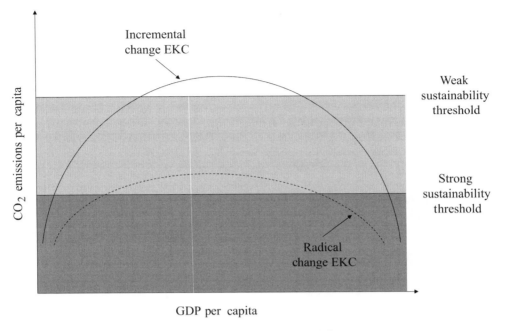

Figure 5.3 Environmental Kuznets Curve and strong sustainability
Source: Authors' rendition.

the Gibson principles of sustainability and the strong sustainability pathway (Chapter 1), which can be measured by ecological footprint analyses or the carbon intensity of human well-being (Chapter 9). The second curve continues to climb beyond a strong sustainability threshold and may even exceed a weak sustainability threshold, suggesting that environmental impacts may be sever or irreversible and that natural capital and ecosystem services may be destroyed as a tradeoff for increasing human capital and human made capital. In this latter case, rising incomes support the use of strategies and instruments that lead to incremental changes to technology, institutions, and infrastructure. These changes may eventually force the downward trend of the EKC to fall back within a sustainable threshold, but there is no guarantee that this will happened in time to avoid changes to biodiversity or global climate cycles that cannot easily be undone.

Economic development and sustainable energy development co-evolving

The success or failure of sustainability transitions relates directly to energy system transitions because of the carbon content of electricity and transportation systems. Linking energy development with economic development can lead to sustainability benefits. Energy-based economic development is defined by Carley et al. (2011, p. 287) as:

> a process by which economic developers; energy policymakers and planners; government officials; industry, utility, and business leaders; and other stakeholders in a given region strive to increase energy efficiency or diversify energy resources in ways that contribute to job creation, job retention, and regional wealth creation.

Energy-based economic development focuses on technologies that are innovative, efficient, or cleaner than conventional options (Carley et al., 2011). It occurs largely at the state and local levels, where experimentation in economic development policy and in energy policy is converging based on public–private partnerships, state and local policy instruments, and strategies to develop local energy resources (Carley et al., 2011). The goals of energy-based economic development include wealth and job creation, self-sufficiency, and diversification (Carley et al., 2011).

Carley et al. (2011) described how different energy strategies and instruments intersect with economic development strategies and instruments (Figure 5.4). For example, *business attraction* and *business retention* strategies relate to energy policies like *renewable portfolio standards* and *feed-in tariffs* that encourage businesses to meet the demands for new energy supply. *Entrepreneurship* is associated with the creation of technologies that co-evolve with social practices into distributed energy systems, including solar PV and blockchain systems that allow distributed energy markets to emerge (Green and Newman, 2017; Sikorski et al., 2017). Industry *cluster* development relates to energy research and development that occurs in conjunction with university research parks, municipal incubators, or accelerator centers (Chapter 6). Quality of life enhancements can be achieved by weathering and efficiency programs or energy technology and infrastructure upgrades.

Carley et al. (2012) outlined a process for energy-based economic development, which starts with engaging a wide range of stakeholders who can help identify goals and objectives (e.g., create jobs, create wealth, diversify the economy, reduce GHG emissions,

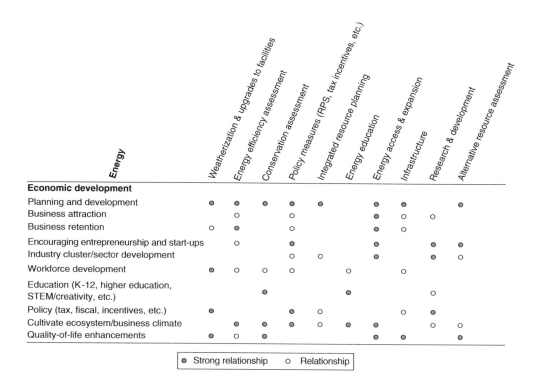

Figure 5.4 Intersection of energy and economic development strategies and instruments

Source: Carley et al. (2011, p. 287).

diversify energy sources, increase energy self-sufficiency). Next, an analysis is conducted to identify assets and gaps in local industries/sectors (e.g., location quotients, firm creation and growth rates), workforce (e.g., education performance metrics, industry needs), energy system (e.g., natural resource potential, utility capacity), and innovation (e.g., research and development activity, university–industry partnerships, firm creation, patent filings). Based on this analysis, energy-based economic developers choose and implement a variety of strategies and instruments (e.g., business incentives, green energy standards, green energy cluster and value chain initiatives, green energy research and development, incubator and accelerator centers). The strategies and instruments are then monitored and evaluated over time against a set of economic (e.g., employment, income, business revenues, energy cost savings), energy (e.g., new MW installed, saved energy, and costs per energy unit saved), environmental (e.g., GHG emissions saved or offset), and social (e.g., perceived benefits, human capital development) indicators. Based on the evaluation results, stakeholders are re-engaged and goals adjusted as part of ongoing learning processes similar to adaptive co-management and the co-production of knowledge (Chapter 3).

Green job creation strategies and instruments

Jung (2015) highlighted the importance of creating good quality green jobs, which are full time, high wage, knowledge and technology based, and having the potential for influencing radical changes in institutions and infrastructure. Sustainable niche experiments as entrepreneurship processes help create technologies, solutions, jobs, and sustainability value. But other economic development strategies are also important for the creation of sustainability solutions. These include *business attraction strategies* (e.g., convincing a solar manufacturer to move from Canada to Germany), *business retention strategies* (e.g., incentivizing a wind manufacturer to stay in Oklahoma rather than moving to Texas), and *business expansion strategies* (e.g., helping a local water filtration start-up company develop new technology applications for additional export markets). Economic development strategies continue to shift from supply side (e.g., tax cuts for business attraction) to demand side (e.g., investments in human capital to encourage entrepreneurship and innovation) (Carley et al., 2011). Strategies have also shifted from targeting basic manufacturing firms to targeting specialized and advanced manufacturing that is more adaptable to changing trends and better able to bring competitive advantages. This last category describes many green energy technologies (e.g., solar, electric cars, batteries) that require new manufacturing processes, higher levels of robotics and automation, more flexible production processes, and higher levels of constantly evolving human capital. What policy instruments can sustainability professionals use to support the aforementioned green job creation strategies?

Policy instruments to support renewable energy could also support green job creation strategies. Renewable portfolio standards, feed-in tariffs, and carbon taxes lead to environmental as well as economic benefits. Inglesi-Lotz (2016) analyzed the influence of renewable energy on economic development in 30 Organization for Economic Co-operation and Development (OECD) countries from 1990–2010 and found a positive relationship between GDP per capita and renewable energy consumption. Wei et al. (2010) found that energy efficiency policies when coupled with a 30 percent renewable portfolio standard target for 2030 would lead to the creation of 4 million full-time equivalent job years by 2030 in the United States. Renewable portfolio standards that are in place for longer periods of time allow for consistency and stability in business strategies and investments

(Lee, 2017), leading to additional green business growth (Bowen et al., 2013). Interestingly, green business growth was not related to the stringency of the renewable portfolio standard or the extent that it increased in stringency over time. Bowen et al. (2013) also found that states with higher GDP per capita, larger investments in public infrastructure, and larger energy subsidies were more likely to see growth in green jobs and businesses.

South Korea's green jobs policy (2008) aimed to reduce GHG emissions and contribute to economic development (Jung, 2015). The policy was led by the government and focused on green growth (weak sustainability pathway) with little citizen participation in the process and few radical changes to regime subsystems. Job creation was largely focused on reducing pollution rather than on proactively driving innovation in new green sectors. South Korea has undergone rapid industrialization and had a high rate of increase in GHG emissions between 2007 and 2015 partly due to a high energy intensity per GDP, and also because of an almost exclusive reliance on energy imports to meet its growing economic demands (Jung, 2015).

Economy-wide policy instruments like a carbon tax are essential but insufficient to solve climate change because they are susceptible to control by dominant economic and political regime actors (John, 2008) like large utilities that have the resources and capabilities to make changes and therefore benefit from reducing emissions more so than smaller businesses. To address these power dynamics, carbon tax revenues can be redistributed to federal-state-local actors or to governance partnerships to develop sustainability technologies as an economic development strategy. This would allow for investments in infrastructure, institutional capacity, and research and development (R&D) in a competitive manner. This approach would reward states/cities that demonstrate plans to efficiently reduce GHG emissions, leading to a virtuous cycle where federal funds are used for entrepreneurship, business attraction, and business expansion strategies for local green energy firms.

The federal government could play a guiding and enabling role by setting standards for emissions reduction performance without picking winners and losers for technology choices. All actors would have an incentive to improve the emissions performance of their technologies if they wish to tap into these economic development funds. Picking winners and losers can have unintended consequences for sustainability transitions. For example, regulating, taxing, or banning certain technologies like nuclear or natural gas could lead to increases in coal development and production. Furthermore, providing tax incentives for solar or electric cars could narrow the focus of entrepreneurs and manufacturers to those technologies while in the process ignoring or slowing R&D in other options that could potentially have more radical impacts on changing institutions and infrastructures.

The relationship between economic development, sustainability, and entrepreneurship continues to evolve (Hall et al., 2010) and new models are constantly being created. For example, Belz and Binder (2017) described a sustainable entrepreneurship model that merged two double-bottom-line processes (social and economic) and (environmental and economic) into a triple-bottom-line solution process. Alternatively, Schaltegger and Wagner (2011) separated four types of sustainability-oriented entrepreneurship as ecopreneurship, social entrepreneurship, institutional entrepreneurship, and sustainable entrepreneurship. All four types make important contributions to sustainability transitions while differing in the extent that economic goals are the primary (ends) objective, or are secondary (means) objective to achieving a primary (ends) objective such as reducing environmental pollution or disparities between rich and poor (Table 5.1). Social entrepreneurship alters the social and cultural subsystems of the regime by changing behavior, norms, and culture, while institutional entrepreneurship alters the political,

Table 5.1 Different types of sustainability–oriented entrepreneurship

	Ecopreneurship	Social entrepreneurship	Institutional entrepreneurship	Sustainable entrepreneurship
Core motivation	Contribute to solving environmental problems and create economic value	Contribute to solving societal problems and create value for society	Contribute to changing regulatory, societal and market institutions	Contribute to solving societal and environmental problems through the realization of a successful business
Main goal	Earn money by solving environmental problems	Achieve societal goals and secure funding to achieve this	Changing institutions as direct goal	Creating sustainable development through entrepreneurial corporate activities
Role of economic goals	Ends	Means	Means or ends	Means and ends
Role of non-market goals	Environmental issues as integrated core element	Societal goals as ends	Changing institutions as core element	Core element of integrated ends to contribute to sustainable development
Organizational development challenges	From focus on environmental issues to integrating economic issues	From focus on societal issues to integrating economic issues	From changing institutions to integrating sustainability	From small contribution to large contribution to sustainable development

Source: Schaltegger and Wagner (2011, p. 224).

policy, and institutional subsystems of the regime by changing policies and rules. These regime subsystem changes make it easier for ecopreneurship experiments (focused on creating economic value by solving environmental problems) and sustainable entrepreneurship experiments (focused on solving social and environmental problems through green business development) to succeed and amplify *sustainability value* throughout the socio-technical system.

Practice of triple-bottom-line economic development

The following case studies outline triple-bottom-line economic development experiences in the United States and Canada.

Case study: Triple-bottom-line economic development in the United States

In 2011, there were more than 3.4 million green goods and services jobs in the United States (BLS, 2011). More than 2.5 million Americans worked in the clean tech sub-segment of green jobs as of 2016 (Ecotech Institute, 2016), which are part of a broader 4.5 million *sustainability jobs* that the Environmental Defense Fund estimates for the United States (Gessesse et al., 2017). Green job creation strategies could further contribute to sustainability goals and enhance an already growing sustainability sector by following the triple-bottom-line approach (Hammer and Pivo, 2016). Investment in renewable energy and energy efficiency generated as many as three times more direct and indirect jobs than investments in the fossil fuel industry (Garrett-Peltier, 2017). The same analysis concluded that for every US$1 million moved from fossil fuels to energy efficiency or renewable energy, an additional increase of five jobs will occur. The rapid growth of the wind and solar industries in the United States demonstrates the impressive job creation potential of triple-bottom-line economic development. Total installed wind capacity increased by nearly 30 times between 1999 (2,472 MW) and the end of 2015 (74,472 MW) (AWEA, 2016). Wind energy was responsible for 40 percent of new power capacity additions in 2015. More than 40 states now operate utility scale wind turbines, with Texas leading with over 18,000 MW of installed capacity. In the last decade, the wind industry has invested $1.2 billion in new wind projects. This led to 88,000 wind-related jobs largely in manufacturing, with 500 wind manufacturing facilities in the United States (AWEA, 2016).

The solar industry is growing by 43 percent per year (SEIA, 2016). The same report shows that as installations increased, costs to install solar declined by 70 percent over the last decade. The average cost of commercial solar projects dropped by a third within the last three years alone. Like wind, the most appealing aspect for an economic development strategy is job creation, with more than 209,000 solar workers employed in 2015 and 260,000 in 2016 (SEIA, 2017), doubling the number of jobs in 2010. This is expected to double again within the next five years to more than 420,000 workers with 8,000 solar companies operating across the country (SEIA, 2016). Texas and Utah experienced the fastest growth, but the overall United States solar industry was expected to exceed an annual growth rate of 80 percent in 2016 (SEIA, 2016). When combined, wind and solar powered more than 26 million homes in the United States (AWEA, 2016; SEIA, 2016).

Public polling before the 2016 presidential election demonstrated that a bi-partisan and increasing majority of Americans believed it is important to transition to a cleaner and more energy efficient economy (Lazard, 2016) and that alternative energy should be prioritized over oil and gas (Gallup, 2016). Similar results were found in a large national survey conducted immediately after the election (Leiserowitz et al., 2016). Politicians focusing on creating green jobs can benefit politically because those jobs contribute economic as well as social and environmental value to society (Bleys and Whitby, 2015; Boos, 2015; Kubiszewski et al., 2015; Lawn, 2005; Posner and Costanza, 2011; Wu and Heberling, 2016). Green jobs are manufacturing intensive, generate high export values (Muro et al., 2011), and have high multiplier effects for indirect and induced jobs (Garrett-Peltier, 2017; Sooriyaarachchi et al., 2015).

Direct jobs are "created in the design, manufacturing, delivery, construction/installation, project management, and operation and maintenance of the direct components of the technology" (Wei et al., 2010, p. 921). *Indirect jobs* include the suppliers of parts made for the technologies created by the direct jobs. *Induced jobs* result from "the expenditure-induced effects in the general economy due to the economic activity and spending of direct and indirect employees" (Wei et al., 2010, p. 921). For example, a residential energy efficiency program helps homeowners improve the efficiency of their home to reduce their energy bills. Homeowners may spend on technologies that directly create green jobs in the air conditioning, insulation, or window businesses. Those businesses order parts from other suppliers, which creates indirect jobs. The money saved by the homeowner over time can be spent in the local community, which leads to induced jobs. Income of the employees of the energy efficiency manufacturing and parts supply businesses can also be spent in the local community on food and entertainment to further create induced jobs.

Another example is a wind power firm that hires 20 new employees (direct jobs) for the manufacturing facility in order to meet increasing demand for their product from a neighboring state. If demand for wind turbines continues to increase, a new supplier of turbine blades, an input to the manufacturing firm's production needs, may move to the area bringing 30 additional indirect jobs. These 50 combined workers in the wind sector now live in the local area and spend a portion of their income at restaurants, shopping malls, grocery stores, and sporting events, leading to the creation of 40 additional induced jobs, as well as contributing to the local tax base. The combination of indirect and induced jobs as a ratio of direct jobs represents the *multiplier effect*, which differs by sectors in the economy. In the aforementioned wind power manufacturing example, 20 direct jobs would lead to 70 additional indirect and induced jobs for a total of 90 jobs. Taking the 90 total jobs divided by 20 direct jobs gives a multiplier of 4.5. This suggests that for every new direct job created, sustainability professionals could expect to create an additional 4.5 indirect and induced jobs. Green manufacturing jobs tend to have higher multiplier effects than green service jobs because they require extensive value chains composed of indirect jobs to support their production. Multiplier effects can also be calculated as a ratio of jobs created per unit of energy saved due to energy efficiency technology investments (Wei et al., 2010).

Triple-bottom-line economic development has many benefits including helping to offset job losses in traditional manufacturing sectors during recessions, growing faster than jobs in fossil fuel industries, paying more than other jobs of similar skill-sets, offering a broader range of employment opportunities (service or manufacturing), and are increasing in every region of the United States (Gkatsou et al., 2014). Gkatsou et al. (2014, p. 31) pointed out that "more jobs are created for each unit of electricity generated from renewable sources than from fossil fuels" because green energy jobs are more labor intensive while fossil fuel jobs are more technology intensive. While southern states have the highest number of green jobs, three-quarters of all green jobs created in the United States between 2003 and 2010 are in urban areas (Muro et al., 2011). Rural areas also benefit from green export job creation in the green chemicals, biofuels, and organic food and farming sectors (Muro et al., 2011), as well as from revenue from renewable energy installations (Greene and Geisken, 2013; Pender et al., 2014) that can even be used to support struggling school districts (Castleberry and Greene, 2017).

Policy instruments designed to jump-start the economy after a recession can contribute to green jobs. Investments in new technology and infrastructure provided by the American Recovery and Reinvestment Act likely saved many renewable energy projects that would have collapsed during the 2008 recession (Carley et al., 2012). The investment provided by the Act led to a ten-fold leveraging of additional state and private investment in energy development. The Act has contributed to energy innovation leading to a significant reduction in solar costs and an increase in renewable energy manufacturing capacity.

The Clean Power Plan of 2015 represented an enabling policy that could encourage states to create policies to mitigate CO_2 emissions. If implemented and fully enforced with a carbon price, the Clean Power Plan would generate substantial revenues for states in some cases exceeding $1 billion annually (Fullerton and Karney, 2018). The aforementioned study found that this could alleviate state budget deficits and even completely replace corporate tax revenues for 13 states. Corporate tax cuts could then be used as a green business attraction strategy that is paid for by the carbon tax revenues. Businesses in states that enforce a carbon tax as part of the Clean Power Plan would have a double incentive to create green jobs: first via strategies to reduce CO_2 emissions and get out of having to pay that tax, and second as a result of making new investments with the savings from the corporate tax cut. The Clean Power Plan is considered an instrument that guides other actors at the state and municipal level to generate *sustainability value*.

Case study: Portland green building cluster

Portland, Oregon was an early adopter of green buildings, which led to clusters that included all types of businesses related to green buildings (e.g., architects, designers, developers, builders, manufacturers, material reclamation companies, and engineers) (Allen and Potiowsky, 2008). The State of Oregon provided funding to help develop this cluster as a triple-bottom-line economic development strategy to turn research into technology and business development. The cluster provided a competitive advantage for triple-bottom-line economic development based on the combination of strong demand for green building-related products and services, a diverse mix of industry leading green building companies, a network of enabling institutions, a high skilled labor market, and a strong value chain (Allen and Potiowsky, 2008). In order to continue innovating, sustainability professionals can help with education, training, and R&D capacity. They can also help develop export markets for the technologies created in the cluster because the market in Portland is relatively small and already saturated. Economic developers should focus on highlighting the cost savings and other factors that reduce the premium price paid for green buildings (Leland et al., 2015) in order to turn LEED (Leadership in Energy and Environmental Design) buildings into a green business attraction strategy.

Despite policy and innovation performance in Oregon and Portland, Oregon's CO_2 emissions have actually increased by 0.3 percent per year from 1997–2014 as explained by the *KAYA Identity* components in (Table 5.2). One reason was the high rate of economic development (2.5 percent per year) and population growth (1.2 percent per year) that Oregon experienced during that time period. As a result, the carbon intensity of the energy system increased by 1.0 percent per year as coal (34 percent as of 2014) and natural

Table 5.2 KAYA Identity for Oregon, U.S.: average annual percent change

Oregon	1997–1999	1999–2001	2001–2003	2003–2005	2005–2007	2007–2009	2009–2011	2011–2014	1997–2014
CO_2 emissions	6.5	-1.9	-0.9	1.3	2.1	-2.1	-3.0	0.7	0.3
Population	0.9	0.7	0.8	0.6	1.0	0.8	0.5	0.9	1.2
GDP/capita	1.6	1.5	1.5	3.2	3.1	0.7	2.6	-1.9	2.5
Energy intensity (energy/GDP)	-1.3	-5.0	-3.0	-2.4	-3.0	-2.9	-3.3	0.6	-2.8
Carbon intensity (carbon/energy)	5.2	1.4	-0.1	0.1	1.2	-0.6	-2.7	1.2	1.0

Source: Data from EIA (2017b, 2017c); calculations by the authors.

gas (14 percent) have remained a large part of the electricity mix (Oregon, 2017) to meet the increase in demand from population and economic development. The increase in CO_2 emissions is also skewed by the 6.5 percent annual increase between 1997 and 1999 due to an increase in coal production for electricity, which is reflected by the 5.2 percent annual increase in carbon intensity during the same period. However, Oregon has achieved impressive improvements in energy intensity of 2.8 percent per year as a result of transitioning from manufacturing to service and creative sectors that are less energy intensive. This has helped to offset what would have been a more significant increase in annual CO_2 emissions. It appears that supply-side bottlenecks have overpowered demand-side improvements in the energy system.

To address this challenge, Oregon plans to close its final coal plant by 2020 while cutting electricity supply carbon emissions in half by 2030 (Renew Oregon, 2016). Oregon aims to reduce state GHG emissions to 75 percent below 1990 by 2050 with strategies and instruments including a renewable portfolio standard for 50 percent renewables by 2040 (Oregon, 2018) and the Oregon Clean Electricity and Coal Transition Act (SB 1547, 2016). Oregon also adopted bills to reduce the carbon intensity in transportation fuels (HB 2186, 2009) and to define in law green jobs while mandating that a plan is developed for creating green jobs, industries, technologies, and innovations (HB 3300, 2009).

Case study: From rust belt to green belt: SolarCity 1-GW solar factory in Buffalo, NY

New York is undergoing an economic transition from old and abandoned manufacturing facilities (brownfield sites) to high-tech and flexible manufacturing facilities. One example is the plan by Elon Musk and SolarCity to build a solar PV manufacturing plant in an abandoned steel factory in Buffalo, New York (Mullaney, 2015). The plant, named Riverbend, is expected to create thousands of direct, indirect, and induced jobs as part of a triple-bottom-line economic development strategy to rebuild the rust belt by turning brownfield sites into engines for triple-bottom-line economic development. Riverbend will allow SolarCity to shift much of its manufacturing capacity from Asia to the United States. The plant will produce enough solar panels annually to supply 1 percent of the total power requirements of the United States (1 gigawatt). Plans for a further five-fold expansion of solar manufacturing in New York will make the state the national leader in solar manufacturing.

The government of the State of New York contributed $750 million to help SolarCity build the factory and purchase the machinery for the facility. In exchange, the State will retain ownership of the plant to prevent SolarCity from moving. SolarCity for its part is required to invest at least $5 billion into the community as part of this project. SolarCity is also required to pay a $42 million penalty for each year that the target of 5,000 jobs is not achieved. This is a new type of triple-bottom-line economic development strategy that partners a dynamic and innovative company in a green industry with a government that is committed to economic revitalization of a former manufacturing region. The State of New York has achieved a 1 percent annual reduction in CO_2 emissions between 1997 and 2014, despite increasing GDP per capita of 1.7 percent per year (Table 5.3). Modest improvements in energy and carbon intensity have helped to achieve these emission reductions. The 2008 recession was partly responsible for a 4.3 percent reduction in annual emissions between 2007 and 2009 due to a 2.3 percent annual improvement in carbon intensity during that period.

Table 5.3 KAYA Identity for New York, U.S.: average annual percent change

New York	1997–1999	1999–2001	2001–2003	2003–2005	2005–2007	2007–2009	2009–2011	2011–2014	1997–2014
CO_2 emissions	0.2	0.2	0.7	−0.1	−1.9	−4.3	−1.7	1.0	−1.0
Population	0.4	0.4	0.2	−0.1	0.0	0.3	0.4	0.3	0.3
GDP/capita	2.3	1.9	−0.4	2.3	0.9	−0.3	1.0	1.2	1.7
Energy intensity (energy/GDP)	−2.1	−2.4	1.4	−2.1	−2.2	−2.2	−2.1	−0.3	−1.8
Carbon intensity (carbon/energy)	−0.2	0.5	−0.5	0.0	−0.5	−2.3	−0.9	−0.3	−0.7

Source: Data from EIA (2017b, 2017c); calculations by the authors.

Case study: Green energy and economic development in Canada

During the past decade, Canada has undergone a transition in political, policy, and economic subsystems of the energy regime. This was enabled in part by a sustainability-focused Liberal government replacing the fossil fuel-entrenched Conservative government at the federal level in 2015. It was also supported by political changes at the provincial level including the socially progressive New Democrats sweeping the Conservatives out of office in oil-rich Alberta in 2015, and the Liberal party winning a majority in Ontario in 2013, which bolstered the green energy transition that was already underway. British Columbia's introduction of a revenue neutral carbon tax in 2008 and Québec's sustainability-oriented culture are also emblematic of sustainability transitions that are emerging from the provincial levels.

A new report from Statistics Canada (2017) tabulated more than 270,000 green jobs in Canada as of the end of 2016, and these jobs pay an average salary of CA\$92,000 as compared to the average Canadian worker earning \$59,000 per year. Green jobs now make up 1.5 percent of the total jobs in the Canadian economy, but were responsible 3.1 percent of Canadian GDP. Environmental and clean technology products were responsible for 1.9 percent of total Canadian exports (an increase of 33.8 percent from 2007–16) and 1.6 percent of total imports (an increase of 41.1 percent from 2007–16) in 2016. These figures suggest that the green economy is an important part of the overall Canadian economy and that triple-bottom-line economic development strategies are paying off.

Case study: Ontario Green Energy and Green Economy Act

Ontario's Green Energy and Green Economy Act (2015) helped achieve an increase in renewable energy manufacturing capacity, an increase in green jobs, an increase in installed renewable energy capacity, the closing of all coal plants in the province, and a reduction in GHG emissions. The Act centered on a feed-in tariff and a local content requirement for manufacturing wind and solar in Ontario, but also included many other triple-bottom-line economic development strategies and instruments. As a result, Ontario's GHG emissions were 7 percent below 1990 levels as of 2014 (Environment and Climate Change Canada, 2017). Ontario has begun to decouple CO_2 emissions from economic development as emissions are now decreasing with increasing GDP per capita.

One drawback of a large-scale province wide plan to generate renewable energy is that prices for domestic consumers are fixed while prices paid from export markets can be variable. In 2016, Ontario generated an excess of 14.6 terawatt hours of green electricity that was exported to neighboring jurisdictions (e.g., New York, Michigan) at a net financial loss to Ontario of \$0.5 billion (Ontario Society of Professional Engineers, 2017). Ontario is selling surplus electricity to its neighbors for less than it costs to produce it. One solution would be to reduce residential and commercial electricity rates in Ontario, but this may discourage conservation and lead to a rebound effect (Ontario Society of Professional Engineers, 2017). Another solution would be to change the electricity market in Ontario to allow consumers to purchase green energy at the same price available to external markets. If domestic consumers can purchase electricity at the same rate as external markets, the local economy would benefit and businesses could be enticed to stay in the province and not leave to other jurisdictions with cheaper electricity. A final solution would be to phase out natural gas for home heating, a drastic measure that would require shifting to electric heating (Morrow and Keenan, 2016). This would increase residential demand for electricity, which could reduce the current surplus and allow higher electricity prices to be paid for green electricity.

The Green Energy and Green Economy Act and its supporting mechanisms have provided incentive and complimentary plans for an additional $7 billion to encourage climate change actions. These plans call for more incentives for building retrofits, rebates for electric vehicle purchases, requirements for less carbon intensive gasoline in the province, changes to building codes to require all new homes to be heated with electricity or geothermal by 2030, a cap-and-trade system and a green bank to offer financing for green energy projects, and a target for 12 percent of new vehicle sales to be electric by 2025 (Morrow and Keenan, 2016). The goal is to get GHG emissions to 15 percent below 1990 levels by 2020, 37 percent by 2030, and 80 percent by 2050. Acceleration Point: Creating a triple-bottom-line economic development policy like the Green Energy and Green Economy Act can amplify sustainability value creation (e.g., increases to economic, social, *and* environmental value in line with the strong sustainability definition in Chapter 1) by providing institutional support for state/province and city actors to create and implement additional strategies and instruments. A mix of complimentary policies is critical to simultaneously encouraging niche creation and regime change as described in Chapter 8.

Case study: Québec sustainable development and climate change mitigation

The provincial electricity utility in Québec called Hydro-Québec combines sustainable development planning and climate change mitigation instruments as part of a triple-bottom-line economic development strategy (Hydro-Québec, 2015). They focus on greening all stages of the value chain including construction, generation, transmission, distribution, customer service, management operations, and technological innovation. At each stage, Hydro-Québec generates sustainability value by focusing on job creation, preserving biodiversity, reducing the environmental footprint of its goods and services, reducing electricity prices for low-income customers, and facilitating ongoing communication and engagement with surrounding communities. Hydro-Québec has created numerous sustainability reports and a Sustainable Development Action Plan that are available to read online to learn more about the process of a sustainable energy transition.

Central to its sustainability efforts is a green innovation strategy based on partnerships with universities, research centers, and other industries. Hydro-Québec views technology innovation as the core of its sustainability value creation strategy. In 2016 alone, Hydro-Québec invested $134 million in R&D focused on extra-high-voltage transmission technology, energy storage and conversion technology, and electric transportation including installing and experimenting with a network of 794 charging stations. The R&D investments generated 1,156 patents for new technologies, which will provide a competitive advantage for Hydro-Québec going forward.

The province of Québec is characterized by a progressive culture and high public agreement that humans are accelerating climate change. This culture supports the creation of triple-bottom-line economic development strategies and sustainability transition instruments. Québec gets 99 percent of its electricity from hydropower, as well as exporting a substantial amount to neighboring jurisdictions, which offsets emissions that would have occurred because those jurisdictions' electricity systems are powered in part by fossil fuels. Benefiting from these pre-existing regime subsystem advantages, Hydro-Québec has reduced its GHG emissions by 91 percent since 1990.

Another major driving force for the actions taken by Hydro-Québec is the Provincial Sustainable Development Act. Québec was one of the first jurisdictions in the world to pass a Sustainable Development Act in 2006 (Québec Sustainable Development Act, 2017). The Act established a definition of sustainable development, a commitment to creating a sustainable development strategy, a responsibility for the head of the government of the province (the premier) to report progress frequently, a requirement for departments/agencies to find actions to achieve the objectives, and a guideline to incorporate sustainable development indicators and evaluation mechanisms. Perhaps most importantly, the Act introduced a set of 16 principles to guide sustainable development actions in the province:

1 *Health and quality of life*: People, human health and improved quality of life are at the center of sustainable development concerns. People are entitled to a healthy and productive life in harmony with nature;
2 *Social equity and solidarity*: Development must be undertaken in a spirit of intra- and inter-generational equity and social ethics and solidarity;
3 *Environmental protection*: To achieve sustainable development, environmental protection must constitute an integral part of the development process;
4 *Economic efficiency*: The economy of Québec and its regions must be effective, geared toward innovation and economic prosperity that is conducive to social progress and respectful of the environment;
5 *Participation and commitment*: The participation and commitment of citizens and citizens' groups are needed to define a concerted vision of development and to ensure its environmental, social and economic sustainability;
6 *Access to knowledge*: Measures favorable to education, access to information and research must be encouraged in order to stimulate innovation, raise awareness and ensure effective participation of the public in the implementation of sustainable development;
7 *Subsidiarity*: Powers and responsibilities must be delegated to the appropriate level of authority. Decision-making centers should be adequately distributed and as close as possible to the citizens and communities concerned;
8 *Inter-governmental partnership and cooperation*: Governments must collaborate to ensure that development is sustainable from an environmental, social and economic standpoint. The external impact of actions in a given territory must be taken into consideration;
9 *Prevention*: In the presence of a known risk, preventive, mitigating and corrective actions must be taken, with priority given to actions at the source;
10 *Precaution*: When there are threats of serious or irreversible damage, lack of full scientific certainty must not be used as a reason for postponing the adoption of effective measures to prevent environmental degradation;
11 *Protection of cultural heritage*: The cultural heritage, made up of property, sites, landscapes, traditions and knowledge, reflects the identity of a society. It passes on the values of a society from generation to generation, and the preservation of this heritage fosters the sustainability of development. Cultural heritage components must be identified, protected and enhanced, taking their intrinsic rarity and fragility into account;
12 *Biodiversity preservation*: Biological diversity offers incalculable advantages and must be preserved for the benefit of present and future generations. The protection of species, ecosystems and the natural processes that maintain life is essential if quality of human life is to be maintained;

13 *Respect for ecosystem support capacity*: Human activities must be respectful of the support capacity of ecosystems and ensure the perenniality of ecosystems;

14 *Responsible production and consumption*: Production and consumption patterns must be changed in order to make production and consumption more viable and more socially and environmentally responsible, in particular through an ecoefficient approach that avoids waste and optimizes the use of resources;

15 *Polluter pays*: Those who generate pollution or whose actions otherwise degrade the environment must bear their share of the cost of measures to prevent, reduce, control and mitigate environmental damage;

16 *Internalization of costs*: The value of goods and services must reflect all the costs they generate for society during their whole life cycle, from their design to their final consumption and their disposal.

These principles share similarities with the Gibson sustainability principles in Chapter 1, but also add context specific principles (protection of cultural heritage), ecological principles (biodiversity preservation; respect for ecosystem support capacity), and economic principles (polluter pays; internalization of costs).

Québec provides a case of co-evolving electricity supply infrastructure and transportation technology in the direction of sustainability principles. The technological innovation system for electric vehicles has evolved in part due to structural changes in the electricity regime and niche experiments in the transportation regime (Haley, 2015). The technological innovation system structure including technology, organizations, and institutions overlaps both the electricity and the transportation regime (Figure 5.5). The structure influences the functions of technological innovation systems, which were outlined in Chapter 4. Haley (2015) found that the hydroelectricity regime enabled

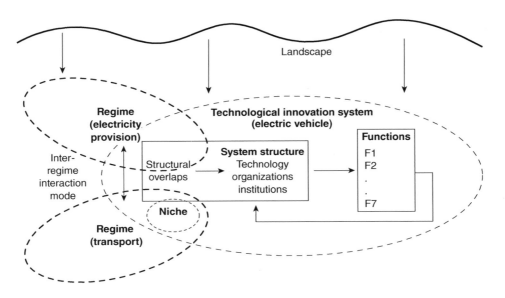

Figure 5.5 Technological innovation system for electric vehicles in Quebec: co-evolving hydroelectricity regime and transport regime supporting electric vehicle niche experiments

Source: Haley (2015, p. 8).

the development of electric vehicles in the province. Many technology overlaps were identified that related to GHG emission reductions, energy independence from switching away from fossil fuels, and the existence of an electricity distribution infrastructure that can handle increased loads due to an increase in electric vehicles. The implication is that creating sustainable niche experiments aimed at changing transportation technology and infrastructure requires understanding the connections between the electricity supply regime and the transportation regime. Engaging entrepreneurs, universities, government agencies, and large incumbent actors like automakers and utility companies in a transition arena may be more successful if sustainability professionals emphasize the triple-bottom-line economic development benefits from upgrading both the energy and transportation systems simultaneously.

Case study: Alberta electricity market transition

Alberta is undergoing a transition in its electricity market that will allow for more renewable electricity at prices competitive with fossil fuels. In 2017, the Alberta Electric System Operator revealed the results of a competitive bidding process for adding 5,000 MW of wind power to Alberta's grid by 2030 (Pittis, 2017). Competitive bids were introduced that claim to be able to generate electricity at prices as low as five cents per kilowatt hour. This will help drive down prices that consumers pay when bundled with current electricity contracts. These changes are part of Alberta's Renewable Electricity Program launched in 2017 aiming to reach 30 percent renewables by 2030 while phasing out coal plants during that time. Microgeneration rules were also changed to allow five megawatt systems (up from one megawatt) and to allow new micro-generators to supply consumers directly through distributive generation (Energy Alberta, 2017). These changes are even more significant given Alberta's legacy of fossil fuel-driven economic development, and the fact that the electricity supply mix is still 51 percent coal, 40 percent natural gas, and only 9 percent renewables. The goal is to use market forces to drive innovation and infrastructure upgrades that will generate triple-bottom-line value for Alberta: cheaper electricity, greener electricity, and a more stable electricity system.

Challenges for triple-bottom-line economic development

Sustainability professionals aiming to follow a strong sustainability pathway must address the potential for uneven economic and social impacts of triple-bottom-line economic development on different groups (Balta-Ozkan et al., 2015). First, solar and wind energy tend to cluster in areas with high energy and economic potential. Necessary upgrades to transmission systems may require public investment as a means of securing private investment in energy production. Convincing citizens to pay more in taxes to fund these upgrades is a challenge in most jurisdictions. Sustainability professionals can help governments communicate the public goods provided by renewable energy via a modernized transmission grid as well as royalties and government revenues that can be redistributed from areas with high solar and wind potential to areas with lower potential. Deciding where to generate new energy is a complex problem because of differing wind/solar potential and transmission cost regimes. Lamy et al. (2016) examined the economics of adding wind capacity in remote areas (Iowa and Minnesota; North and South Dakota) to connect to the United States midwestern electricity grid, which is far from markets and therefore requires upgrading the transmission system, versus adding wind near the markets

(Illinois), which would require less investment in transmission but generate less energy yields. They found that the decision depended on the transmission cost premium, which ranged from US$250 per kilowatt in Minnesota and Iowa to $360 per kilowatt in North and South Dakota. This is compared to the transmission cost premium in Illinois of $33 per kilowatt. Therefore, the cost per kilowatt of new installed capacity would have to be added to the transmission cost premiums to decide the location to expand wind capacity in order to minimize costs. Governments can manipulate the transmission cost premium as one form of green business attraction strategy to incentivize renewable energy producers to come to their state.

Second, rural and urban differences in energy demand and sources as well as perceptions about energy sources, impacts, and distributed generation can lead to uneven economic development patterns and technology winners and losers (Balta-Ozkan et al., 2015). Sustainability professionals can help match the skills and education required for green energy jobs to the characteristics of the local people through retraining and engagement programs similar to those going on in coal country. For example, Bloomberg Philanthropies created a $3 million initiative to support on-the-job training, economic development, and new career opportunities in communities impacted by the declining coal industry in the United States (Bloomberg Philanthropies, 2017). The funding helps organizations like Coal-Field Development Corporation, a community-based non-profit in West Virginia, hire and train workers based on a 42-hour weekly program: 33 hours in sustainable construction, solar installation, mine-land reclamation, sustainable agriculture, and artisanship; six hours of higher education; and three hours of mentorship. Figure 5.6 shows the changing energy production landscape in the United States and the Kentucky to West Virginia coal corridor where these retraining programs are badly needed.

Third, while economic development benefits arise from *agglomeration economies* associated with the manufacturing of solar and wind technologies in clusters (e.g., manufacturers locate near suppliers, competitors, high-skilled labor, universities), additional costs can result from agglomerations of production that lead to energy network constraints if solar and wind generators all located in the same areas (Balta-Ozkan et al., 2015) as shown in Figure 5.6. Sustainability professionals can work with green energy producers, transmission companies, and storage companies to alleviate these constraints. Clean Line is one company in the United States that is working to install new transmission capacity to get renewable energy from production locations to markets where affordable and stable energy is needed (Clean Line, 2017). This will help overcome network constraints and facilitate the development of additional production capacity by creating new markets. In the case of Oklahoma, the wind resource is driving *business expansion strategies* focusing on integrated energy generation and transmission systems like the Wind Catcher Energy Connection Project proposed for the panhandle of Oklahoma. This will include the largest wind farm in the United States (2,000 MW) and a dedicated powerline to get the power to markets where it is needed (American Electric Power, 2017). Not only will this project create jobs, it will save electricity customers over $7 billion during the first 25 years.

Fourth, if a region or country pursues a carbon reduction policy that encourages local wind and solar manufacturing and microgrid development, the benefits of green job creation and local multiplier effects will result from clustering. If however governments pursue centralized generation of nuclear, natural gas, or carbon capture and storage, these technologies may be produced elsewhere and imported into the region leading to fewer indirect and induced jobs (Balta-Ozkan et al., 2015). Ontario's Green Energy and Green Economy Act and feed-in tariff was an example of a sustainability policy designed to create local jobs and economic

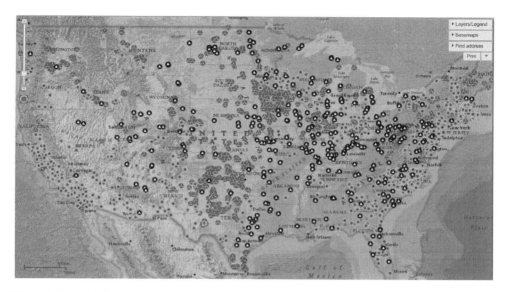

Figure 5.6 America's changing energy production landscape: coal, solar, and wind

Source: EIA (2017a).

Legend: The triangle symbols represent coal plants, the turbine blade symbols are wind farms, and the sun symbols are solar plants.

development benefits by requiring local manufacturing of the wind and solar systems. The local content requirement was challenged by Japan at the World Trade Organization on the grounds that it was an unfair protectionist trade provision that disadvantaged renewable energy manufactures in Japan (WTO, 2017). The result was that Canada was forced to remove domestic requirements for large renewable electricity purchases and reduce domestic content requirements for small and microFIT purchasing that were part of the feed-in tariff program for wind and solar electricity. This case demonstrates a challenge for triple-bottom-line economic development when considering the extent that economies are connected and trade rules are bottlenecks to domestic green energy policies, which sustainability professionals who are environmental lawyers can help overcome.

Measuring progress towards triple-bottom-line economic development

One way to measure progress towards triple-bottom-line economic development is through the green jobs location quotient (LQ) (Chapple et al., 2011). The LQ is used to calculate the concentration of economic activity in a county for a particular sector compared to the activity in the state/province for that same sector. It can also be used to calculate the proportion of green jobs in a county relative to the total jobs in the state. Chapple et al. (2011) found that the five largest metro areas in California have approximately 70 percent of the green jobs in California. Los Angeles had the highest number of green jobs in the state focused on areas that it has a competitive advantage, namely, manufacturing, transportation, and recycling. The East Bay area had the highest concentration of green jobs (LQ of 2.67) due to the presence of three national laboratories focused on energy R&D. San Diego (environmental services), San Francisco (green transportation), and Sacramento (environmental services) also had LQs greater than 1, suggesting that the portion of green jobs surpassed the portion of total jobs and that economic activity in the green sectors was leading to exports after meeting local demands. The fastest growth in green jobs was in Sacramento (environmental services), Upper San Joaquin (green building), and the Riverside-San Bernardino areas (recycling/remediation).

The number of clean tech startups and the amount of venture capital focusing on clean tech increased rapidly from 2007–08 in California, but still remained a small portion of the overall economy (Chapple et al., 2011). This trend is similar to the number of patents, where green/clean tech patents were less than 1 percent of the total patents in California. Large incumbent actors held a significant proportion of the green tech patents. Chapple et al. (2011) discovered that there were more rapidly growing green firms than rapidly growing firms in the overall economy.

The United States Bureau of Labor Statistics conducted a national survey to measure the number and type of green jobs in 2010 and 2011 (BLS, 2011). The following figures show the total number of green jobs (Figure 5.7) and the number of green jobs per capita (Figure 5.8) in each state relative to the per capita CO_2 emissions for 2011. While the larger states tend to have more green jobs, the states with the highest numbers of green jobs per capita are Vermont, Oregon, and Iowa. Only Massachusetts and Pennsylvania are in the top ten on both graphs, suggesting that they have created a large number of green jobs, but also, that their triple-bottom-line economic development strategies and policy mix instruments are efficient at creating green jobs when controlling for population. There are weak associations between the total number of green jobs and CO_2 emissions per capita (R = -0.29) and between the number of green jobs per capita and CO_2 emissions per capita (R = -0.14), suggesting that increasing the number of green jobs may be related to decreases in CO_2 emissions in some states. Many states that created a large and diverse energy efficiency and renewable energy policy mix (Chapter 8) also created large numbers of green jobs. Sustainability professionals can create strategies and instruments tailored to each state's industry mix. For example, some coal-producing states have created few green jobs (e.g., West Virginia, North Dakota, Wyoming). But unlike West Virginia, North Dakota and Wyoming rank in the middle of the pack when it comes to green jobs per capita. Wyoming has created wind installation jobs and receives 11 percent of its electricity from wind, but is still dependent on coal for 88 percent of its electricity while producing more than 40 percent of the total coal mined in the United States (EIA, 2017a).

The number of green goods and services jobs in 2010 is presented in Figure 5.9 by sector and compared to the total number of jobs in the United States in the same sector. The sectors with the highest numbers of green jobs include manufacturing, local governments, construction, and the professional, scientific, and technical services sector. The fewest green jobs were in the financial services sector. LQs were calculated and the values are included on Figure 5.9 above each bar, which demonstrate the concentration of green jobs relative to employment in the same sector overall in the United States. The utilities sector has the highest concentration of green jobs with a LQ of 4.93, followed by construction, the federal government, and transportation and warehousing. The sectors with the lowest concentration of green jobs include financial activities, education and health services, and leisure and hospitality. It is important to note that all three levels of government had a LQ over 1, suggesting that green jobs are over represented relative to other government jobs.

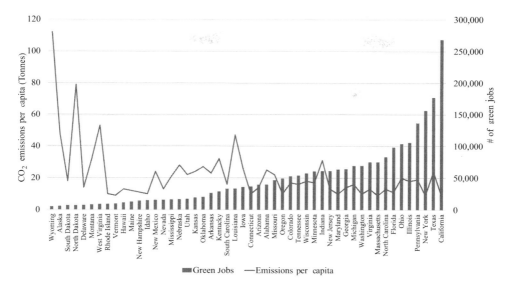

Figure 5.7 Total number of green jobs relative to CO_2 emissions per capita, U.S. states
Source: Emission data from EIA (2017b); green jobs numbers from BLS (2011).

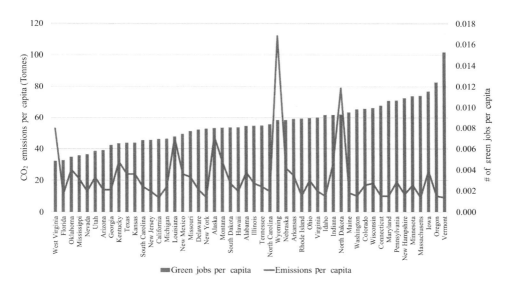

Figure 5.8 Number of green jobs per capita relative to CO_2 emissions per capita, U.S. states
Source: Emission data from EIA (2017b); green jobs numbers from BLS (2011).

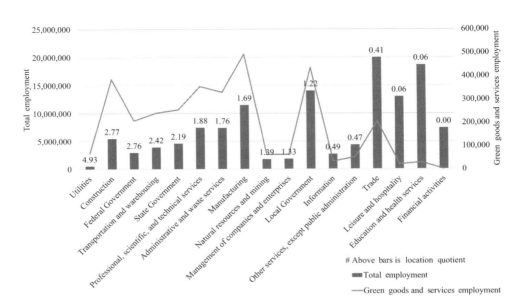

Figure 5.9 U.S. green goods and services jobs relative to total jobs by sector, 2010

Source: Data from BLS (2011); LQ calculations by the authors.

A green regional economic analysis was conducted for the two states with the highest number of green jobs, California and Texas, focusing on private sector jobs only. First, LQs for each sector were calculated for 2010 and 2011 for California and Texas (Table 5.4). Each state's LQ was calculated using the number of state-level green jobs relative to the number of jobs for the same green sector at the national level. The LQs tell us something about the concentration of green employment in these states relative to the country. Notable differences include natural resources and mining, administrative/waste services, and leisure/hospitality sectors where California had a higher concentration of green jobs than Texas. However, Texas had a higher concentration of green jobs in the construction and the professional, scientific, and technical services sector.

Second, a shift share analysis was conducted to examine the structure of the state green economies as a function of location aspects, exogenous forces, and the mix of green industries. The shift share analysis allows sustainability professionals to explore change in green jobs in a state between time periods and to understand the competitive position of the state green economy. There are three components of the shift share: the national component (RS), the industry mix (IM), and the differential shift (DS). The RS growth component measures the state change that could have occurred if the state green economy had grown at the same rate as the national green economy. The IM component measures the share of state change that could be attributed to the national green economies industry mix. This reflects the degree that the state green economy specializes in industries that are fast/slow growing in the national green economy. The DS component measures the difference between the green industry's state growth rate (or rate of decline) and the industry's national growth rate or decline. The differential shift component is considered to reflect a state's green competitive advantage, since it measures how well a given sector is performing in the state relative to how that sector is performing in the country. In this case, if a green industry in the state creates jobs faster than the same industry in the nation even during times of overall economic prosperity, that signifies a green competitive advantage in that industry in the state. The shift share formula is as follows:

$$\Delta X_{\delta,j} = X_{1,j}\left(\frac{T_2}{T_1} - 1.0\right) + X_{1,j}\left(\frac{B_{2,j}}{B_{1,j}} - \frac{T_2}{T_1}\right) + X_{I,j}\left(\frac{X_{2,j}}{X_{1,j}} - \frac{B_{2,j}}{B_{1,j}}\right)$$

Where $\Delta X_{\delta,j}$ reflects the change in green jobs in the state from time period one to time period two, B is the **green employment in a sector in the nation**, T is the **total green employment in the nation**, and X is the **green employment in a sector in the state**. The RS, IM, and DS components are outlined below.

$$RS_j = X_{1,j}\left(\frac{T_2}{T_1} - 1\right) \quad IM_j = X_{1,j}\left(\frac{B_{2,j}}{B_{1,j}} - \frac{T_2}{T_I}\right) \quad DS_j = X_{1,j}\left(\frac{X_{2,j}}{X_{1,j}} - \frac{B_{2,j}}{B_{1,j}}\right)$$

Using the LQs and the shift share analysis, a Carvalho Classification was undertaken for California and Texas. This classification system was created by economics professor E. Carvalho to offer a descriptive scale for how a particular economic sector is performing. The Classification is combined with industry targeting descriptions (McLean and Voytek, 1992) in Figure 5.10 to inform a series of strategies for economic development. Table 5.4 shows that green employment increased in every sector in California except for transportation and warehousing. In contrast, many sectors saw a decline in green employment in Texas between 2010 and 2011. These changes can be explained by the shift share components. For example, in California, of the 30,725 new green jobs created, 17,816 were because of activity in the overall green economy in the United States (RS), 201 were due to the mix of green industries in the national economy (IM), and 12,709 were due to local competitive advantages in California (DS). This suggests that while the green economy overall was doing well during this time period in the United States, the California green economy was outperforming the national green economy.

In Texas, there was a decline of 2,978 green jobs from 2010 to 2011. This change is explained by an RS of 13,401, an IM of 3,284, and a DS of –19,663. In other words, the overall United States green economy led to positive job growth in green sectors in Texas, in particular in construction and trade where green employment increased. However, the negative DS suggests that the local green economy was not performing well, which stifled potential triple-bottom-line economic development that could have occurred if the Texas green economy was growing at the same rate as the nation's green economy. This suggests that the Texas green economy did not have a competitive advantage during the 2010 to 2011 period.

Review the full Carvalho Classification legend and McLean and Voytek (1992) industry targeting descriptions in Figure 5.10. To interpret the classification system, compare the LQ, IM, and DS figures for each sector. For example, if the LQ is above 1.25, the IM is positive (leading), and the DS is positive (leading), then the Carvalho Classification is driving, which is categorized as current strength. The Carvalho Classification for California shows that the construction sector and the other services except public administration sector are current strengths with high growth potential. Natural resources and mining, utilities, and the administrative and waste services sectors are evolving and in

Table 5.4 Green jobs and green economy performance analysis for California and Texas

California

| | LQ 2010 | LQ 2011 | Green employment numbers | | | Shift share | | | Carvalho Classification |
			2010	2011	Change	RS	IM	DS	
Natural resources and mining	2.49	2.40	16,313	16,906	593	1,269	−923	247	Evolving
Utilities	0.64	1.02	4,528	7,899	3,371	352	−215	3,233	Transitional
Construction	0.93	1.02	37,180	54,070	16,890	2,893	6,931	7,066	Accelerating
Manufacturing	0.63	0.66	31,957	36,417	4,460	2,486	−1,567	3,541	Moderate
Trade	1.08	0.98	22,915	23,789	874	1,783	169	−1,078	Yielding
Transportation and warehousing	0.60	0.55	15,076	14,151	−925	1,173	−1,384	−714	Marginal
Professional, scientific, and technical services	1.13	1.04	41,596	43,279	1,683	3,236	−124	−1,430	Vulnerable
Administrative and waste services	1.39	1.37	47,464	50,022	2,558	3,693	−3,009	1,874	Evolving
Leisure and hospitality	1.74	1.59	3,701	4,103	402	288	260	−146	Promising
Other services, except public administration	1.54	1.48	8,250	9,069	819	642	61	116	Driving
Total			**228,980**	**259,705**	**30,725**	**17,816**	**201**	**12,709**	

Texas

	LQ 2010	LQ 2011	Green employment numbers			Shift share			Carvalho Classification
			2010	2011	Change	RS	IM	DS	
Natural resources and mining	0.61	0.51	3,023	2,341	–682	235	–171	–746	Marginal
Utilities	1.08	1.00	5,789	5,021	–768	450	–274	–944	Vulnerable
Construction	1.34	1.35	40,171	46,559	6,388	3,125	7,489	–4,226	Promising
Manufacturing	0.79	0.77	30,198	27,554	–2,644	2,350	–1,481	–3,513	Vulnerable
Trade	1.08	1.19	17,240	18,727	1,487	1,341	127	18	Accelerating
Transportation and warehousing	0.54	0.56	10,153	9,476	–677	790	–932	–535	Marginal
Professional, scientific, and technical services	1.30	1.24	35,897	33,558	–2,339	2,793	–107	–5,025	Vulnerable
Administrative and waste services	0.92	0.89	23,685	21,159	–2,526	1,843	–1,501	–2,867	Marginal
Leisure and hospitality	0.88	0.94	1,413	1,574	161	110	99	–48	Yielding
Other services, except public administration	1.16	0.83	4,677	3,299	–1,378	364	35	–1,776	Yielding
Total			172,246	169,268	**–2,978**	**13,401**	**3,284**	**–19,663**	

Source: Data from BLS (2011); calculations by the authors.

transition, but their prospects for future growth are limited by external trends in the United States green economy. The manufacturing sector is categorized as moderate, which means that its prospects are limited by a weak export base and by external trends in the United States green economy. The trade sector is yielding and the leisure and hospitality sector is promising, which suggests that these sectors are high priority retention targets that triple-bottom-line economic developers could focus on incentivizing to stay in the area to tap into positive trends in the national sectors. The professional, scientific, and technical services sector is vulnerable, which suggests that its prospects are limited by external trends and declining competitiveness in the state sector.

When looking at the Carvalho Classification for Texas, the trade sector is accelerating and is a current strength with high growth potential. Manufacturing, utilities, and the professional, scientific, and technical services sectors are vulnerable and their prospects are limited by external trends and declining competitiveness in the state sectors. Construction, leisure and hospitality, and other services except public administration are high retention targets due to positive trends in those sectors in the national green economy. Acceleration Point: Sustainability professionals can jump-start sustainability transitions in institutions and infrastructures by supporting industries that are growing rapidly, are identified as high retention targets, or that have a competitive advantage in a particular state. These industries will generally have political support and are easy to justify based on the direct, indirect, and induced jobs that they will generate.

Location quotient (LQ)	Industrial mix (IM)	Differential shift (DS)	Carvalho classification	Industry targeting classification	
> 1.25 (High)	Leading (+)	Leading (+)	Driving	Current strength	**High growth**
0.75 – 1.25 (Medium)	Leading (+)	Leading (+)	Accelerating	Current strength	
< 0.75 (Low)	Leading (+)	Leading (+)	Rising	Emerging strength	
> 1.25 (High)	Lagging (-)	Leading (+)	Evolving	Prospects limited by external trends	
0.75 – 1.25 (Medium)	Lagging (-)	Leading (+)	Transitional	Prospects limited by external trends	
< 0.75 (Low)	Lagging (-)	Leading (+)	Moderate	Prospects limited by weak base and external trends	
> 1.25 (High)	Leading (+)	Lagging (-)	Promising	High priority retention target	
0.75 – 1.25 (Medium)	Leading (+)	Lagging (-)	Yielding	High priority retention target	
< 0.75 (Low)	Leading (+)	Lagging (-)	Modest	Prospects limited by weak base and declining competitiveness	
> 1.25 (High)	Lagging (-)	Lagging (-)	Challenging	Prospects limited by external trends and declining competitiveness	
0.75 – 1.25 (Medium)	Lagging (-)	Lagging (-)	Vulnerable	Prospects limited by external trends and declining competitiveness	
< 0.75 (Low)	Lagging (-)	Lagging (-)	Marginal	Prospects limited overall	**Declining**

Figure 5.10 Carvalho Classification legend and industry targeting descriptions

Source: Adapted from Thompson et al. (2009).

Triple-bottom-line economic developers can conduct similar analyses of the green economy for other jurisdictions. This type of analysis can be undertaken for cities and metropolitan areas in relation to the broader state/provincial economy. The challenge for sustainability professionals is to help triple-bottom-line economic developers collect accurate and ongoing data on the type and number of green jobs. The BLS (2011) survey was discontinued after two years, and a suitable replacement has not yet been undertaken for the United States. One reason is that it is expensive and time consuming to collect this type of data. A second reason is that defining a green job is getting more difficult, as all industries and sectors are creating jobs that achieve some degree of sustainability benefits. It is incumbent on sustainability professionals to continue pushing the envelope and require greener jobs that generate *sustainability value* in line with *strong sustainability* principles. In order to increase employment in green sectors, businesses, nonprofits, and governments can incentivize green innovation (Ceschin and Gaziulusoy, 2016), focus on radical innovation in sectors with high multiplier effects like the aircraft manufacturing industry (Slayton and Spinardi, 2015), use triple-bottom-line strategies to gain a competitive advantage (Schulz and Flanigan, 2016), reward sustainability solutions (Vasileiadou et al., 2015), and support sustainable investment strategies (Unruh et al., 2016).

Check on learning

- Describe in your own words the functional domains of the green economy. Thinking about connections between the functional domains, outline one or two strategies and instruments that sustainability professionals can use to encourage infrastructure changes.
- What is ecological modernization theory and how could it be used to explain sustainability transitions in countries like Brazil, India, and China?
- Outline a plan for developing and implementing a triple-bottom-line economic development strategy for your town or city. What actors would be involved? How would you, as a sustainability professional, convince those actors to participate, invest their funds, help mobilize resources, and develop capabilities that could contribute to triple-bottom-line economic development?
- Some jurisdictions including Ontario and Québec are able to generate more electricity than they can consume. They then export a substantial amount of low emission electricity to neighboring jurisdictions. Think about the sustainability implications both for the exporting and the importing regions. How do the economic, political, technological, and environmental barriers and benefits differ for the importers and the exporters?
- Review Québec's 16 principles to guide sustainable development actions. Which three of these principles do you believe are most important for encouraging a sustainability transition? Think about how you would design a set of integrated sub-principles to measure and track progress of these principles at the community level.

Assignments

- Conducting an environmental cost-benefit analysis in order to choose between sustainable transportation alternatives at the regional level
- Understanding competitive advantages in the green economy

References

Allen, J. H., & Potiowsky, T. (2008). Portland's green building cluster economic trends and impacts. *Economic Development Quarterly*, 22(4), 303–315.

American Electric Power. (2017). Wind Catcher Energy Connection Project. *American Electric Power*. Available at: www.aep.com/about/MajorBusinesses/PowerGeneration/WindCatcherProject.aspx

Apergis, N., Christou, C., & Gupta, R. (2017). Are there environmental Kuznets Curves for US state-level CO_2 emissions? *Renewable and Sustainable Energy Reviews*, 69, 551–558.

Arrow, K., B. Bolin, R. Costanza, P. Dasgupta, C. Folke, C. S. Holling, B.-O. Jansson, S. Levin, K.-G. Meller, C. Perrings, & D. Pimentel. (1995). Economic growth, carrying capacity and the environment. *Science*, 268, 520–521.

Atasoy, B. S. (2017). Testing the environmental Kuznets curve hypothesis across the US: Evidence from panel mean group estimators. *Renewable and Sustainable Energy Reviews*, 77, 731–747.

Austin Technology Incubator. (2017). About the Austin Technology Incubator. University of Texas at Austin and the IC^2 Institute. Available at: http://ati.utexas.edu/about-us/

AWEA. (2016). Wind energy facts at a glance. U.S. Wind Energy Statistics. Available at: www.awea.org/Resources/Content.aspx?ItemNumber=5059&navItemNumber=742

Bailey, I., & Caprotti, F. (2014). The green economy: Functional domains and theoretical directions of enquiry. *Environment and Planning A*, 46, 1797–1813.

Bakari, M. E. K. (2014). Sustainability's inner conflicts: From 'Ecologism' to 'Ecological Modernization'. *Journal of Sustainable Development Studies*, 6(1), 1–28.

Balta-Ozkan, N., Watson, T., & Mocca, E. (2015). Spatially uneven development and low carbon transitions: Insights from urban and regional planning. *Energy Policy*, 85, 500–510.

Belz, F. M., & Binder, J. K. (2017). Sustainable entrepreneurship: A convergent process model. *Business Strategy and the Environment*, 26(1), 1–17.

Bleys, B., & Whitby, A. (2015). Barriers and opportunities for alternative measures of economic welfare. *Ecological Economics*, 117(C), 162–172.

Bloomberg Philanthropies. (2017). From the ashes. Available at: www.fromtheashesfilm.com/; www.crowdrise.com/fromtheashesfilm

BLS. (2011). Green goods and services (GGS). Bureau of Labor Statistics. *United States Department of Labor*. Available at: www.bls.gov/ggs/

Boos, A. (2015). Genuine savings as an indicator for 'weak' sustainability: Critical survey and possible ways forward in practical measuring. *Sustainability*, 7(4), 4146–4182.

Bowen, W. M., Park, S., & Elvery, J. A. (2013). Empirical estimates of the influence of renewable energy portfolio standards on the green economies of states. *Economic Development Quarterly*, 27(4), 338–351.

Buttel, F. H. (2000). Ecological modernization as social theory. *Geoforum*, 31(1), 57–65.

Carley, S., Lawrence, S., Brown, A., Nourafshan, A., & Benami, E. (2011). Energy-based economic development. *Renewable and Sustainable Energy Reviews*, 15(1), 282–295.

Carley, S., Brown, A., & Lawrence, S. (2012). Economic development and energy from fad to a sustainable discipline? *Economic Development Quarterly*, 26(2), 111–123.

Castleberry, B., & Greene, J. S. (2017). Impacts of wind power development on Oklahoma's public schools. *Energy, Sustainability and Society*, 7(1), 34.

Ceschin, F., & Gaziulusoy, I. (2016). Evolution of design for sustainability: From product design to design for system innovations and transitions. *Design Studies*, 47, 118–163.

Chapple, K., Kroll, C., Lester, T. W., & Montero, S. (2011). Innovation in the green economy: An extension of the regional innovation system model? *Economic Development Quarterly*, 25(1), 5–25.

Clean Line. (2017). Clean Line projects. Clean Line Energy Partners. Available at: www.cleanlineenergy.com/projects

Ecotech Institute. (2016). Clean jobs index. Available at: www.ecotechinstitute.com/careers/clean-jobs-index.

EIA. (2017a). U.S. states state profiles and energy estimates. U.S. *Energy Information Administration*. Available at: www.eia.gov/state/maps.php?src=home-f3

EIA. (2017b). CO_2 emissions data. U.S. *Energy Information Administration*. Available at: www.eia.gov/environment/emissions/state/

EIA. (2017c). Population, energy demand, and GDP data. State Energy Data System. U.S. *Energy Information Administration*. Available at: www.eia.gov/state/seds/seds-data-complete.php?sid=US

Elliott, R. J., & Lindley, J. K. (2017). Environmental jobs and growth in the United States. *Ecological Economics*, 132, 232–244.

Energy Alberta. (2017). Renewable Electricity Program and energy transition plans. Available at: www.energy.alberta.ca/OurBusiness/Electricity.asp; www.alberta.ca/electricity-capacity-market.aspx

Environment and Climate Change Canada. (2017). GHG emissions by province and territory, Canada, 1990, 2005, 2014. Available at: www.ec.gc.ca/indicateurs-indicators/default.asp?lang=en&n=18F3BB9C-1

Fullerton, D., & Karney, D. H. (2018). Potential state-level carbon revenue under the Clean Power Plan. *Contemporary Economic Policy*, 36(1), 149–166.

Gallup. (2016). In the U.S., 75% now prioritize alternative energy over oil, gas. Available at: www.gallup.com/poll/190268/prioritize-alternative-energy-oil-gas.aspx?g_source=CATEGORY_ENVIRONMENT_AND_ENERGY&g_medium=topic&g_campaign=tiles

Garrett-Peltier, H. (2017). Green versus brown: Comparing the employment impacts of energy efficiency, renewable energy, and fossil fuels using an input-output model. *Economic Modelling*, 61, 439–447.

Gessesse, E., Grady, N., Whitehouse, K., Crowe, J., Delaney, L., Hanley, K., Marchyshyn, A., & McKeon, N. (2017). *Now Hiring: The Growth of America's Clean Energy and Sustainability Jobs*. Environmental Defense Fund. Climate Corps. Meister Consultants Group.

Gkatsou, S., Kounenou, M., Papanagiotou, P., Seremeti, D., & Georgakellos, D. (2014). The impact of green energy on employment: A preliminary analysis. *International Journal of Business and Social Science*, 5(1), 29–41.

Green Energy and Green Economy Act. (2015). Ontario Green Energy and Green Economy Act of 2009. Ministry of Energy. Available at: www.energy.gov.on.ca/en/green-energy-act/

Green, J., & Newman, P. (2017). Citizen utilities: The emerging power paradigm. *Energy Policy*, 105, 283–293.

Greene, J. S., & Geisken, M. (2013). Socioeconomic impacts of wind farm development: A case study of Weatherford, Oklahoma. *Energy, Sustainability and Society*, 3(1), 1–9.

Haley, B. (2015). Low-carbon innovation from a hydroelectric base: The case of electric vehicles in Québec. *Environmental Innovation and Societal Transitions*, 14, 5–25.

Hall, J. K., Daneke, G. A., & Lenox, M. J. (2010). Sustainable development and entrepreneurship: Past contributions and future directions. *Journal of Business Venturing*, 25(5), 439–448.

Hammer, J., & Pivo, G. (2017). The triple bottom line and sustainable economic development theory and practice. *Economic Development Quarterly*, 31(1), 25–36.

HB 2186. (2009). House Bill 2186. 75th Oregon Legislative Assembly. Available at: https://olis.leg.state.or.us/liz/2009R1/Downloads/MeasureDocument/HB2186/Enrolled

HB 3300. (2009). House Bill 3300. 75th Oregon Legislative Assembly. Available at: https://olis.leg.state.or.us/liz/2009R1/Downloads/MeasureDocument/HB3300

Hess, D. (2012). *Good Green Jobs in a Global Economy*. MIT Press, Cambridge, MA.

Hydro-Québec. (2015). Sustainable Development Plan for Climate Change Mitigation. Available at: www.hydroquebec.com/sustainable-development/; www.hydroquebec.com/publications/en/corporate-documents/sustainable-development-action-plan.html

Inglesi-Lotz, R. (2016). The impact of renewable energy consumption to economic growth: A panel data application. *Energy Economics*, 53, 58–63.

John, D. (2008). Opportunities for economic and community development in energy and climate change. *Economic Development Quarterly*, 22(2), 107–111.

Jung, Y. M. (2015). Is South Korea's green job policy sustainable? *Sustainability*, 7(7), 8748–8767.

Kubiszewski, I., Costanza, R., Gorko, N. E., Weisdorf, M. A., Carnes, A. W., Collins, C. E., . . . & Schoepfer, J. D. (2015). Estimates of the Genuine Progress Indicator (GPI) for Oregon from 1960–2010 and recommendations for a comprehensive shareholder's report. *Ecological Economics*, 119, 1–7.

Lamy, J. V., Jaramillo, P., Azevedo, I. L., & Wiser, R. (2016). Should we build wind farms close to load or invest in transmission to access better wind resources in remote areas? A case study in the MISO region. *Energy Policy*, 96, 341–350.

Lawn, P. A. (2005). An assessment of the valuation methods used to calculate the index of sustainable economic welfare (ISEW), genuine progress indicator (GPI), and sustainable net benefit index (SNBI). *Environment, Development and Sustainability*, 7(2), 185–208.

Lazard. (2016). Growing percentage of U.S. *voters favor increased commitment to alternative energy*. Available at: www.lazard.com/media/2489/2016-alternative-energy-poll-release.pdf.

Lee, T. (2017). The effect of clean energy regulations and incentives on green jobs: panel analysis of the United States, 1998–2007. *Natural Resources Forum*, 41(3), 145–155.

Leiserowitz, A., Maibach, E., Roser-Renouf, C., Rosenthal, S., & Cutler, M. (2016). Politics & global warming, November 2016. Yale University and George Mason University. New Haven, CT: Yale Program on Climate Change Communication. Available at: http://climatecommunication.yale.edu/publications/politics-global-warming-november-2016/2/

Leland, S. M., Read, D. C., & Wittry, M. (2015). Analyzing the perceived benefits of LEED-certified and Energy Star-certified buildings in the realm of local economic development. *Economic Development Quarterly*, 29(4), 363–375.

McLean, M. L., & Voytek, K. P. (1992). *Understanding Your Economy: Using Analysis to Guide Local Strategic Planning*. Planners Press American Planning Association, Chicago, IL.

Morrow, A., and Keenan, G. (2016). Ontario to spend $7-billion on sweeping climate change plan. Available at: www.theglobeandmail.com/news/national/ontario-to-spend-7-billion-in-sweeping-climate-change-plan/article30029081/?click=sf_globefb

Mullaney, T. (2015). Elon Musk's biggest challenge yet: Recharging Buffalo, NY. *SolarCity's new factory is linchpin of a $1 billion plan to bring back a third of Nickel City's lost manufacturing jobs*. Available at: www.cnbc.com/2015/06/11/elon-musks-biggest-challenge-yet-recharging-buffalo-ny.html

Muro, M., Rothwell, J., & Saha, D. (2011). Sizing the clean economy: A national and regional jobs assessment. The Brookings Institution. Metropolitan Policy Program. *Battelle Technology Partnership Practice*. Available at: www.brookings.edu/wp-content/uploads/2016/06/0713_clean_economy.pdf

Obama, B. (2017). The irreversible momentum of clean energy. *Science*, 355(6321), 126–129.

Ontario Society of Professional Engineers. (2017). Society notes. *Ontario lost more than $500 million exporting clean energy* in 2016. Available at: https://blog.ospe.on.ca/advocacy/ontario-lost-500-million-exporting-clean-energy-2016/

Oregon. (2017). Electricity mix in Oregon. Oregon.*gov*. Available at: www.oregon.gov/energy/energy-oregon/pages/electricity-mix-in-oregon.aspx

Oregon. (2018). Renewable portfolio standard. *Oregon Department of Energy*. Available at: www.oregon.gov/energy/energy-oregon/Pages/Renewable-Portfolio-Standard.aspx.

Panayotou, T. (1997). Demystifying the environmental Kuznets curve: Turning a black box into a policy tool. *Environment and Development Economics*, 2(04), 465–484.

Pender, J. L., Weber, J. G., & Brown, J. P. (2014). Sustainable rural development and wealth creation five observations based on emerging energy opportunities. *Economic Development Quarterly*, 28(1), 73–86.

Pittis, D. (2017). Radically new Alberta auction system will play a part in disrupting the global energy market. *CBC news*. Available at: www.cbc.ca/news/business/electricity-prices-markets-auction-alberta-1.4417616

Posner, S. M., & Costanza, R. (2011). A summary of ISEW and GPI studies at multiple scales and new estimates for Baltimore City, Baltimore County, and the State of Maryland. *Ecological Economics*, 70(11), 1972–1980.

Québec Sustainable Development Act. (2017). The Sustainable Development Act. Available at: www.mddelcc.gouv.qc.ca/developpement/loi_en.htm

Renew Oregon. (2016). Greenhouse gas emission reductions resulting from the clean energy and coal transition plan. Available at: www.reneworegon.org/pollution_reductions_from_clean_electricity_and_coal_transition_plan

SB 1547. (2016). Oregon Clean Electricity and Coal Transition Act. Senate Bill 1547. 78th Oregon Legislative Assembly. Available at: https://olis.leg.state.or.us/liz/2016R1/Downloads/MeasureDocument/SB1547/Enrolled

Schaltegger, S., & Wagner, M. (2011). Sustainable entrepreneurship and sustainability innovation: Categories and interactions. *Business Strategy and the Environment*, 20(4), 222–237.

Schulz, S. A., & Flanigan, R. L. (2016). Developing competitive advantage using the triple bottom line: A conceptual framework. *Journal of Business & Industrial Marketing*, 31(4), 449–458.

SEIA. (2016). Solar Energy Industries Association. U.S. Solar Market Insight. Available at: www.seia.org/research-resources/us-solar-market-insight.

SEIA. (2017). Solar industry data: Top 10 solar states. *Solar Energy Industries Association*. Available at: www.seia.org/research-resources/top-10-solar-states; www.seia.org/solar-industry-data

Sikorski, J. J., Haughton, J., & Kraft, M. (2017). Blockchain technology in the chemical industry: Machine-to-machine electricity market. *Applied Energy*, 195, 234–246.

Slayton, R., & Spinardi, G. (2016). Radical innovation in scaling up: Boeing's Dreamliner and the challenge of socio-technical transitions. *Technovation*, 47, 47–58.

Sooriyaarachchi, T. M., Tsai, I. T., El Khatib, S., Farid, A. M., & Mezher, T. (2015). Job creation potentials and skill requirements in, PV, CSP, wind, water-to-energy and energy efficiency value chains. *Renewable and Sustainable Energy Reviews*, 52, 653–668.

Statistics Canada. (2017). Environmental and clean technology products economic account, 2007–2016. Statistics Canada Daily Report. Available at: www.statcan.gc.ca/daily-quotidien/171213/dq171213g-eng.htm

Stern, D. I. (2004). The rise and fall of the environmental Kuznets curve. *World Development*, 32(8), 1419–1439.

Thompson, S., Carvalho, E., & Marr, S. (2009). Competitive analysis of industries in the City of Port Colborne, Ontario. *Port Colborne Economic & Tourism Development Corporation*. Available at: http://portcolborne.ca/fileBin/library/Competitive%20Analysis%20of%20Industries%20in%20Port%20Colborne.pdf

Unruh, G., Kiron, D., Kruschwitz, N., Reeves, M., Rubel, H., & Zum Felde, A. M. (2016). Investing for a sustainable future: Investors care more about sustainability than many executives believe. *MIT Sloan Management Review*, 57(4), 1–32.

Vasileiadou, E., Huijben, J. C. C. M., & Raven, R. P. J. M. (2016). Three is a crowd? Exploring the potential of crowdfunding for renewable energy in the Netherlands. *Journal of Cleaner Production*, 128, 142–155.

Wei, M., Patadia, S., & Kammen, D. M. (2010). Putting renewable and energy efficiency to work: How many jobs can the clean energy industry generate in the US? *Energy Policy*, 38, 919–931.

World Bank. (2017). DataBank World Development Indicators. Available at: http://databank.worldbank.org/data/reports.aspx?source=world-development-indicators&preview=on#

WTO. (2017). Canada: Certain measures affecting the renewable energy generation sector. Available at: www.wto.org/english/tratop_e/dispu_e/cases_e/ds412_e.htm

Wu, S., & Heberling, M. T. (2016). Estimating green net national product for Puerto Rico: An economic measure of sustainability. *Environmental Management, 57*(4), 822–835.

York, R., & Rosa, E. A. (2003). Key challenges to ecological modernization theory: Institutional efficacy, case study evidence, units of analysis, and the pace of eco-efficiency. *Organization & Environment, 16*(3), 273–288.

6 Intermediaries for sustainability transitions

Learning objectives

- Introduce sustainability-oriented intermediaries as key actors in sustainability transitions
- Discuss processes of interaction between intermediaries and niche and regime actors
- Compare different types of sustainability-oriented intermediaries
- Critique and outline the roles and functions of sustainability-oriented innovation intermediaries

Theories of sustainability intermediaries

Specific types of actors that connect niches and regimes include champions, intermediaries, and policy entrepreneurs. *Environmental champions* link sustainable behavior to organizational level changes. *Intermediaries* carry out important functions for changing institutions and infrastructures including analyzing, filtering, and transferring knowledge between actors as well as building collaborations between organizations via networks and partnerships. *Innovation intermediaries* help connect individual entrepreneurs and organizational decisions to broader green innovation and economic development processes. *Policy entrepreneurs* help amplify green innovation systems into triple-bottom-line economic development strategies through their ability to link policy solutions to problems at key times during windows of opportunity. Sustainability professionals can be champions or policy entrepreneurs. Sustainability professionals can also create, work within, or engage with intermediaries as a means of accelerating sustainability transitions.

Environmental champions linking sustainable behavior to organizational strategy

Environmental champions are individuals who work within an organization (business, non-profit, government) in any role or capacity (e.g., management, office staff, director of sustainability) (Gliedt and Parker, 2010). They first identify a problem that is personally important to them that may relate to something they observed in the operations of the organization (e.g., waste management practices, energy use). They can also identify an issue that does not relate directly to the operations of the organization (e.g., climate change) but for which they believe the organization could make a difference though changing strategies or processes. The champion researches potential solutions that were implemented within other similar organizations. They then present a business plan to organizational leadership that incorporates and explains the economic, social, and environmental benefits of the solution. This could take the form of *sustainability value creation* strategies encompassing multiple dimensions of the organization (Chapter 3), or it could focus on innovation strategies in combination with other actors within technological innovation systems (Chapter 4) designed to create products, services, or programs for sale or delivery to markets. Another important technique of champions is to gather support for their solution from key members of the organization who may hold positions of authority or positions of direct influence on the ability to make the changes desired by the champion (Andersson and Bateman, 2000; Gattiker and Carter, 2010). Timing is important because the chances of successful championship events increase if the solution is implemented during a time when the organization could most benefit (e.g., investing in solar panels prior to rolling out a new green product line to coordinate the messaging and maximize the public relations benefits), or a time when the barriers to making the change are lowest (e.g., when the electricity contract is up for renewal) (Juravle and Lewis, 2009; Wichmann et al., 2015).

Environmental champions play a critical role at linking sustainable behavior (e.g., their individual preferences for making sustainability changes) to organizational sustainability changes. Their values, personality, drive, knowledge, and in some cases past experiences with sustainability decisions are drawn upon to instigate organizational changes that have the potential to magnify the impact of the original idea or behavior. Environmental champions may emerge on their own (Gliedt et al., 2010), can be created by the organization with help of incentives (e.g., rewards for green new programs or products created), or may be appointed as leaders of green teams that are tasked with creating win–win–win solutions to economic–social–environmental problems that the organization faces (Swaffield and Bell, 2012). Champions themselves can act as intermediaries (Martiskainen and Kivimaa, 2017), and can use structures (e.g., environmental committees) or linking agents (e.g., sustainability manager or senior corporate social responsibility officer) in the process of gathering support for their solution (Gliedt and Parker, 2010). It is important to engage senior managers as sustainability godparents (Exter, 2013) who provide mentoring, institutional memory, structural support, and symbolic support to the champions' initiative. Acceleration Point: Organizations can encourage/incentivize environmental champions as a way to create sustainability value by supporting changes to programs, products, structures, partnerships, or services, which in turn, help to influence or accelerate sustainability improvements in the broader community.

Champions can play important roles and use key strategies to link organizations to innovation intermediaries (Gliedt et al., 2018). They identify problems and potential solutions through their own research independent of the organization. Champions can then gather support for new strategies to solve those problems by building coalitions of individuals within a sustainability-oriented start-up, or between the intermediary organization and other actors within a cluster or network. Champions are able to frame issues as important or timely and use selling techniques to convince key decision-makers to implement their strategy (Galvin and Terry, 2016). Individual champions within intermediaries are able to help influence radical sustainability innovations (Küçüksayraç et al., 2015). Acceleration Point: Champions within intermediaries use **anticipatory competence** to identify windows of opportunity when they can apply **strategic** and **interpersonal relations competence** to align green innovation processes from technology entrepreneurs with triple-bottom-line economic development strategies and supportive policy mixes at the regime level.

Sustainability-oriented innovation intermediaries

Sustainability-oriented innovation intermediaries are defined as organizations that influence, facilitate, support, or drive the creation and diffusion of new technologies, products, or services that have the potential to shift or accelerate changes to socio-technical systems. Sustainability-oriented innovation intermediaries include *incubator and accelerator centers* and university research parks that help entrepreneurs understand and implement sustainability value creation as a strategy for business and technology creation and development (Gliedt et al., 2018). The goal of sustainability-oriented innovation intermediaries is to contribute to triple-bottom-line economic development (Chapter 5) by incorporating sustainability principles into entrepreneurship processes as a means of shaping pathways of innovation towards strong sustainability. These intermediaries aim to change the conditions in the regime subsystems to support the scaling of niche experiments to influence technology and infrastructure changes.

Sustainability-oriented innovation intermediaries build networks during times of political or institutional instability and draw upon or develop relationships with entrepreneurs, businesses, and researchers (Gliedt et al., 2018). They can help outline technology innovation pathways related to strong sustainability principles, minimize risks through developing capabilities that allow for adaptive strategies in clusters, provide niche protection (Chapter 7) through financial, human, and other resources, and link entrepreneurs to markets for their products or services. Sustainability professionals working within innovation intermediaries can use their *sustainability competencies* to develop scenarios, anticipate alternative outcomes of ongoing changes in regime subsystems, and understand the connections between niche processes and regime changes. **Interpersonal relations competence** (Chapter 1) is critical for working with many different actors from entrepreneurs to government and industry leadership.

Recent studies highlight the roles and functions of sustainability-oriented innovation intermediaries (Bush et al., 2017; Hannon et al., 2014; Hargreaves et al., 2013; Kivimaa, 2014; Kivimaa et al., 2017; Methner et al., 2015; Nilsson and Sia-Ljungström, 2013; Nolden et al., 2016). They can work to convince small businesses and entrepreneurs to use triple-bottom-line criteria and help entrepreneurs connect to external actors who have sustainability skills and competencies (Kanda et al., 2014). Intermediaries can scan for sustainability related ideas that researchers are developing within university laboratories or research and technology parks. They can help start-ups prototype, test, and commercialize green technology (Kanda et al., 2015). In some cases, they may select certain entrepreneurs over others to enter the incubator based on the extent that their product or technology relates to key sustainability areas including sustainable IT, green building, solar and wind energy, energy storage, energy efficiency, or smart grids (Bank and Kanda, 2016).

Sustainability-oriented innovation intermediaries can help integrate sustainability into different functions and services that support innovation as well as into the business plans of the entrepreneurs (Kivimaa et al., 2017). Intermediaries use sustainability metrics and decision-making tools like lifecycle analysis to evaluate proposals for new green technologies. They can then require that current or potential tenants of the incubator or accelerator center perform well against a set of sustainability criteria and sustainability performance levels in order to continue receiving support services (Abbate and Coppolino, 2012). Staff within intermediaries can measure or anticipate the sustainability performance of niche experiments including the potential impact of new technologies on behavior and infrastructure change in socio-technical systems (Antikainen et al., 2017).

Incubators, accelerators, and sustainability principles

Incubators help entrepreneurs turn ideas into innovations and then into businesses. They are often created as public–private partnerships between municipalities, universities, chambers of commerce, and other business networks to provide mentoring and guidance, technical and legal assistance for seeking intellectual property protections and negotiating contracts, marketing and accounting services, networking and partnership building, as well as access to seed funding and angel investors. Incubators provide office space and materials at low or no cost, and can help entrepreneurs build networks with investors and other stakeholders to reduce transaction costs for developing their business. Incubators help to screen ideas, analyze potential growth, develop business plans, and create growth strategies for graduating out of the incubator and into their own office space or into accelerator centers.

Accelerator centers accept graduates from incubators that are ready to scale rapidly within domestic markets or through global networks because they have a dynamic leader, an innovative technology, or a sound business strategy. Accelerator centers provide many of the same services as incubators, but are focused on protecting small and rapidly growing businesses from market forces while they scale. Accelerator centers may also tailor specific programs to university students at the early stages of business creation, or to postgraduates who have already left the accelerator but continue to benefit from mentoring services. Accelerator centers also incentivize entrepreneurship by awarding seed funding, access to market research, and connections to investors to the winners of competitions (Waterloo Accelerator, 2016). Incubator and accelerator centers are increasingly focused on clean technology start-ups that have the potential for triple-bottom-line economic development benefits. The centers themselves also lead to thousands of direct and indirect jobs and hundreds of millions of dollars of raised capital and local economic impacts (New York Incubator, 2016).

Blankenship et al. (2009) examined a business incubator in Sweden that integrated strategic sustainable development principles into the process of entrepreneurship. They found that integrating sustainability into the incubator can provide value to the entrepreneurs and to their start-ups. The incubator staff questioned prospective entrepreneurs at the early stages of business development regarding sustainability principles. The entrepreneurs shifted their sustainability views from cost minimization to analyzing ways of integrating sustainability principles into all dimensions of operations (triple-bottom-line), selecting or creating business solutions that generate sustainability benefits, incorporating environmental dimensions in marketing and public relations, and meeting environmental regulatory requirements. The entrepreneurs began to view sustainability and business development as integrated, introducing strategic sustainability initiatives including (Blankenship et al., 2009, p. 258):

- eco-labelling of their products,
- conducting market analysis of sustainability demands by consumers,
- creating sustainability requirements for their suppliers,
- developing a service based model for one of their current products to reduce the environmental impacts and expand the scope of product delivery,
- fostering a partnership for research with a university, and
- incorporating human and social dimensions into business planning.

As part of the incubation process, incubator staff incorporated sustainability into the screening stage (e.g., add value to the start-ups), the analysis stage (e.g., show examples of opportunities where sustainability enhanced business performance), the business development stage (e.g., a key intervention point when business leaders choose partners, investors, and market opportunities where sustainability could be a strategic advantage), and the growth stage (e.g., bring graduates of the incubator back to teach sustainability as a competitive advantage) (Blankenship et al., 2009). Further research is needed to examine how the connections between *niche actors* (e.g., green champions and entrepreneurs), *regime actors* (e.g., policy entrepreneurs), and *innovation intermediaries* (e.g., incubator and accelerator centers) can help accelerate triple-bottom-line economic development (Gliedt et al., 2018).

Linking niche to regime

The functions of sustainability-oriented innovation intermediaries are critical for helping niche actors including entrepreneurs and champions transform innovation processes into green job creation and triple-bottom-line economic development benefits (Gliedt et al., 2018). For example, intermediaries are able to outline sustainability pathways including the role of technology to help entrepreneurs see the bigger picture impacts of their work (Kivimaa, 2014). Intermediaries can use **strategic** and **anticipatory competence** to provide niche protection (Barrie et al., 2017) and niche empowerment (Bush et al., 2017) as outlined in Chapter 7. Intermediaries can use **integrated sustainability research and problem-solving competence** to help develop internal resources and capabilities to support sustainability-focused innovation (Klewitz et al., 2012). One of the main functions of sustainability-oriented innovation intermediaries is to help lower transaction costs so that green technologies and services can become more competitive and scale-up to gain broader diffusion throughout the socio-technical system (Nolden et al., 2016).

Sustainability-oriented innovation intermediaries use **interpersonal relations competence** to connect entrepreneurs with external knowledge and resources (Klewitz et al., 2012) including programs offering subsidies, grants, tax credits, angel investors, or venture capital (Polzin et al., 2016). Intermediaries can act as champions to help entrepreneurs make connections to firms and other actors through networks and transition arenas to scale niche experiments (Klerkx and Aarts, 2013). This includes strategic partnerships with industry and universities as well as connections between other intermediaries that focus on green technology through national or international networks (Hannon et al., 2014). Intermediaries can help prospective green entrepreneurs break into regime subsystems by transferring knowledge and technologies and managing the innovation process (Küçüksayraç et al., 2015). Intermediaries can also use their **interpersonal relations competence** to turn conflicts between entrepreneurs into a means of encouraging research and development (Agogué et al., 2017).

Linking regime to niche

The magnitude of success of sustainability-oriented innovation intermediaries depends in part on changing the institutional regime to create a more favorable policy mix for green innovation and triple-bottom-line economic development. Regime actors including policy entrepreneurs can help innovation intermediaries create the conditions for niche experiments to develop into green technologies and diffuse into green job creation strategies. Intermediaries facilitate regime changes that can make it more likely for niche experiments to scale-up and change the regime (Bush et al., 2017). Staff within intermediaries can brand the green technology sector and clusters (Kanda et al., 2015) in order to convince regime actors to invest in green technology innovation and business development as a triple-bottom-line economic development strategy (Chapter 5).

Mattes et al. (2015) described an *intermediary subsystem* that includes labor unions, chambers of commerce, networks of actors, and enabling organizations. This intermediary subsystem fostered connections between the other regime subsystems (Chapter 7) to accelerate niche experiments and regime changes. Intermediaries are able to influence changes to the regime to reduce barriers to green innovation by entrepreneurs including by supporting science, technology, and innovation policy, and by developing strategic partnerships and mobilizing private finance from banks (Polzin et al., 2016). Intermediaries can act as gatekeepers within the regime to enable innovation networks and transfer knowledge about green innovation processes between different clusters (McLennan et al., 2016). One type of regime actor who can link the regime to the niche are policy entrepreneurs.

Policy entrepreneurs for regime change

Kingdon's (1984) policy streams approach helps understand how actors are linked to institutions and how policies can be changed during times of uncertainty. A problem stream, a policy stream, and a politics stream are constantly flowing in a 'soup' of potential that is waiting to be aligned at key times by policy entrepreneurs. The **problem stream** involves recognizing an issue, framing it in a way that necessitates change, and using focusing events to highlight the impacts for society. The **policy stream** recognizes that many ideas are circulating amongst civil servants, which policy entrepreneurs could bring to the agenda and shape as solutions to one or more of the problems flowing in the problem stream. *Policy entrepreneurs* are defined as elected or non-elected government or governance actors who "try to effect change" and who "use their agency to do so" by "using the resources and strategies available to them to achieve their desired outcome" (Green, 2017, p. 1473). The **politics stream** is the current political landscape, which is shaped by power dynamics, elections, legislation, administrations, social economy groups, and public sentiment. The politics stream influences and constrains the types of policy solutions that may be feasible. Sustainability professionals can help policy entrepreneurs figure out how the problem, policy, and politics streams can come into alignment during a window of opportunity when the regime subsystems are vulnerable to new sociotechnical solutions.

Policy entrepreneurs can play specific roles when it comes to regime subsystems. The roles include identifying problems, searching for solutions, matching problems with solutions, and navigating the political subsystems in order to reduce barriers for innovation intermediaries. Policy entrepreneurs can support niche and regime changes by drawing upon political connections, encouraging a policy mix for regime change and for niche creation, and providing coherence during political transitions (Gliedt et al., 2018). Acceleration Point: Policy entrepreneurs can be sustainability professionals if they work to create sustainability policies from within a regime while mobilizing support for infrastructure funding bills and innovation support instruments as a means of driving sustainability transitions. Sustainability professionals can also help identify potential policy entrepreneurs as well as the connections between them and other actors including entrepreneurs, champions, and innovation intermediaries.

Policy entrepreneurs are critical to changing institutional frameworks and developing policy mixes to support green innovation. Huitema and Meijerink (2010) outlined various techniques used by policy entrepreneurs to foster water system transitions, which include creating new ideas, building coalitions, selling ideas to decision-makers, and recognizing and capitalizing on windows of opportunity. Policy entrepreneurs successfully used persuasive framing techniques to instigate a biofuels policy creation process (Palmer, 2015). This involved linking the problem (e.g., greenhouse gas emissions and climate change) with a solution, which in this case was a biofuels policy. The policy entrepreneur connected across boundaries to defend the policy once it was enacted. Palmer (2015) suggested that persuasive framing may help open new policy windows at key times of uncertainty prior to new policy agendas becoming locked-in. Limitations of policy entrepreneurs were also identified, including that framing and boundary spanning techniques were not effective for the politics stream, and that in some cases, policy entrepreneurs were able to prevent change by using their boundary position to slow or undermine a potential new policy (Palmer, 2015). Sustainability professionals as boundary spanners can develop boundary chains to link the government's environmental institutions to municipal and state actors to encourage sustainability ideas and solutions.

Boundary spanners and boundary chains

Based on Williams (2002) and Berardo and Scholz (2010), Edelenbos and van Meerkerk (2015) defined boundary spanners as "organizational members who are able to link the organization they represent with its environment" (p. 27). This can include linking science and policy makers, or linking niche and regime levels. For example, boundary spanner organizations (e.g., between science and policy makers) act as knowledge sources and brokers and support policy entrepreneurs (Kalafatis et al., 2015). Knowledge sources and brokers can have direct impacts on policy creation by helping link the problem with solutions, and indirect impacts by changing ideas flowing within the policy subsystems of the regime. Alternatively, Smink et al. (2015) outlined boundary spanners who linked the biomethane niche to the natural gas regime in the Netherlands. The boundary spanners conducted various activities including convening, translation of information, facilitating collaboration, and mediation between actors at different levels in the energy system. Boundary spanners can link large-scale energy system actors with small-scale energy projects. Smink et al. (2015) also identified *intra-organizational boundary shaking*, which occurs when champions attempt to gain support for an initiative from others within the organization by disrupting strategies, structures, or plans.

Kalafatis et al. (2015) described boundary chains as partnerships or networks that translate and present climate science for practical consumption in municipal departments. Examples given of boundary chains were the National Oceanic and Atmospheric Association's (NOAA) Regional Integrated Sciences and Assessment (RISA) program in the United States (see Lemos et al., 2014) and Climate Proof Cities in the Netherlands (see Albers et al., 2015). Boundary chains are important for linking climate and sustainability problems and solutions across governance scales. They can help transfer information and funding in the form of grants to cities or universities. Boundary chains can be leveraged by policy entrepreneurs at the state and city level to gain support for local initiatives. They are particularly important for making changes in energy and water systems, which involve connections between technology, infrastructure, and institutional actors.

Boundary spanners in water governance: The Netherlands

Water systems are fragmented into various institutional and organizational roles and responsibilities ranging from water supply and demand management, to water quality and health concerns, to technology innovation and policy creation. Van Meerkerk et al. (2015) and Edelenbos and van Meerkerk (2015) described the case of water governance in the Netherlands and the role of boundary spanners in creating and using connective capacity for multi-level water system changes. This involved boundary spanners creating conditions for interactions and trust between the actors in the water system. To achieve sustainable outcomes, boundary spanners fostered "the inclusion of relevant and affected actors, the willingness of the participants to exchange or pool resources, and the development of common conceptions of problems, solutions, and decision-making premises" (Edelenbos and van Meerkerk, 2015, p. 27). They also argued that boundary spanners "play a key translating and bridging role between informal networks on the one hand and formal decision-making structures and policy processes on the other hand" (p. 27). Boundary spanners create a space for interaction across levels and scales, and play a critical role in linking science to policy making and implementation (Kalafatis et al., 2015). Success of boundary spanning may depend on the organization type with private and social economy organizations found in one study to be more likely to foster boundary spanners than government organizations (van Meerkerk and Edelenbos, 2014). Governments may invest in additional structures within the government hierarchy (van Meerkerk and Edelenbos, 2014) rather than develop boundary organizations that connect to the private sector or to higher/lower levels of government.

Practice of sustainability intermediaries

Sustainability professionals can be champions, policy entrepreneurs, or boundary spanners, or alternatively, they can work with those individuals and organizations to drive and support changes in niches and regimes. Networks of sustainability professionals can therefore contribute to socio-technical system change when centered around intermediaries as linking and amplifying agents. The multi-level perspective (MLP) framework relies upon mechanisms for facilitating cross-level flows of knowledge, experience, financial capital, behavior and practices, technology applications, and policy changes. An important capability for sustainability professionals is to understand these flows and connections between ongoing innovation and policy change processes to enable cross-level interactions between niche and regime actors. Sustainability-oriented intermediaries carry out functions and equip sustainability professionals with tools and competencies to support the creation and implementation of strategies and instruments that guide pathways connecting innovation and policy change processes towards sustainability principles. The following case studies highlight the roles, functions, and impacts of sustainability intermediaries within energy system transitions.

Case study: Clean technology intermediaries in the United Kingdom

One well-known clean technology intermediary in the United Kingdom is Cambridge Cleantech, which is a non-profit intermediary organization focused on promoting

Cambridge as a clean technology cluster, supporting business development and value creation opportunities in clean technology, and facilitating networks of government, university, and private sector actors involved in clean technology (Cambridge Cleantech, 2017). This intermediary has identified and supported more than 500 clean technology entrepreneurs located in the area, which focus on research, development, and manufacturing of green energy technologies (wind, solar, wave, tidal, biomass, geothermal), alternative fuels, sustainability transportation technologies, recovery and recycling processes, automated energy and waste management systems, energy transmission and grids, carbon finance, sustainable building technologies, information and communication technologies related to clean tech, air pollution reduction technologies, and water supply and waste water treatment systems. Cambridge Cleantech developed an action plan to guide triple-bottom-line economic development strategies in the region. This multi-stage approach included setting a vision, outlining a set of breakthrough objectives, identifying key themes to pursue the objectives, defining an action plan to carry out each of the objectives, identifying a champion for each action plan, creating a set of outcome metrics and key milestone dates to measure progress towards the objectives, and linking the action plans to budgets to be developed by each champion. Example themes around which green innovation and triple-bottom-line economic development processes would coalesce included early stage financing, development, and commercialization; accelerated prototyping; sustainability; strategic alliances; showcase capabilities; and leadership. Each theme can guide niche and regime strategies and instruments related to idea creation, proof of concept, scaling, business development and supporting infrastructure, and political influence and lobbying.

Hannon et al. (2014), Bush et al. (2017), and Nolden et al. (2016) analyzed other cases of sustainability-oriented energy intermediaries in the United Kingdom. Hannon et al. (2014) identified different types of intermediaries operating at different levels within the *socio-technical system*. **Systemic intermediaries** helped coordinate activities of multiple niche actors and carry out the technological innovation system functions described in Chapter 4. A **super-intermediary** operated at the regime level and coordinated activities of multiple systemic intermediaries at and between niches. Two systemic intermediaries were the Research Councils and the Technology Strategy Board, while the super-intermediary was the Low Carbon Innovation and Coordination Group. The Research Councils identified research and training needs, fostered national and international networks and partnerships, developed capacity for energy innovation, and disseminated knowledge through various subprograms. The Technology Strategy Board developed numerous strategies for networking and knowledge dissemination including collaborative research and development projects, innovation vouchers, small business research initiatives, accelerator (catapult) centers, and annual innovation conferences. The accelerator centers focused on offshore renewable energy, future cities, transport systems, and the digital economy, with a fifth accelerator center in the works to address energy system innovation. The Board also helped coordinate research grant proposals with other innovation related agencies. The Low Carbon Innovation and Coordination Group acted as an overarching governance intermediary that facilitated communication and collaboration between leaders of the niche level intermediaries. It conducted and disseminated research to help identify strengths, weaknesses, opportunities, and threats in the innovation system, which informed the creation of a strategic framework for energy innovation in the United Kingdom. Hannon et al. (2014) concluded that intermediaries often developed as a reaction to bottlenecks in the innovation system, rather than as a proactive strategy to create innovations.

Bush et al. (2017) used a decision theater approach similar to the one outlined in Chapter 3 to examine the roles and functions of municipal and national intermediaries at empowering a niche focused on district heating in the United Kingdom. The decision theatre allowed for participatory action research by simultaneously studying and enabling interactions between niche and regime actors involved in the innovation process. District heating was being introduced as a means of decentralizing low carbon energy innovation, which required numerous technology, infrastructure, and institutional changes. The national intermediary developed networks and partnerships and facilitated knowledge diffusion. It also interacted with and provided capacity to municipal intermediaries. The municipal intermediaries aided in "persuading local stakeholders of the value of district heating, and building the social networks required to deliver projects" (p. 143). Municipal intermediary activities included building teams of experts needed for the transition such as planners, cartographers, lawyers, financers, energy managers, community energy groups, and private district heating companies. Bush et al. (2017) found that intermediaries at the municipal and national level were able to support the restructuring of the regime to make it more likely that radical innovations could expand.

Nolden et al. (2016) analyzed the energy service contracting market in the United Kingdom and found that intermediaries provided "a legal framework for establishing contracts" as well as "an organizational framework that facilitates contract negation and execution" (p. 420). Intermediaries facilitated transactions between clients and energy service companies. Energy service companies deliver and guarantee energy savings to clients as a return-on-investment that is protected by a contract. Energy service contracts help to encourage innovation as part of sustainable niche experiments "by specifying outputs (e.g., energy savings) rather than inputs (e.g., specific technologies)" (p. 420), which rewards contractors who are able to design energy management programs including technology and automation that achieve the greatest energy savings for the lowest price. Nolden et al. (2016) discovered that these public-sector intermediaries "can encourage learning from one contract to another, increase trust between the relevant parties and reduce the costs faced by both the client and contractor in establishing and executing the contract" (p. 424). Sustainability professionals can design energy service contracts in a way to encourage more radical niche experiments requiring different risk–reward assessment frameworks.

Champions as intermediaries for zero carbon homes

Different types of intermediaries and champions work together to encourage sustainability improvements to buildings in the United Kingdom (Martiskainen and Kivimaa, 2017). Some champions are also intermediaries because they carry out networking and connecting functions in addition to being agents for change. With respect to zero carbon buildings, *non-championing intermediaries* facilitated learning through education, advice, knowledge sharing, and creating spaces for new ideas, while using networking skills to mobilize resources and connect different project actors. *Championing intermediaries* have a personal interest in green buildings and sustainability principles and worked to actualize their views through pilot projects, lobbying for policy and industry changes, or helping create new zero carbon building standards. They also facilitated learning and networking to support zero carbon building experiments. These individuals can be considered **process champions**.

Non-intermediary champions worked to advance their personal vision for zero carbon building technologies and sustainability principles, but did not use networking as a strategy (Martiskainen and Kivimaa, 2017). They were advocates or creators of new technologies/applications (considered **technology champions**) or sponsors of other actors by smoothing a pathway and helping remove barriers for their initiatives (considered **power champions**). While intermediaries and champions are both examples of sustainability professionals (Chapter 11), championing intermediaries represent a new type of actor that requires further examination within ongoing sustainability transition processes.

Case study: Local energy development and sustainability transitions in Germany

Mattes et al. (2015) compared two places in Germany (Emden and Bottrop) undergoing local transitions partially guided by the German *Energiewende* (energy transition plan). For an overview of challenges facing the *Energiewende*, see *The Economist* (2012). Mattes et al. (2015) concluded that local energy transitions are "complex, multidimensional change processes involving a variety of stakeholders from different subsystems" (p. 261) of the regime. Some processes may be deliberately instigated (like in the case of Bottrop) while others emerged without initial planning (as was the case in Emden). The interactions between the subsystems of the regime were informal in both cases, drawing upon personal networks and contacts. Formal communication mechanisms were also used in Bottrop with committees/roundtables focusing on making energy transition processes more frequent. An intermediary organization was created in Bottrop specifically to facilitate coordination between the actors of the other subsystems of the regime. Increasing levels of coordination occurred in both cases over time as more actors became involved in the transition. The two towns are summarized from Mattes et al. (2015) below:

Emden:

- Population: 50,000.
- Location: northwest Germany within a region with broad support for renewable energy.
- Economy: historically shipbuilding but transitioned to wind manufacturing businesses.
- Energy system context: 1987: municipal utility installed windmill; 1990: first wind farm; 2008: joined the Climate Alliance, set climate targets for 10 percent CO_2 reduction every five years and 50 percent by 2030 below 1990 levels.
- Political subsystem: policy makers used business attraction strategies for wind manufacturers; ex-mayor was a key champion acting as a facilitator and connector through his networks.
- Industrial subsystem: businesses viewed wind energy as an economic opportunity; new companies were created and existing companies reworked their business models to focus on wind manufacturing (e.g., a shipbuilder started to manufacture parts for offshore wind turbines); municipal utility company used personal networks and drove the energy transition by aiming to supply the city with 100 percent renewable energy by 2030.
- Public administration subsystem: Department of Urban Development influenced the city to participate in European Energy Award and Climate Alliance programs; it promoted residential energy efficiency programs and supported industrial actors by reducing red tape.

- Science subsystem: the university offers a degree on energy efficiency and supports offshore wind energy.
- Intermediary organization subsystem: chamber of commerce and business networks offered training to companies; but unlike Bottrop, no intermediary was created specifically for the energy transition.
- Civil society subsystem: environmental non-governmental organizations (NGOs) and citizens groups played education and engagement roles.
- Financial subsystem: local banks offered loans for energy efficiency and solar projects.
- Energy transition process: informal and loosely coordinated; led by political, industrial, and administration actors.

Bottrop:

- Population: 116,000.
- Location: west central Germany within a region transitioning away from coal.
- Economy: historically dominated by steel production and coal mining.
- Energy system context: 1990s: hired energy manager and aimed to retrofit public buildings; 2010: city won an innovation award for a plan to transform a large portion of the residential, commercial, and industrial zones to reduce CO_2 emissions by 50 percent below 2010 by 2020.
- Political subsystem: passive role; willing enablers of energy transition.

  o   Provided stability by approving initiatives suggested by city departments.
  o   Mayor identified as a champion.
  o   Strong political support from state and federal levels.

- Industrial subsystem: companies conducting numerous niche experiments with technologies; most are from outside the city.
- Public administration subsystem: strong personal relationships between Departments for Urban Planning, Urban Renewal, Environment and Greenery, and Economic Development.

  o   Pragmatic, solution-oriented environment.
  o   Strong communication and mutual trust.

- Science subsystem: local universities involved in energy systems research focused on smart buildings and grids; conducting analysis of the transition to a low-carbon city.
- Intermediary organization subsystem: new intermediary organization called Innovation City GmbH was created to coordinate the energy innovation transition.

  o   Helps bridge gaps between different cultures and between industrial and administration actors.
  o   Helps overcome bottlenecks e.g., legal, red tape.

- Civil society subsystem: households, farmers, and a solar cooperative have invested in PV and wind energy; environmental NGOs only a small part of the energy transition because they were focused on other priorities related to the environment.
- Energy transition process: highly coordinated; steered by technical experts from the intermediary, government, companies, and universities.

A limitation of the Bottrop process was that it was driven and controlled by a few powerful actors within a few subsystems, while only marginally including citizens in the process.

While Emden had a more open and informal process, it was also largely driven by elite actors. An important finding is that change was initiated from different subsystems in each case; in Bottrop, the political, administration, and intermediary subsystems led the transition, while in Emden, the political subsystem in combination with key individuals from the administration and industry subsystems led the transition process. Acceleration Point: Sustainability professionals need to engage actors from as many regime subsystems as possible and monitor trends, anticipate shocks and windows of opportunity, and highlight the specific triple-bottom-line economic development benefits that will accrue to actors in each subsystem.

Renewable energy leaders: China, U.S., India, Germany

Renewable energy transitions are well underway in China, the United States, India, and Germany. Each country has followed a different path to the point where renewable energy began to take off. China's high economic development rates were enabled by high energy requirements and resulting greenhouse gas (GHG) emissions. China has now overtaken the United States as the largest global emitter (Bretschger and Zhang, 2017). China has a number of social and environmental challenges that relate to its rapidly growing population and resource demands (Lewis, 2009). These challenges include widening inequality between urban and rural areas and between western (agricultural) and eastern (industrial and political power) states, a lack of clean water for a majority of cities, forced human relocations and biodiversity impacts from massive hydropower dams, and urban air pollution that is many times the level deemed safe even for young healthy adults (McCann, 2017). India faces similar population and economic development challenges including a high reliance on coal and high air and water pollution levels.

China and India began to address these challenges by becoming world leaders in climate change mitigation and renewable energy installation (Condliffe, 2017). A report by Ernst and Young ranks China and India as the two leading destinations for green energy investment ahead of the United States and Western European countries (Condliffe, 2017). China has already installed 145 GW of wind (Figure 6.1) with a plan to reach 1 TW of wind power installed by 2050 at massive wind power bases (IEA, 2011). China has built some of the world's largest solar plants, including a 40 MW floating solar plant that was connected to the grid in 2017 (Adams, 2017). The advantages of floating solar plants include that they do not require high-valued agricultural and urban lands. Floating solar plants also reduce water evaporation from the lake or reservoir where they exist. The air is cooler on water compared to solar panels in a desert, which can help maintain performance of the solar systems over time (Adams, 2017).

China and the United States have similar patterns of installing solar and wind power (Figure 6.1). Growth rates for wind began to accelerate in the early 2000s and for solar a decade later. Despite many policies at the federal level (e.g., the Solar Investment Tax Credit) and the state level (e.g., feed-in tariffs, renewable portfolio standards) in the United States to achieve this growth, China has overtaken the United States as well as Germany for both wind and solar installed capacity. Figure 6.2

(continued)

(continued)

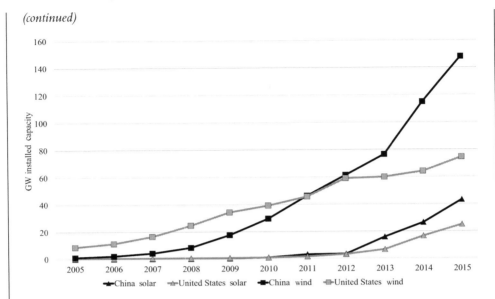

Figure 6.1 Installed wind and solar capacity comparison: China and the U.S.

Source: EIA (2017a).

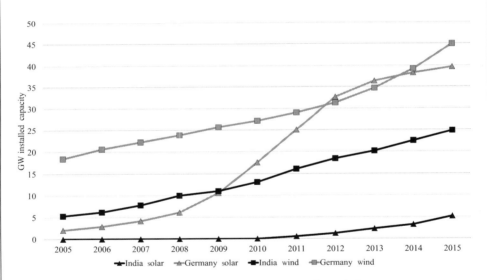

Figure 6.2 Installed wind and solar capacity comparison: India and Germany

Source: EIA (2017a).

shows solar and wind installation capacity for India as compared to Germany. While Germany rapidly increased solar installations from 2006 to 2012, India has steadily increased its wind capacity and began to increase its solar capacity between 2012 and 2015. The world's largest solar plant on land is in India, generating 648 MW of electricity, enough to power 150,000 homes (Thompson, 2016). The Kamuthi Solar Power Project covers four square miles of land and cost $679 million to build in eight months. This is only a small part of India's goal of generating enough solar energy to power 60 million homes (Thompson, 2016) as part of a plan to generate 175 GW of renewable energy by 2022 (Condliffe, 2017). These countries are driving installation rates of wind and solar for climate mitigation (Germany), for energy system innovation and transformation (United States), and for economic development (India and China).

A triple-bottom-line economic development strategy for India and China could have significant benefits for climate change mitigation as well as for poverty reduction and the creation of sustainable livelihood opportunities. Sustainability professionals can help foster private sector investment in technology innovation processes to create export industries for India similar to how China has become a world leader in solar manufacturing and exports. Modified versions of sustainability-oriented innovation intermediary organizations could be created in India and China that learn from experiences in Germany and the United States. These intermediaries could support sustainable niche experiments in technology innovation while engaging policy entrepreneurs to foster institutional changes. Given the differences in the political-economic systems, sustainability researchers can conduct comparative analyses to examine how intermediaries operate differently within each national socio-technical system context.

Case study: Sustainability-oriented innovation intermediaries in the United States

Green energy transitions and intermediaries in Massachusetts

McCauley and Stephens (2012) outlined a green energy transition in central Massachusetts. They focused on Worcester, a city that faced regional economic challenges, a reduction in property values, and declining municipal tax revenues. Worcester began the process of creating a sustainable energy cluster in 2008. This approach included politicians, universities, businesses, citizen groups, and activists. The goal was to capitalize on the interrelated problems of economic and energy system transitions. To accelerate this process, an intermediary organization called the Institute for Energy and Sustainability was created to help make Worcester known as a national leader in sustainability. The intermediary organization used various triple-bottom-line economic development strategies including: (1) marketing the area as supportive for green businesses, (2) attracting, expanding, and retaining green firms through zoning changes as well as permitting and tax breaks, (3) supporting sustainability science and socio-technical transition research at the local universities, (4) coordinating labor development, training, and outreach related to energy efficiency improvements, and (5) supporting cluster development (McCauley and Stephens, 2012). The full set of sustainability accomplishments achieved by Worcester, including official resolutions, pledges, recognitions, partnerships, climate action planning, building energy efficiency improvements, municipal electricity greening and lighting retrofits, waste and recycling programs, renewable energy changes, and community outreach and engagement programs are described in further detail in Worcester (2017).

Massachusetts applied for and won hundreds of millions of dollars from the American Recovery and Reinvestment Act in 2009 for sustainable energy developments (McCauley and Stephens, 2012). The recession in 2008 provided a window of opportunity and the sustainability intermediary capitalized on this opportunity by coordinating action from local and state governments, universities, and private businesses. The cluster pulled investment into the region aided by the climate action plan of Worcester, as well as a new energy and conservation manager staff position. As part of the cluster, creative financing options became available and new types of partnerships were developed for energy projects. The learning and network benefits of the cluster created excitement and an *institutional thickness* that attracted sustainability professionals and green companies to the region (McCauley and Stephens, 2012). As a result of the triple-bottom-line economic development strategy, Massachusetts witnessed clean energy become the tenth largest industry with over 60 clean energy businesses that are part of the cluster. Massachusetts achieved an average annual CO_2 emission reduction of 1.5 percent between 1997 and 2014, while at the same time increasing gross domestic product (GDP) per capita by 1.9 percent per year (Table 6.1). The *KAYA Identity* shows that significant improvements to the carbon intensity of energy were achieved after the 2008 recession, averaging 1.6 percent per year between 2009 and 2011 and 2.8 percent per year between 2011 and 2014.

Although intermediaries, champions, policy entrepreneurs, and boundary spanners can accelerate sustainability transitions, in some cases, powerful actors that span many subsystems of the regime can slow or inhibit sustainability transitions. The automotive industry provides an illustrative case of regime resistance and the role of actors in overcoming bottlenecks to transitions.

Automotive industry transitions and regime resistance

Penna and Geels (2015) examined the United States car industry over the three decades between 1979 and 2012 when major automotive manufacturing companies were inhibitors to policy change and innovation. Although the industry has made major changes and now offers a full line of electric, hybrid electric, and other sustainable options, it took many failed attempts from environmental groups, state governments, public outcry, consumer demand, and federal-level political changes before the automobile companies began to embrace climate change and develop a market for greener products.

Penna and Geels (2015) combined two theoretical frameworks to help understand the transitions that occurred and the barriers that were overcome. The first is the Triple Embeddedness Framework, which explains how firms in the automotive industry are embedded within an **economic environment** with resource pressures from markets and suppliers, a **socio–political environment** with *legitimacy* pressures from social movements, public sentiment, and policy makers, and an **industry regime** that is characterized by locked in regulations, laws, standards, mission identities, norms, technical knowledge and capabilities, and mindsets and belief systems (Figure 6.3). Penna and Geels (2015) outlined different strategies that auto companies used to respond to these pressures. For example, *innovation strategies* were used to address the economic pressures. These strategies related to supply chain management, operations management, and marketing. However, corporate *political influence strategies* (lobbying, financial contributions to political parties, constituency building, information strategies), and *socio-cultural strategies* (public relations, advertising) were used to respond to pressures from the socio–political environment. The companies generally fought against or slowed attempts to transition the automotive sector towards sustainability. What was missing from the transition attempts was a sustainability-oriented intermediary organization, which could have helped to support a transition by

Table 6.1 KAYA Identity for Massachusetts, U.S.: average annual percent change

Massachusetts	1997–1999	1999–2001	2001–2003	2003–2005	2005–2007	2007–2009	2009–2011	2011–2014	1997–2014
CO_2 emissions	-1.7	0.4	0.8	0.0	-1.8	-4.0	-1.1	-2.1	-1.5
Population	0.5	0.4	0.1	-0.1	0.2	0.4	0.5	0.7	0.5
GDP/capita	2.7	2.7	0.8	1.4	1.2	-1.0	1.5	0.4	1.9
Energy intensity (energy/GDP)	-2.4	-1.9	-1.3	-1.4	-2.0	-1.4	-1.4	-0.3	-1.8
Carbon intensity (carbon/ energy)	-2.3	-0.7	1.3	0.1	-1.1	-2.2	-1.6	-2.8	-1.5

Source: EIA (2017b, EIAc), with calculations by the authors.

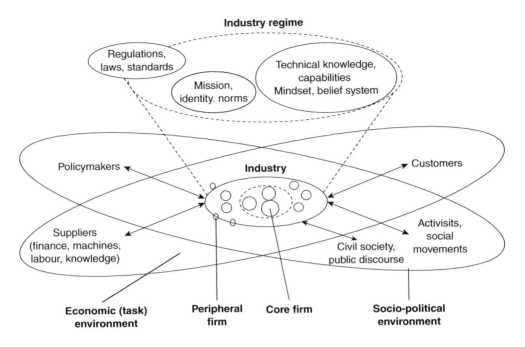

Figure 6.3 Triple Embeddedness Framework for automotive industry

Source: Penna and Geels (2015, p. 1031).

aligning technological innovation processes with institutional changes in the socio-political environment and infrastructure changes in the economic environment.

The second framework is the dialectic issue lifecycle model with five phases of transition for how climate change was handled by the major automakers (Penna and Geels, 2015). In phase one, firms downplayed the problem of climate change and suggested that it was not real or not important. In phase two and three, firms were forced to recognize the problem due to public pressure or political changes, and as a response created *industry associations* to band together against political pressures and instigate collective strategies to frame the issue differently. Industry associations are a form of intermediary organization designed in this case to slow rather than accelerate change. Firms used *incremental* innovation to defend the existing regime by making small changes to existing product lines. This included focusing on flex-fuel cars that can run on gasoline or ethanol or a mixture of both, or focusing on improving the engine efficiency or aerodynamics of existing models. During phase three, some firms began to conduct research and development on *radical* innovations as a hedge against anticipated competition or potential policy changes. This included a focus on hybrid gas-electric vehicles, plug-in electric vehicles, and fuel cell vehicles.

The transition to phase four and five strategies occurred when the climate change problem started to have effects on the economy (Penna and Geels, 2015). At this point, the political system implemented laws to change the economic conditions in response to climate change impacts. Eventually the problem recognition, policy response, and impact on the economy started to influence consumer demand for greener or more efficient products. Firms responded by investing in radical innovation and fostering new markets for greener products. Diversifying the product line and investing in innovation led to competitive advantages. However, the wide range of technological solutions (e.g., hybrids, fuel cell, electric, biofuels, flexfuels) created uncertainty as to which products would appeal to consumers and become mass manufactured. This caused firms to hedge and delay radical changes to their production lineups. Penna and Geels (2015) differentiated between *symbolic changes* that used communication, marketing, and lobbying to frame the climate change issue, and *substantive actions* that involved actual investments of resources. Technology development was sometimes used for symbolic purposes to enhance public reputation or to pre-empt and avoid regulations.

The actions of the automotive actors were mostly reactive rather than proactive. While the automobile industry did eventually respond to the various pressures, these reactions were slow and there was little willingness to proactively embrace a green transition. The downside of a reactive approach is that transitions towards strong sustainability take longer and may miss out on potential system changing radical innovations that could lead to triple-bottom-line economic development benefits for the jurisdiction. The lack of consensus on what actions to take made the transition in the automotive sector more difficult. In contrast, consensus about the need and general direction for a transition was higher in other jurisdictions where proactive and radical transitions took place, including Ontario and Quebec (Chapter 5) as well as in the United Kingdom, Germany, and Central Massachusetts described above. One case that highlights the potential for proactive actions is Puerto Rico.

Green champions as intermediaries for energy system transitions in Puerto Rico

Puerto Rico is an interesting case study in sustainability because it was nearly 100 percent reliant on fossil fuels for transportation and electricity. Rapid urbanization took place and land-use changes destroyed much of the mangroves that were critical for flood protection. A key point that could be a bottleneck or a seedbed for sustainability transitions is the massive recovery and rebuilding efforts after Hurricane Maria in 2017. Most of the electricity grid was destroyed and proposals for rebuilding ranged from replacing the grid with similar fossil fuel powered supply options, to Tesla's proposal to use solar and battery storage to build a resilient and green grid for the island (Korosec, 2017). Tesla sent Powerwall storage systems to be linked to solar generation capacity to provide immediate microgrids. Other solar companies sent portable solar trailers to create movable microgrids (Chow, 2017). But plans are being discussed with the United States Department of Economic Development and Commerce to expand these microgrids to a broader energy system transition. Replacing the entire electricity grid that was once powered by fossil fuels with a solar and battery system could greatly improve the sustainability of Puerto Rico by reducing the carbon intensity of electricity and enhancing the resilience of the grid to future storms and disruptions. In this case, green champions like Tesla acted as intermediaries by driving sustainable niche experiments within Puerto Rico as well as regime changes at the United States federal government level that could support a sustainability transition.

The challenge for sustainability professionals is to coordinate innovation, political, and socio-cultural strategies so that niche experiments and changes to regime subsystems can be co-shaped in the direction of sustainability principles. Sustainability-oriented innovation intermediaries can help with coordinating these strategies by working with industry leaders, technology entrepreneurs, and policy entrepreneurs. Places that are developing green technology as a triple-bottom-line economic development strategy can benefit from intermediaries that work to amplify niche and regime changes to accelerate a sustainability transition in institutions, technologies, and infrastructures.

Check on learning

- How can sustainability-oriented innovation intermediaries integrate sustainability principles into green innovation processes?
- What are some ways that niche actors, regime actors, and innovation intermediaries can collaborate to support socio-technical transitions?
- How can boundary spanners help foster the incorporation of sustainability principles into water or infrastructure system changes?
- What are energy service companies and how can they contribute to sustainability?
- Read Penna and Geels (2015) and devise a set of strategies and instruments to encourage a transition in the transportation, water, or energy sector in your country or state/province. What lessons from this study are important? How could the creation and use of a sustainability-oriented innovation intermediary have helped overcome barriers by working with industry and government agencies to accelerate this transition?

Assignments

- Turning a sustainability idea into an initiative via collaborative green championship
- Designing an innovation incubator for sustainability value creation

References

Abbate, T., & Coppolino, R. (2012). Leading Sustainable Innovation: the Role of innovation intermediaries. In G. Calabro, A. D'Amico, M. Lanfranchi, L. Pulejo, & R. Salomone (Eds). *Moving from the Crisis to Sustainability. Emerging Issues in the International Context*, pp. 189–198. FrancoAngeli, Milan, Italy.

Adams, D. (2017). The world's largest floating solar power plant just went online in China. Digital Trends. Available at: www.digitaltrends.com/cool-tech/china-floating-solar-power-plant/

Agogué, M., Agogué, M., Berthet, E., Berthet, E., Fredberg, T., Fredberg, T., . . . & Stoetzel, M. (2017). Explicating the role of innovation intermediaries in the 'unknown': A contingency approach. *Journal of Strategy and Management*, 10(1), 19–39.

Albers, R. A. W., Bosch, P. R., Blocken, B., Van Den Dobbelsteen, A. A. J. F., Van Hove, L. W. A., Spit, T. J. M., . . . & Rovers, V. (2015). Overview of challenges and achievements in the climate adaptation of cities and in the Climate Proof Cities program. *Building and Environment*, 83, 1–10.

Andersson, L. M., & Bateman, T. S. (2000). Individual environmental initiative: Championing natural environmental issues. *Academy of Management Journal*, 43(4), 548–570.

Antikainen, R., Alhola, K., & Jääskeläinen, T. (2017). Experiments as a means towards sustainable societies: Lessons learnt and future outlooks from a Finnish perspective. *Journal of Cleaner Production*, 169, 216–224.

Bank, N., & Kanda, W. (2016). Tenant recruitment and support processes in sustainability-profiled business incubators. *Industry and Higher Education*, 30(4), 267–277.

Barrie, J., Zawdie, G., & João, E. (2017). Leveraging triple helix and system intermediaries to enhance effectiveness of protected spaces and strategic niche management for transitioning to circular economy. *International Journal of Technology Management & Sustainable Development*, 16(1), 25–47.

Berardo, R., & Scholz, J. T. (2010). Self-organizing policy networks: Risk, partner selection, and cooperation in estuaries. *American Journal of Political Science*, 54(3), 632–649.

Blankenship, H., Kulhavy, V., & Lagneryd, J. (2009). Introducing strategic sustainable development in a business incubator. *Progress in Industrial Ecology, an International Journal*, 6(3), 243–264.

Bretschger, L., & Zhang, L. (2017). Carbon policy in a high-growth economy: The case of China. *Resource and Energy Economics*, 47, 1–19.

Bush, R. E., Bale, C. S., Powell, M., Gouldson, A., Taylor, P. G., & Gale, W. F. (2017). The role of intermediaries in low carbon transitions: Empowering innovations to unlock district heating in the UK. *Journal of Cleaner Production*, 148, 137–147.

Cambridge Cleantech. (2017). Cambridge Cleantech about us. Available at: www.cambridge cleantech.org.uk/about-us

Chow, L. (2017). This brilliant initiative is sending 100 solar trailers to Puerto Rico for free. EcoWatch. Available at: www.ecowatch.com/power-puerto-rico-solar-project-2512174871.html

Condliffe, J. (2017). India and China are emerging as climate icons. Sustainable Energy. MIT Technology Review. Available at: www.technologyreview.com/s/607881/india-and-china-are-emerging-as-climate-icons/

Economist. (2012). Germany's energy transformation: *Energiewende*. German plans to cut carbon emissions with renewable energy are ambitious, but they are also risky. *The Economist*. Available at: www.economist.com/node/21559667

Edelenbos, J., & van Meerkerk, I. (2015). Connective capacity in water governance practices: The meaning of trust and boundary spanning for integrated performance. *Current Opinion in Environmental Sustainability*, 12, 25–29.

EIA. (2017a). International energy statistics. U.S. Energy Information Administration. Available at: www.eia.gov/beta/international/data/browser/#/?pa=000000200000000000000000g2&c=ruvvvvvfvtvnvv1urvvvvfvvvvvvfvvvou20evvvvvvvvvnvvuvs&ct=0&tl_id=2-A&vs=INTL.2-2-AFG-BKWH.A&cy=2014&vo=0&v=H&end=2015

EIA. (2017b). CO_2 emissions data. U.S. Energy Information Administration. Available at: www.eia.gov/environment/emissions/state/

EIA. (2017c). Population, energy demand, and GDP data. State Energy Data System. U.S. Energy Information Administration. Available at: www.eia.gov/state/seds/seds-data-complete.php?sid=US

Exter, N. (2013). *Employee Engagement with Sustainable Business: How to Change the World Whilst Keeping Your Day Job*. Routledge, New York, NY.

Galvin, R., & Terry, N. (2016). Selling energy savings in the United Kingdom: A case study of top-down pro-environmental behaviour change in commercial office buildings. *Energy Research & Social Science*, 11, 155–163.

Gattiker, T. F., & Carter, C. R. (2010). Understanding project champions' ability to gain intra-organizational commitment for environmental projects. *Journal of Operations Management*, 28, 72–85.

Gliedt, T., & Parker, P. (2010). Dynamic capabilities for strategic green advantage: Green electricity purchasing in North American firms, SMEs, NGOs and agencies. *Global Business and Economics Review*, 12(3), 171–195.

Gliedt, T., Berkhout, T., Parker, P., & Doucet, J. (2010). Voluntary environmental decision making in firms: Green electricity purchases and the role of champions. *International Journal of Business Environment*, 3(3), 308–328.

Gliedt, T., Hoicka, C. E., & Jackson, N. (2018). Innovation intermediaries accelerating environmental sustainability transitions. *Journal of Cleaner Production*, 174, 1247–1261.

Green, J. F. (2017). Policy entrepreneurship in climate governance: Toward a comparative approach. *Environment and Planning C: Politics and Space*, 35(8), 1471–1482.

Hannon, M., Skea, J., & Rhodes, A. (2014). Facilitating and coordinating UK energy innovation through systemic innovation intermediaries. 5th International Conference Sustainability Transitions. Utrecht, the Netherlands, August.

Hargreaves, T., Hielscher, S., Seyfang, G., & Smith, A. (2013). Grassroots innovations in community energy: The role of intermediaries in niche development. *Global Environmental Change*, 23(5), 868–880.

Huitema, D., & Meijerink, S. (2010). Realizing water transitions: The role of policy entrepreneurs in water policy change. *Ecology and Society*, 15(2), 26.

IEA. (2011). Technology roadmap: China wind energy development roadmap 2050. International Energy Agency. Energy Research Institute. Available at: www.iea.org/publications/freepublications/publication/china_wind.pdf

Juravle, C., & Lewis, A. (2009). The role of championship in the mainstreaming of sustainable investment (SI). What can we learn from SI pioneers in the United Kingdom? *Organization & Environment*, 22(1), 75–98.

Kalafatis, S. E., Grace, A., & Gibbons, E. (2015). Making climate science accessible in Toledo: The linked boundary chain approach. *Climate Risk Management*, 9, 30–40.

Kanda, W., Hjelm, O., & Bienkowska, D. (2014). Boosting eco-innovation: The role of public support organizations. In *ISPIM Conference Proceedings*. p. 1. The International Society for Professional Innovation Management (ISPIM), Dublin, Ireland.

Kanda, W., Clausen, J., Hjelm, O., & Bienkowska, D. (2015). Functions of intermediaries in eco-innovation: A study of business development organizations and cluster initiatives in a Swedish and a German region. Global Cleaner Production and Sustainable Consumption Conference, 1–4 November, Sitges-Barcelona, Spain.

Kingdon, J. W. (1984). *Agendas, Alternatives, and Public Policies*. Vol. 45. Little, Brown, Boston, MA.

Kivimaa, P. (2014). Government-affiliated intermediary organisations as actors in system-level transitions. *Research Policy*, 43(8), 1370–1380.

Kivimaa, P., Boon, W., & Antikainen, R. (2017). Commercialising university inventions for sustainability: A case study of (non-) intermediating 'cleantech' at Aalto University. *Science and Public Policy*, 44(5), 631–644.

Klerkx, L., & Aarts, N. (2013). The interaction of multiple champions in orchestrating innovation networks: Conflicts and complementarities. *Technovation*, 33(6), 193–210.

Klewitz, J., Zeyen, A., & Hansen, E. G. (2012). Intermediaries driving eco-innovation in SMEs: A qualitative investigation. *European Journal of Innovation Management*, 15(4), 442–467.

Korosec, K. (2017). Tesla could be tapped to rebuild Puerto Rico's electrical grid. Fortune. Available at: http://fortune.com/2017/10/23/tesla-could-be-tapped-to-rebuild-puerto-ricos-electrical-grid/

Küçüksayraç, E., Keskin, D., & Brezet, H. (2015). Intermediaries and innovation support in the design for sustainability field: Cases from the Netherlands, Turkey and the United Kingdom. *Journal of Cleaner Production*, 101, 38–48.

Lemos, M. C., Kirchhoff, C. J., Kalafatis, S. E., Scavia, D., & Rood, R. B. (2014). Moving climate information off the shelf: Boundary chains and the role of RISAs as adaptive organizations. *Weather, Climate, and Society*, 6(2), 273–285.

Lewis, J. I. (2009). Climate change and security: Examining China's challenges in a warming world. *International Affairs*, 85(6), 1195–1213.

Martiskainen, M., & Kivimaa, P. (2017). Creating innovative zero carbon homes in the United Kingdom: Intermediaries and champions in building projects. *Environmental Innovation and Societal Transitions*. Available at: www.sciencedirect.com/science/article/pii/S2210422416301277

Mattes, J., Huber, A., & Koehrsen, J. (2015). Energy transitions in small-scale regions: What we can learn from a regional innovation systems perspective. *Energy Policy*, 78, 255–264.

McCann, E. (2017). Life in China, smothered by smog. *The New York Times*. Available at: www.nytimes.com/2016/12/22/world/asia/china-smog-toxic.html

McCauley, S. M., & Stephens, J. C. (2012). Green energy clusters and socio-technical transitions: Analysis of a sustainable energy cluster for regional economic development in Central Massachusetts, USA. *Sustainability Science*, 7(2), 213–225.

McLennan, C. J., Becken, S., & Watt, M. (2016). Learning through a cluster approach: Lessons from the implementation of six Australian tourism business sustainability programs. *Journal of Cleaner Production*, 111, 348–357.

Methner, N., Hamann, R., & Nilsson, W. (2015). The evolution of a sustainability leader: The development of strategic and boundary spanning organizational innovation capabilities in Woolworths. In V. Bitzer, R. Hamann, M. Hall, E. Wosu Griffin-EL (Eds). *The Business of Social and Environmental Innovation*. pp. 87–104. Springer International Publishing, Cham, Switzerland.

New York Incubator. (2016). New York University Tandon Labs. Available at: http://engineering.nyu.edu/business/future-labs.

Nilsson, M., & Sia-Ljungström, C. (2013). The role of innovation intermediaries in innovation systems. *Proceedings in Food System Dynamics*, 160–180.

Nolden, C., Sorrell, S., & Polzin, F. (2016). Catalysing the energy service market: The role of intermediaries. *Energy Policy*, 98, 420–430.

Palmer, J. R. (2015). How do policy entrepreneurs influence policy change? Framing and boundary work in EU transport biofuels policy. *Environmental Politics*, 24(2), 270–287.

Penna, C. C., & Geels, F. W. (2015). Climate change and the slow reorientation of the American car industry (1979–2012): An application and extension of the Dialectic Issue LifeCycle (DILC) model. *Research Policy*, 44(5), 1029–1048.

Polzin, F., von Flotow, P., & Klerkx, L. (2016). Addressing barriers to eco-innovation: Exploring the finance mobilisation functions of institutional innovation intermediaries. *Technological Forecasting and Social Change*, 103, 34–46.

Smink, M., Negro, S. O., Niesten, E., & Hekkert, M. P. (2015). How mismatching institutional logics hinder niche–regime interaction and how boundary spanners intervene. *Technological Forecasting and Social Change*, 100, 225–237.

Swaffield, J., & Bell, D. (2012). Can 'climate champions' save the planet? A critical reflection on neoliberal social change. *Environmental Politics*, 21(2), 248–267.

Thompson, A. (2016). The world's largest solar plant is now online in India. *Popular Mechanics*. Available at: www.popularmechanics.com/science/green-tech/a24063/worlds-largest-solar-plant-india/

van Meerkerk, I., & Edelenbos, J. (2014). The effects of boundary spanners on trust and performance of urban governance networks: Findings from survey research on urban development projects in the Netherlands. *Policy Sciences*, 47(1), 3–24.

van Meerkerk, I., Edelenbos, J., & Klijn, E. H. (2015). Connective management and governance network performance: the mediating role of throughput legitimacy. Findings from survey research on complex water projects in the Netherlands. *Environ. Plan. C Gov. Policy*, 33, 746–764.

Waterloo Accelerator. (2016). The Accelerator Center. University of Waterloo. Available at: http://acceleratorcentre.com/about/

Wichmann, B. K., Carter, C. R., & Kaufmann, L. (2015). How to become central in an informal social network: An investigation of the antecedents to network centrality in an environmental SCM initiative. *Journal of Business Logistics*, 36(1), 102–119.

Williams, P. (2002). The competent boundary spanner. *Public Administration*, 80(1), 103–124.

Worcester. (2017). Worcester: A greener future, today. Worcester's Sustainability Accomplishments. Available at: www.worcesterenergy.org/leading-by-example/sustainability-accomplishments

7 Sustainability-oriented socio-technical systems in relation to transition theory

Learning objectives

- Define sustainability-oriented socio-technical systems in relation to transition theory
- Discuss the interactions between sustainable behavior and practices, organizations as agents of sustainability, green innovation systems, triple-bottom-line economic development strategies, and the role of the intermediaries within the multi-level perspective (MLP) sustainability transitions framework
- Highlight the interconnections between infrastructure change processes and institutional change processes
- Outline various niche and regime processes, strategies, and pathways for transitioning socio-technical systems towards the principles of sustainability

Theories of sustainability transitions

Sustainability transitions theory has been approached and conceptualized from many angles including governance, management, innovation, and complex systems, as well as sectoral, regional, or city-level analyses. It is important to view institutions, technologies, and infrastructures as inter-connected within *socio-technical systems* because making changes to one often requires changes to the others. Additionally, major infrastructures (e.g., energy, water, transportation) overlap regulatory and governance levels including cities, states/provinces, and federal governments. Focusing on processes, strategies, and instruments for changing institutions can enable or accelerate changes to technologies and infrastructures. Correspondingly, making changes to infrastructures can enable private sector innovation in new technologies that benefit from institutional changes. Overcoming bottlenecks that slow or undermine efforts to change institutions and infrastructures (Chapter 9) also requires coordinating niche and regime processes. Key actors within industries can help change the *subsystems of the regime* by working to shift institutions and infrastructures within which they are integrated. But how do these changes and transitions occur? How are changes instigated as part of multi-level processes, who does the instigating, and does this differ based on the country, region, or place?

A sustainability transition is complex for a number of reasons (Markard et al., 2012). First, it requires radical changes to multiple interrelated socio-technical systems including energy, food, water, and transportation. Second, within each socio-technical system, incremental and radical changes are necessary to the subsystems of the regime (e.g., technological, organizational, institutional, political, economic, socio-cultural) that must be aligned with ongoing niche experiments. Third, the functions of numerous actors with different preferences and skill sets (e.g., niche and regime actors, intermediaries) have to be directly or indirectly coordinated as part of transition processes. Fourth, long time-frames (e.g., 50+ years) for infrastructure change as part of *techno-economic paradigm* shifts must be accelerated if sustainability problems including climate change are to be solved. Finally, organizations need to realign products/services and business models based on sustainability principles and sustainability value creation frameworks. According to Smith et al. (2010), the *multi-level perspective* can help by providing "a relatively straight-forward way of ordering and simplifying the analysis of complex, large-scale structural transformations in production and consumption demanded by the normative goal of sustainable development" (p. 441). Sustainability professionals can therefore use the MLP as a means of structuring and coordinating a set of strategies and instruments designed to both create niche experiments and change the regime.

The transition processes that are described in this chapter are composed of interactions between and changes to niches and regime subsystems within the MLP outlined in Figure 7.1. These interactions and changes may lead to rapid and radical transitions in institutions, technologies, and infrastructures. The MLP helps sustainability professionals recognize the timing and alignment between external pressures from the landscape and internal processes that either slow the rate of change in socio-technical systems (e.g., the path dependence and lock-in characteristics of the regime subsystems described as bottlenecks in Chapter 9), or initiate and accelerate the rate of change in socio-technical systems (e.g., the entrepreneurship and innovation processes in Chapter 4; the triple-bottom-line economic development strategies in Chapter 5; the role of intermediaries in Chapter 6). While windows of opportunity can be identified by historical analysis (e.g., looking backward) of innovation processes that led to new technology creation and diffusion (Wesseling et al., 2015), the challenge for sustainability professionals is to predict when a new window of opportunity will occur (e.g., looking forward) and to align it with ongoing or anticipated institutional and infrastructure change processes. Sustainability professionals can collaborate with other key actors described below to influence transition processes with the help of *transition management, strategic niche management*, or governance in the form of *transition arenas* (Avelino and Grin, 2017).

Using the **normative competence**, sustainability professionals set goals to begin a transition process. These goals help select decision-making tools and capabilities that draw upon the **strategic** and **anticipatory competences** to develop pathways to strong sustainability similar to those outlined in Figure 1.10 in Chapter 1: (1) Proactive, (2) Pragmatic, and (3) Reactive. Sustainability professionals use the **systems thinking competence** to examine the interconnections between the niche, regime, and landscape as a means of understanding transition processes. Transition processes described below include regime destruction and change, niche creation and protection, niche-to-regime interactions, regime-to-niche interactions, niche-to-niche interactions, and regime-to-regime interactions. Sustainability professionals can use the **integrated sustainability research and problem-solving competence** to devise *strategies and instruments* that help actors within the aforementioned transition processes accelerate or guide movement along and between the strong sustainability pathways. Sustainability professionals engage with niche and regime actors using the **interpersonal relations competence** in order to build momentum for changing institutions, technologies, and infrastructures in the direction of sustainability principles.

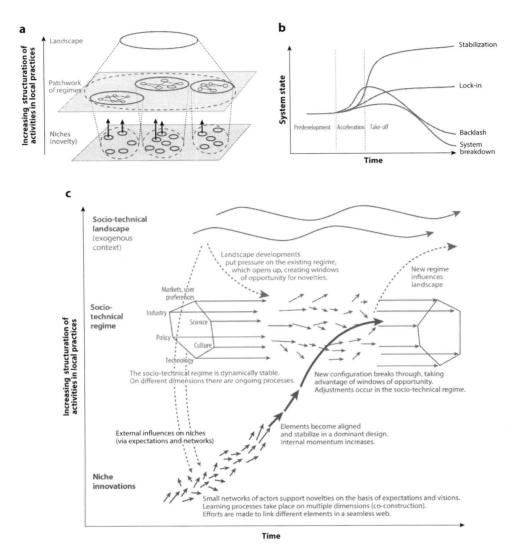

Figure 7.1 The multi-level perspective on sustainability transitions

Source: Loorbach et al. (2017, p. 606).

Although many of these pathways and processes have helped countries like the Netherlands, the United Kingdom, and Germany encourage and guide transitions in socio-technical systems, the formalized *transition management* approach utilizing a *transition arena* may not apply in the same way in other contexts like the United States or Canada where top-down strategically planned transitions may not be politically feasible. An important question for sustainability professionals is, therefore, whether to influence transition pathways and processes based on criteria related to normative sufficiency, economic efficiency, or political feasibility. For example, transitions in European countries may be deemed successful if they achieve normative sufficiency goals (e.g., greenhouse gas [GHG] emissions reduced per year) outlined by the transition team at the outset of the transition process. However, transitions in some U.S. states and Canadian provinces may require improvements to economic efficiency criteria to be considered successful (e.g., GHG emissions reduced per public dollar invested per year). Combining sufficiency with efficiency criteria may make some transitions more politically feasible if job creation and value creation to the broader community can be shown to be competitive with alternative public project options. However, combining efficiency with sufficiency criteria may reduce the political feasibility of some transitions if the initial projections of return-on-investment are not competitive with alternative project options. This highlights the importance of critiquing the transition management approach while offering alternative frameworks that include actors and processes for bottom-up and industry driven sustainability transitions. It also emphasizes that actors within transition processes need to frame and sell interventions aimed at institutional, technology, and infrastructure changes by using strategies and instruments that will appeal to the key funders, financers, or investors in a particular place.

Transition actors

Actors play key roles in sustainability transitions including maintaining institutions (e.g., activities that enforce or conform to the current regime rules), creating institutions (e.g., activities that question the assumptions of current regime rules and aim to create new rules), and disrupting institutions (e.g., activities that challenge regime rules and undermine their legitimacy) (Bettini et al., 2015). The aforementioned study suggested that different places may have different actors working on each of these roles and that locations lacking the creating and disrupting roles may be less likely to experience a sustainability transition. To operationalize socio-technical system change, actors in sustainability transitions focus on strategic activities (e.g., problem structuring, establishing of arena, and envisioning), tactical activities (e.g., developing coalitions and agendas), operational activities (e.g., mobilizing actors, executing projects and experiments), and reflexive activities (e.g., monitoring, evaluating, and learning) (Bettini et al., 2015).

Transition pathways may be led by government, business, or civil society actors (Foxon, 2013). Government driven pathways focus more on infrastructure and institutional changes, while business driven pathways center on technology, entrepreneurship, and product development. Civil society driven pathways include education, behavior, and culture changes through partnerships, community engagement, and social innovation. A fourth integrated pathway combines contributions from each of the government, business, and civil society actors. The importance of the integrated pathway is emphasized in this book because strong sustainability pathways (Figure 1.10) combine strategies and instruments that are led by actors from government, businesses, and civil society. The roles of actors and the extent that they may collaborate in sustainability transitions differs depending on the level of risk each deems acceptable, the level of investment that is necessary, and the degree that institutional changes are needed to enable successful changes to technologies and infrastructures. Acceleration Point: Sustainability-oriented intermediary organizations (Chapter 6) can accelerate a transition by coordinating transition actors, strategies, and instruments to avoid overlap and build synergies between transition processes.

Fischer and Newig (2016) categorized actors that are important to a sustainability transition based on their functions, the extent that they are dependent on other actors and resources, and the potential of each actor to influence transitions (Table 7.1). Although some actors support transitions and others oppose them, actor functions vary and the same person or organization can fall into more than one category. The key actors in sustainability transitions are the niche and regime actors and the intermediaries (Fischer and Newig, 2016). Niche actors drive technology innovation processes, which are constrained or enabled by policy changes instigated by other actors at the governance levels. Regime actors focus on changing institutions and policies but often in a manner consistent with the preferences of current and dominant industry and governance actors. This may lead to incremental changes to infrastructures consistent with weak sustainability pathways. Regime actors can also slow a transition by convincing other actors that changes to regime subsystems are not necessary. Other important actors include those at the national governance level who can lead or structure a transition by creating the conditions for sustainability-oriented innovation to be driven by businesses (technology innovation), lower levels of government (institutional and policy innovation), and civil society (social innovation).

Sustainability professionals could work or volunteer for any of these transition actors. For example, a sustainability professional could be a sustainability coordinator within a non-profit organization, a corporate social responsibility manager within a firm, or a minister/director heading a government agency. The *sustainability competencies* outlined in Chapter 1 are related to skills and capabilities that would benefit sustainability professionals within these industries. The most important is **interpersonal relations competence**, which will help sustainability professionals foster collaborations between the transition actors. Knowing how to do computer modelling, scenario development, or visioning analyses is useful to the extent that sustainability professionals can leverage the resulting outputs (e.g., information and reports) to mobilize transition actors. Sustainability intermediaries in particular will benefit from hiring sustainability professionals with **interpersonal relations competence** because these organizations overlap and connect niche and regime levels and many different types of actors with different objectives and functions. Intermediaries are critical for influencing transitions because niche and regime actors themselves have limited agency (e.g., the ability to make changes in the socio-technical system). Rather, it is the niche and regime levels that are composed of multiple actors, as well as the interactions between the levels facilitated by intermediaries, which provides agency for instigating transitions (Table 7.1).

Socio-technical system change is a function of changes to institutions, technologies, and infrastructures that are instigated by niches and regimes and coordinated by intermediaries (Figure 7.2). Socio-technical system change can be driven by *transition management*, which integrates top-down or bottom-up approaches, learning from experiments, and develops adaptive capacity for adjusting to shocks and pressures (Foxon et al., 2009). Transition management can become a mechanism for collaboration between niche and regime actors that is centered on a series of functions designed to (Loorbach and Rotmans, 2010, p. 238):

- manage uncertainties (e.g., use scenarios),
- keep options open,
- deal with fragmented policies,
- take a long-term orientation when creating short-term policies,
- focus on international aspects of change processes,
- find solutions on the right scale, and
- recognize the special role of governments (e.g., stimulate, mediate, engage in brokering services, create the right conditions, enforce laws, and engage in steering).

Table 7.1 Functions, dependencies, and influence of actors in sustainability transitions

Type	Actor	Functions	Dependencies on other actors and resources	Potential influence on transitions
MLP	Niche actor	New, radical social and technological ideas emerge, knowledge development and diffusion, articulation of visions, entrepreneurial activities, market formation, guidance of search activities, mobilization of resources, creation of legitimacy, overcoming of resistance to change, can create a starting point for systemic change.	Successful niche emergence depends on changes in government policy and support.	Niche level is a protective space which supports more agency, niche actors have limited agency.
	Regime actor	Supporters of transition by forming powerful coalitions to push through a reform agenda that fits incumbent regimes interest. Opponents of transition by downplaying the need for transformation.	In order to build up adaptive capacity, regime actors must articulate problems or direction and get involved in networks to share and coordinate resources.	The regime level itself can be either a source of or structure of agency, regime actors have limited agency.
	Landscape actor	Provides pressure on the regime, encourages or discourages interactions between actors in multiple regimes and niches.	Changes at the landscape level have, for example, influence on civil societies participation in community-based innovative initiatives.	No activities; level itself provides no room for agency.
State, market, civil society and citizens	Government	Traditional role of providing financial resources at the early non-competitive state of innovations. New role of creating niches through institutional work enabling experimentation.	Depend on job availability, tax incomes, economic growth and new technologies. Depend on the wider public for re-election.	Limited agency (often perceived as leading actor in transitions).

(continued)

Table 7.1 (continued)

Type	Actor	Functions	Dependencies on other actors and resources	Potential influence on transitions
	Market	Bring competitive products and services to the market. Supporters of transition when being entrants, seeking new business opportunities. Opponents of transition when business with established technologies, not eager about alternatives.	Consumer pressure.	Limited room for unilateral agency: reasons for new ideas not spreading – overarching structures of markets, patterns of final consumer demand, institutional and regulatory systems and inadequate infrastructure for change.
	Civil society	Ability to get engaged to both regime stability and the pressuring of the regime. Pressuring of the regime: diffusing innovative niche ideas and practices, using lobbying and protests to unsettle the regime, pushing and encouraging regime actors to seek new solutions from niches, representing general landscape-level trends.	Through markets and politics, they can help to shape the landscape. Civil society can unsettle the regime or contribute to stability.	Limited, for example, by reaching a critical mass.
Actors on different levels of governance	Local governance level	Framing issues of sustainability and the creation of effective policies. Successful bottom up approaches for behavior changes. Might create local acceptability for certain national policies and fiscal measures. Developing infrastructure and providing locations for experimentation. Niche managers.	Local initiatives depend on linkages with transition arenas on a higher level to be able to scale-up.	Limited (see also actors on the regional governance level).
	Regional governance level	May help to promote transitions on a broader scale when national/global actors can draw on successful regional transitions (dependency). Helps to transform a technology experiment to reality.	Achieve the greatest impacts with the help of their human and institutional capacities.	Weak agency. Few laws can be changed. Legal enforcement of action is hardly possible. Administrative capacity is limited. Many incumbents are out of reach.

National governance level	Organize key resource flows efficiently by managing flexibly targeted supply and pricing strategies. Can establish markets for sustainable innovation together with entrepreneurs (also dependencies).	Managing transitions depends on national actors and their real and perceived power.	Leading or structuring actor.
Global governance level	Can guide reform processes enacted by the government. Priority for governing seems to be wealth accumulation.	National governments have partly given up political and economic sovereignty to multinational corporations and financial institutions.	Limited agency.
Intermediaries	Providing and distributing necessary information. Mediating function. Provide services. Connecting niche-level activities with regime-level institutions. Diffuse new technologies and practice through the regional level.	Resource dependency.	Active agents.

Source: Modified from Fischer and Newig (2016, pp. 13–14).

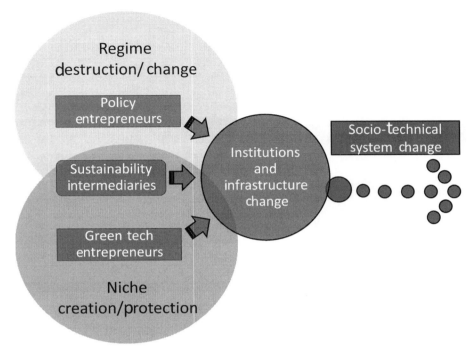

Figure 7.2 Key actors in sustainability transitions

Source: Authors' rendition.

Regime actors like policy entrepreneurs can work to change institutions while green entrepreneurs develop technologies that will offer new options to coordinate with infrastructure change (Gliedt et al., 2018). The extent that these changes lead to sustainability transitions may depend on the ability of sustainability intermediaries to amplify and guide them in the direction of sustainability principles. Intermediaries play the most active and direct role in sustainability transitions because they are specifically designed to foster innovation, encourage connections between entrepreneurs and policy makers, and scale-up new technologies into broader triple-bottom-line economic development benefits (Fischer and Newig, 2016). Sustainability-oriented intermediaries can help accelerate transitions by encouraging and facilitating cross-level interactions between actors operating within the *landscape*, the *regime*, and the *niches* (Kivimaa and Kern, 2016). Acceleration Point: It is important to remember that sustainability transitions arise not just from encouraging and facilitating interactions between niche and regime levels, but from encouraging and facilitating with a sustainability purpose. Sustainability-oriented intermediaries and the sustainability professionals working within them combine their skills and competencies with a passion for making change and addressing social and environmental problems in society.

Transition processes

Transition actors including sustainability professionals focus on regime destruction and niche creation processes. Given that many niches are nested within each regime, and many regimes are nested within a landscape (Figure 7.1A), it is also important to examine how interactions and collaborations between niches and regimes could accelerate transitions. Therefore, sustainability professionals must develop capabilities for connecting niches to regimes, regimes to niches, niches to niches, and regimes to regimes in order to accelerate transition processes.

Regime change and regime destruction

Regime change and *regime destruction* are two processes for changing the *subsystems of the regime* towards sustainability principles (Foxon et al., 2009; Voß et al., 2009; Smith et al., 2010). The subsystems are visualized as streams of society that are constantly flowing and interacting (Figure 7.1C), and taken together they represent the dominant conditions at a specific time in a particular society. Subsystems include **science** (e.g., science and education), **political** (e.g., political parties and actors), **public administration** (e.g., municipal and regional administration), **industry** (e.g., companies compete or cooperate), **intermediaries** (e.g., labour unions, chambers of commerce, network connectors), **financial** (e.g., funding, venture capital, banks), and **civil society** (e.g., non-governmental organizations [NGOs], mobilized citizens) (Mattes et al., 2015).

Regime change can occur slowly through co-evolutionary processes. In cases where subsystems are co-evolving, changes to one subsystem like science (e.g., a new breakthrough in research and development focused on more efficient solar panels) can lead to changes in other subsystems like market and policy (e.g., new businesses are created to manufacture and export this solar technology; new regulations are created to either support or slow down development and diffusion of this technology). Regime change occurs incrementally when actors alter subsystems of the regime to indirectly influence changes in other subsystems (e.g., public education to influence culture change; policy change to influence the development of new markets and industries). Co-evolution occurs when the resulting subsystems and their interactions are unrecognizable from where they were prior to the scientific breakthrough. While this co-evolutionary model explains incremental changes to the regime that occur over long periods of time through a series of phases (Figure 7.1B), sustainability as both a normative and ecological imperative requires more immediate and radical changes.

Regime destruction can be accelerated by natural shocks from the landscape or via interventions with strategies and instruments that aim to change the nature and extent of interactions between the subsystems (Figure 7.1C). Regime destruction occurs when actors work to radically change the subsystems of the regime directly (e.g., institutional and policy change). Mattes et al. (2015) suggested that "change may be triggered, pushed or hindered by either subsystem, and the interaction between them increases the necessity to coordinate" (p. 257). For example, competition within the industry and scientific subsystems can drive research and development (R&D) and innovation, but policy entrepreneurship (Chapter 6) within the political subsystem can help to coordinate and accelerate those innovation processes. In places where radical institutional changes are politically feasible, pathways to strong sustainability can be driven and coordinated by regime destruction processes. In situations where incremental changes to subsystems are more likely, additional processes are needed to move from weak to strong sustainability pathways. These include niche creation and protection processes. Acceleration Point: Sustainability professionals could instigate a transition by mobilizing change from within any of these subsystems; however, it is more likely that a transition will change the regime if changes in more than one subsystem are coordinated.

Niche creation

Niche creation processes include niche experiments and niche empowerment strategies. *Niche experiments* can be carried out as part of green entrepreneurship strategies or encouraged by strategic niche management (Kern et al., 2015; Kivimaa and Kern, 2016; Raven et al., 2016; Sengers and Raven, 2015). Sengers et al. (2017) defined an experiment as "an inclusive, practice-based and challenge-led initiative, which is designed to promote system innovation through social learning under conditions of uncertainty" (p. 1). The goal of niche experiments is to create new technologies and solutions to societal problems that can also generate revenue and/or profit for the policy and technology entrepreneurs and their organizations. Intermediary organizations including incubator and accelerator centers and university science and technology research parks (Chapter 6) can help accelerate the process of niche creation and can also provide *niche protection* and *empowerment* for the early stages of technology development.

The first step for niche creation processes is to identify and mobilize a set of actors that are dedicated to making radical changes in society and to encourage them to collaborate based on mutually beneficial outcomes of the process. Smith et al. (2010) suggested that actors doing niche experiments are "relatively more supportive of the social and environmental qualities of the niche socio-technical practice, and more forgiving of teething troubles, owing to their different expectations of future performance compared to regime members" (p. 441). In other words, actors who are interested in encouraging changes to technologies, infrastructures, and institutions may be willing to accept more risk and lower financial returns in exchange for participating in changing the subsystems of the regime in a manner that can foster long-term sustainability value to society and to the individual actors. If a niche experiment is expected to generate sustainability value (e.g., increases to economic, social, *and* environmental value consistent with the strong sustainability definition in Chapter 1), it can be termed a *sustainable niche experiment*.

Sustainable niche experiments

Sustainable niche experiments are processes that lead to the creation and diffusion of technological, social, or policy innovations that have the potential to influence changes to the regime subsystems. Sengers et al. (2017, p. 8) highlighted different forms of experiments that relate to technological innovation studies and sustainability transitions theory: *niche experiments*, bounded socio-technical experiments, *transitions experiments*, grassroots experiments, and *sustainability experiments* (Table 7.2). These types of experiments differ in many ways. For example, niche experiments are based on nurturing strategies of learning, alignment of expectations, and the formation of actor networks. However, transition experiments focus on strategies for expanding sustainability innovation benefits by deepening, broadening, and upscaling processes. Sustainability experiments are defined by Sengers et al. (2017, p. 6) as:

> tests of new sustainability transition ideas (that are) highly novel meaning that they radically differ from the known and prevailing solutions and ways of providing human needs within a specific context...they are planned, which implies that they are conscious choices and not accidents or accidental occurrences...they are expected to lead to substantial sustainability gains...(and they may) result from activities at various societal levels.

Table 7.2 Sustainable niche experiments from the sustainability transitions literature

Concept	Normative orientation (success factors)	Theoretical foundations	Analytical emphasis	Main actors
Niche experiment	Creation of market niches for radical innovation in the context of socio-technical transitions.	Socio-technical systems and evolutionary economics, part of strategic niche management and the MLP.	Three niche nurturing processes: building networks, articulating expectations, second order learning.	Regime-outsiders, important role for users.
Bounded socio-technical experiment	Social learning towards new socio-technical systems.	Social learning theory.	Social learning processes.	Civil society (but as part of a diverse set of stakeholders).
Grassroots experiment	Inclusive green niche development with the potential for wider transformation of mainstream society.	Social movement theory, draws on niche based approaches (i.e. strategic niche management/MLP).	Sustainable consumption indicators: localization, reduction of ecological footprint, community building, collective action, new social infrastructure.	Civil society (especially local communities, ecological citizens as initiators).
Transition experiment	Stimulating transitions towards societal goals.	Complex systems theory, part of transition management.	Three processes: broadening, deepening, scaling-up.	Frontrunners as initiators.
Sustainability experiment	Sustainability gains, avoiding environmental convergence.	Geography and innovation studies in developing country context, influenced by strategic niche management/MLP.	Transnational linkages: actors, technology, knowledge, capital, institutions.	Multi-scalar innovation networks.

Source: Modified from Sengers et al. (2017).

Sustainability experiments follow a normative sustainability vision and goals and are part of a strategic effort to change the regime and its subsystems. They can be planned by groups of societal actors or encouraged from higher governance levels through competitions (Chapter 4). Actors may support the creation of a green innovation cluster in a particular place in order to create the conditions for sustainability experiments to occur without actually dictating which technologies or specific experiments should be conducted. Actors within these clusters may collaborate through networks with other clusters and form a transnational innovation system. The goal would be to encourage both collaboration within and between clusters and competition between actors within clusters to drive the entrepreneurship (experimentation) processes. Sustainability experiments can also help connect ongoing transition processes in developed and developing countries. The questions for sustainability professionals include how to encourage and support sustainable niche experiments, how to scale them up, how to coordinate regime changes with the sustainable niche experiments, and what actors need to be engaged in the process. Three important processes for sustainability professionals to consider are niche empowerment, niche protection, and niche nurturing.

Niche empowerment

Smith and Raven (2012) defined *niche empowerment* processes as two strategies that aim to support niche experiments either in the context of the existing regime (fit-and-conform) or with the help of regime changes (stretch-and-transform). According to Smith and Raven (2012, p. 1033) **fit-and-conform strategies** aim to:

> convince the wider social world that the niche can become competitive on conventional, regime criteria … it will perform profitably in existing markets, and does not require radical changes to institutions, infrastructures, skills and knowledge bases, user relations … shielding measures will be represented as temporary, and nurturing processes will value lessons that direct development towards enhancing competitiveness.

Stretch-and-transform strategies (Smith and Raven, 2012, p. 1033) are designed to:

> convince the wider social world that the rules of the game need to be changed. The selection pressures constituted by prevailing regimes need to be transformed in order that niche-derived forms of sustainable solutions may flourish … the promise of the niche has to have considerable appeal in order to instill confidence and commitment to the broader sustainability vision which it embodies, but niche performance and legitimacy will be judged against sustainability criteria rather than the status quo … shielding measures will be represented as manifesting widely desired sustainability criteria and requiring institutionalization, and nurturing processes will value lessons that direct development towards improving sustainability.

Raven et al. (2016) argued that fit-and-conform niche empowering strategies are designed to demonstrate the competitiveness of new technologies within existing regimes to various stakeholders including government regulators and agencies, consultants, business networks, investors, and users. Stretch-and-transform empowering strategies involve changing the regime subsystems to increase the chances that the new technology can gain market acceptance. Policy entrepreneurs (Chapter 6) are critical to stretch-and-transform niche empowering strategies including changing laws, institutions, and norms. Policy mixes (Chapter 8) are also important empowering strategies that focus on changing the regime in order to enable niche technology breakthroughs. Sustainability professionals aiming to initiate transitions as part of the reactive sustainability pathway (Chapter 1) can identify and engage actors that could be important to empowering niche experiments by making the case for creating value via incremental improvements that fit within the existing subsystems. Acceleration Point: Sustainability professionals working to accelerate strong sustainability pathways can identify and engage actors who are making incremental changes and work to convince them of the merits of changing the regime subsystems including institutions thereby enabling radical innovations.

Niche protection and shielding

A major challenge to the practice of green innovation is how best to create a protective environment for new technologies and entrepreneurs. Huijben et al. (2016) defined *niche shielding* as the financial and resource support that can protect innovations from market forces by reducing transaction costs in the early stages of development. Niche shielding can influence how competitive new green technologies are once they expand into the market. Shielding is important until the performance, price, and supporting infrastructure improves enough for the new technology to compete with incumbent technologies that have built-in structural advantages. Actors that help create these protective spaces include technology developers, lobby groups, environmental non-profit organizations, government decision-makers, and the users of the technology.

Raven et al. (2016) argued that niche shielding occurs first in passive spaces and second in active spaces. An example of a *passive protective space* is when technology developers create off-grid solar or wind generation systems that may be combined with storage, and therefore, are buffered from the market selection pressures of grid-connected systems where the dominant energy companies with powerful political lobbies can limit expansion of the new technologies. Installing solar panels or small wind turbines with fuel cell storage systems in remote First Nations communities in northern Canada is another example where a pre-existing passive space provides protection from selection pressures because the alternative is to fly in expensive diesel fuel, which makes the new technology solution competitive on price within that passive protected space (Rogers, 2018). The broader place-based characteristics including networks and culture also provide passive niche protection. An example of an *active protective space* would be incubator centers (Chapter 6), which are created to buffer new technology start-ups from selection pressures during the critical early stages. Other active protective spaces include developing and using strategic and dynamic capabilities (Chapter 3) to give a new business competitive advantages, and the implementation of subsidies and other policy buffers (e.g., renewable portfolio standards, feed-in tariffs) that provide political and economic protection for new energy companies (Chapter 8).

Huijben et al. (2016) found that the choice of business model by the green entrepreneur was influenced by the amount of niche shielding that they received in the initial phases of development. Higher levels of niche shielding led to the choice of a less creative business model, while lower levels of niche shielding led to a more radical and risk-taking business model. This demonstrated that the choice of strategy for scaling-up a green innovation may relate to the initial entrepreneurship strategies that were followed in response to levels of niche shielding as financial and resource support. The lesson is that if green entrepreneurs receive high levels of niche protection, they may become complacent and thus vulnerable once they graduate from the incubator centers and start to scale through the market.

Niche nurturing

Sustainability professionals can help encourage niche protection by supporting *niche nurturing* processes via social learning and social network development (Raven et al., 2016). This could include intermediaries working to link technology creators to market adoption processes. An example of nurturing would be accelerator centers (Chapter 6) helping a renewable energy technology start-up by buffering it from market and institutional forces within the existing regime. Accelerator centers can aid entrepreneurs by connecting them to networks of funders (e.g., angel investors), skilled labor, government or university researchers working on similar technologies, or lawyers with international expertise in preparation for entering new markets. Niche nurturing can also occur as a consequence of *institutional thickness* (McCauley and Stephens, 2012) that results from the collection of countercultural institutions, networks, groups, and practices that characterize certain places including green clusters (Longhurst, 2015).

Transition arena

Niche creation, empowerment, protection, and nurturing can all be facilitated by groups of actors within a transition arena. A *transition arena* can be employed "to develop new substance (ideas, agendas visions); to support a process (of network/coalition building, learning); and to subtly influence existing regimes or regime actors" (Loorbach and Rotmans, 2010, p. 243). Transition arenas act as intermediary platforms for actors to interact, ideas to clash, power to be displayed and eventually coalesce around a pathway to a new regime, and solutions to be created and supported through competitive and collaborative dynamics. Loorbach and Rotmans (2010, p. 243) described a transition arena based on their experiences in the Netherlands:

> An arena process is an evolutionary process with continuous mutations. We also learned how important a balance is between niche players and change-inclined, innovative regime players. In fact, the latter are also niche players, but with invested power operating within the regime. In a transition process we need both pioneers operating outside and inside the incumbent power structures.

Strategic niche management can be coordinated within a transition arena using a strategic planning approach. It involves identifying opportunities and building teams of actors interested in niche creation as a means of initiating or supporting a sustainability transition and to guide the process of creating and scaling-up new technologies and practices. Sustainability professionals can use sustainability competencies (Chapter 1) to first understand the current situation and then devise a plan for change in relation to a normative goal. Devising a plan concerns the 'how we are going to get there' component of strategic planning and requires sustainability-oriented intermediaries, boundary organizations, and other linking agents to use **interpersonal relations competence** to mobilize support from key actors and build momentum towards achieving the normative goal. The process

of strategic niche management involves five phases: (1) identifying a new technology/
solution, (2) designing an experiment for that technology/solution, (3) implementing an
experiment, (4) expanding an experiment to a niche, and (5) protecting an experiment
(Weber et al., 1999, p. 32). Strategic niche management requires managing expectations
by communicating niche strategies and actions to external actors, building social networks,
and supporting first order learning (daily knowledge and expertise) and second order
learning (questioning assumptions and constraints of regimes) (Seyfang and Haxeltine,
2012). According to Sengers et al. (2017), "strategic niche management assumes that
creating new technological niches through protective policy measures and strategically
exploiting existing market niches can facilitate this innovation journey" (p. 3).

Loorbach and Rotmans (2010, p. 243) described a transition arena in theory as a:

> relatively safe and free, protected environment without any power hierarchy which
> is aimed to stimulate the development of creative, innovative ideas and which can be
> used to generate more time and space to develop ideas and to create distance from
> the existing regime without losing touch.

In practice, however, transition arenas are subject to power dynamics both from within
and from outside the arena. The case of Los Angeles's urban energy transition highlights
this in Chapter 8. Powerful actors from outside the arena also have a stake in keeping the
regime the same or slowing down a transition. Even in cases where the arena is composed
of actors who share a common vision and are working well together, other actors from
the broader political landscape (e.g., national governments or international coalitions) or
from within the regime (e.g., the Koch Brothers discussed in Chapter 9) are able to act as
bottlenecks to the transition arena.

Given that much of the experience with transition arenas comes from Europe, is
it possible for these mechanisms to work in North America, South America, Asia, or
Africa? Bringing together actors from various sectors with the idea of strategically planning and negotiating a pathway to regime change in the direction of sustainability goals
may pose challenges that require sustainability professionals who organize the arena to
make a compelling case for participation. The following sub-sections describe a series of
interactions that could offer alternative mechanisms in cases where a formal transition
arena is not possible.

Niche-to-regime interactions

The MLP sustainability transitions framework is based on the assumption that niche
experiments will be scaled-up and break through the regime during windows of opportunity where regime subsystems are vulnerable to change. Niches are made up of actors
that "serve as 'global carriers' of best practice, standards, institutionalized learning, and
other intermediating resources such as networking and lobbying, which are informed by,
and in turn inform, concrete local projects (experiments)" (Seyfang and Haxeltine, 2012,
p. 383). How can sustainability professionals help encourage or accelerate niche-to-
regime interactions during periods where the regime is not vulnerable to change or in
cases where there is no transition arena?

Raven et al. (2016) argued that actors supporting new technologies should create narratives that highlight how the new technology is a solution to existing problems facing
actors in the regime. Both the United Kingdom and the Netherlands off-shore wind cases

explain how technology advocates aligned messaging with existing government agendas focusing on transitioning the economy and creating jobs. In contrast to off-shore wind, attempts to frame solar PV as a job creation strategy were complicated by the fact that solar PV modules were largely made in China as compared to the wind turbines manufactured in England and Scotland. Therefore, it was easier to frame off-shore wind as a job creation and economic development strategy than it was solar PV (Raven et al., 2016). Intermediaries can help accelerate niche-to-regime interactions (Gliedt et al., 2018) and sustainability professionals can help regime actors understand the benefits of niche experiments. This could include clearly articulating the economic benefits to each specific actor as well as the broader public goods benefits and sustainability value to society.

Regime-to-niche interactions

Sustainability professionals need to find new ways of supporting regime actors at empowering niche development. This can include using institutional support that may exist for broad sustainability initiatives (e.g., climate change) at the regime level to instigate specific green energy technology development (e.g., solar or wind) at the niche level (Kern et al., 2015). Actors in the regime can have a direct or indirect effect on niche experiments by changing institutions, policies, and programs. Regime actors can encourage and support niche experiments, for example, by capitalizing on the interacting relationships between the subsystems of the regime that influence niche creation including how "institutions coordinate investment in infrastructure and production technology" as well as how "technology choices affect production, which affects relations between users and the ecosystem" (Smith and Stirling, 2010, p. 2). The cultural subsystem is also critical to how technologies are created and adapted over time: "social movements, lifestyle expectations, environmental stresses, behavioral patterns, and resource endowments exercise important influences on patterns of technology development and use" (Smith and Stirling, 2010, p. 2).

Although some national governments have set stringent emissions targets and created climate change and other environmental policies that will influence niche experiments, other countries that lack a top-down guiding or enabling policy regime can focus on engaging lower levels of government as regime actors to support niche experiments. Cities, states/provinces, and other sub-national governments focus on planning and land-use changes, building code changes, and feed-in tariffs that encourage sustainability-oriented businesses to come to the region, stay in the region, and expand within the region. These policy and regulatory changes can support green technology innovation processes (Chapter 4) as niche experiments that are part of triple-bottom-line economic development strategies (Chapter 5) regardless of whether a transition arena is formed.

Niche-to-niche interactions

Niche-to-niche interactions can occur both within a regime or between two or more niches in different regimes. Within a regime, multiple green technologies can be developed simultaneously, many of which have complimentary uses and applications. For example, battery innovation niches can benefit from coordination with electric car innovation niches and residential solar development niches, as changes within the former niche can directly affect the technological performance and market demand for the latter two niches. Intermediary organizations can play important roles at searching for complimentary technology development niches and fostering communication and collaboration between the niche actors within the same regime. Intermediaries can also search for social and policy innovation niches at the city level, which could support the success of green technology development niches within the same regime.

Niche experiments can benefit from connections to other niches in other regimes including in other parts of the world that are working on comparable technologies. The example of solar PV in India demonstrates the importance of transnational connections between niches. Wieczorek et al. (2015) discovered that nearly all of the solar PV experiments in India showed evidence of one transnational linkage, and a majority of the experiments showed evidence of two or more. The transnational linkages included actor-related, knowledge-related, capital-related, institutions-related, and technology-related interactions. Transnational linkages connecting niches-to-niches have been understudied (Wieczorek et al., 2015), and require further examination to understand their role in innovation processes on a strong sustainability pathway.

Kivimaa et al. (2017) reviewed the literature on experiments in climate governance that helped achieve sustainability transitions. The experiments focused on different scales of change, ranging from niche creation within protected spaces to market creation combining several niches, and from spatial development patterns at the city planning level to societal problem solving at the state or federal policy level. These experiments led to different types of change, including discourse, technology, human-made capital/infrastructure, policy/institutional, business practices, market changes, and new consumer/citizen practices. Experiments differed in their outputs and outcomes (Kivimaa et al., 2017). For example, in the case of technology changes, outputs included the creation of new solar PV applications, new technology solutions for energy efficiency, and new types of smart meters, while outcomes included the broader learning processes for how to apply and adopt successful experiments as new energy systems. In the case of infrastructure, outputs included temporary changes to land-use planning to encourage green buildings and developments, while outcomes included learning how to make broader changes to infrastructure with sustainability benefits. With respect to policy and institutional change, outputs included new district planning practices for green construction, renovation, transportation, as well as incorporating additional actors into policy making, while outcomes included the creation of new political spaces and governance practices, which have the potential for supporting further experiments at the regime and niche levels.

Niche-to-niche interactions are important for encouraging and coordinating experiments that lead to technology, infrastructure, and policy/institutional changes within a regime. Institutional changes within city planning departments can be outputs from one niche experiment, which then encourages the creation of other niche experiments focused on technology and infrastructure innovation. Niche experiments focused on energy system transitions and transportation system changes are important independent of each other simply because of the scale of annual GHG emissions from these sectors (Figure 7.3), where over 80 percent of the total GHG emissions in 2015 were from CO_2 and a further 10 percent were from methane (EPA, 2017). When these niche experiments are coordinated, however, they can lead to even larger impacts on the socio-technical system due to the complementarity between these sectors (Chapter 8). Acceleration Point: Sustainability professionals can search for ongoing or emerging niche experiments that could be coordinated to build momentum and develop synergies within a regime.

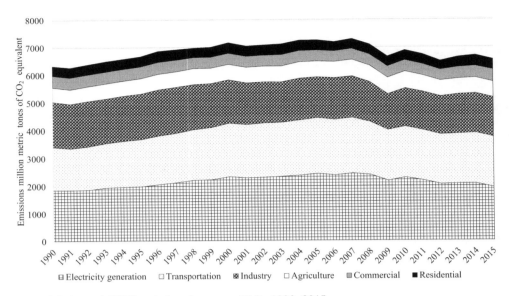

Figure 7.3 Annual GHG emissions by sector, U.S., 1990–2015

Source: Graph by the authors based on data from EPA (2017).

Regime-to-regime interactions

Regime-to-regime interactions have the potential to improve the sustainability of major socio-technical systems. For example, the United States agriculture industry faces sustainability challenges related to pesticide and fertilizer use, declining soil fertility, GHG emissions from technology use, and water quality concerns from chemical runoff. The corn growing industry in Iowa uses pesticides and fertilizers to increase yields. Demand for corn is increasing from United States food consumers, from ethanol producers, as well as from other countries via exports. Runoff in the form of nitrates goes into the Mississippi river and ends up in the Gulf of Mexico where it creates a dead zone. This dead zone impacts the fishing and shrimping industry in Louisiana. The livelihoods of the fishers and shrimpers are directly impacted by decisions hundreds of miles away in another governance regime. Each industry is connected to different subsystems of regimes. In the case of Iowa, industry actors may act as bottlenecks to limit transitions away from high rates of pesticide and fertilizer application for agriculture. In the case of Louisiana, choices by external actors from beyond their regime are constraining the functions and services provided by food, energy, and water systems within the state. While the United States Environmental Protection Agency provides guidelines on which chemicals should be banned and best practices for application rates and techniques, individual states are left to enforce the guidelines.

One potential solution is for the Iowa corn growers to collaborate with the Louisiana fishing industry directly to alleviate a *collection action dilemma*. Both industries can benefit from a change in farming practices in Iowa, and the Louisiana fishing industry has an incentive to compensate the Iowa corn industry to encourage a change in practices to either use less chemical inputs or to drive niche innovation for new types of fertilizers or pesticides. Corn yields may decline in the short term, but long-term productivity may be sustained due to a rejuvenation of soil fertility. The sustainability of two different regimes in different places is interconnected, and this provides an incentive for regime-to-regime collaboration. Regime-to-regime collaboration can act as a driver of niche experiments in agriculture technology and practices.

The *KAYA Identity* in Table 7.3 shows that Louisiana's CO_2 emissions declined by 0.2 percent per year between 1997 and 2014 due to slow population and economic growth and a 1.0 percent annual improvement in energy intensity. Iowa's CO_2 emissions increased by 0.9 percent per year during the same period due in part to a faster economic growth rate of 1.9 percent per year. Iowa has successfully improved its carbon intensity over time while Louisiana only started to improve its carbon intensity during the 2011–14 period. There is an opportunity for these states to collaborate by sharing technology development strategies to reduce CO_2 emissions for Iowa while reducing chemical runoff that goes down the river and impacts Louisiana. Both state governments and other actors within each regime have an incentive to contribute to triple-bottom-line economic development while reducing environmental pollution. Industries from other regimes contributing to the dead zone through new meat production processes (Gallagher, 2017) also have an incentive to participate in collaboration through adaptive co-management (Chapter 3). Sustainability professionals can constantly scan the landscape for major focusing events like the growing dead zone in the Gulf of Mexico, which can be used to put social and political pressure on actors in multiple regimes to encourage collaborative solutions that can benefit all actors in the socio-ecological system.

Landscape awareness: capitalizing on external pressures

Regimes and niches are influenced by landscape processes such as "environmental and demographic change, new social movements, shifts in general political ideology, broad economic restructuring, emerging scientific paradigms, and cultural developments" (Smith et al., 2010, p. 441). *Landscape awareness* is a capability of transition actors to capitalize on external pressures during windows of opportunity (e.g., national, state, or city level political changes) (Wittmayer et al., 2015). Sustainability professionals use **anticipatory competence** to understand landscape trends and to help transition actors encourage niche experiments and regime change strategies. Sustainability-oriented intermediaries can focus on landscape awareness through search mechanisms and social science methods like public opinion surveys, industry surveys, and visioning exercises.

Scanning and understanding the landscape can be a source of ideas and resources for niche experiments. Cities for example often choose visions for sustainability transitions based on what has been done elsewhere (Sengers and Raven, 2015). Knowledge for niche experiments is partly derived from local capabilities and practical experiences but also based on connections through networks to expertise from other regimes. Sengers and Raven's (2015) local-global niche model recognizes networks as multi-scalar *transition arenas* where negotiations between multiple actors take place as part of the niche development process. Key actors move through networks and bring expertise from one place to another to instigate a niche experiment. The local and global are connected and niches for developing a sustainable technology or infrastructure can extend beyond a place through networks.

Sustainability professionals can apply their *sustainability competencies* towards understanding the interactions between niche, regime, and landscape processes. The competencies

Table 7.3 KAYA Identity for Louisiana and Iowa: average annual percent change

Louisiana	1997–1999	1999–2001	2001–2003	2003–2005	2005–2007	2007–2009	2009–2011	2011–2014	1997–2014
CO_2 emissions	-2.2	-1.2	0.8	0.6	2.7	-1.9	3.6	-2.7	-0.2
Population	0.3	0.1	0.3	0.4	-1.5	0.9	0.6	0.5	0.3
GDP/capita	1.2	-0.7	1.6	2.9	-0.1	0.1	-0.9	-1.1	0.5
Energy intensity (energy/GDP)	-3.4	-1.1	-2.0	-2.7	3.9	-2.7	3.0	-0.4	-1.0
Carbon intensity (carbon/ energy)	-0.2	0.5	1.0	0.2	0.5	0.0	0.8	-1.8	0.2

Iowa	1997–1999	1999–2001	2001–2003	2003–2005	2005–2007	2007–2009	2009–2011	2011–2014	1997–2014
CO_2 emissions	2.7	0.0	0.0	1.0	2.8	-0.5	0.6	-1.4	0.9
Population	0.3	0.2	0.1	0.2	0.4	0.4	0.4	0.5	0.4
GDP/capita	0.6	0.9	2.3	3.1	1.4	-1.6	1.0	1.9	1.9
Energy intensity (energy/GDP)	0.8	-1.9	-1.6	-0.8	0.8	3.1	-0.2	-1.4	-0.3
Carbon intensity (carbon/ energy)	0.9	0.9	-0.6	-1.4	0.1	-2.1	-0.5	-2.3	-0.9

Source: EIA (2017a, 2017b), with calculations by the authors.

can both help to develop new strategies and instruments but also to improve the timing and use of existing strategies and instruments at accelerating sustainability transitions and shifting transition actors, processes, and formal and informal arenas from weak towards strong sustainability pathways.

Check on learning

- Read the literature review by Loorbach et al. (2017) and write one to two pages to summarize five important points about sustainability transitions theory. How would you teach these concepts to your friends or classmates, including the common themes and the important interactions between the niche, regime, and landscape levels in the MLP? What are three important definitions you learned from the article, and how do they help you understand sustainability transitions as a complex problem?
- Review the Foxon (2013) article and summarize and compare the different transition pathways. Thinking about your home town or city, identify key actors who would be involved in each type of transition pathway. Given the importance of collaboration to energy initiatives (Pitt and Bassett, 2013), how could the actors that you identified collaborate? How could civil society actors encourage government and business actors to contribute to a transition?
- Read Foxon et al. (2009) and summarize into your own words the differences and similarities between the adaptive management and the transition management frameworks. What roles are played by agents/actors within each framework? How does each framework treat spatial scales and time scales? How do Foxon et al. (2009) propose combining the transitions management and adaptive management approaches? Finally, how is the Foxon et al. (2009) combined framework different from or similar to the solutions-oriented sustainability transition framework in Chapter 1 with respect to change and resilience?
- Read Kivimaa et al. (2017) and identify two outputs and two outcomes that you believe are critical to sustainability transitions. What specific steps would you take, if you were a mayor, governor, or civil servant, to create strategies and instruments that could lead to each of those outputs and outcomes in your town or city?
- As a sustainability professional, how would you encourage niche-to-niche interactions between two complimentary niches in your country that could help accelerate or amplify sustainability transitions?
- How could the concept of landscape awareness be used by sustainability professionals to support the development of the next international climate change agreement?
- Do some research and find one emerging technology that you believe will have a large impact on sustainability in the coming decade. Write one page that describes a set of steps that you would follow to design a combined regime change-niche creation strategy that will increase the chances that the technology will succeed at improving the Gibson principles of sustainability in your country.

Assignments

- Green job creation transition arena at the state/provincial level

References

Avelino, F., & Grin, J. (2017). Beyond deconstruction: A reconstructive perspective on sustainability transition governance. *Environmental Innovation and Societal Transitions*, 22, 15–25.

Bettini, Y., Brown, R. R., de Haan, F. J., & Farrelly, M. (2015). Understanding institutional capacity for urban water transitions. *Technological Forecasting and Social Change*, 94, 65–79.

EIA. (2017a). CO_2 emissions data. U.S. Energy Information Administration. Available at: www.eia.gov/environment/emissions/state/

EIA. (2017b). Population, energy demand, and GDP data. State Energy Data System. U.S. Energy Information Administration. Available at: www.eia.gov/state/seds/seds-data-complete.php?sid=US

EPA. (2017). Inventory of US greenhouse gas emissions and sinks. About the Emissions Inventory. Environmental Protection Agency. Available at: www.epa.gov/ghgemissions/inventory-us-greenhouse-gas-emissions-and-sinks

Fischer, L. B., & Newig, J. (2016). Importance of actors and agency in sustainability transitions: A systematic exploration of the literature. *Sustainability*, 8(5), 476.

Foxon, T. J. (2013). Transition pathways for a UK low carbon electricity future. *Energy Policy*, 52, 10–24.

Foxon, T. J., Reed, M. S., & Stringer, L. C. (2009). Governing long-term social–ecological change: What can the adaptive management and transition management approaches learn from each other? *Environmental Policy and Governance*, 19(1), 3–20.

Gallagher, S. (2017). Tyson foods linked to largest toxic dead zone in U.S. history. Earth Island Journal. Available at: www.earthisland.org/journal/index.php/elist/eListRead/tyson_foods_linked_largest_toxic_dead_zone_us_history/

Gliedt, T., Hoicka, C. E., & Jackson, N. (2018). Innovation intermediaries accelerating environmental sustainability transitions. *Journal of Cleaner Production*, 174, 1247–1261.

Huijben, J. C. C. M., Verbong, G. P. J., & Podoynitsyna, K. S. (2016). Mainstreaming solar: Stretching the regulatory regime through business model innovation. *Environmental Innovation and Societal Transitions*, 20, 1–15.

Kern, F., Verhees, B., Raven, R., & Smith, A. (2015). Empowering sustainable niches: Comparing UK and Dutch offshore wind developments. *Technological Forecasting and Social Change*, 100, 344–355.

Kivimaa, P., & Kern, F. (2016). Creative destruction or mere niche support? Innovation policy mixes for sustainability transitions. *Research Policy*, 45(1), 205–217.

Kivimaa, P., Hilden, M., Huitema, D., Jordan, A., & Newig, J. (2017). Experiments in climate governance–a systematic review of research on energy and built environment transitions. *Journal of Cleaner Production*, 169, 17–29.

Longhurst, N. (2015). Towards an 'alternative' geography of innovation: Alternative milieu, socio-cognitive protection and sustainability experimentation. *Environmental Innovation and Societal Transitions*, 17, 183–198.

Loorbach, D., & Rotmans, J. (2010). The practice of transition management: Examples and lessons from four distinct cases. *Futures*, 42(3), 237–246.

Loorbach, D., Frantzeskaki, N., & Avelino, F. (2017). Sustainability transitions research: Transforming science and practice for societal change. *Annual Review of Environment and Resources*, 42(1), 599–626.

Markard, J., Raven, R., & Truffer, B. (2012). Sustainability transitions: An emerging field of research and its prospects. *Research Policy*, 41(6), 955–967.

Mattes, J., Huber, A., & Koehrsen, J. (2015). Energy transitions in small-scale regions: What we can learn from a regional innovation systems perspective. *Energy Policy*, 78, 255–264.

McCauley, S. M., & Stephens, J. C. (2012). Green energy clusters and socio-technical transitions: analysis of a sustainable energy cluster for regional economic development in Central Massachusetts, USA. *Sustainability Science*, 7(2), 213–225.

Pitt, D., & Bassett, E. (2013). Collaborative planning for clean energy initiatives in small to mid-sized cities. *Journal of the American Planning Association*, 79(4), 280–294.

Raven, R., Kern, F., Verhees, B., & Smith, A. (2016). Niche construction and empowerment through socio-political work. A meta-analysis of six low-carbon technology cases. *Environmental Innovation and Societal Transitions*, 18, 164–180.

Rogers, S. (2018). Nunavut community to expand solar project with new federal funds. Kugluktut's arena to get 144 new solar panels in 2018. Nunatsiaq Online. Available at: www.nunatsiaqonline.ca/stories/article/65674nunavut_community_to_expand_solar_project_with_new_federal_funds/

Sengers, F., & Raven, R. (2015). Toward a spatial perspective on niche development: The case of Bus Rapid Transit. *Environmental Innovation and Societal Transitions*, 17, 166–182.

Sengers, F., Wieczorek, A. J., & Raven, R. (2017). Experimenting for sustainability transitions: A systematic literature review. *Technological Forecasting and Social Change*. Available at: www.sciencedirect.com/science/article/pii/S0040162516302530

Seyfang, G., & Haxeltine, A. (2012). Growing grassroots innovations: Exploring the role of community-based initiatives in governing sustainable energy transitions. *Environment and Planning-Part C*, 30(3), 381.

Smith, A., & Raven, R. (2012). What is protective space? Reconsidering niches in transitions to sustainability. *Research Policy*, 41(6), 1025–1036.

Smith, A., & Stirling, A. (2010). The politics of social-ecological resilience and sustainable socio-technical transitions. *Ecology and Society*, 15(1), 11.

Smith, A., Voß, J. P., & Grin, J. (2010). Innovation studies and sustainability transitions: The allure of the multi-level perspective and its challenges. *Research Policy*, 39(4), 435–448.

Voß, J. P., Smith, A., & Grin, J. (2009). Designing long-term policy: Rethinking transition management. *Policy Sciences*, 42(4), 275–302.

Weber, M., Hoogma, R., Lane, B., & Schot, J. (1999). Experimenting with Sustainable Transport Innovations: A Workbook for Strategic Niche Management. Institute for Prospective Technological Studies, Joint Research Centre in Seville, Spain.

Wesseling, J. H., Farla, J. C. M., & Hekkert, M. P. (2015a). Exploring car manufacturers' responses to technology-forcing regulation: The case of California's ZEV mandate. *Environmental Innovation and Societal Transitions*, 16, 87–105.

Wieczorek, A. J., Raven, R., & Berkhout, F. (2015). Transnational linkages in sustainability experiments: A typology and the case of solar photovoltaic energy in India. *Environmental Innovation and Societal Transitions*, 17, 149–165.

Wittmayer, J. M., van Steenbergen, F., Rok, A., & Roorda, C. (2016). Governing sustainability: A dialogue between Local Agenda 21 and transition management. *Local Environment*, 21(8), 939–955.

8 Practice of sustainability-oriented socio-technical system transitions

Learning objectives

- Examine cases that show sustainability transitions and the underlying changes to niches and regimes
- Introduce policy mixes as a way to integrate niche experiments, regime changes, and sustainability principles and sub-indicators
- Review KAYA Identity trends for understanding the drivers of change for CO_2 emissions
- Develop a comprehensive indicator for measuring socio-technical system change towards a sustainability transition

Practice of sustainability transitions

The case studies in this chapter highlight key change processes within socio-technical systems to identify lessons learned for sustainability professionals wishing to instigate sustainability transitions. Sustainability professionals can start by following a four-step strategic planning process: (1) discover where are we now, (2) decide where we want to be at some point in the future, (3) strategically plan for how we are going to get there, and (4) continually reassess progress against sustainability principles and adjust accordingly.

Discovering where are we now necessitates research including primary and secondary data collection and analysis. This step requires **systems thinking competence**. It can be time consuming and resource intensive and even when new information, knowledge, or insight is generated it can be politically contentious. The challenge is to translate knowledge into a format that is clear and powerful for informing the next two steps in the process. Impartial data collection and analysis is sometimes difficult, as biases could be attributed to the source of funding for the research. Furthermore, assumptions can relate to the type of methods used to collect and analyze the data, the choice of variables for inclusion in models, or the selection of specific findings to highlight as a result of the analysis. Identifying biases and assumptions can help to improve transparency and add validity to the information.

Deciding where we want to be at some point in the future includes normative goal-setting as part of participatory action research, co-producing knowledge, adaptive co-management, or transition arenas. This step requires **anticipatory competence** and **normative competence**. The challenge is to figure out who decides and how much power is equated to the actors involved in the decision. This is particularly important in the multi-level perspective (MLP) because transition management has been critiqued for treating the political economy as neutral and not incorporating citizens except as consumers (Kenis et al., 2016). Transition management does not explicitly highlight the role of individual agency as a driver of transitions (Rauschmayer et al., 2015), and power is often ignored, discounted, or misunderstood within the MLP (Lawhon and Murphy, 2012). This is because transition management and arenas are driven by small groups of actors chosen for their expertise, which may undermine the democratic or pluralistic nature of the transition (Lawhon and Murphy, 2012). A team of industry and political elites agrees on a vision and pathway based on their attitudes and beliefs, and can steer the transition in a direction towards technological and institutional changes that will benefit them. As a result, transition management may be too narrow to incorporate normative targets to guide sustainability transitions (Rauschmayer et al., 2015). Sustainability professionals need to focus on how actors can contribute in a way that is fair and supports empowering rather than marginalizing voices of those who may not be powerful actors in the regime. Acceleration Point: Sustainability professionals can use sufficiency rather than efficiency goals in order to structure social justice objectives into transition processes. How far into the future should the goal be set? Should there be incremental targets, sub-goals, different levels of achievement, or an overarching single objective?

Creating a strategic plan for how we are going to get to the normative target or achieve the sufficiency goals is important to the practice of sustainability transitions. This step requires **strategic competence** and **interpersonal relations competence**. Strategic plans for sustainability transitions support the creation of policy instruments (e.g., regulations, guidelines, laws), guide the development of new partnerships or alliances (e.g., public–private partnerships, multi-level networks), and instigate innovation processes (e.g., research and development, expansion, adaptation). The challenge is to use the strategic planning process to mobilize public and private sector support for changing the locked-in and path-dependent subsystems through policy mixes for niche and regime transitions.

Sustainability professionals will **continually reassess progress against a set of sustainability principles and adjust the strategies and instruments accordingly**. This requires **integrated sustainability research and problem–solving competence**. The strong sustainability pathways in Chapter 1 outlined different options for linking goals to strategies and instruments at the niche and regime levels. A direct pathway to strong sustainability could use formal strategic management plans to strictly guide progress and make course corrections as necessary. Indirect pathways can involve formal or informal governance arrangements that loosely guide progress in the general direction of strong sustainability. A formal strategic management plan can include market-based instruments like carbon taxes or cap-and-trade systems that provide flexibility in the choice and combination of technology and infrastructure solutions. To reach strong sustainability, a pathway must ensure that socio-ecological systems stay within a range of tolerance, which can be calculated based on critical natural capital levels or functions of ecosystem services that must be maintained, or rates of materials and energy throughput that must not be exceeded. The principles of sustainability can be used as indicators for the range of tolerance within an ends–means diagram (see Figure 8.5), and other metrics like the KAYA Identity and a comprehensive indicator for measuring socio-technical system change (described later in this chapter) can inform adjustments to strategies and instruments.

Sustainability professionals attempting to initiate a transition process need to incorporate strategies and instruments to encourage and coordinate sustainable behavior and practices with organizational changes, the development of green innovation systems, and the implementation of triple-bottom-line economic development. Sustainability professionals can learn from case studies of previous transitions by focusing on what worked and what did not work to change the subsystems of the regime.

Electric mobility as system innovation

The transportation sector provides many challenges to sustainability professionals both because of the scale of greenhouse gas (GHG) emissions and the entrenched regime subsystems that have resisted change for many decades (Wesseling et al., 2015a, 2015b). Incremental changes are occurring as evidenced by a gradual shift from fossil fuel-powered internal combustion engine vehicles, to hybrids, plug-in and fully electric, fuel cells, natural gas, and flex fuel vehicles. These technologies offer promise for sustainability in that they can improve efficiency or reduce the carbon intensity of the automotive sector. Several challenges remain, however, including the need to reduce manufacturing costs (e.g., fuel cell vehicles), improve lifecycle environmental performance (e.g., flex fuel vehicles), build necessary supporting infrastructure (e.g., fully electric vehicles), or increase public demand for these products (e.g., natural gas vehicles).

The advantage of hybrid vehicles (gas and electric engines with friction breaking technology and battery systems) is that they do not require a supporting infrastructure and do not significantly disrupt the existing regime. This represents a **fit-and-conform strategy** (Chapter 7). Hybrid technology allows automakers to continue producing internal combustion vehicles; oil companies to continue extracting, refining, and selling gasoline; and city and state governments to continue building roadways and interstate highways in the same manner that they have for the past several decades. Additionally, consumers do not have to change their behavior or practices because they can continue driving to work and filling their vehicles with gasoline. While this is good for automakers and oil companies in the short term, it reduces the need for investing in innovation processes that could radically improve the efficiency and emissions performance of vehicles in the long term.

Transforming the transportation sector requires viewing it as a multi-level system of nested niches and regimes. Changing the transportation sector regime involves sustainable behavior change, organizational strategies, green innovation and economic development, and policy and institutional changes. Sustainability professionals can help to coordinate changes to each of these levels as part of a **stretch-and-transform strategy** (Chapter 7). The following case study focuses on electric mobility as an example of system innovation in the MLP. Innovation creation and diffusion processes involve many niche experiments and changes to multiple regime subsystems. In particular, changes to consumer behavior, technology, policy, and business strategies can be understood as interactions between niche and regime actors in order to accelerate a transition.

Consumer behavior change

A primary challenge for sustainability professionals is to investigate how to convince consumers to purchase fully electric vehicles, which involves strategies to overcome barriers to purchasing and user practices. Rezvani et al. (2015) revealed different motivations and barriers to consumer adoption of electric vehicles, including technical, contextual, cost, and individual/social factors. **Technical factors** like performance (e.g., speed, range, recharge time, safety, noise, and reliability) and aesthetics (e.g., look and style) were listed as barriers to adoption for early electric models and by consumers who did not hold personal environmental values. Car companies responded by improving these factors over the past decade, thereby reducing the barriers. For example, speed and range are now comparable with internal combustion engine vehicles and charge time can be as little as 15 minutes with certain systems. Other technical factors related to environmental attributes (e.g., decreased use of oil, GHG emissions, energy efficiency, battery materials) were a motivating factor for purchasing electric vehicles among an environmentally conscious segment of the population. Car companies can benefit from leveraging these improvements into strategic green advantages by creating and disseminating a sustainability assessment reporting system. Strategic advantages can accrue to the company as a result of preemptively improving sustainability performance prior to the creation of new legislation. This can be accomplished by leveraging new products to attract sustainability-oriented investments from public and private actors, and by using green innovation processes to develop new technologies that could spin-off into new segments. The green innovation process itself will force companies to develop new technology capabilities that are hard to imitate and therefore create a barrier for competitors to enter the electric vehicle segment. One example of technology capabilities is found in Tesla factories that use state-of-the-art automation and robotics invented specifically for those factories, which makes them difficult for competitors to imitate.

Contextual factors include charging concerns (e.g., station locations on roads and in public places) and jurisdictional differences (e.g., tax incentives/rebates, government regulations, and fuel prices) (Rezvani et al., 2015). Sustainability professionals can help to mitigate these concerns by fostering communication between the electric vehicle manufacturers and government agencies. Governments benefit when car companies in their jurisdiction develop and export new technologies, and companies benefit from governments investing in the supporting institutions and infrastructure for electric vehicles. Companies can also benefit from other companies that make investments in electric vehicle infrastructure and renewable energy supply and transmission systems. Sustainability-oriented intermediaries can focus on showing each set of actors the mutually beneficial outputs and outcomes of working together in this manner.

Diffusion rates of electric vehicles in most markets will relate in part to **cost factors**, which include purchase price, operating costs, fuel cost savings, and payback period (Rezvani et al., 2015). While some *first movers and early adopter* consumers (Rogers, 2010) are willing to pay a premium price for electric vehicles because of **individual and social factors**, including lifestyle (e.g., pro-environmental, technology oriented) or symbolic meaning (e.g., what it means to drive an electric vehicle, emotions, norms, social status), the mainstream consumer is less likely to switch to an electric vehicle until the costs are comparable with internal combustion vehicles (Rezvani et al., 2015). Sustainability professionals can help producers create strategies to overcome consumer barriers like the perceived difficulty in changing driving habits (e.g., recharging, driving behavior, and social etiquette) by delivering community engagement programs that allow people to gain personal experience driving electric vehicles. The best way to develop new practices is to walk someone through every stage of the process, and although this is time and resource intensive, social capital and social norms can be used to amplify initial investments in programs to change practices. The community-based social marketing process and the social practices perspective outlined in Chapter 2 can be used to design a behavior change strategy based on the unique combinations of technical, contextual, cost, individual, and social factors that are important to vehicle owners in different jurisdictions or demographics. Sustainability professionals working for business or government actors can benefit from social science research methods like surveys and interviews to identify trends in consumer perceptions.

Manufacturers of electric vehicles need to understand the innovation processes of competitors who promise more affordable and better performing electric vehicles. This requires sustainability professionals who may also be green champions to use scanning capabilities and **interpersonal relations competence** to connect with and potentially collaborate with actors conducting similar types of niche experiments for technology change.

Technology change

The second challenge for sustainability professionals is to understand and accelerate the rate of technology change in electric vehicles. In contrast to hybrid vehicles, Augenstein (2015) argued that a high transformative potential of battery electric vehicles means that they may be less likely to succeed as part of a transition because they do not conform to the existing transportation regime. Regime actors will push back and attempt to slow the development of this technology (Wesseling et al., 2015a). However, the radical potential of battery electric vehicles could instigate broader changes to institutions, infrastructures, and user acceptance that are important for supporting the demand for these innovations. The extent that a new technology has the potential to stretch and transform the subsystems of the regime and encourage new connections between niche and regime actors is termed *transformative capacity* (Augenstein, 2015). Augenstein (2015) concluded that although there was public and private interest in having a transition to battery electric vehicles in Germany, the extent of use of regime transition mechanisms including the level of government funding was relatively low and the dominant regime of gasoline cars acted as a bottleneck to radical transitions.

An electric mobility system can deliver greater sustainability benefits if it is based on a lifecycle analysis of the components of the system. A recent study (reported by Neslen, 2017) found that lifecycle GHG emissions are significantly less for electric vehicles than diesel cars in Europe even when the grid is powered largely by coal. Switching to renewable energy options to power the electric mobility system will create additional *sustainability value*. The success of a transition in transportation systems therefore depends on "how the established sectoral structures, institutions and actors react to a new technology" (Augenstein, 2015, p. 104), and in particular, how the other subsystems of the regime change in coordination with electric vehicle development pathways. The following sections discuss policy and business strategy changes that occur as a reaction to the deployment of electric vehicles or as a means to accelerate their development.

Policy change

The third challenge for sustainability professionals interested in instigating or accelerating a transition in the transportation sector is to select policy and regulatory instruments that are effective at generating sustainability value while minimizing the amount of public investment required. For example, does an increase in public subsidies encourage market uptake of electric vehicles and corresponding sustainability benefits? Olson (2015) found that the costs of public subsidies for battery electric vehicles in Norway were high relative to the social (e.g., health) and environmental (e.g., emissions reduced) benefits generated by the policy. Norway is a special case because the size of its entire car fleet is small compared to most cities in North America, and because Norway generates much of its power from hydro-electricity and has a carbon tax on fuel for gasoline-powered cars. Therefore, the social and environmental benefits of a public subsidy aimed at encouraging more electric vehicle purchases may be less than in other countries that have larger numbers of internal combustion vehicles and that lack other supportive policies like a carbon tax.

Figenbaum (2017) outlined Norway's electric vehicle policy. Although incentives for battery electric vehicles were available since 1990, they were not effective at increasing the uptake of electric vehicles until manufactures switched to using lithium ion batteries in 2010. The combination of battery technology innovation and policy changes helped increase the market share of electric vehicles in Norway to 17 percent in 2015. Figure 8.1 outlines the global landscape and national governance factors that put pressure on the Norwegian internal combustion engine (ICE) vehicle regime to create a *window of opportunity* for local, regional, and national niche experiments to scale-up. This shows that niche experiments can occur at different levels and are not tied to local or place-based factors.

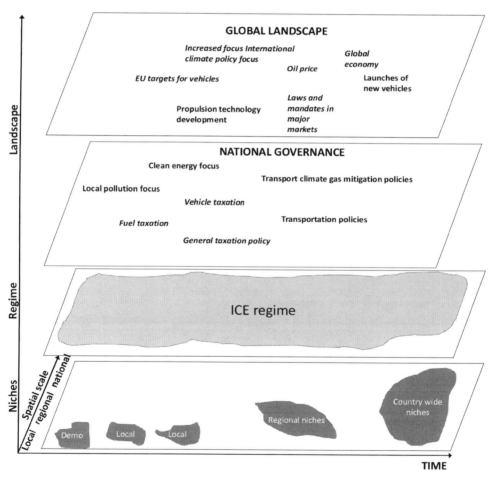

Figure 8.1 MLP for Norway's electric vehicle transition
Source: Figenbaum (2017, p. 18).

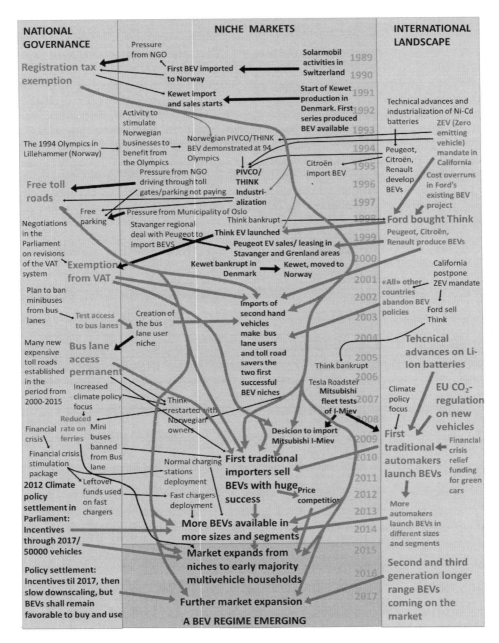

Figure 8.2 Emerging regime for battery electric vehicles in Norway
Source: Figenbaum (2017, p. 27).

The national and international factors including strategy and instrument changes that influenced Norwegian niche experiments coalesced around Acceleration Points (depicted where multiple arrows meet on Figure 8.2) when specific policies were implemented, infrastructure changes were made, and technology breakthroughs were achieved. The result is a complex set of pathways and interactions across scales and time periods where changes to producer and consumer behavior and practices, organizational investments, green innovation systems, triple-bottom-line economic development strategies, and policy mixes helped create a new regime focused on battery electric vehicles (Figure 8.2). Sustainability professionals can study these pathways and interactions in order to learn how bottlenecks were overcome and how *sustainable niche experiments* were scaled-up within the Norwegian socio-technical system.

Another policy and regulatory option is to introduce a fuel economy standard for vehicles that aims to force car companies to innovate in order to reduce fossil fuel consumption (e.g., by efficiency, design, or fuel switching) and increase market demand for the product line based on the assumption that greener cars can save consumers money. Some technology innovations that result may be radical and depend on major changes to infrastructure and institutions to support their market development. For example, electric cars may require policy changes in order to build the charging infrastructure, as well as insurance industry changes to allow new types of vehicles on the road in some jurisdictions. Large incumbent firms may resist developing these technologies without a supporting or encouraging policy mix because they add risk by requiring significant changes to their operating position (Wesseling et al., 2015a).

Wesseling et al. (2015a) analyzed how car companies in the United States responded to the Zero Emission Vehicle Mandate between 1990 and 2013, which was adopted by California and nine other states. They found that some companies used innovation strategies in response to proposed environmental regulations while others developed political influence strategies to mitigate or reduce the stringency of impending regulations. Alternatively, firms that are sustainability leaders can lobby the government for more supply supporting regulations (e.g., fuel economy standards) and demand supporting regulations (e.g., carbon tax, subsidies for users) for electric vehicles (Wesseling et al., 2015b) as a niche-to-regime interaction strategy, which can solidify their leadership position by providing protection for further *sustainable niche experiments* (Chapter 7). Policy changes at the governance level can lead to business strategy changes that either inhibit or accelerate the recalibration of long-term innovation pathways towards electric mobility technologies and infrastructures.

Business strategy change

In response to the zero-emission mandate in the United States, car manufacturers (General Motors, Chrysler, Toyota, Nissan) followed business strategies that focused on different combinations of innovation (as measured by patent applications) and political influence (as measured by arguments, litigation, compliance) (Wesseling et al., 2015a). Political influence strategies changed over time, with manufacturers preferring **defensive strategies** to oppose the mandate early on (2000–2006), but then gradually switching to **proactive strategies** to shape the mandate or support the mandate (2007–2013) (Wesseling et al., 2015a). GM in particular used defensive strategies to oppose the mandate initially and also bought electric vehicle and hybrid electric vehicle credits from Tesla, Toyota, and Honda as part of their compliance strategy instead of investing in innovation. Tesla welcomed a stricter regulation as part of a proactive strategy because additional demand from GM for electric vehicle credits would allow Tesla to expand its market share. As of April 2017, Tesla had overtaken Ford (BBC, 2017) and GM (GN, 2017) as the largest automaker by market value, and now faces production challenges to meet increasing orders for its electric vehicles.

As GM increased innovation rates and commercialization of greener car options, it gradually switched its political influence strategy from opposing to shaping the mandate in the direction of plug-in hybrid electric vehicles (Wesseling et al., 2015a). While all companies initially opposed the mandate (1990–1999) and were laggards (Rogers, 2010) with respect to innovation, political influence strategies supporting the mandate were adopted by Toyota and Nissan between 2007 and 2013. GM and Chrysler eventually moved from opposing to shaping strategies in 2007–2013. Chrysler never became an innovation leader in any green technology. Wesseling et al. (2015a) concluded that strategies can change over time from maintaining and protecting existing product lines through defensive political influence to creating value through new product lines via technology innovation and proactive political influence. Firms that were the least innovative had the strongest political influence strategies focused on opposing or weakening the mandate. Firms that were most innovative had political influence strategies focused on shaping or supporting the mandate. Firms that were using *sustainable niche experiments* and regime change mechanisms simultaneously (Chapter 7) were able to increase market share for new transportation technologies.

Wesseling et al. (2015b) argued that car makers need both an **incentive** (e.g., does it enhance competitiveness and increase market share) and **opportunity** (e.g., has the company developed capabilities and built assets necessary for developing radical technologies) to innovate. The combination of incentive and opportunity to innovate influences the choice of business strategy of the firm (e.g., first mover, quick follower, laggard). Mitsubishi, Renault, and Nissan had a high incentive to innovate and a strong opportunity to innovate and were considered first movers that successfully developed and sold large numbers of electric vehicles. By contrast, BMW, Ford, Honda, and Daimler had average incentive to innovate and some opportunity to innovate. These companies began developing and marketing electric vehicles and were characterized as quick followers. A first group of laggards included GM, Volkswagen, and Toyota, which had little incentive (above average profitability) but a strong opportunity (electric vehicle asset position above average) to develop electric vehicles. A second group of laggards included Fiat, Suzuki, and Mazda, which had a high incentive to innovate due to their below average profitability but little opportunity to innovate because their electric vehicle asset position was below average.

Automakers can choose to collaborate as a strategy to foster further innovation in electric vehicles (Wesseling et al., 2015b). In particular, large incumbent firms can partner with electric vehicle entrepreneurs to gain a competitive advantage by being able to monitor and guide the development of cutting-edge electric vehicle technologies. This represents a niche-to-niche interaction strategy (Chapter 7) that helps spread risk and encourage larger investments in research and development (R&D). Another niche-to-niche interaction opportunity exists for residential solar system manufactures to collaborate with electric car makers. Electric cars can be used as storage devices to power homes during peak times, saving money and helping to shift electricity demand (Brush et al., 2015). Homeowners would not have to pay for battery storage systems because the car batteries could serve the double role of powering the vehicle when in use, charging during off-peak times, and powering the home during peak times. Manufacturers of home battery storage systems like Tesla can respond by further innovating and improving the performance and cost of their systems. This represents niche-to-niche competition across sectors, which can lead to strategic partnerships and alliances or to the development of *dynamic capabilities* as a means of fortifying against competition.

Electric vehicles represent a key technology that when integrated with institutional and infrastructure changes can drive triple-bottom-line economic development for car producing regions. Recent projections suggest that electric vehicles may grow from one percent to over 30 percent of the car market by 2030 with over 100 electric models expected in the next few years (Randall, 2017). With battery prices declining by 20 percent every year, Toyota is planning to phase out fossil fuel combustion engines from all of its vehicles by the middle of this century (Randall, 2017). Much of the growth in electric vehicle sales is expected to come from China (Randall, 2017). In fact, GM aims to sell 20 fully electric vehicles by 2023 largely because of demand from China. This is supported by China's plan to cap CO_2 emissions by 2030 (a top-down enabling policy), which influenced a requirement for 12 percent of vehicles to be zero or low-emission. GM is therefore focusing a *sustainable niche experiment* to meet expected demand for electric vehicles instigated by a policy from within a different regime (Welch, 2017). This regime-to-niche interaction can serve as a model of innovation within a globalized economy where *value cycles* and markets are interconnected.

Transitions in transportation socio-technical systems require changes to renewable energy production and delivery, storage systems, and urban energy systems if they are to be consistent with sustainability principles. Understanding the interactions between the regimes and niche experiments in these areas is critical to sustainability transitions.

Wind and solar photovoltaics as system innovations

Sustainability professionals can compare renewable energy installation rates between different countries in order to understand how innovation diffusion can be accelerated. For example, offshore wind installations have increased in the United Kingdom while installations in the Netherlands have flatlined (Kern et al., 2015). Both countries have significant offshore wind potential (natural resource landscape), governments that publicly support offshore wind (policy and political regime subsystems), and share many large wind companies that have substantial investments in offshore wind in each country (industry regime subsystem). The difference was that offshore wind expansion in the United Kingdom occurred due to *niche empowerment* strategies that were more successful than what occurred in the Netherlands. As Kern et al. (2015, p. 353) explained:

> while advocates in both countries pursued both 'fit and conform' as well as 'stretch and transform' strategies, only in the case of the UK were the latter successful and led to significant offshore wind deployment. The difference is mainly attributed to the existence of a system builder in the form of the Crown Estate (niche empowering actor) as well as the salience of climate change and renewable energy targets in the UK.

The style of policy making is also important in the innovation process for offshore wind. Reichardt et al. (2017) examined and compared adaptive and participatory styles between the German energy policy processes that led to (1) the Renewable Energy Act and (2) the Energy Economy Law. They found that an **adaptive style** had a negative effect on certain functions of technological innovation systems (Chapter 4), including entrepreneurial activities, knowledge development, and resource mobilization within the Energy

Economy Law policy process, while a **participatory style** had a positive effect on entrepreneurial activities, knowledge development, knowledge exchange, guidance of the search, and creation of legitimacy in both policy processes. Uncertainties in the adaptive style had a negative effect on the entrepreneurial activities, knowledge development, guidance of the search, and resource mobilization in the Renewable Energy Act process. Sustainability professionals can examine styles of policy making in order to enhance green innovation processes in socio-technical systems. **Interpersonal relations competence** can also be used to mitigate uncertainties that come with adaptive governance styles by clearly communicating a vision and guidelines, and by reassuring actors who are part of the process that minor *turbulence* and frequent adjustments are to be expected.

Similar to the global wind industry, the rate of growth in the global solar industry is changing rapidly. This has led to a reduction of manufacturing costs for solar PV and an increasing competitiveness relative to other energy technologies. For example, the United States installed more solar capacity than any other energy source for the first time in 2016 (SEIA, 2017). Sustainability professionals are helping actors within niches create and scale-up solar technologies. But regime actors are working to inhibit this transition. How are strategies of businesses changing in response to the rapid growth rates and emerging bottlenecks in the industry?

Dewald and Fromhold-Eisebith (2015) used a case study of solar PV in Germany to show that different actor networks (*transition arenas*) and different geographic scales (institutional spaces) are important at different stages of the innovation process. German solar PV technology is more than 60 years old and has gone through stages of growth, stagnation, and decline. While early growth was supported by policies including the 100,000 solar roofs program, which provided low-interest loans with zero down payment requirements (Mundo-Hernández et al., 2014), the German *Energiewende* and accompanying *feed-in tariff* provided a mechanism to continue domestic demand for solar. One of the reasons for the recent decline is the "inappropriate scaling of processes" that have included "a focus on national markets, subsidies and protection laws" (Dewald and Fromhold-Eisebith, 2015, p. 111). The focus on national market development acted as a bottleneck to solar actors in Germany by inhibiting them from upgrading their innovation systems in response to emerging competition from solar companies in Asia. The implication is that nationalism or protectionism of an industry can reduce the incentive for innovation by insulating manufacturers from external competition. This may even overpower support from federal policies aimed at encouraging an energy transition. The United States is going through similar discussions and debating whether to institute a tariff on solar technology imports from countries like China (Natter and Martin, 2017). In the long-term, this may reduce innovation rates and research and development within the United States solar industry, which are currently competitive with the other major solar players including Japan, Germany, and China (Zheng and Kammen, 2014).

Figure 8.3 shows that Germany, Japan, and the United States were leaders in solar technology patents and innovation in 2000, while China had minimal research and development, manufacturing, or installed capacity until 2008 (Zheng and Kammen, 2014). By 2010, the United States was a leader in patents, R&D, and innovation, while China led in manufacturing and Germany in market installation capacity. Japan has continued to be balanced between innovation, manufacturing, and installation. While rapid growth in manufacturing and installed capacity (48 percent per year between 2002 and 2012) has led to a consistent decline in prices, the flipside is that it also led to an oversupply of solar production relative to demand (Zheng and Kammen, 2014). Oversupply created a situation where there was a declining incentive for innovation, and lower prices for solar caused many companies to go out of business or

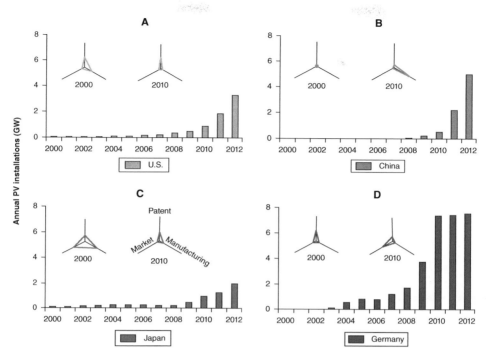

Figure 8.3 Evolution of innovation, manufacturing, and market demand in four key nations in
the PV industry

Source: Zheng and Kammen (2014, p. 162).

to become less profitable. These trends have destabilized the environment for investment in
R&D, and in particular, for new types of solar like thin film technologies, which find it difficult to compete with large-scale solar PV manufacturers (Zheng and Kammen, 2014).

Despite market challenges and uncertainty, solar and wind energy consumption rates
have been increasing in the United States, exceeding 1.8 quadrillion BTU in 2014. Using
data from the Energy Information Administration (EIA, 2017b), Figure 8.4 shows patterns of solar and wind development in the United States (Figure 8.4A) and key states
(Figures 8.4B, 8.4C, 8.4D). Rapid growth in wind consumption during the early 2000s
in Colorado, Hawaii, Illinois, Kansas, Oklahoma, Oregon, and Texas was followed by
solar consumption rates accelerating during the late 2000s in Arizona, California, Hawaii,
Massachusetts, and Nevada. North Carolina has emerged on the solar scene in a major
way and now has the second largest installed capacity in the nation as of 2016 (SEIA,
2017). Despite significantly less solar potential as measured by kilowatt hours per square
meter per day (NREL, 2017), New Jersey was consuming about the same amount of solar
power as Nevada as of 2015 ranking in the top five solar states. California is a large consumer of both solar and wind energy and had more than 100,000 solar jobs in 2016 (SEIA,
2017). Massachusetts, Texas, Nevada, Florida, and New York followed with more than
8,000 solar workers each in the same year. One reason why the solar industry accelerated
in the United States was the introduction of the Solar Investment Tax Credit in 2006,
which was extended and expanded in 2008 and again extended in 2015 (SEIA, 2017).

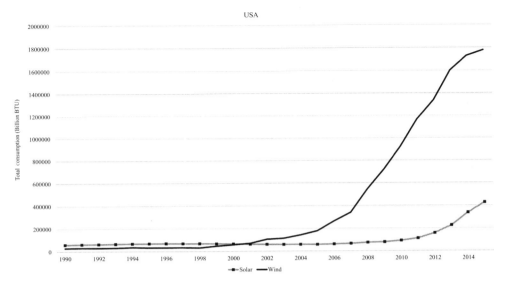

Figure 8.4A Patterns of solar and wind development in the U.S.

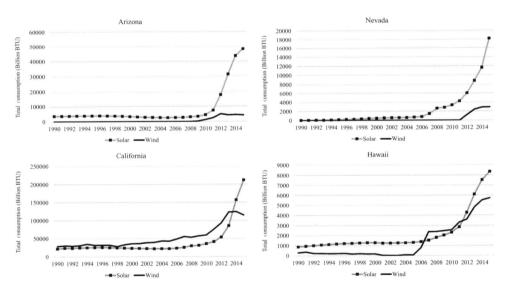

Figure 8.4B Patterns of solar and wind development in Arizona, Nevada, California, and Hawaii

This tax credit can be justified on economic grounds because it has helped create more than 260,000 solar jobs as of 2016, which is double the amount in 2012 (SEIA, 2017). More than 9,000 solar companies now operate in the United States and the resulting increase in manufacturing capacity helped to reduce solar prices by more than 70 percent between 2010 and 2016 (SEIA, 2017).

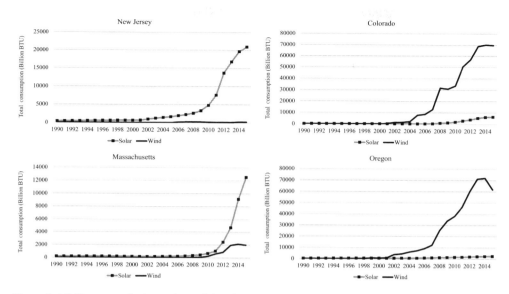

Figure 8.4C Patterns of solar and wind development in New Jersey, Colorado, Massachusetts, and Oregon

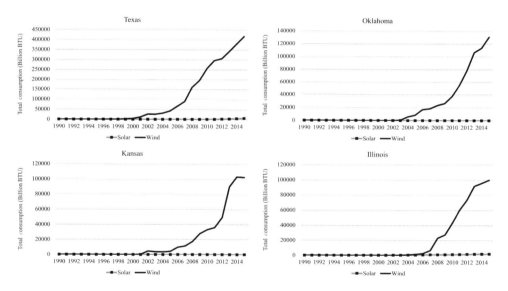

Figure 8.4D Patterns of solar and wind development in Texas, Oklahoma, Kansas, and Illinois
Source: U.S. Energy Information Administration (EIA, 2017d).

The solar industry depends on connections between local (regional) innovation systems and national and international innovation systems (Dewald and Fromhold-Eisebith, 2015). First, similar innovations are developing simultaneously in different places with little or no interaction between those places. Increasing the interaction between places instigates competition or in some cases collaboration, which could lead to modified versions of the technology through *economies of scope* strategies. Second, different drivers of innovation including R&D, technology production, market formation, and policy making can be located at different levels (e.g., local, regional, national, supranational, international). These drivers may complement each other (e.g., national economic development policy may support local technology entrepreneurship at the early stages). Drivers at different levels may be important at different phases in the innovation process including the pioneer stage, the industrial reluctance stage, the market formation stage, the internationalization stage, and the crisis stage (Dewald and Fromhold-Eisebith, 2015). Sustainability professionals can create policy mixes that match interventions at different levels to the phases of innovation as is discussed in Chapter 11. This coordination can avoid duplication of resources, but it does entail *transaction costs* and political challenges of working, trusting, and agreeing with actors at different levels. Transnational linkages may also bolster solar industry development against regime resistance strategies within different countries.

Within the United States, utility companies are using regime resistance strategies to impede and slow distributed solar energy development (Hess, 2016). Major utilities that have political and economic power aim to reverse policies that support distributive solar initiatives including net metering programs. Similar to automotive companies, utility companies work to influence the political opportunity structure to create or bolster conditions that protect their interests. Regime actors use a range of strategies in state legislatures, courts, and even within markets through acquisitions of emerging competitors. Many strategies focus on creating laws that increase costs for distributive solar generators to make it less economically beneficial, or to add connection fees to make it less likely that residential or commercial producers would want to connect to the grid. Numerous lawsuits were filed aiming to undermine distributed solar industries. Laws like SB1456 in Oklahoma were created and passed to increase the electricity rates for distributed generation solar and wind companies that buy from the grid when the sun and wind are not producing enough energy to meet their demands. Regime actors test many strategies in different states as experiments in order to learn and improve future regime resistance strategies (Hess, 2016).

To counteract the power of regime actors, niche actors focusing on scaling solar developments can partner with political parties, seek support from investment banks and large private companies, and align with social movements that support solar energy and distributed energy systems (Hess, 2016). Intermediary organizations can foster these relationships and build networks of actors with complimentary interests (Chapter 6). While finding political parties that support solar in some states or cities may be difficult, partnerships can be created with political actors in other jurisdictions to build momentum and influence change within the overarching governance regime at the federal/national level. Partnering or creating informal relationships with banks interested in technology development can have mutually beneficial outcomes in that the bank provides credibility to the solar industry during the entrepreneurship stage, and the solar industry provides financial returns during the product diffusion stage as manufacturing costs come down because of *economies of scale*. Solar actors can build alliances with large companies in other industries (e.g., Goggle, Facebook, Twitter) to gain public support and fulfill corporate social responsibility imperatives. Environmental non–profits also build alliances with solar companies as a means of strengthening the position of both partners (Lyakhov and Gliedt, 2017). Partnerships and networks can accelerate institutional change and innovation processes and can mobilize support to win court cases against regime actors aiming to slow solar industry growth (Hess, 2016).

Transition towns in the United Kingdom

Transition towns are driven by two interrelated *landscape* factors that put pressure on the regime: climate change and peak oil. Transition towns in the United Kingdom are an example of a community-based innovation that enables a network of best practices for redesigning society for sustainability transitions (Seyfang and Haxeltine, 2012). A major challenge for community-based innovation is "the struggle to maintain a viable sustainable socio-technical space within a wider unsustainable regime" (Seyfang and Haxeltine, 2012, p. 384). This protective space could be fostered by policies, culture, values, structures, or practices as described in Chapter 7. Transition towns combine elements of each and thus represent an integrated mechanism for *niche creation* (e.g., as seedbeds for innovation) and *niche protection* (e.g., by buffering *agents of change* against regime actors attempting to slow down a transition).

As a low-tech alternative to the radical technological changes and market reforms advocated by *ecological modernization theory*, transition towns are a lifestyle and cultural change involving simple practices to improve quality of life. Although expanding membership beyond the original environmentalists who created a town proved difficult, Seyfang and Haxeltine (2012) found that transition towns have been replicated in other parts of the world. *Strategic niche management* could be used by sustainability professionals to expand the transition town movement to influence broader regime changes (Seyfang and Haxeltine, 2012). Transition towns are effective within regimes characterized by a supportive culture for climate change mitigation based on sustainability values; however, they may be less effective at changing the regime within entrenched urban systems. The case of Los Angeles outlines how large cities can encourage sustainability transitions and overcome the path dependence of energy regimes.

Urban energy transition: city of Los Angeles

Although historically considered as one of the more unsustainable cities in the United States due to sprawling development and urban air pollution, Los Angeles created a Green L.A. Plan in 2007 and started to switch electricity contracts from coal to wind and solar suppliers in 2011 (Monstadt and Wolff, 2015). Urban energy transitions are a function of the transformative capacity of urban sustainability policies and the socio-technical adaptability of the regime (Monstadt and Wolff, 2015). Urban sustainability policies have a high **transformative capacity** if they influence changes to technology, institutional arrangements, practices in energy use, power dynamics between actors, and the labor and human capital supply of the regime. Regimes that are easily able to integrate new green technologies, are composed of organizations that are able to adopt new socio-technical solutions, routines, products, or strategies, and where institutions are open and flexible to change would represent high **socio-technical adaptability**.

Policy changes at the state level were a major driving force for initiating climate and energy policies at the municipal level in Los Angeles (Monstadt and Wolff, 2015). A California renewable portfolio standard was adjusted to include a focus on municipal energy systems to require 33 percent renewable energy by 2020. The California Global Warming Solutions Act (AB 32) passed in 2006 aimed to reduce GHG emissions from electricity to 35 percent below 1990 levels by 2030 (Monstadt and Wolff, 2015). As a way to accelerate achievement of the AB 32 mandate, the state created the California Climate Strategy (2015) with a more stringent target to reduce GHG emissions to

40 percent below 1990 levels by 2030. This overarching strategy is supported by a number of sub-targets to increase renewable electricity production to 50 percent, reduce petroleum use in vehicles by 50 percent, and double the energy efficiency of existing buildings. Each of these state-level targets, strategies, and instruments is designed to encourage and enable sustainability innovation and investments by businesses and municipalities. To what extent have these policy shifts led to measurable improvements in climate change mitigation and innovation within the Los Angeles urban energy regime?

Coal declined from 51 percent of Los Angeles' electricity supply mix in 2003 to 39 percent in 2010, while renewables increased from three to 20 percent in the same time period (Monstadt and Wolff, 2015). As a result, the Los Angeles electricity system was able to reduce GHG emissions to 22 percent below 1990 levels by 2013. To achieve these reductions, many initial renewable energy contracts were awarded to out-of-state companies. The challenge was that many supply contracts were only short-term (five years) and once those contracts expired, they had to be replaced by the Los Angeles utility. The need for replacement supply capacity led to the creation of a solar rooftop feed-in tariff that aimed for 100 MW of locally produced green energy by 2016. City council members acted as regime resistance actors (bottlenecks) by limiting the program to larger solar producers, which slowed the development of small-scale solar installations (Monstadt and Wolff, 2015). Monstadt and Wolff (2015) concluded that despite the rapid switching from coal to renewable suppliers, the continued use of large, centralized suppliers for the majority of Los Angeles' energy demonstrates that the regime was not transformed, and in fact, was reinforced. The networks of energy actors were not disrupted, and the routines and corporate strategies of the utility were not significantly changed. The goal of transitioning to a decentralized generation regime was not yet achieved.

California represents an interesting case for sustainability professionals. On May 13, 2017, a new record was set in the state as 67.2 percent of electricity was generated by renewables (excluding hydropower) or 80.7 percent when including hydropower (Lant, 2017). California and Los Angeles are not alone in making major investments into renewable energy transitions in the United States. Cities like Atlanta and Chicago plan to run solely on renewable energy by 2035 and 2025, while Las Vegas is already 100 percent powered by renewables. Nevada, Massachusetts, and Hawaii have similar targets for their states (Lant, 2017). For comparison, the entire country of Germany set its own record, generating 85 percent of its electricity from renewables on April 30, 2017 (Houser, 2017). Germany even generated an excess of renewable energy in December 2017 and had to pay consumers to use more of it as prices went negative (Berke, 2018). More remarkable is that in 2016, 90 percent of all new electricity added to Europe's grid was renewable (Houser, 2017).

States and cities are interconnected because the regime subsystems of each overlap. Changes to regime subsystems at the state level can influence or enable niche experiments at the city level. Policy mixes become even more important when considering how to coordinate city and state policies to more effectively encourage transitions.

Policy mixes for creation and destruction within sustainability transitions

A key question of interest for sustainability professionals is how to create technological innovations while simultaneously changing the existing regime. *Policy mixes* can be used to foster technological and infrastructure innovations, as well as institutional innovations that help destabilize the regime and create openings for new technologies (Kivimaa and Kern, 2016). The particular combination of policies can be important to support "the development of specific niche innovations and new technological innovation systems with attention to regime destabilization. . .in a mutually re-enforcing way" (Kivimaa and Kern, 2016, p. 206). Simply adding more policies could lead to negative effects, however, by creating overlaps and confusion between actors across governance levels (Costantini et al., 2017). The policy mix should lead to a simplified and easy-to-understand institutional environment. In other words, if a collection of policies that are well coordinated and complimentary are able to both encourage the creation and adoption of technologies and the destruction or weakening of the existing institutional regime, then the chances of successfully transitioning society towards sustainability are enhanced (Kivimaa and Kern, 2016).

Policy mixes for sustainability transitions are composed of objectives, sub-targets, strategies, and instruments (Rogge and Reichardt, 2016). **Objectives** can be set to a long-term sustainability oriented target such as a 75 percent GHG emission cut from 1990 levels by 2050. **Sub-targets** can be used to integrate or encourage cross-level interactions between different components of the sustainability framework (e.g., from green innovation processes to triple-bottom-line economic development) in order to measure progress towards an overarching objective. Sub-targets could include, for example, the number of export-oriented green manufacturing jobs created per public dollar invested in R&D. The sub-targets help link objectives to long-term plans that contain **strategies** to mobilize financial and institutional support. **Instruments** include specific tools and techniques for changing the regime subsystems and may focus on encouraging the creation and production of new technologies, increasing demand for those technologies, and altering the institutions and infrastructure systems to help scale-up and protect those technologies.

Rogge and Reichardt (2016) created a typology of different combinations of **instrument type** (economic, regulation, information) and **instrument purpose** (technology push, demand pull, systemic change). For example, **economic instruments** included research, development, and demonstration grants/loans, tax incentives (technology push), subsidies, feed-in tariffs, emissions trading systems (demand pull), and infrastructure provisions (systemic change). Examples of **regulation instruments** included patent laws, intellectual property rights (technology push), technology and performance standards (demand pull), grid access guarantees, and environmental liability laws (systemic change). Finally, **information instruments** included entrepreneurship training, scientific workshops (technology push), rating and labeling systems, public information campaigns (demand pull), education system changes, and cluster development (systemic change). Any of these policy instruments on their own may generate important changes to regimes or work to foster and protect *niche experiments*, but sustainability professionals can find a mix of instruments that not only complement each other, but also create positive impacts (synergies) that are greater than the sum of the effects of each.

Kivimaa and Kern's (2016) policy mix framework focused on creating niche innovations and destroying regimes. Technology entrepreneurs (Chapter 4) and *policy entrepreneurs* (Chapter 6) as well as the interrelationships between them are important to the creation and use of policy mixes for sustainability transitions. The policy mix framework combines the *technological innovation systems framework* (Chapter 4) and the *strategic niche management* theory (Chapter 7) to outline a number of policies that could lead to the creation of innovations. Policy mixes can be used to encourage creative destruction of a socio-technical system by simultaneously encouraging technology solutions while weakening the path dependent and locked-in subsystems of the regime (Kivimaa and Kern, 2016). What do policy mixes look like in practice, and what are the implications of policy mixes for sustainability outcomes?

Kern et al. (2017) compared the development of policy mixes for energy efficiency between Finland and the United Kingdom. They discovered that policy mixes for both nations became more complex over time as many additional policies were added and few were removed. There was a need identified for both countries to better coordinate policies and evaluate the outcomes of the policy mix. Kern et al. (2017) also noted that many of the energy efficiency policies created in the United Kingdom and Finland were driven by energy efficiency directives from the European Union, which acted as guiding and enabling policies. The specific policy choices differed by country, which suggests that guiding and enabling policies can be effective at influencing countries to take action while tailoring those actions to allow flexibility for place and context specificities. For example, the United Kingdom reduced the number of voluntary energy efficiency programs over time while Finland found these programs successful and continued to use them.

Measuring the outcomes of policy mixes can be accomplished by linking them to the sustainability principles outlined in Chapter 1. Ontario, Canada, serves as an example of policy mixes that have contributed to improving the sustainability principles. Ontario's policy mix includes the Green Energy and Green Economy Act (2015), which was linked to other policies like the feed-in tariff. A set of policies focusing on sustainable behavior included smart meter and time-of-use pricing programs, which aimed to maximize conservation and demand management (CDM) improvements. Another set of policies intended to maximize the use of renewable energy included a renewable portfolio standard. Major outcomes of the Green Energy and Green Economy Act included the creation of green jobs and green manufacturing capacity within Ontario. As a compliment to the Act, city and regional policies like smart growth planning (e.g., integrated transportation, land-use and energy system changes) were implemented across the province to minimize fossil fuel use through green transit, minimize urban sprawl, and maximize population density along transportation corridors.

Each of these policies aim to either encourage/protect niche experiments by driving the development and scaling of new technologies and infrastructures, or to instigate change to the subsystems of the regime. Some policies used **economic instruments** designed to be flexible to allow for competition including feed-in tariffs, while others used **regulation instruments** like transportation planning changes and mandatory smart meter programs. **Information instruments** were also deployed to communicate the other instruments and programs to citizens and organizations and to coordinate green innovation processes in clusters with the help of intermediaries (Chapter 6). All of the policies are interrelated and collectively work to achieve the sustainability principles outlined in Chapter 1, including maximizing resource maintenance and efficiency, socio-ecological system integrity, livelihood sufficiency, and intra- and inter-generational equity. An ends–means diagram (Figure 8.5) can be used to connect an overarching goal of achieving a sustainability transition by 2050 to the sustainability principles and sub-indicators that are part of the **ends objectives hierarchy**. These ends objectives are further linked to a **means objectives network,** which includes sub-indicators that measure the first and second order impacts of the policy mix. Acceleration Point: Sustainability-oriented policy mixes focus on coordinating actors and resources to most efficiently and effectively improve performance of the sustainability principles and sub-indicators that are part of the ends objectives hierarchy, which include minimizing GHG emissions, maximizing health and safety, maximizing access to affordable energy, and maximizing green jobs created.

An example impact of policy mixes can be seen when comparing U.S. state-level energy policies to per capita CO_2 emissions (Figure 8.6). The states are sorted from lowest to highest CO_2 emissions per capita in 2014 (from left to right) and are displayed in

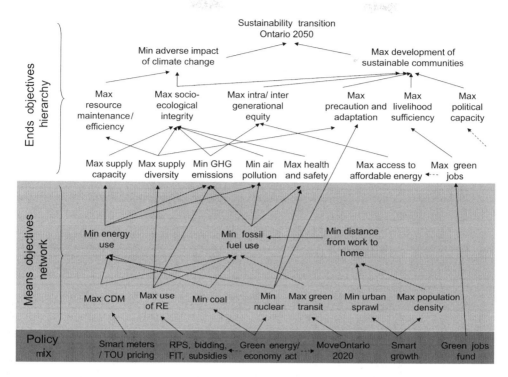

Figure 8.5 Policy mix linked to sustainability principles: Ontario sustainability transition
Source: Authors' rendition.

three groups. The group of states with the lowest average CO_2 emissions per capita (10 tonnes) also had the highest average number of energy efficiency and renewable energy policies (103). The second group averaged 17 tonnes per capita with 90 policies, while the third group averaged 41 tonnes per capita with only 66 policies per state. While the association between the average number of policies and per capita emissions is weak ($R = -0.3$), it suggests that adding certain combinations of energy efficiency and renewable energy policies may contribute to a reduction in per capita CO_2 emissions in some cases. States like California (CA), Oregon (OR), Washington (WA), Minnesota (MN), Colorado (CO), and Texas (TX) stand out for having a mix of policies focused on **financial incentives** for energy efficiency and renewable energy, **regulatory policies** for energy efficiency and renewable energy, and **technical resources** for energy efficiency and renewable energy. Other states like Kansas (KS), North Dakota (ND), and West Virginia (WV) had few **financial incentive** policies and lacked a diverse policy mix. Mississippi (MS) and Tennessee (TN) had few **regulatory policies**, but instead focused on **financial incentives** (MS) or **technical resources** (TN).

New York (NY), Michigan (MI), Vermont (VT), Washington (WA), Indiana (IN), Hawaii (HI), and California (CA) had feed-in tariffs, an example of a **financial incentive** for renewable energy. Of the aforementioned states with feed-in tariffs, all but New York also had a *renewable portfolio standard*, an example of a **regulatory policy** for renewable

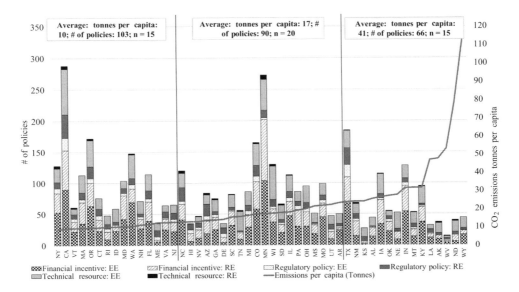

Figure 8.6 CO_2 emissions per capita versus the number and type of energy efficiency and renewable energy policies by state, 2014

Source: Data from EIA (2017a) and DSIRE (2017). Authors' calculations.

energy. In total, 38 states including Massachusetts (MA), Rhode Island (RI), Delaware (DI), Connecticut (CT), Maine (ME), Maryland (MD), Ohio (OH), Pennsylvania (PA), New Mexico (NM), New Hampshire (NH), Wisconsin (WI), Texas (TX), New Jersey (NJ), Kansas (KS), Oregon (OR), Colorado (CO), and North Carolina (NC) had a renewable portfolio standard.

Minnesota (MN), Texas (TX), and Indiana (IN) stand out with high numbers of policies compared to their relatively high emissions per capita. Vermont (VT), Rhode Island (RI), and Maine (ME) are outliers with low numbers of policies compared to their relatively low emissions per capita. This suggests that it is not just the number of policies that is important to sustainability outcomes, but how they interact and complement each other. Sustainability professionals could examine Minnesota (MN) and Indiana (IN) to see if some of their policies could be merged, modified, or removed to improve efficiency or effectiveness for reducing emissions per capita.

Measuring progress towards socio-technical system change

The KAYA Identity

The KAYA Identity was created by Kaya and Yokoburi (1997) and is introduced here as a method for measuring progress towards sustainability-oriented socio-technical system transitions. Growth in CO_2 emissions = population growth rate + economic development growth rate (GDP/population) + rate of change in energy efficiency (energy/GDP) + rate of change in carbon intensity (CO_2/energy). The KAYA Identity is an expansion of Ehrlich and Holdren's (1971) I=PAT equation, which argued that environmental

Table 8.1 KAYA Identity for the U.S.: Average annual percent change

USA	1997–1999	1999–2001	2001–2003	2003–2005	2005–2007	2007–2009	2009–2011	2011–2014	1997–2014
CO_2 emissions	0.5	0.4	0.5	0.8	0.1	–3.4	0.4	–0.2	–0.2
Population	0.8	0.7	0.6	0.6	0.6	0.6	0.5	0.7	1.0
GDP/capita	2.3	1.0	0.9	1.8	0.8	–1.6	0.8	1.4	1.4
Energy intensity (energy/GDP)	–2.2	–1.8	–0.9	–1.5	–1.2	–1.3	–0.4	–1.5	–1.7
Carbon intensity (carbon/energy)	–0.2	0.6	–0.1	0.0	–0.1	–1.2	–0.6	–0.7	–0.4

Source: EIA (2017a, 2017b). Authors' calculations.

impacts (I) are a product of population (P), affluence (A), and technology (T). The KAYA Identity adds specific categories for technology change related to energy efficiency and carbon intensity as drivers of CO_2 emissions. The implication is that reducing emissions will require improvements in the energy intensity and carbon intensity rates by more than the percentage increase in population and economic development.

Between 1990 and 2014, the CO_2 emissions in the United States increased by 7.5 percent (EIA, 2017a) despite a target of 6 percent below 1990 that was part of the original Kyoto Protocol. The following analysis focuses on the time period of 1997–2014 in order to accentuate the impact of recent policy changes. Although some states that were early movers on CO_2 emission reductions such as Oregon may not get the full credit they deserve, this time period highlights important trends and regional differences that help explain changes in CO_2 emissions as a function of the four driving forces outlined by the KAYA Identity. While CO_2 emissions increased in the United States between 1990 and 2014, they declined between 1997 and 2014 by 0.2 percent per year (Table 8.1). This occurred despite an average annual increase in population of 1.0 percent and GDP per capita of 1.4 percent. This is explained in part by average annual improvements to the energy intensity and carbon intensity of the economy by 1.7 and 0.4 percent respectively. Another contributing factor was the 2008 recession, which is reflected in the period of 2007–09 when CO_2 emissions declined by more than 3 percent per year as a result of a decline in GDP per capita of 1.6 percent per year. Importantly, the period of 2011 to 2014 shows that the United States achieved an average annual reduction in CO_2 emissions of 0.2 percent despite an increase in population and economic growth. This period was characterized by the Clean Power Plan that led to the closure of many older coal power plants, policy instruments aimed at improving the average fuel economy of vehicles, and other federal policies attempting to achieve a green energy transition (Obama, 2017). How did the change in emissions differ by states?

Figure 8.7 shows the KAYA Identity components for all 50 states sorted by size of CO_2 emission reduction between 1997 and 2014 from largest reducers to largest increasers. Three groups are evident based on whether a state saw a reduction of greater than 5 percent, relatively no change between -5 and 5 percent, or an increase of more than 5 percent. The group of states that reduced CO_2 emissions by more than 5 percent (n = 23) had an average increase in population of 13 percent and an average increase in GDP per capita of 18 percent. The group that saw their average emissions increase by more than 5 percent (n = 15) had an average population increase of 20 percent and GDP per capita increase of 33 percent. While average improvements in energy intensity (energy/GDP) were similar in all three groups, average improvements in carbon intensity were three times greater for the largest reducers group (-12 percent) relative to the other two groups (-5 and -4 percent respectively). This suggests that CO_2 emissions would have been much higher in the largest reducers group if not for significant improvements in carbon intensity during this time period. Large improvements in carbon intensity were achieved by policy instruments aimed at increasing renewable electricity and switching away from coal as Massachusetts demonstrated. As of 2014, the average CO_2 emissions per capita was 18 tonnes for the largest reducers group and 31 tonnes for the largest increasers group.

Some individual states stand out including North Dakota (ND), which experienced rapid economic growth from fracking and other fossil fuel energy developments that drove CO_2 emissions and overpowered significant improvements in energy and carbon intensity. Nevada (NV) had rapid population growth despite a contracting economy,

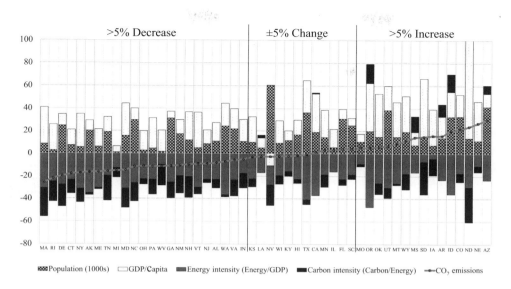

Figure 8.7 KAYA Identity for all 50 U.S. states: percent change CO_2 emissions, 1997–2014
Source: EIA (2017a, 2017b). Authors' calculations.

which helped to keep CO_2 emissions from increasing. Michigan (MI) had almost no economic or population growth, which allowed CO_2 emissions to decline despite only marginal improvements in energy and carbon intensity. Arizona's (AZ) rapid population growth pushed emissions up by the highest of any state. Seven states saw carbon intensity get worse including Oregon (OR), and California (CA), and Mississippi (MS). Massachusetts (MA), Rhode Island (RI), Delaware (DE), Connecticut (CT), and New York (NY) achieved the most significant CO_2 emission reductions due to large improvements in energy and carbon intensity despite economic and population growth during that period. How can sustainability professionals understand and measure ongoing changes in socio-technical systems as a function of niche and regime strategies and instruments that lead to energy and carbon intensity improvements?

A comprehensive indicator for measuring socio-technical system change

The following formula could be used to measure and track the extent that a sustainability transition is occurring in socio-technical systems. This is a modified version of the shift share formula introduced in Chapter 5. The goal is to monitor rates of change in niche creation and regime destruction, while measuring the development rates of green technology and infrastructure. The formula emphasizes the role of innovation intermediaries at integrating levels through their activities and interactions with niche actors (champions) and regime actors (policy entrepreneurs). It also emphasizes the transition policy mix as an important driver of regime destruction and for enabling green innovation and job creation. This formula could be modified with the incorporation of additional sub-indicators and metrics of innovation, including human capital development rates, information and communication technology, ease of access to credit, knowledge workforce diversification, and knowledge diffusion rates (Global Innovation Index, 2014).

The challenge for sustainability professionals is to collect the type of data required for this formula on an ongoing basis. For example, data on green patents, dollar amounts invested in R&D, the number of contracts for infrastructure improvements, and the dollar amounts of public and private investment in infrastructure are easy to find in most countries' statistical databases or as part of ongoing data collection by government departments. Other data are more difficult and may require costly and time-consuming surveys or interviews by government or governance actors. Sustainability professionals working for intermediary organizations can help collect this data by surveying business leaders agbout their innovation strategies and their championing activities within the organizations; local officials about their attempts to form transition arenas or other collaborative approaches to strategic niche management; and government civil servants to identify and track the activities of policy entrepreneurs working to change the institutional conditions of the regime. Researchers can also identify the number and type of green jobs policies with the help of interviews of government officials, and analyze the nature of sustainability-focused policy mixes using content analysis and interviews.

$$\Delta STS = \left(TC\left(\frac{GP_2}{GP_1} \div \frac{IRD_2}{IRD_1}\right) + IC\left(\frac{C_2}{C_1} \div \frac{PPI_2}{PPI_1}\right) + NC\left(\frac{OIS_2}{OIS_1} \div \frac{PA_2}{PA_1}\right) + RD\left(\frac{GJP_2}{GJP_1} \div \frac{TPM_2}{TPM_1}\right) \right) \times$$
$$\left(IM\left(\frac{CA_2}{CA_1} + \frac{IAA_2}{IAA_1} + \frac{PEA_2}{PEA_1}\right) + \frac{CLI_2}{CLI_1} \right)$$

Where ΔSTS = change in socio-technical systems

TC = technology change

GP = green patents

IRD = investment in R&D

IC = infrastructure change

C = contracts

PPI = public private investment

NC = niche creation

OIS = organizational innovation strategies

PA = policy arena development

RD = regime destruction

GJP = green jobs policies

TPM = transition policy mix

IM = intermediary multiplier

CA = champion activity

IAA = incubator and accelerator center activity

PEA = policy entrepreneur activity

CLI = champion $\rightarrow$ incubator/accelerator $\rightarrow$ policy entrepreneur cross-level interactions

$_1$ = previous time period

$_2$ = most recent time period

The focus for sustainability professionals wishing to understand if a transition is occurring is on the intermediary multiplier, which is a combination of champion activity, incubator and accelerator center activity, policy entrepreneur activity, and the cross-level connections between each of these actors. While collecting data about these activities and connections will pose many challenges, the hypothesis is that if intermediary activity increases over time, then a sustainability transition in technology, infrastructure, and institutions will be more likely to accelerate (Gliedt et al., 2018). Acceleration Point: Sustainability professionals should focus on developing and implementing strategies and instruments to support the intermediary multiplier.

Check on learning

- In two pages or less, first, describe how electric mobility is a system innovation, and second, outline key actors, strategies, and processes that are important in sustainability transitions focused on the transportation sector.
- Read Figenbaum (2017) and review the emerging regime diagram that is displayed in this chapter as Figure 8.2. Thinking about your country, do some research and draw a similar diagram to show how a new sustainable technology and its supporting infrastructure and institutional changes have co-evolved over time.
- Thinking of the state/province or city where you live, find and examine sustainability-related policies that have been implemented and choose one that would be considered a niche creation policy and a second that would be considered a regime destabilization or destruction policy (following definitions in Kivimaa and Kern, 2016). Describe in one or two paragraphs how the two policies may complement or contradict each other. How can the mix of niche creation and regime destruction policies help accelerate a sustainability transition? What role could sustainability professionals play in creating a more effective policy mix?
- Read Table 1 in Reichardt et al. (2017) and summarize the descriptions of technological innovation system functions. Thinking about your city or community, identify at least one important actor who would be involved in each of the functions. How could a sustainability-oriented innovation intermediary (Chapter 6) contribute to each of these functions?
- Examine the KAYA Identity components. Do some research of publicly available data sources like the World Bank, the Energy Information Administration, the International Energy Agency, or the Organization for Economic Co-operation and Development. Find and download the necessary data to calculate the KAYA Identity for your country and/or state/province. How have the components changed over time? What explanation can you think of for why energy intensity and carbon intensity have changed?
- Examine the comprehensive indicator for socio-technical system change. What type of collection techniques would be necessary to gather the different types of data for this indicator? What other variables would you want to include in this type of indicator in order to measure progress towards sustainability?

Assignments

• Building a sustainability app for socio-technical system change

References

AB 32. (2006). Assembly Bill No. 23. Chapter 488. Nunez. Air pollution: greenhouse gases: California Global Warming Solutions Act of 2006. Available at: www.leginfo.ca.gov/pub/ 05-06/bill/asm/ab_0001-0050/ab_32_bill_20060927_chaptered.pdf

Augenstein, K. (2015). Analysing the potential for sustainable e-mobility: The case of Germany. *Environmental Innovation and Societal Transitions*, 14, 101–115.

BBC. (2017). Tesla's market value overtakes Ford. Available at: www.bbc.com/news/ business-39485200

Berke, J. (2018). Germany had so much renewable energy over Christmas it had to pay people to use it. Science Alert. Available at: www.sciencealert.com/germany-actually-paid-people-use-clean-renewable-electricity-over-holidays-christmas

Brush, A. J., Krumm, J., Gupta, S., & Patel, S. (2015). EVHomeShifter: Evaluating intelligent techniques for using electrical vehicle batteries to shift when homes draw energy from the grid. In *Proceedings of the 2015 ACM International Joint Conference on Pervasive and Ubiquitous Computing* (pp. 1077–1088). September. ACM.

California Climate Strategy. (2015). California Climate Strategy. An integrated plan for addressing climate change. Available at: http://climatechange.ca.gov/

Costantini, V., Crespi, F., & Palma, A. (2017). Characterizing the policy mix and its impact on eco-innovation: A patent analysis of energy-efficient technologies. *Research Policy*, 46(4), 799–819.

Dewald, U., & Fromhold-Eisebith, M. (2015). Trajectories of sustainability transitions in scale-transcending innovation systems: The case of photovoltaics. *Environmental Innovation and Societal Transitions*, 17, 110–125.

DSIRE. (2017). Database of state incentives for renewables and efficiency. N.C. Clean Energy Technology Center. N.C. State University. U.S. Department of Energy. Available at: www. dsireusa.org/

Ehrlich, P. R., & Holdren, J. P. (1971). Impact of population growth. *Science*, 171(3977), 1212–1217.

EIA. (2017a). CO_2 emissions data. U.S. Energy Information Administration. Available at: www. eia.gov/environment/emissions/state/

EIA. (2017b). Population, energy demand, and GDP data. State Energy Data System. U.S. *Energy Information Administration*. Available at: www.eia.gov/state/seds/seds-data-complete. php?sid=US

Figenbaum, E. (2017). Perspectives on Norway's supercharged electric vehicle policy. *Environmental Innovation and Societal Transitions*, 25, 14–34.

Gliedt, T., Hoicka, C. E., & Jackson, N. (2018). Innovation intermediaries accelerating environmental sustainability transitions. *Journal of Cleaner Production*, 174, 1247–1261.

Global Innovation Index. (2014). The Global Innovation Index 2014: The Human Factors in Innovation. Cornell University. Eds: Soumitra Dutta, Bruno Lanvin, & Sacha Wunsch-Vincent. Available at: www.wipo.int/edocs/pubdocs/en/economics/gii/gii_2014.pdf

GN. (2017). Tesla overtakes market value of Ford and GM. GineersNow. Available at: www. gineersnow.com/industries/tesla-overtakes-market-value-ford-gm

Green Energy and Green Economy Act. (2015). Ontario Green Energy and Green Economy Act of 2009. Ministry of Energy. Available at: www.energy.gov.on.ca/en/green-energy-act/

Hess, D. J. (2016). The politics of niche-regime conflicts: Distributed solar energy in the United States. *Environmental Innovation and Societal Transitions*, 19, 42–50.

Houser, K. (2017). Germany just smashed an energy record, generating 85% electricity from renewables. Futurism. Available at: https://futurism.com/germany-just-smashed-an-energy-record-generating-85-electricity-from-renewables/

Kaya, Y., & Yokobori, K. (Eds). (1997). *Environment, Energy, and Economy: Strategies for Sustainability*. United Nations University Press, Tokyo, Japan.

Kenis, A., Bono, F., & Mathijs, E. (2016). Unravelling the (post-) political in transition management: Interrogating pathways towards sustainable change. *Journal of Environmental Policy & Planning*, 18(5), 568–584.

Kern, F., Verhees, B., Raven, R., & Smith, A. (2015). Empowering sustainable niches: Comparing UK and Dutch offshore wind developments. *Technological Forecasting and Social Change*, 100, 344–355.

Kern, F., Kivimaa, P., & Martiskainen, M. (2017). Policy packaging or policy patching? The development of complex energy efficiency policy mixes. *Energy Research & Social Science*, 23, 11–25.

Kivimaa, P., & Kern, F. (2016). Creative destruction or mere niche support? Innovation policy mixes for sustainability transitions. *Research Policy*, 45(1), 205–217.

Lant, K. (2017). California grid smashes record, gets 67% of energy from renewables. Futurism. Available at: https://futurism.com/california-grid-smashes-record-gets-67-energy-renewables/

Lawhon, M., & Murphy, J. T. (2012). Socio-technical regimes and sustainability transitions Insights from political ecology. *Progress in Human Geography*, 36(3), 354–378.

Lyakhov, A., & Gliedt, T. (2017). Understanding collaborative value creation by environmental nonprofit and renewable energy business partnerships. *VOLUNTAS: International Journal of Voluntary and Nonprofit Organizations*, 28(4), 1448–1472.

Monstadt, J., & Wolff, A. (2015). Energy transition or incremental change? Green policy agendas and the adaptability of the urban energy regime in Los Angeles. *Energy Policy*, 78, 213–224.

Mundo-Hernández, J., de Celis Alonso, B., Hernández-Álvarez, J., & de Celis-Carrillo, B. (2014). An overview of solar photovoltaic energy in Mexico and Germany. *Renewable and Sustainable Energy Reviews*, 31, 639–649.

Natter, A., & Martin, C. (2017). U.S. solar developers relieved at small import tariff proposals. Bloomberg. Available at: www.bloomberg.com/news/articles/2017-10-31/u-s-trade-panel-proposes-duties-of-up-to-35-in-solar-case-j9frwy6w?cmpId=flipboard

NREL. (2017). Photovoltaic solar resources of the United States. National Renewable Energy Laboratory. Available at: www.nrel.gov/gis/solar.html

Neslen, A. (2017). Electric cars emit 50% less greenhouse gas than diesel, study finds. *The Guardian*. Available at: www.theguardian.com/environment/2017/oct/25/electric-cars-emit-50-less-greenhouse-gas-than-diesel-study-finds

Obama, B. (2017). The irreversible momentum of clean energy. *Science*, 355(6321), 126–129.

Olson, E. L. (2015). The financial and environmental costs and benefits for Norwegian electric car subsidies: Are they good public policy? *International Journal of Technology, Policy and Management*, 15(3), 277–296.

Randall, T. (2017). The electric-car boom is so real even oil companies say it's coming. *Bloomberg*. Available at: www.bloomberg.com/news/articles/2017-04-25/electric-car-boom-seen-triggering-peak-oil-demand-in-2030s

Rauschmayer, F., Bauler, T., & Schäpke, N. (2015). Towards a thick understanding of sustainability transitions: Linking transition management, capabilities and social practices. *Ecological Economics*, 109, 211–221.

Rezvani, Z., Jansson, J., & Bodin, J. (2015). Advances in consumer electric vehicle adoption research: A review and research agenda. *Transportation Research Part D: Transport and Environment*, 34, 122–136.

Reichardt, K., Rogge, K. S., & Negro, S. O. (2017). Unpacking policy processes for addressing systemic problems in technological innovation systems: The case of offshore wind in Germany. *Renewable and Sustainable Energy Reviews*, 80, 1217–1226.

Rogers, E. M. (2010). *Diffusion of Innovations*. 4th Edition. Simon and Schuster. The Free Press, New York, NY.

Rogge, K. S., & Reichardt, K. (2016). Policy mixes for sustainability transitions: An extended concept and framework for analysis. *Research Policy*, 45(8), 1620–1635.

SEIA. (2017). Solar industry data: Top 10 solar states. Solar Energy Industries Association. Available at: www.seia.org/research-resources/top-10-solar-states; and www.seia.org/solar-industry-data

Seyfang, G., & Haxeltine, A. (2012). Growing grassroots innovations: Exploring the role of community-based initiatives in governing sustainable energy transitions. *Environment and Planning-Part C*, 30(3), 381.

Welch, D. (2017). GM plans 20 all-electric models by 2023. Bloomberg Technology. Available at: www.bloomberg.com/news/articles/2017-10-02/gm-pledges-electric-future-with-20-all-electric-models-by-2023

Wesseling, J. H., Farla, J. C. M., & Hekkert, M. P. (2015a). Exploring car manufacturers' responses to technology-forcing regulation: The case of California's ZEV mandate. *Environmental Innovation and Societal Transitions*, 16, 87–105.

Wesseling, J. H., Niesten, E. M. M. I., Faber, J., & Hekkert, M. P. (2015b). Business strategies of incumbents in the market for electric vehicles: Opportunities and incentives for sustainable innovation. *Business Strategy and the Environment*, 24(6), 518–531.

Zheng, C., & Kammen, D. M. (2014). An innovation-focused roadmap for a sustainable global photovoltaic industry. *Energy Policy*, 67, 159–169.

9 Sustainability in transition
Bottlenecks and seedbeds

Learning objectives

- Address the question of whether sustainability is an end state that can be achieved or whether sustainability is an ongoing process
- Outline major reasons why it is hard to change socio-technical systems under current conditions and conceptions of sustainability
- Identify bottlenecks to sustainability transitions and seedbeds for instigating and supporting sustainability transitions
- Critique indicators for sustainability and question whether they are effective at encouraging transitions

Bottlenecks to sustainability

This chapter reflects on sustainability transitions theory and practice and contemplates sustainability as a process based on continual efforts aimed at overcoming bottlenecks and creating and supporting seedbeds. Bottlenecks are things that slow down, inhibit, undermine, cast uncertainty on, or stop altogether sustainability movements or transition attempts in society. They are sometimes obvious such as financial barriers that inhibit sustainability initiatives in businesses or political barriers that undermine sustainability policies in government agencies. Other times bottlenecks are less obvious and even invisible until sustainability professionals dig beneath the surface. This section reviews regime bottlenecks that relate to the policy and political subsystem, those that occur as a result of the new abundance of fossil fuels related to the technology and industry subsystems, the various bottlenecks associated with the institutional subsystem that have limited any serious global action on climate change, and the classic and yet still relevant bottleneck provided by *NIMBY* (Not In My Back Yard) and how it relates to the ability of stakeholders to shape the narrative within the social and cultural subsystems.

Policy and political subsystems: Strategies of regime actors including ALEC and the Koch Brothers in resisting transitions

Sustainability professionals focus on strategies and instruments for destabilizing the regime to pave the way for sustainable niche experiments to successfully scale-up. This is made more challenging because of *regime stability*, which is the result of "active resistance by incumbent actors" (Geels, 2014, p. 23) reflecting the role of power dynamics between actors. Power becomes entrenched when policy makers and business leaders form alliances based on mutual dependencies. These dependencies include firms relying on governments for property rights, market rules and norms, and governance structures, while governments support and shape economic sectors with tariffs, loans, grants, government procurement, patents, tax reform, and research (Geels, 2014). These alliances and dependencies explain how regimes resist change: both dominant actor groups benefit from maintaining the current system and power structures, and success of each group is dependent on the other. Geels (2014, p. 28) outlined four different forms of power that help to maintain regime stability and resist change:

1   Instrumental forms of power:

    • Actors use resources (e.g., positions of authority, money, access to media, capabilities) to influence other actors to help achieve their goals and interests.

2   Discursive forms of power:

    • Actors use discourses that shape what and how issues are discussed (thus setting agendas).

3   Material forms of power:

    • Actors draw on technical capabilities and financial resources to change the technical dimension of socio-technical regimes (infrastructure) in their favor.

4   Institutional forms of power:

    • Actors use institutional contexts to facilitate strategies and thus assist regime resistance.

These forms of power can help regime actors set the agenda for selecting potential sustainability solutions. Power can help to portray a particular socio-technical solution as the only option, thereby removing debate, discussion, critique, and learning about multiple possible pathways (Geels, 2014). As Geels (2014) explained, "this post-political technocratic style therefore favors existing regimes and makes it difficult to open up choices for wider political and cultural debate, which again helps explain why alternative transition pathways are side-lined" (p. 35). Policy makers may support sustainability solutions that match up with the current interests of actors in the regime (weak sustainability) rather than exploring radical options that may not fit with prevailing interests and agendas (strong sustainability).

When transition processes start to take shape and gain momentum, the regime tends to reassert power with command-and-control mechanisms (Loorbach and Rotmans, 2010). Loorbach and Rotmans (2010, p. 244) argued that the regime actors may:

> attempt to build up new institutional constituencies, such as task forces, advisory boards, and sounding boards. This arises mainly out of fear to give away the steering and control of the transition processes: it is a mere reflex to remain a handle on a complicated process the regime wants to be in charge of.

The result of regime actors pushing back is a reduction in the creative, supportive, and protective spaces for front runners and first movers that are critical for intermediaries and other niche and regime actors to instigate sustainability transitions (Chapter 7).

In contrast to sustainability transitions in many European countries where socio-technical solutions could be created and implemented independent of political differences, politics in North America is arguably the biggest bottleneck to sustainability transitions and has served to lock in the existing regime subsystems for decades. Many political barriers are well known and relate to politicians voting for or against legislation based on how it would affect their constituencies (e.g., West Virginia and coal miners). Additionally, the amount of pressure from lobbyists representing various dominant actors in the regime (e.g., ALEC and the Koch Brothers) represents a political bottleneck to change as described below. The extent to which politicians toe the party line in cases where political parties have traditionally supported fossil fuels (e.g., the United States Republican Party) is also a bottleneck when considering political and ethical debates about choosing country over party, or in the case of sustainability, choosing the earth over party.

Other policy and political bottlenecks are more difficult to interpret. Take for example the Oklahoma Solar Law. The act, S.B. 1456, permitted centralized electric utilities to levy a surcharge on customers who produced power using distributed generation systems (Griffin et al., 2014). This act essentially protected centralized power producers from individuals or businesses who wished to install solar panels on their own properties, which could in theory lead to decreased demand for their electricity supply product. On its face, this appears to be a protectionist policy for the fossil fuel industry. But the issue becomes more complicated when you consider that some utilities in Oklahoma have already installed solar farms themselves, while others are major supporters of wind production and transmission capacity upgrades as part of an energy transition in the state. The bottleneck in this case relates to traditional economic protectionist arguments where powerful regime actors attempt to influence policies to reinforce the path dependence of the existing systems. At the point when niche opportunities emerge (e.g., the cost of solar declines or the demand for solar credits increases), the dominant regime actors then work to corner a new market by making it harder for new entrants (e.g., small scale or individual generators) to compete.

Another example of political barriers is the American Legislative Exchange Council (ALEC). ALEC is a political lobbying organization that writes *model legislation* for policy makers, holds conferences to teach politicians and business leaders how to speak about climate change and other sustainability issues, and works to systematically weaken and dismantle state and federal environmental legislation. One of ALEC's main goals is to remove actual or perceived barriers to further fossil fuel development (Goldenberg and Pilkington, 2013). The current director of the United States Environmental Protection Agency (EPA), Scott Pruitt, was a former member of ALEC who even held a chair position in the organization (Jervey, 2017). Pruitt, who during his time as the Attorney General of Oklahoma filed 14 lawsuits against the EPA, including targeting the Clean Power Plan that aimed to limit CO_2 emissions from power plants (DeSmogBlog, 2017), also has connections to many oil companies and legal associations that support and are supported by fossil fuel actors. The director of the agency in charge of protecting the environment is therefore himself a bottleneck to sustainability.

ALEC has had a direct and measurable effect on slowing the electric vehicle demand in the United States. For example, in Georgia, an ALEC member and state representative introduced *model legislation* that was adopted by the state. Georgia both removed incentives for electric vehicles and began charging electric vehicle drivers extra fees, which caused electric vehicle sales to decline by 90 percent (Jervey, 2017). The Koch Brothers, who are powerful oil industry actors and funders of anti-climate science campaigns, also fund ALEC

and have worked to build opposition within states that provide incentives for electric vehicles. For more information on ALEC and the Koch Brothers, explore the DeSmogBlog
(2017), a non-profit group of environmental researchers and reporters focused on uncov-
ering the political and institutional bottlenecks that reinforce the path dependence of fossil
fuel technology and infrastructure systems. The volunteers and workers at DeSmogBlog
could therefore be considered sustainability professionals who investigate, compile, and
communicate critical information about regime resistance strategies. Acceleration Point:
When it comes to understanding how fossil fuel actors protect the regime, sustainability
professionals need to follow the money and devise a strategy for decoupling the linkages
between regime actors who are political bottlenecks and the policy-making process.

Technology and industry subsystems: the new supply glut of fracking, methyl-hydrates, and the Keystone Pipeline-oil sands dilemma

Although some environmental movements (e.g., transition towns) were born out of the
worry that peak oil and related supply shortages will impact society in uncertain and
potentially destructive ways, some studies suggest that the main problem preventing us
from solving sustainability challenges is that there is too much fossil fuels left in the ground
(Jaccard, 2006). In this case, a solution would be to use fossil fuels more sustainably. But
is this even possible? How does this argument relate to the Environmental Kuznets Curve
discussed in Chapter 5? Using fossil fuels more sustainably could involve clean coal, fracking, and carbon capture and storage, but are technologies and industries able and willing
to develop and support these options?

The idea of clean coal has proven difficult to achieve in practice and the first large-scale
clean coal energy production facility in the United States, the Kemper County plant in
Mississippi, was cancelled after racking up US$4 billion in cost overruns while failing to
achieve carbon capture and storage (Fountain, 2017). The stakeholders involved decided
to give up on the clean coal technology and switch to burning natural gas. The result: a
nearly $8 billion experiment has demonstrated that the technology is flawed and far from
economically viable. This will not stop industry subsystem researchers from continuing
to invent new technologies to capture and store carbon from coal plants, which is seen as
the holy grail for continuing the global coal industry.

A similar story exists for the oil sands industry. The process of mining, extracting,
refining, conditioning, and transporting the Alberta oil sands poses many environmental
challenges that are well documented (Mosher, 2017). One of the less talked about issues
is the extensive use of natural gas to thin and extract the bitumen and pump it out of
the ground. The most shocking statistic is that nearly one third of Canada's total natural
gas consumption (averaging 2.4 billion cubic feet per day) was used for this process in
the Alberta oil sands in 2016, which was four times higher than in 2005 (BNN, 2017).
Natural gas makes an ideal home heating fuel and is cleaner burning than oil or coal. But
when burned to produce oil sands, the sustainability benefits are dubious at best. Are capture and storage technologies ever going to be viable for the oil sands producers? At what
price point will innovation processes activate and solve this dilemma?

A further infrastructure dimension that can either inhibit or enable oil sands development was the decision of whether or not to expand the Keystone XL Pipeline. This decision was debated for many years during which time an environmental impact assessment
was conducted (Eilperin and Mufson, 2014; read the entire statement at Keystone XL
Project, 2014). The pipeline was eventually approved, which will allow for higher vol-
umes of oil from the Alberta oil sands to be sent to refineries in the United States. Hall and

Shultz (2015) found that United States senators who voted for the Keystone XL Pipeline bill in 2015 did so partly because they believed they were representing the political will of their constituents and partly due to the proportion of campaign funding from fossil fuel energy regime actors. This infrastructure change will bolster further development of the oil sands as a source of energy for the United States, therefore acting as a bottleneck to sustainability transitions.

Another technology development that will act as a bottleneck to sustainability transitions is hydraulic fracturing or fracking, which is a process that enables previously unrecoverable oil and gas to be retrieved and refined. It involves new technologies including horizontal drilling to break rocks with the help of water and chemicals to release natural gas or oil. Fracking requires large quantities of water from already drought stricken areas and produces chemical wastes that must be managed to minimize the impact on water quality (Vengosh et al., 2014). Injecting the waste water back into the ground has been associated with an increase in earthquake activity in Oklahoma and Texas (Jones, 2013), which has caused damage to buildings and infrastructure. Another implication is the increase in local air pollution, which in some cases has been recorded at levels well above the EPA limits (Davis, 2012). For a comparison of the environmental and economic implications of fracking, see Howarth et al. (2011) and Mehany and Guggemos (2015).

Differences in the subsystems of the regime can influence industry fracking developments. Davis (2012) compared the subsystems of the regime in Texas and Colorado with respect to how they have shaped fracking strategies. The oil and gas industries are responsible for more than 20 percent ($200 billion) of the Texas economy while employing over 200,000 workers in the state. The natural gas industry employs 137,000 in Colorado. The two states differ in their regulations, with industry actors in Colorado required to notify land owners before drilling while actors in Texas are not. Colorado actors are required to conduct an environmental review prior to new fracking operations, and are required to limit the impact of fracking on wildlife and biodiversity, while actors in Texas are not. Additionally, Colorado had a more supportive political climate for sustainability policies than Texas as well as a governor who acted as a policy entrepreneur for new environmental regulations on fracking (Davis, 2012). Acceleration Point: Sustainability professionals can work to gain the support of key political actors as well as influence broader changes to the political climate prior to introducing strategies and instruments designed to disrupt the fossil fuel regime.

Absent a carbon policy, economic conditions will continue to influence when and how much of the remaining coal, oil, and gas *resources* are transformed into *reserves* and brought to market. As long as prices remain high enough, the fossil fuel industries will develop new technologies that extend and protect the regime. This includes developing and exploiting new frontiers in the Arctic, which holds tremendous amounts of unconventional gas resources (Palmer, 2015). Methyl-hydrates are locked within the ice and permafrost of northern Canada and Russia. As the permafrost melts, methyl-hydrates bubble to the surface and escape to the atmosphere. This presents a potential tipping point for climate change because of the quantity and the global warming potential of the methyl-hydrates (Ruppel, 2011). Should sustainability scientists focus on strategies and instruments for trapping and transporting methyl-hydrates to markets as a cleaner burning alternative (relative to coal)? As global average temperatures melt the northern latitudes, energy companies can access these resources with new technologies to increase the amount of *economically recoverable reserves*. Along with fracking, the Keystone XL Pipeline, and clean coal technologies, methyl-hydrates may serve to extend the *reserve-to-production ratio* for fossil fuels. This will enable the fossil fuel regime to reinforce its subsystems against sustainability transition attempts focused on climate change mitigation.

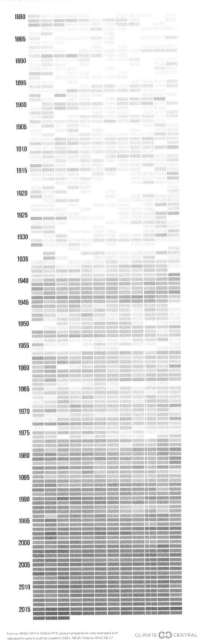

Figure 9.1 Annual global average temperatures relative to early industrialization

Source: Kahn (2017). Data updated as of April 19, 2017. For a colour version, see the Climate Central Website.

Institutional and science subsystems: sustainability's Achilles heel – climate change

There is an abundance of evidence that climate change is accelerated or amplified by human decisions as part of socio-technical systems that are entrenched and reliant on the continued use of fossil fuels (Hansen et al., 2012; IPCC, 2014; Paris, 2015). Most scientists agree that it is important to reduce greenhouse gas (GHG) emissions immediately if there is any hope of slowing increases to global average temperature. As of April 2017, the world reached another milestone by passing 410 parts per million (ppm) CO_2 for the first time in millions of years (Kahn, 2017). Climate scientists have argued that 450 ppm should not be exceeded if the world is to stay below the 2-degree Celsius increase in average temperature (Geels, 2014). Current trends suggest that the world may surpass those levels, as changes to global average temperature patterns are already recognizable. Figure 9.1 shows that the world has experienced 627 straight months of above-normal temperatures. This trend is becoming even more pronounced with numerous annual temperature records falling in the past two decades.

Global and national institutions have been used to compel actors to work together on climate change mitigation. The result has been numerous agreements from Kyoto to Paris with little-to-no enforceable punishments for noncompliance. One reason is that powerful fossil fuel regime actors have continued to create bottlenecks to prevent enforceable compliance mechanisms from being included in international agreements. Given this track record, do societies have the capacity and willingness to adjust institutions and infrastructure in a more rapid and radical way (Kern and Rogge, 2016)? Jordan et al. (2013) argued that new strategies are needed that take into account country-level differences (pp. 755–756):

1   Mitigate for 2 degrees Celsius but adapt for 4 degrees Celsius:

- Even pursuing 2 degrees Celsius to the maximum does not eliminate the risk of 4 degrees Celsius. Society should hedge its bets by taking steps to adapt to a much warmer world while maintaining a high level of ambition regarding mitigation.

2   Adopt new metrics and targets:

- Because a long-term temperature-based target appears unable to stimulate short-term policy responses and does not represent current understandings of global climate system sensitivities, more specific and near-term targets should be adopted.

3   Be politically more pragmatic:

- Society should accept that adopting science-informed targets such as 2 degrees Celsius has failed to drive social change and leaders should instead concentrate on delivering what is politically achievable in the short to medium term.

4   Recommit to staying within 2 degrees Celsius:

- The growing probability of highly risky rates of warming makes it even more important to recommit to low stabilization rates.

Can actors collaborate to adopt these types of proactive and pragmatic strategies to internalize the impacts of climate change into societal decision-making (Ostrom, 2012)? Or will societies collectively settle for adaptation as the dominant strategy (Pelling, 2010; Shi et al., 2015) because it is more politically feasible and generates ancillary benefits including economic development, disaster resilience, and infrastructure upgrades? Sustainability professionals must address these questions as they work to foster sustainable behavior, create green technologies, develop triple-bottom-line economic development strategies, and encourage niche creation and regime change policy mixes.

In 2017, the United States signaled that it would withdraw from the Paris Climate Agreement based on the notion that it would hurt job creation (Beggin et al., 2017). This would leave the United States as the only country in the world not part of the Paris Agreement after Syria signed in November 2017 (Harvey, 2017). Although the current United States federal government does not appear interested in taking significant action on mitigating climate change, states and cities are acting as *laboratories of democracy* for climate change legislation experiments and *laboratories of innovation* for technology creation experiments (Deitchman, 2014). Deitchman (2014) found that some states also acted as *laboratories of opposition* by using policies to slow down transitions to more sustainable energy systems. In cases where leadership was personally interested in climate change and clean energy, the state level was "an effective venue for facilitating the expansion of energy savings and carbon dioxide programs" (Deitchman, 2014, p. xvii). Some states were able and willing to accept support from an enabling policy (the State Energy Program Recovery Act as part of the American Recovery and Reinvestment Act [ARRA] of 2009) to develop clean energy financing and supportive regulations (e.g., building code changes). Leadership in some states used the ARRA to help frame climate change mitigation and clean energy investments as economic development strategies rather than as environmental policies to gain political support, which fits with a pragmatic strategy for addressing climate change. Acceleration Point: Sustainability-oriented intermediaries can help coordinate experiments as part of laboratories of democracy with experiments as part of laboratories of innovation to amplify technology and institutional change. Policy entrepreneurs can help overcome laboratories of opposition by creating new alliances and framing sustainability strategies and instruments as economic development opportunities. One example experiment that could be conducted as part of laboratories of democracy would be to test the effectiveness of *voluntary-to-mandatory escalator mechanisms* designed to encourage a shift from reactive and weak sustainability strategies and instruments to proactive and strong sustainability strategies and instruments. These escalator mechanisms could incrementally increase the legal requirements for technology change or carbon intensity improvements annually to allow industries to adapt.

Comparing Brazil's sugar cane ethanol to Venezuela's oil revolution

Biofuels represent a parallel yet interconnected socio-technical system to oil. Sugar cane ethanol produced in Brazil has a higher energy and lower emissions content than other biofuels including corn based ethanol in the United States. Local environmental and social impacts exist due to emissions from mechanical or burning harvesting techniques (Garcia and Von Sperling, 2017), degrading soils, water systems, and ecosystem services (de Oliveira Cervone et al., 2017), and exploiting the health and wellbeing of workers (Martinelli and Filoso, 2008). These impacts must be considered in lifecycle analyses of sugar cane ethanol as a potential solution to climate change and energy system transitions. Improving the performance of sugar cane ethanol can therefore be considered a sustainable niche experiment in the liquid fuels sector (Goldemberg et al., 2008) that must overcome institutional and scientific bottlenecks.

Unlike Brazil, Venezuela did not diversify its economy after the 1970s oil crisis and is heavily dependent on oil for over 95 percent of its export revenue (Clemente, 2017). As a result, lower oil prices in the past few years have led to a reduction in gross domestic product (GDP) and rapid inflation rates (Toumi et al., 2017). National institutional challenges and population growth rates also hamper sustainability efforts, despite participating in international climate agreements (Toumi et al., 2017). Venezuela may be an example of the *natural resource curse*, defined as "the paradox that countries endowed with natural resources such as oil, natural gas, minerals etc. tend to have lower economic growth and worse development outcomes than countries with fewer natural resources" (Badeeb et al., 2017, p. 124). Venezuela may also exhibit elements of Dutch Disease, which Badeeb et al. (2017, p. 125) argued occurs when:

> natural resource booms increase domestic income and the demand for goods. This increase generates inflation and appreciation of the real exchange rate. As a result, the relative prices of non-resource commodities increase, and their export becomes expensive relative to world market prices. This leads to a decrease in the competitiveness of these non-resource commodities and in the investment they attract.

When comparing Brazil and Venezuela, Venezuela's oil exports are declining while Brazil's oil exports are actually increasing (Nogueira and Teixeira, 2017). One reason is that environmental standards in China, India, Europe, and the United States are influencing these regions to import Brazil's light crude, which has lower sulphur content and is therefore more cost effective to refine. Brazil has made massive investments in sugar cane ethanol to fuel its domestic transportation sector while at the same time investing in exploration and development of offshore oil for export markets. This strategy is helping boost Brazil's economy at the same time when Venezuela's economy is struggling due to, among other things, a lack of diversification.

Social and cultural subsystems: NIMBY as a bottleneck to sustainability transitions

To what extent can cultural and historical lessons guide social changes at the community level that can impact climate change and sustainability pathways (Offen, 2014)? One way of examining the impact of social and cultural regime subsystems on sustainability transitions is by viewing changes to the NIMBY syndrome. NIMBY suggests that people may be accepting of new energy or other technology developments as long as those developments are not located near them (Burningham et al., 2015). They may not want to see them in the case of solar panels in neighborhoods with homeowner's associations. They may legitimately worry about the consequences of accidents as in the case of nuclear power plants. Or they may fear a series of perceived illnesses in the case of wind turbines (Chapman, 2017). Many examples of NIMBY are found around the world, a classic case in the United States being the Kennedy family, including well-known environmentalist Robert F. Kennedy Jr., opposing wind farm development off the coast of Cape Cod (Kennedy, 2005; Seelye, 2010). Another case from Ontario involved residents of a wealthy suburb near Toronto not willing to accept new natural gas generating stations in their community, forcing the government to cancel the project at a cost to taxpayers of more than CA\$1 billion (Morrow, 2015). Aas et al. (2014) conducted a large survey of residents in the United Kingdom, Norway, and Sweden and found a significant difference between those who would support and those who would accept overhead powerlines. Acceptance was higher than support and general acceptance was higher than local acceptance. This verifies the NIMBY hypothesis that people are unlikely to support a large-scale change in their place but are more likely to accept it if it occurs elsewhere. What can sustainability professionals do to help overcome NIMBY?

Sustainability professionals can reframe how green energy developments are communicated as a socio-technical process that combines social change and technology change (Batel and Devine-Wright, 2015a, 2015b). Batel and Devine-Wright (2015a) suggested that "it is not change per se that needs to be understood, but the relation between change and stability" (p. 316). People may agree in principle that wind power is good when considered as a global issue, but may not accept that their lives should be affected by technology installations when considered as a local issue – supporting the notion that social representations of societal change are multidimensional (Batel and Devine-Wright, 2015a). Social representations of societal change are further complicated by socio-political views that shape perceptions and decisions related to technology change. Batel and Devine-Wright (2015a, p. 318) argued that:

> When there is opposition against a given techno-scientific innovation, those opposing it may not be opposing or questioning the object in itself, but rather the assumptions others make about them and their relation with that object . . . which, in turn, will impact on people's responses to the technology.

One example is when landowners in rural areas may be more concerned that their neighbors will associate them with liberals or socialists if they support wind, and therefore, they latch onto negative perceptions of wind technology that swirl through local social networks. Sustainability professionals need to examine the multidimensional nature of social representations of societal change within each specific context in order to better design community-based social marketing strategies to build acceptance for renewable energy technology and infrastructure changes.

Cultural bottlenecks to sustainability transitions are evident in survey data conducted in the United States. One example is a study by Hamilton and Saito (2015) that examined public concern about environmental issues in New Hampshire. They compared responses of Democrats, Republicans, Independents, and Tea Party supporters and found that Tea Party supporters were less likely to trust scientists, believe in human evolution, believe in human-caused climate change, climate science, or measurable changes in Arctic ice, glaciers, or CO_2. Despite demonstrating the lowest level of knowledge about climate change, the Tea Party supporters were the most likely to be confident in their own knowledge of climate change. Interestingly, the higher the education level of Tea Party respondents, the less likely they were to believe in human-caused climate change. Democrats, Republicans, and Independents were more likely to believe in human-caused climate change and this increased with education levels.

Hamilton and Saito (2015) postulated that these findings may even underestimate the differences compared to other states with higher Evangelical populations, which are more likely to be Tea Party supporters, and less likely to make sustainability-oriented decisions (Smith and Leiserowitz, 2013). Sustainability professionals should replicate this study after the 2016 election of President Trump, whose voters included large numbers of Tea Party supporters in addition to former Democrats and Independents. Given that this coalition was largely built on social and cultural issues, it will be interesting to examine how the drastic changes in environmental policies that are occurring under the Trump administration either align or conflict with the diversity of Trump supporters' views on sustainability problems and solutions.

The previous sections have applied the socio-technical systems framework to understand how change in multi-level systems is resisted by bottlenecks from within the regime subsystems that are locked in and path dependent. Learning how to overcome the bottlenecks by drawing upon seedbeds of sustainability is the purpose of the next section.

Seedbeds of sustainability

Seedbeds are important to sustainability transitions because they provide ideas, energy, and support to actors wishing to make changes to socio-technical systems. Seedbeds offer hope that changes can occur, and in some cases, a vision based on changes that have occurred in other places. Seedbeds provide a spark for sustainable niche experiments that could radically change technologies and infrastructure. Seedbeds also provide a structure to enable incremental changes at the regime levels, which in turn support experiments from the niche levels.

Engaging a new sustainability youth movement

Learning and doing sustainability requires an additional dimension that is sometimes ignored: political engagement. With voting rates among millennials in parts of the United States ranging from 10 to 20 percent (U.S. Census Bureau, 2017), and only slightly higher in the United Kingdom (Parkinson, 2016), it is apparent that the enthusiasm for sustainability demonstrated on social media and in survey responses (Rayapura, 2014) does not always translate into political action. How can a new sustainability youth movement be instigated that will endure over time and lead to higher voter participation?

Ziegler (2015) suggested a potential solution with the idea of a youth quota that would require policy innovation. The proposal would set aside a number of seats in parliament/congress based on age cohorts in proportion to the population representation. The hypothesis is that greater representation by youth would encourage greater participation in the voting system by the same demographic. Millennials are concerned with and knowledgeable about sustainability given that it will directly impact their lives. More representation would provide more power to influence institutional changes that can lead to radical infrastructure innovations in socio-technical systems. This idea would require testing in practice to see if higher levels of representation actually lead to policy changes in the direction of sustainability.

One indicator of an increasing level of engagement among millennials in politics was the global March for Science that took place April 22, 2017 (March for Science, 2017). Students participated in public marches and a week of activism to highlight the importance of science including research and development (R&D), and in particular, climate change and sustainability science. Scientists of all ages are now running for office in order to increase participation in the political system in response to anti-science policies and rhetoric (Yong, 2017). A political action group called 314Action was created to support scientists who wish to run for office including training sessions and support networks (314Action, 2017). Support for their campaigns reflects views and policy platforms in line with sustainability principles, climate change mitigation targets, and triple-bottom-line economic development strategies. A new generation of sustainability professionals would therefore have an opportunity to influence regime change from within the political system as green politicians, which is important for developing an environmental state.

Greening the state and politics

Sustainability professionals must focus on the political dynamics of socio-technical systems and niche and regime transitions: "politics is the constant companion of socio-technical transitions, serving alternatively (and often simultaneously) as context, arena, obstacle, enabler, arbiter, and manager of repercussions" (Meadowcroft, 2011, p. 71). Meadowcroft (2011, p. 71) described the role of politics at each of the levels of the multi-level perspective (MLP) sustainability transitions framework that was described in Chapter 7:

- Landscape:
  - o Influences the general economic climate, the orientation of innovation, and the ways technologies are deployed;
- Regime:
  - o Legal structures and regulatory initiatives support (or undercut) dominant regimes; states are dependent on revenues drawn from prevailing economic practices; and political and economic actors become entangled;
- Niche:
  - o Specific government programs can protect or expose niches and encourage or discourage innovation. Choices among alternative technological pathways involve struggle among rival groups, and this spills over into conflicts over regulation and property rights. Governments may explicitly encourage certain technological paths.

Meadowcroft (2011, p. 73) suggested viewing the politics of sustainability transitions through the integrated concepts of interests, institutions, and ideas, which leads to a number of important questions that will be critical for sustainability professionals:

- Interests:
  - o Which strategies are most successful for building impetus for change in specific societal subsystems?
  - o Which kinds of changes create positive feedbacks driving further changes?
  - o What resistance strategies are most popular with transition opponents?
  - o How are these resistance strategies countered by transitions supporters?

- Institutions:

  o What institutional contexts are favorable to orienting and accelerating sustainability transitions?

  o Which changes to democratic institutions can improve their capacity to negotiate sustainability transitions?

  o What sorts of institutional innovations focused on sustainability can make a difference?

- Ideas:

  o How are values supportive of sustainability incorporated in direct political ideologies?

  o How can a political culture favorable to sustainability be nurtured?

  o How can the public and politicians come to change their perceptions?

Sustainability professionals attempting to answer these questions can focus on *strategies and instruments* that will encourage technological innovation, improve social justness of environment and resource decisions and outcomes, and maximize economic efficiency while also ensuring that targets are met within the necessary timeframes for mitigating climate change. Achieving this goal in line with strong sustainability may ultimately require the creation of an environmental state.

The environmental state is characterized as a government that "actively addresses negative environmental externalities of economic activities" (Sommerer and Lim, 2016, p. 92). Environmental states could contain elements of green state theory, free market environmentalism, and ecological modernization theories (Greenwood, 2015). The green state theory is governance-oriented and is derived from the ecological economics tradition of strong sustainability and the non-substitutability of natural capital and ecosystem services. Free market environmentalism and ecological modernization theories are market-oriented and tend to align with technology innovation, efficiency improvements, and economic development. Duit et al. (2016) argued for a new focus on the environmental state because states have the ability to "structure political, economic, and social interactions, maintain legal frameworks (including systems of property rights) backed by coercive power, and deploy significant economic and administrative resources through taxation/expenditure and their bureaucratic apparatus" (p. 3). Governments are responsible for implementing and monitoring progress of environmental policies to meet international environmental agreements. The extent to which an environmental state exists may be measured by the strength of the institutional capacity created to address environmental concerns, the amount and type of environmental legislation, and the size of public spending on environmental projects. While each of these areas is important, it is the combination of all three that signifies a resilient environmental state that will survive leadership changes and political pendulum swings (Sommerer and Lim, 2016).

How would conservatives view an environmental state, which often involves intervention by governments into markets and policies that constrain the behavior of businesses? Peifer et al. (2016) cited a number of studies suggesting that conservatives (Republicans) are more likely than liberals (Democrats) to support the existing regime, and that conservatives tend to resist the type of radical changes needed for sustainability transitions. Acceleration Point: Sustainability professionals can work within conservative political groups, including green evangelicals, to build support for sustainability strategies and instruments by tailoring communication and engagement strategies to align with their values. Community-based social marketing strategies that aim to reduce perceived barriers to the outputs and outcomes of sustainability transitions including new technology, infrastructure, and livelihoods could be used.

Comparing Germany and Norway as environmental states

Eckersley (2016) compared two leading environmental states' (Norway and Germany) framings of the issue of climate change. Both states have ambitious GHG emission reduction targets of 30–40 percent below 1990 levels by 2020; powerful fossil fuel regimes (coal in Germany still at 45 percent of the electricity mix, and oil and gas being a major export in Norway); and have moved away from technology options that would reinforce the fossil fuel regime like carbon capture and storage. Germany faces the additional challenge of rising energy prices due to the feed-in tariff, which was paid for by a fee added to electricity bills. Despite pressure from businesses pushing back against these rising prices, the national energy plan *Energiewende* had a strong political coalition that acted as a protective boundary in support of this regime change. This reinforces the idea of consensus, which is why even against some resistance, the energy plan in Germany persists.

Eckersley (2016) found that the most important frames for Germany were leadership, responsibility, green growth, justice, and security. Messaging strategies implemented within the German political arena framed the nation as a leader in climate change negotiations on the international stage, as an innovator in green technology development, and as a leader in GHG emission reductions. These messaging strategies drew upon the *common but differentiated responsibilities* principle of the United Nations Framework Convention on Climate Change that Germany has "an international responsibility to take the lead in mitigation by virtue of their historical responsibility and superior economic capacity, and to assist developing countries in mitigation and adaptation" (Eckersley, 2016, p. 187). Germany's green growth framing is based on the principle of decoupling economic growth from GHG emissions by investing in renewable energy, energy efficiency, enhancing energy security, driving technological innovation, and creating green jobs. Although based on market principles, supportive of carbon markets, and aiming to foster competitive advantages for German industry, Germany recognized the importance of "a regulatory state to guide and channel market behavior towards socially desirable ends" (Eckersley, 2016, p. 188). The framing of the energy transition in Germany therefore had similarities to environmental economic geography, which combines ecological modernization with regulations (Chapter 4).

Norway framed itself as a pioneer in climate change mitigation and viewed climate change as an international action to be addressed with carbon trading and offsetting (Eckersley, 2016). Unlike Germany, Norway tied its domestic commitments to international achievements where it would raise its GHG emissions target from 30 to 40 percent by 2020 if an international agreement is reached to hold the world to the 2-degree Celsius level. Norway would also aim to achieve carbon neutrality by 2030, 20 years earlier than its current target of 2050. A government change in 2013 led to backing off these strict commitments but a general agreement that climate change was still a priority. Although Norway generates almost all of its electricity from hydro power, its manufacturing, transport, and oil and gas industries saw GHG emissions increase. To address these trends, Norway used a carbon tax, emissions trading, and voluntarily agreed not to count international forest management as carbon credits towards their target. Norway, like Germany, accepts that they must take a leadership role in mitigation, adaptation, climate finance, and financial assistance to developing countries to take climate actions and develop new technologies.

To compensate for their oil and gas industry contribution to GHG emissions, Norway framed its domestic climate change actions around international development that coupled poverty reduction to climate change mitigation through investment in forest protection, carbon capture and storage technology creation, and participation in international carbon markets (Eckersley, 2016). Norway was the first country to put a carbon tax on its oil and gas industry, and the domestic fossil fuel industry is framed as a partner in climate change action because of its technology development and its legacy as generating wealth for the country, which now facilitates strict climate change policies. The themes of leadership and technology pioneership were linked to the history of economic development in Norway as a means of supporting the climate change mitigation actions. This fits with the new conservative government's focus on environmental stewardship and ecological modernization.

Norway and Germany both faced the challenge of having strict climate change goals, framing the country as a climate change mitigation leader, and yet being heavily invested in domestic fossil fuel production. Eckersley (2016) concluded that green growth and ecological modernization are important frames for climate change action in Norway and Germany. One reason is that ecological modernization fits with most political ideologies and this may make it more appealing as a means of gaining support from opposition parties for strategies and instruments that lead to climate change mitigation outcomes. Both countries framing strategies went well beyond technology, however, to include national identities (Norway) or European identities (Germany) of leadership and international responsibilities.

Replacing coal with renewables

Sustainability professionals often think about the difficulty of transforming society in the direction of a normative goal that seems unattainable. It can become disheartening when seemingly obvious solutions are routinely ignored or discounted for various reasons. But every once in a while, certain cases offer hope that this type of transition is possible. Take for example the United Kingdom, which used no coal for electricity for an entire 24-hour period in April 2017 for the first time since the industrial revolution (Brown, 2017). This is a remarkable accomplishment and part of a broader switch away from coal to renewables and natural gas. This transition has been driven largely due to the United Kingdom's plan to phase out fossil fuels to meet its climate change commitments by 2025.

Ontario, Canada, was the first major jurisdiction in North America to completely eliminate coal from the supply mix as of 2014 (Ontario Ministry of Energy, 2017). This included switching coal plants to run on locally produced biomass. Additionally, Ontario invested in energy efficiency, upgrades to transmission lines, new wind and solar supply, hydro capacity expansion, refurbishment of nuclear facilities, and new natural gas plants. Ontario's electricity supply mix is now 35 percent nuclear, 28 percent gas, 23 percent hydro, 11 percent wind, 1 percent solar and 1 percent biofuel (IESO, 2017). These electricity system transitions have not harmed the economy, as Ontario's GDP has increased by 17 percent between 2012 and 2016 (Statistics Canada, 2017). During the same time period, Canada's GDP increased by 12 percent, and Alberta's GDP rose by less than 1 percent (Statistics Canada, 2017). The resulting jobs and business development benefits of the Ontario transition were outlined in Chapter 5, which represent a decoupling of economic development from energy related emissions.

The environmental benefits included an 87 percent reduction in GHG emissions, an 86 percent reduction in NOx, a 99.6 percent reduction in SOx, and a 100 percent reduction in mercury emissions from Ontario's electricity sector between 2005 and 2015 (Ontario Ministry of Energy, 2017). Another metric of progress is the declining number of smog days. For example, in 2003 and 2004, while coal was still 25 percent of the supply mix, Ontario experienced 19 and 20 smog days respectively. Smog days spiked at 53 in 2005, before hitting 39 in 2007 and 30 in 2012 (Ontario Ministry of Environment and Climate Change, 2017). Ontario closed its final coal plant in 2014 and the number of smog days declined to two in 2013 and zero in 2014. Air quality improvements will reduce hospital visits and improve quality of life for residents and visitors to southern Ontario where hot summer days used to include a yellow-brown haze that blocked out the Toronto and Hamilton skylines. This transition directly contributed to improvements in the socio-ecological system integrity, livelihood sufficiency and opportunity, intra- and inter-generational equity, and resource maintenance and efficiency principles of sustainability.

How did Ontario achieve this energy transition away from coal? They developed a broad implementation team composed of all major actors in the energy system including producers, transmission, market operators, labor unions, government, and private sector stakeholders. They also created a public outreach and communication strategy as an intermediary mechanism to engage the public and coalesce the major actors around a common vision. Sustainability professionals that were part of the Ontario transition adopted a long-term and collaborative strategic plan that focused on changing infrastructure, policies, and market conditions. Can other coal-reliant jurisdictions follow Ontario and the United Kingdom's lead?

A coal company in Kentucky called Berkeley Energy Group is developing two solar farms at the location of a retired coal mine. They aim to use the land and employ workers in partnership with a solar company called EDF Renewable Energy while creating the first solar farm in the Appalachia coal-producing region of the United States (Lumb, 2017). The transition from coal to renewable energy in Kentucky may seem odd to some, as the state has a long history of unionized coal miners fiercely dedicated to protecting the regime. A fourth-generation coal miner in Harlan County, Kentucky, became a green energy champion driving change in the direction of solar. This champion's actions were not carried out in the name of environmental progress, but for the potential cost savings and economic benefits for homeowners who are coal industry decedents. The champion ran for city council, won, then started a campaign to raise money for demonstration projects to show that solar could help reduce electricity bills. An initial demonstration project on a single home led to additional projects and eventually to the Kentucky Coal Mining Museum agreeing to install 80 solar panels to reduce their energy bills by up to $10,000 annually (Kaufman, 2017). Although Kentucky still generates 83 percent of its electricity from coal (EIA, 2017), it did begin to close some coal power plants in 2016.

This is perhaps an early indicator of individual and organization level changes instigating a broader transition in culture, politics, and eventually infrastructure.

Instigating a roadmap for radical innovation

Radical innovation involves the creation of new technologies (e.g., thin film solar photovoltaics) or systems of networked technology and infrastructure changes (e.g., *the internet of things*). In this roadmap, there are several routes that can be taken to achieve the same goals. People often try to follow very similar paths that are either the most travelled or seem the safest. Since radical innovations are critical to sustainability transitions, it is important to emphasize that radical minds and imaginations are required to achieve radical transitions towards sustainability. That is crucial for careers as sustainability professionals, which are described in Chapter 11.

Radical innovation has helped the United Kingdom continue to be a leader in climate change mitigation in partnership with energy innovation going on in other parts of Europe. In 2017, a wind farm in Liverpool Bay went online that contained the world's largest turbines at 8 MW each (Vaughan, 2017). These turbines are more than double the standard 3.6 MW offshore wind turbines, and were installed by a Danish company. The 195-meter-tall turbines can provide greater efficiency. The United Kingdom now has 5.3 GW of installed offshore wind capacity, enough to power over 4 million homes. While government subsidies were used to partly fund this wind farm, the same company has just partnered with Germany to create the world's first subsidy-free offshore wind farm that is anticipated to have turbines as large as 15 MW (Vaughan, 2017). This represents a technology breakthrough that will also change the policy and political regime subsystems by removing a barrier to new energy options (e.g., the need for public dollars) that had previously acted as a bottleneck in many countries. Germany is known for its willingness to innovate in wind technology and is installing the first integrated wind–hydro power turbines in 2017 (Green Energy Tribune, 2017). These turbines are connected to reservoirs at their base and further down a hill, which allow water to be pumped up during times when the wind is blowing or when demand for electricity is lower, and then released downhill to generate hydroelectricity when the wind is not blowing or when demand increases. These integrated and radical system innovations can improve the economics of renewable energy. They can also help build broader and more powerful coalitions of support with actors from different industries being part of these large-scale infrastructure projects.

Radical innovations can also have social and institutional dimensions. Take for example the CALFED Bay-Delta Program (CALFED, 2017), which some have called "the most ambitious experiment in collaborative environmental policy and adaptive management the world has seen to date" (Kallis et al., 2009, p. 631). Collaboration between dozens of federal, state, and local government and non-governmental actors helped restore a water system that provides drinking water for more than 20 million people (Kallis et al., 2009). This project leveraged over $3 billion to fund restoration, research, and water banking projects from 1994 to 2006. Adaptive co-management (Chapter 3) was the core governance framework used to build support, participation, and legitimacy for CALFED. Adaptive co-management was effective due to the informality, self-organizing relationships, and the boundary spanners that helped to link the various stakeholders across levels and scales. A key finding was that these informal forms of environmental governance needed to better coordinate with existing forms of government in order to not overlap responsibilities. Although adaptive co-management provided a mechanism for generating innovative ideas, it was less successful at transforming those ideas into sustainable water management out-comes (Kallis et al., 2009). Acceleration Point: Sustainability professionals can improve the outcomes of adaptive co-management by incorporating triple-bottom-line metrics that are designed to generate sustainability value. This will nudge project decisions in the direction of strong sustainability outcomes.

There are many experiments involving radical innovations around the world that hold the potential to make giant leaps towards sustainability. One example involves Ceramic Piezoelectric arrays that are about to be tested on a large scale in California as a means of generating electricity when cars pass over roadways (Alexander, 2017). The pressure applied to the roadway by the cars driving over them is enough to generate a charge that could be used to power nearby homes or university campus buildings. The California Energy Commission is supporting two pilot projects, one at the University of California – Merced campus, and the other in San Jose on a half mile stretch of highway. One of the driv-ing forces behind the development and demonstration of this technology is the California Legislature's target to generate half of the state's electricity from renewable energy by 2030. This target is spurring radical innovation processes and a series of corresponding institutional changes required to adopt the technology. This particular innovation may face technologi-cal challenges (e.g., to improve efficiency to make it economically viable), infrastructure challenges (e.g., to build a road that is able to vibrate without causing damage and requiring frequent repairs), user challenges (e.g., to encourage consumers to accept a bumpier or dif-ferent ride experience), and political challenges (e.g., to convince politicians of the need to fund this public infrastructure project). The process of improving these issues may lead to additional and even more effective solutions and spin-off innovations. Acceleration Point: Sustainability professionals should monitor ongoing innovation processes for potential solu-tions that could be adapted to other socio-technical system transition contexts.

Identifying seedbeds in the media

One way for sustainability professionals to scan external environments for ideas and solu-tions is to monitor the media. On a daily basis, new headlines emerge in international newspapers and online forums. Take for example *Can this tiny African nation lead the world forward?* (Taylor, 2017). This article details a plan by Cabo Verde, a country off the west coast of Africa, to use 100 percent renewable energy by 2025. The plan consists of solar, wind, ocean, and battery energy storage. The objective is to help the economy by provid-ing sustainable, low-cost, and stable energy for all 550,000 residents including all of its ten islands. This would be the first country to be 100 percent reliant on renewable energy that does not include substantial hydropower sources. Acceleration Point: Sustainability pro-fessionals from other jurisdictions of similar size and type can study the sustainable niche experiments as well as the institutional and infrastructure changes that occurred, and adapt the lessons learned to design their own transition arenas and pathways.

The following headlines published in newspapers during 2017 give a snapshot of seedbeds for sustainability based on socio-technical solutions that are being created and implemented. They suggest that sustainability progress is being made based on green innovation, triple-bottom-line economic development, policy change, culture change, and behavior and practices changes:

- *Algae helps Sweden reach zero emissions*
- *Young people don't want to work in oil companies*
- *America's hungriest wind and solar power users are big companies*

- *Google is officially 100% sun and wind powered – 3.0 gigawatts' worth*
- *One of the biggest U.S. oil fields turns to an unexpected power source: solar*
- *Why wave power may be the next big thing in green energy*
- *Big oil joins with environmental groups to back carbon tax*
- *Tesla is changing the electric grid*
- *Toyota's new power plant will create clean energy from manure*
- *Solar will kill coal fast*
- *Solar powered supercapacitor produces hydrogen fuel and electricity*
- *Chernobyl is going to become a solar farm*
- *U.S. energy grid almost to 1990 CO_2 levels*
- *Australia can meet carbon emissions target at zero net cost*
- *EV battery life extended by feeding energy back into the grid*
- *New solar paint lets you transform your entire home into a source of clean energy*
- *How Zero Mass is using solar panels to pull drinkable water directly from the air*
- *MIT membrane produces fuel from CO_2 emissions*
- *Dutch households will use servers to heat their showers for free*
- *Panasonic joins push to put photovoltaics on more car roofs*
- *World's biggest coal company closes 37 mines as solar prices plummet*
- *It's so windy in Britain that the price of electricity went negative*
- *Heirs to Rockefeller oil fortune divest from fossil fuels over climate change*
- *Sustainable investing gains ground in boardrooms everywhere*
- *Chile is producing so much solar power, it's giving it away for free*
- *Costa Rica breaks own record, runs entirely on renewable energy for 300 days*

Do some research in major national newspapers and find a few headlines that provide evidence of seedbeds for a sustainability transition. When reading the articles, think about how different niche-to-regime and regime-to-niche functions were likely important to make sustainability changes. Who were the key actors that were involved? What strategies and instruments were necessary to support the niche experiments or regime subsystem changes? Which principles of sustainability will likely improve as a result of the solutions outlined in the article? How would progress towards a sustainability transition be measured and understood?

Measuring progress towards sustainability

Understanding the extent that a sustainability transition is occurring is important to verify progress and make necessary adjustments, to lend *legitimacy* to niche experiments and regime changes, and to build support for further investments and policy changes. Choosing the right metrics is critical for measuring the integrated and ongoing process of sustainability and the extent that economic, social, and environmental capital is being enhanced or maintained and that sustainability value is being created.

Comparing the Human Development Index to CO_2 emissions per capita

One integrated metric of progress towards strong sustainability is presented in Figure 9.2, which shows the *Human Development Index* (HDI) and CO_2 emissions per capita for all countries in the world in 2014. Only three countries have been able to achieve an HDI above 0.9 and CO_2 emissions per capita below 5 metric tons: Liechtenstein, Switzerland,

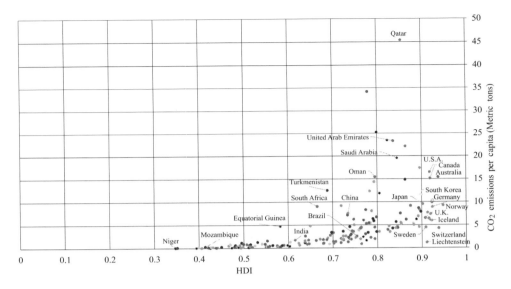

Figure 9.2 Comparing the Human Development Index and CO_2 emissions per capita by country, 2014

Source: HDI data from UNDP (2017); CO_2 emissions per capita from the World Bank (2017). Figure by the authors.

and Sweden. Countries that have achieved an HDI above 0.9 and per capita CO_2 emissions below 10 metric tons include Iceland, the United Kingdom, Ireland, New Zealand, Germany, Norway, the Netherlands, Japan, Denmark, and Hong Kong. Countries that have an HDI of 0.9 or higher and per capita CO_2 emissions between 10 and 15 metric tons are Singapore and South Korea. Resource rich countries that have high HDI and high CO_2 emissions per capita are Australia, the United States, and Canada. The emerging powers of China, Brazil, and India are increasing the HDI and CO_2 emissions per capita rapidly. One outlier is Qatar, which exceeded 45 metric tons per capita of CO_2 emissions. Other petroleum producing countries including the United Arab Emirates and Kuwait exceeded 20 metric tons per capita. Many African countries such as Niger, Burundi, and Mozambique have a low HDI and CO_2 emissions per capita. The low HDI limits progress towards technology and infrastructure development. As these countries continue to develop, the CO_2 emissions per capita will likely increase and follow the trend of moving east and then northeast on Figure 9.2.

Are any countries on Figure 9.2 sustainable? Even though Liechtenstein, Switzerland, and Sweden managed to achieve a high HDI while keeping CO_2 emissions below 5 metric tons per capita, further improvements can still be made. No country has achieved an HDI index of 0.95 and CO_2 emissions per capita less than 2 metric tons. And even if a country, state, or city achieves that goal, other factors still require improvement including reducing the disparities between rich and poor, improving the availability of sustainable livelihoods for all, and enhancing technological innovation capacity that could help create solutions to future problems. What other metrics would have to be considered? Review the country-level ecological footprints and overshoot days at the Global Footprint Network (2017). How do they change your perception of sustainability relative to the country placement on Figure 9.2?

Previous studies have compared the *ecological footprint* to the HDI. The HDI is a composite index that combines income, health, and education, and is calculated every year for countries (UNDP, 2017). When comparing the ecological footprint and the HDI, several important trends are evident. First, as the level of HDI goes up for a country, the ecological footprint also goes up (UNEP, 2011). In other words, as income, health, and education improve, the impact on the natural environment increases. Second, no countries in the world had achieved both an HDI value higher than 0.8 and had an ecological footprint value lower than 1.7 global hectares per capita (Global Footprint Network, 2017; UNEP, 2011), which is considered a sustainable level relative to earths biocapacity, as described in Chapter 2. The problem facing sustainability professionals working towards strong sustainability transition pathways is how to reorient strategies and instruments to simultaneously increase the HDI and lower the ecological footprint. Consistent with the strong sustainability definition in Chapter 1, sustainability is an ongoing and continuous process that requires constant monitoring and adjustment. Sustainability professionals face a challenge that never ends. One way to measure the ongoing process of sustainability is the ecological intensity of human well-being.

The ecological and carbon intensity of human well-being

The ecological intensity of human well-being is a measure of the ratio between an indicator of environmental stress, in this case the per capita ecological footprint, and an indicator of human well-being, in this case average life expectancy at birth (Jorgenson and Dietz, 2015). The goal is to reduce the intensity of environmental stress required to produce another unit of human well-being. The aforementioned study found that the United States is inefficient at producing another unit of human well-being relative to the impact on the environment. They also found that when developed countries increase their GDP per capita, the ecological intensity of human well-being also increases. This means that increases in wealth per person add additional impacts on the environment that are disproportionally greater than improvements in human well-being. Developing countries, by contrast, have been able to increase GDP per capita without increasing the ecological intensity of human well-being. The question for sustainability professionals is what type of strategies and instruments are needed to guide niche creation and regime subsystem change in a manner than can reduce the environmental impacts per new unit of human well-being created?

A modified version of the ecological intensity of human well-being can be calculated by substituting CO_2 emissions per capita for per capita ecological footprint as the measure of environmental stress to represent the carbon intensity of human well-being (Jorgenson, 2014). This can act as a measure of the contribution to climate change for each new unit of human well-being created. Average life expectancy at birth is used as the indicator of human well-being. Figure 9.3 shows that the carbon intensity of human well-being increased from 1960–70 for the United States, Canada, and the Netherlands, but then steadily declined through 2014. The lower the value, the better for sustainability because there are less emissions per capita per unit of human well-being. The United States and Canada have a higher carbon intensity per unit of well-being than European countries with similar life expectancies (Netherlands, United Kingdom, Norway). China's carbon intensity of human well-being started to increase rapidly in 2002, while India has only recently started to increase the rate slowly in 2012. The carbon intensity of human well-being for Saudi Arabia has increased rapidly and now exceeds the United States, Australia, and Canada. Denmark in particular has made large improvements in the carbon intensity

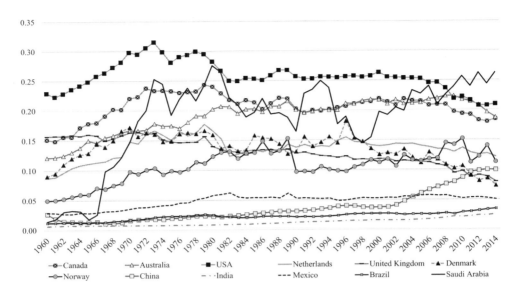

Figure 9.3 Carbon intensity of human well-being: CO_2 emissions per capita/life expectancy
Source: Data from the World Bank (2017); Calculations by the authors.

of human well-being. Most countries in Africa and South America still have an extremely low carbon intensity of human well-being, but this will likely increase over time with industrialization and growing average income.

Mexico: Sustainability transitions case study

Mexico is an important case study for energy transitions because it faces challenges and also has opportunities for greener energy options. Mexico has been able to increase average life expectancy over time (Figure 9.4) with little change to the carbon intensity of human well-being (Figure 9.3). How has Mexico achieved these results?

On the challenge side, Mexico is largely reliant on fossil fuels (92 percent of energy used in 2011) and in particular on oil (65 percent of energy used in 2011) (Mundo-Hernández et al., 2014). Like most other countries at a similar level of development, Mexico only generates a small portion of its energy from renewables and most of that is from biomass, geothermal, and hydro. Furthermore, Mexico struggles to meet its annual increase in consumption of 2 percent when its annual production of energy decreased by 0.3 percent between 2000 and 2011 (Mundo-Hernández et al., 2014). Mexico's oil reserves will only last between 10 and 33 years at current production rates (Mundo-Hernández et al., 2014). Energy security is therefore a critical national strategy, which is coupled with a desire to produce energy more efficiently and at competitive prices, as well as a goal to improve the environmental sustainability of the national energy production (Mundo-Hernández et al., 2014).

In comparison, renewables met over 20 percent of electricity needs in Germany in 2011, which will grow to 80 percent by 2050 due to many policies including the Renewable Energy Sources Act and the feed-in tariff that guarantees a fixed price paid to generators for 20 years. The feed-in tariff also declines by 5 percent every year as manufacturing costs decline and the incentive is no longer needed (Mundo-Hernández et al., 2014). The solar PV manufacturing sector in Germany alone had 110,000 full time employees in 2011, which will triple by 2030, along with additional demands for training and education programs for this type of high-skilled work (Mundo-Hernández et al., 2014). This is compared to the estimated 146 solar PV manufacturing jobs in Mexico in 2010. What is even more striking is the difference in solar potential between Germany (3.2 kWh/meter squared/day) and Mexico (5 to 6 kWh/meter squared/day) (Mundo-Hernández et al., 2014).

To take advantage of this renewable energy potential, Mexico passed a General Law for Climate Change in 2012 that aims to generate 35 percent of energy from renewables (e.g., biomass, geothermal, wind, solar) by 2024 (Alemán-Nava et al., 2014). Mexico also passed the Use of Renewable Energy and Finance of the Energy Transition law, which created a fund and a technical committee to oversee financing of green energy technologies. Mexico is home to the largest solar PV manufacturer in Latin America (Alemán-Nava et al., 2014). Nevertheless, Alemán-Nava et al. (2014) argued that Mexico needs a longer-term energy strategy that both integrates and highlights the benefits of renewable energy for providing stable energy prices and energy security, and provides targets and mechanisms to guarantee these targets are met. They also recommended financing programs for small producers, standardizing and simplifying rules for connecting renewables to the grid, and additional educational and R&D programs based on public–private partnerships.

Figure 9.4 compares the relationship between CO_2 emissions per capita, average life expectancy at birth, and GDP per capita (constant 2010 US dollars) for selected countries. Mexico experienced fluctuations in GDP per capita and continual increases in life expectancy, while CO_2 emissions per capita increased from 1960 through 1989 where it remained relatively stable until 2014. In the case of Denmark, GDP per capita has grown

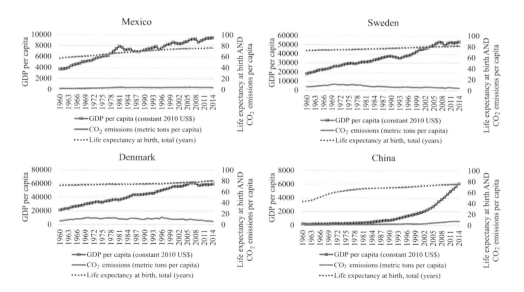

Figure 9.4 Relationship between CO_2 emissions per capita, average life expectancy, and GDP per capita

Source: Data from the World Bank (2017); Calculations by the authors.

rapidly with increases to average life expectancy at birth, while CO_2 emissions per capita increased from 1960 to 1996 before declining to 2014. A similar pattern was found for Sweden except that CO_2 emissions per capita began to decline earlier in 1976. China has experienced a rapid increase in GDP per capita between 1988 and 2014 as well as a steady increase in life expectancy. CO_2 emissions per capita have continued to increase through 2014. As Mexico continues to develop and transition away from fossil fuels, sustainability professionals can examine the lessons from countries like Sweden and Denmark in order to reduce CO_2 emissions per capita while increasing average life expectancy and income per capita at a consistent pace.

Check on learning

- In one or two pages, design a community-based social marketing strategy to overcome NIMBY for renewable energy installations in your community.
- What strategies and instruments do you believe would be most effective to overcome bottlenecks associated with actors from the fossil fuel industry?
- The United States Environmental Protection Agency administrator Scott Pruitt said in May 2017 that fracking and horizontal drilling are largely why the United States has reduced GHG emissions. Pruitt used this as a reason why the United States should pull out of the Paris Climate Agreement and as evidence that businesses are creating new solutions to climate change without the need for regulations. Is Scott Pruitt correct? Find statistical evidence to support or refute this claim. What are some alternative explanations for why the United States reduced GHG emissions?
- As a sustainability professional, what would you recommend to Brazil and to Venezuela to guide energy system transitions in relation to sustainability value creation?
- Do some research and in one page or less, make an argument why Liechtenstein, Switzerland, and Sweden have or have not achieved strong sustainability.
- How does the ecological intensity of human well-being differ from using an ecological footprint as a measure of progress towards sustainability? How does the carbon intensity of human well-being differ from using CO_2 emissions per capita as a measure of progress towards sustainability?
- Choose two countries on Figure 9.3 and write one paragraph explaining why you believe the trendlines for each have changed over time.
- Critical thinking exercise: do some research into the Energy Trilemma Index (energy security, energy equity, and environmental sustainability) (Alemán-Nava et al., 2014; Mundo-Hernández et al., 2014; World Energy Council, 2015). Write a five-point plan for Mexico that would focus on triple-bottom-line economic development, technology innovation, and policy change to improve performance on the Index.

Assignments

- Debating sustainability problems and solutions as cross-level interactions

References

314Action. (2017). 314Action. Available at: www.314action.org/home/

Aas, Ø., Devine-Wright, P., Tangeland, T., Batel, S., & Ruud, A. (2014). Public beliefs about high-voltage powerlines in Norway, Sweden and the United Kingdom: A comparative survey. *Energy Research & Social Science*, 2, 30–37.

Alemán-Nava, G. S., Casiano-Flores, V. H., Cárdenas-Chávez, D. L., Díaz-Chavez, R., Scarlat, N., Mahlknecht, J., . . . & Parra, R. (2014). Renewable energy research progress in Mexico: A review. *Renewable and Sustainable Energy Reviews*, 32, 140–153.

Alexander, K. (2017). California's jammed highways hold hope as power source. San Francisco Chronicle. Available at: www.sfchronicle.com/bayarea/article/California-s-jammed-highways-hold-hope-as-power-11075037.php

Badeeb, R. A., Lean, H. H., & Clark, J. (2017). The evolution of the natural resource curse thesis: A critical literature survey. *Resources Policy*, 51, 123–134.

Batel, S., & Devine-Wright, P. (2015a). Towards a better understanding of people's responses to renewable energy technologies: Insights from Social Representations Theory. *Public Understanding of Science*, 24(3), 311–325.

Batel, S., & Devine-Wright, P. (2015b). A critical and empirical analysis of the national-local 'gap' in public responses to large-scale energy infrastructures. *Journal of Environmental Planning and Management*, 58(6), 1076–1095.

Beggin, R., Ebbs, S., & Fishel, J. (2017). What's next in US withdrawal from Paris Climate Agreement. ABC News. Available at: http://abcnews.go.com/Politics/us-withdrawal-paris-climate-agreement/story?id=47778917

BNN. (2017). Oil sands production using nearly one-third of Canada's natural gas. Business News Network. The Canadian Press. Available at: www.bnn.ca/oil-sands-production-using-nearly-one-third-of-canada-s-natural-gas-1.728578

Brown, G. (2017). British power generation achieved first ever coal-free day. National Grid hails milestone as other sources like gas, nuclear, wind and solar allow UK to keep lights on with all coal-fired powerplants offline. *The Guardian*. Available at: www.the-guardian.com/environment/2017/apr/21/britain-set-for-first-coal-free-day-since-the-industrial-revolution

Burningham, K., Barnett, J., & Walker, G. (2015). An array of deficits: Unpacking NIMBY discourses in wind energy developers' conceptualizations of their local opponents. *Society & Natural Resources*, 28(3), 246–260.

CALFED. (2017). History of CALFED Bay-Delta Program. Available at: http://calwater.ca.gov/calfed/about/History/Detailed.html

Chapman, S. (2017). How to catch 'wind turbine syndrome': By hearing about it and then worrying. Renewable Energy Opinion. *The Guardian*. Available at: www.the-guardian.com/commentisfree/2017/nov/29/how-to-catch-wind-turbine-syndrome-by-hearing-about-it-and-then-worrying

Clemente, J. (2017). Venezuela's oil problems abound. Forbes. Available at: www.forbes.com/sites/judeclemente/2017/11/05/venezuelas-oil-problems-abound/#4695a2fa6104

Davis, C. (2012). The politics of 'fracking': Regulating natural gas drilling practices in Colorado and Texas. *Review of Policy Research*, 29(2), 177–191.

Deitchman, B. H. (2014). Why US states became leaders in climate and energy policy: Innovation through competition in federalism. PhD Dissertation, Georgia Institute of Technology. Available at: http://hdl.handle.net/1853/52224

de Oliveira Cervone, C. O. F., Walter, A., Guarenghi, M. M., & Favero, C. (2017). Resident perceptions of the impacts of large-scale sugarcane production on ecosystem services in two regions of Brazil. *Biomass and Bioenergy*. Available at: www.sciencedirect.com/science/article/pii/S0961953417302817

DeSmogBlog. (2017). Clearing the PR pollution that clouds climate science. Available at: www.desmogblog.com/ and the Research Database available at: www.desmogblog.com/global-warming-denier-database

Duit, A., Feindt, P. H., & Meadowcroft, J. (2016). Greening Leviathan: The rise of the environmental state? *Environmental Politics*, 25(1), 1–23.

Eckersley, R. (2016). National identities, international roles, and the legitimation of climate leadership: Germany and Norway compared. *Environmental Politics*, 25(1), 180–201.

EIA. (2017). Population, energy demand, and GDP data. State Energy Data System. U.S. Energy Information Administration. Available at: www.eia.gov/state/seds/seds-data-complete.php?sid=US

Eilperin, J. & and Mufson, S. (2014). State Department releases Keystone XL final environmental impact statement. *The Washington Post*. Available at: www.washingtonpost.com/business/economy/state-to-release-keystones-final-environmental-impact-statement-friday/2014/01/3 1/3a9bb25c-8a83-11e3-a5bd-844629433ba3_story.html?utm_term=.ab816479c286

Fountain, H. (2017). In blow to 'clean coal', flawed plant will burn gas instead. *The New York Times*. Available at: www.nytimes.com/2017/06/28/climate/kemper-coal-mississippi-clean-coal-project.html

Garcia, J. C. C., & Von Sperling, E. (2017). Greenhouse gas emissions from sugar cane ethanol: Estimate considering current different production scenarios in Minas Gerais, Brazil. *Renewable and Sustainable Energy Reviews*, 72, 1033–1049.

Geels, F. (2014). Regime resistance against low-carbon energy transitions: Introducing politics and power into the multi-level perspective. *Theory, Culture, and Society*, 31(5), 21–40.

Global Footprint Network. (2017). Country overshoot days. Available at: www.footprintnetwork.org/

Goldemberg, J., Coelho, S. T., & Guardabassi, P. (2008). The sustainability of ethanol production from sugarcane. *Energy Policy*, 36(6), 2086–2097.

Goldenberg, S., & Pilkington, E. (2013). ALEC's Campaign Against Renewable Energy. The Conservative group is pushing back against clean energy programs. The American Legislative Exchange Council. www.motherjones.com/environment/2013/12/alec-calls-penalties-freerider-homeowners-assault-clean-energy

Green Energy Tribune. (2017). Huge wind turbines are to combine with hydropower in a German forest. Available at: https://greenenergytribune.com/huge-wind-turbines-are-to-combine-with-hydropower-in-a-german-forest/

Greenwood, D. (2015). In search of Green political economy: Steering markets, innovation, and the zero carbon homes agenda in England. *Environmental Politics*, 24(3), 423–441.

Griffin et al. (2014). Senate Bill 1456. Oklahoma State Legislature. www.oklegislature.gov/BillInfo. aspx?Bill=SB1456&Session=1400; http://webserver1.lsb.state.ok.us/cf_pdf/2013-14%20 ENR/SB/SB1456%20ENR.PDF; www.climatecentral.org/news/oklahoma-solar-surcharge-bill-becomes-law-17335

Hall, J. C., & Shultz, C. (2015). Determinants of voting behaviour on the Keystone XL Pipeline. *Applied Economics Letters*, 23(7), 498–500.

Hamilton, L. C., & Saito, K. (2015). A four-party view of US environmental concern. *Environmental Politics*, 24(2), 212–227.

Hansen, J., Sato, M., Ruedy, R. (2012). Perception of climate change. *Proceedings of the National Academy of Sciences*, 109(37), 14726–14727.

Harvey, F. (2017). Syria signs Paris climate agreement and leaves US isolated. *The Guardian*. Available at: www.theguardian.com/environment/2017/nov/07/syria-signs-paris-climate-agreement-and-leaves-us-isolated

Howarth, R. W., Ingraffea, A., & Engelder, T. (2011). Natural gas: Should fracking stop? *Nature*, 477(7364), 271–275.

IESO. (2017). Ontario's supply mix. Ontario's Energy Capacity. Independent Electricity Supply Operator. Available at: www.ieso.ca/learn/ontario-supply-mix/ontario-energy-capacity

IPCC. (2014). 5th Assessment Report (AR5), Synthesis Report. Summary for Policy Makers. Intergovernmental Panel on Climate Change. Available at: www.ipcc.ch/; http://ar5-syr.ipcc.ch/

Jaccard, M. (2006). *Sustainable Fossil Fuels: The Unusual Suspect in the Quest for Clean and Enduring Energy*. Cambridge University Press, Cambridge, UK.

Jervey, B. (2017). Mapping EPA nominee Scott Pruitt's many fossil fuel ties. Available at: www.desmogblog.com/2017/01/13/mapping-epa-nominee-scott-pruitt-many-fossil-fuel-ties; and States ramp up attacks on incentives for electric vehicles. Available at: www.desmogblog.com/2017/03/13/states-ramp-attacks-electric-vehicle-incentives

Jones, N. (2013). Wastewater injection cracks open quake concerns. *Nature Geoscience*, 6(5), 329–329.

Jordan, A., Rayner, T., Schroeder, H., Adger, N., Anderson, K., Bows, A., . . . & Whitmarsh, L. (2013). Going beyond two degrees? The risks and opportunities of alternative options. *Climate Policy*, 13(6), 751–769.

Jorgenson, A. K. (2014). Economic development and the carbon intensity of human well-being. *Nature Climate Change*, 4(3), 186–189.

Jorgenson, A. K., & Dietz, T. (2015). Economic growth does not reduce the ecological intensity of human well-being. *Sustainability Science*, 10(1), 149–156.

Kahn, B. (2017). This graphic puts global warming in full perspective. Climate Central. Available at: www.climatecentral.org/news/628-months-since-the-world-had-cool-month-21365; We just breached the 410 parts per million threshold. Climate Central. Available at: www.climatecentral. org/news/we-just-breached-the-410-parts-per-million-threshold-21372

Kallis, G., Kiparsky, M., & Norgaard, R. (2009). Collaborative governance and adaptive management: Lessons from California's CALFED Water Program. *Environmental Science & Policy*, 12(6), 631–643.

Kaufman, A.C. (2017). A coal museum in Kentucky went solar this month. The backstory is even better. *The Huffington Post*. Available at: www.huffingtonpost.com/entry/kentucky-coal-solar_us_58f76a49e4b029063d3590a9

Kennedy, R. F. (2005). An ill wind off Cape Cod. *The New York Times*. Available at: www.nytimes.com/2005/12/16/opinion/an-ill-wind-off-cape-cod.html?_r=0

Kern, F., & Rogge, K. S. (2016). The pace of governed energy transitions: Agency, international dynamics and the global Paris agreement accelerating decarbonisation processes? *Energy Research & Social Science*, 22, 13–17.

Keystone XL Project. (2014). Final supplemental environmental impact statement for the Keystone XL Project. Executive Summary. Applicant for Presidential Permit: TransCanada Keystone Pipeline, LP. United States Department of State, Bureau of Oceans and International Environmental and Scientific Affairs. Available at: https://keystonepipeline-xl.state.gov/documents/organization/221135.pdf

Loorbach, D., & Rotmans, J. (2010). The practice of transition management: Examples and lessons from four distinct cases. *Futures*, 42(3), 237–246.

Lumb, D. (2017). Coal company plans Kentucky's biggest solar farm for old mine site. MSN.com and Engadget. Available at: www.msn.com/en-us/news/technology/coal-company-plans-kentuckys-biggest-solar-farm-for-old-mine-site/ar-BBA3v3G

March for Science. (2017). March for science. Available at: https://satellites.marchforscience.com/

Martinelli, L. A., & Filoso, S. (2008). Expansion of sugarcane ethanol production in Brazil: Environmental and social challenges. *Ecological Applications*, 18(4), 885–898.

Meadowcroft, J. (2011). Engaging with the politics of sustainability transitions. *Environmental Innovation and Societal Transitions*, 1(1), 70–75.

Mehany, M. S. H. M., & Guggemos, A. (2015). A literature survey of the fracking economic and environmental implications in the United States. *Procedia Engineering*, 118, 169–176.

Morrow, A. (2015). Ontario Liberal's gas-plants scandal: Everything you need to know. *The Globe and Mail*. Available at: www.theglobeandmail.com/news/politics/ontario-liberals-gas-plants-scandal-everything-you-need-to-know/article23668386/

Mosher, D. (2017). At one end of the Keystone XL oil pipeline, there is a scene you must see to believe. Futurism. Available at: https://futurism.com/keystone-xl-oil-pipeline-scene-see-believe/

Mundo-Hernández, J., de Celis Alonso, B., Hernández-Álvarez, J., & de Celis-Carrillo, B. (2014). An overview of solar photovoltaic energy in Mexico and Germany. *Renewable and Sustainable Energy Reviews*, 31, 639–649.

Nogueira, M., & Teixeira, M. (2017). Brazil's oil exports set to jump this year, weakening OPEC curbs. Reuters. Available at: www.reuters.com/article/us-brazil-oil-exports-analysis/brazils-oil-exports-set-to-jump-this-year-weakening-opec-curbs-idUSKBN1722IW

Offen, K. (2014). Historical geography III climate matters. *Progress in Human Geography*, 38(3), 476–489.

Ontario Ministry of Energy. (2017). The end of coal. An Ontario primer on modernizing electricity supply. Available at: www.energy.gov.on.ca/en/archive/the-end-of-coal/

Ontario Ministry of Environment and Climate Change. (2017). Smog advisories and smog days by region. Available at: www.airqualityontario.com/history/aqi_advisories_stats.php.

Ostrom, E. (2012). Nested externalities and polycentric institutions: Must we wait for global solutions to climate change before taking actions at other scales? *Econ. Theory*, 49(2), 353–369.

Palmer, A. (2015). Underwater conventional and unconventional oil and gas in the Arctic. *Journal of Environmental Solutions for Oil, Gas, and Mining*, 1(1), 119–130.

Paris. (2015). Conference of the Parties 21. *Paris Climate Change Conference*. November 2015. Available at: http://unfccc.int/meetings/paris_nov_2015/meeting/8926.php

Parkinson, H. J. (2016). Young people are so bad at voting – I'm disappointed in my peers. *The Guardian*. Available at: www.theguardian.com/commentisfree/2016/jun/28/young-people-bad-voting-millennials-eu-vote-politics

Peifer, J. L., Khalsa, S., & Howard Ecklund, E. (2016). Political conservatism, religion, and environmental consumption in the United States. *Environmental Politics*, 25(4), 661–689.

Pelling, M. (2010). *Adaptation to Climate Change: From Resilience to Transformation*. Routledge, London, UK.

Rayapura, A. (2014). Millennials most sustainability-conscious generation yet, but don't call them 'environmentalists'. Sustainable Brands: The Bridge to Better Brands. Available at: www.sustainablebrands.com/news_and_views/stakeholder_trends_insights/aarthi_rayapura/millennials_most_sustainability_conscious

Ruppel, C. D. (2011). Methane hydrates and contemporary climate change. *Nature Education Knowledge*, 3(10), 29.

Smith, N., & Leiserowitz, A. (2013). American evangelicals and global warming. *Global Environmental Change*, 23(5), 1009–1017.

Seelye, K. Q. (2010). Big wind farm off Cape Cod gets approval. *The New York Times*. Available at: www.nytimes.com/2010/04/29/science/earth/29wind.html

Shi, L., Chu, E., & Debats, J. (2015). Explaining progress in climate adaptation planning across 156 US municipalities. *Journal of the American Planning Association*, 81(3) 191–202.

Sommerer, T., & Lim, S. (2016). The environmental state as a model for the world? An analysis of policy repertoires in 37 countries. *Environmental Politics*, 25(1), 92–115.

Statistics Canada. (2017). Gross domestic product, expenditure-based, by province and territory. Statistics Canada. Available at: www.statcan.gc.ca/tables-tableaux/sum-som/l01/cst01/econ15-eng.htm

Taylor, M. (2017). Can this tiny African nation lead the world forward? TravelPulse. Available at: www.travelpulse.com/news/features/can-this-tiny-african-nation-lead-the-world-forward.html

Toumi, O., Le Gallo, J., & Rejeb, J. B. (2017). Assessment of Latin American sustainability. *Renewable and Sustainable Energy Reviews*, 78, 878–885.

UNDP. (2017). Human Rights Reports. Public Data Explorer. Human Development Index Public Data Tool. Available at: http://hdr.undp.org/en/data-explorer

UNEP. (2011). Green Economy Report. United Nations Environment Program. http://web.unep.org/greeneconomy/resources/green-economy-report

U.S. Census Bureau. (2017). Voting and registration. United States Census Bureau. Available at: http://thedataweb.rm.census.gov/TheDataWeb_HotReport2/voting/voting.hrml?GESTFIPS=ALL&INSTANCE=Nov+2014

Vaughan, A. (2017). Mersey feat: World's biggest wind turbines go online near Liverpool. *The Guardian*. Available at: www.theguardian.com/environment/2017/may/17/mersey-wind-turbines-liverpool-uk-wind-technology

Vengosh, A., Jackson, R. B., Warner, N., Darrah, T. H., & Kondash, A. (2014). A critical review of the risks to water resources from unconventional shale gas development and hydraulic fracturing in the United States. *Environmental Science & Technology*, 48(15), 8334–8348.

World Bank. (2017). DataBank World Development Indicators. Available at: http://databank.worldbank.org/data/reports.aspx?source=world-development-indicators&preview=on#

World Energy Council. (2015). Mexico's Energy Trilemma Index. Available at: www.worldenergy. org/data/trilemma-index/country/mexico/

Yong, E. (2017). Professor Smith goes to Washington. In response to the new president's stances on a range of issues, more scientists are preparing to run for political office. The Atlantic. Available at: www.theatlantic.com/science/archive/2017/01/thanks-to-trump-scientists-are-planning-to-run-for-office/514229/

Ziegler, R. (2015). Towards all voices, from all levels and in their own ways? A discussion of the youth quota proposal as an incremental policy innovation for sustainability. In J. Tremmel, A. Mason, P. Haakenstad Godli, & I. Dimitrijoski (Eds). *Youth Quotas and Other Efficient Forms of Youth Participation in Ageing Societies.* pp. 93–107. Springer International Publishing, Cham, Switzerland.

10 Developing sustainability systems

Learning objectives

- Envision sustainability as an ongoing and continuous process requiring constant monitoring and adaption
- Introduce various sustainability solutions related to energy, food, water, buildings, and infrastructure
- Assess indicators that measure progress against strong sustainability criteria
- Describe pathways to strong sustainability as part of socio-technical system change

Sustainability value can be created on an ongoing basis as a result of dramatic shifts in technologies, infrastructures, policies, and institutions that underlie keystone systems of sustainability: energy systems, food and water systems, and buildings and infrastructure systems. These keystone systems change as part of a multi-level socio-technical transition. The core focus is on integrated solutions that combine multiple technologies, sectors, and approaches in ways that have the potential to drastically change the sustainability equation.

Lifecycle energy systems

Many theories and frameworks have been created to help understand how to reduce energy demand through behavioral conservation and technological efficiency improvements. These include *factor 10 theory*, which suggests that to achieve sustainability of materials and energy use, a massive decrease in energy use and material flows (by a factor of 10) in addition to a massive increase in efficiency (by a factor of 10) is required (Schmidt-Bleek, 2008). That equates to a 90 percent cut in resource and energy demands going well beyond *factor 4 theory* (von Weizsäcker et al., 1998), which argued for a 75 percent cut in resource and energy use while doubling wealth creation. To achieve a factor 10 cut to resource and energy demands, significant changes to technologies, institutions, and infrastructure, as well as to the social, cultural, policy, political, economic, industry, and science subsystems of the socio-technical system are required.

One approach to encourage factor 10 changes is the *circular economy perspective* (Moreau et al., 2017), which aims to reduce resource and energy use while taking waste outputs from the traditional linear economy and using them as inputs to additional production processes. It focuses on designing products, technologies, and infrastructure from a lifecycle perspective and on reorienting value chains into value cycles directed towards triple-bottom-line objectives. One component of the circular economy is *upcycling*, defined as the process of transforming what was considered waste into useful materials or technologies (McDonough and Braungart, 2013). Upcycling and the circular economy can help create *sustainability value* rather than simply reducing environmental harms. Sustainability professionals are concerned with creating and amplifying sustainability value by coordinating changes in products and technologies with changes in infrastructure systems.

Connections between technology and infrastructure changes are highlighted by Busch et al. (2017) within circular economy scenarios for hydrogen fuel cell and battery electric vehicles. Many factors go into deciding which type of vehicle technology should or could be supported by policies and market demand. For example, lithium–ion battery electric vehicles are more efficient at transforming input electricity into output electricity (90 percent versus 56 percent for fuel cell). This means that additional materials and energy would be required to enhance the electricity infrastructure if fuel cell vehicles were to be scaled up as a sustainable niche experiment. Of perhaps more importance is the availability of rare earth metals needed for each vehicle as well as the substitutability for those materials within the production process. One option is to reuse platinum from old catalytic converters from internal combustion vehicles, which could reduce the demand for platinum for hydrogen fuel cells by 80 percent by 2030. Current stocks of platinum already exist in older vehicles but for other materials the stocks are not going to be available until after the useful life of the technology. For example, lithium and cobalt are available from lithium–ion batteries from electric vehicles after eight years because the lifespan of the batteries is shorter than the lifespan of the vehicles (13 years). These batteries can be reused for building grid-connected storage systems because there is still two-thirds of the original capacity left in the batteries even though they are no longer acceptable for use in vehicles (Busch et al., 2017).

A broad view of the circular economy as a socio-technical system therefore includes both the resources to make the technology as well as the socio-economic processes that create and use the resources underlying the technology. Busch et al. (2017) pointed out that this type of circular economy requires a systems analysis to understand whether the elimination of material and energy demands for the production of the products exceeds the energy and materials required for the recycling or reuse. Furthermore, some key resources like rare earth metals are critical to various technologies that are important for transportation and energy infrastructure transitions. Social, economic, and political considerations add an additional dimension to the environmental analysis and require sustainability professionals to develop new integrated methods for understanding the permutations of these complex decisions.

Another example of the connections between technologies and infrastructure systems is outlined by Bolton and Foxon (2015) in the case of transitions of large-scale energy distribution infrastructure in the United Kingdom. Energy system infrastructure produces public goods including economic development benefits as well as public costs such as air pollution. Infrastructure change was viewed as a socio-technical process that proceeded through phases from innovation and development of local systems to the building of national grids. Infrastructure decisions were influenced by a co-evolution of social, political, and institutional factors in addition to science, technology, and economic trends. This included the strategies of utility companies, the practices of energy end users, and the instruments of regulators and policy makers.

Bolton and Foxon (2015, pp. 540–541) outlined four phases of energy infrastructure transitions that resemble those of the *complex adaptive cycle* outlined in Chapter 1 and described later as part of a *panarchy*:

1   System building and establishment phase

- New systems are created within niches

  o   Geographically dispersed with a wide range of technologies and practices

2   System expansion and momentum phase

- Systems expand and develop an internal momentum
- Standards develop and dominant designs emerge from the pack

  o   These winning systems connect over space (e.g., across cities, regions, nations)

3   Stagnation and inertia phase

- Long-term investments are made in fixed assets. This produces regime lock-in as investors want to recoup their returns over time.

  o   Benefits of scale economies and network effects provides durability

4   System transition and renewal phase

- Infrastructure assets age
- Landscape pressures build (e.g., climate change, energy security) and start to destabilize the regime
- Regime actors either incrementally adapt to landscape pressures or radically change in response to niche experiments

These transitions were initiated and driven by the coordinated efforts of many types of actors during key phases in the infrastructure cycles. In particular, two types of champions were important in the energy infrastructure transitions: technical champions and political champions (Bolton and Foxon, 2015). **Technical champions** were "typically an employee of a council energy or building services department . . . [who] possess the technical knowledge and capabilities required to develop [energy infrastructure solutions] . . . learn from best practice both nationally and internationally and has project management skills" (p. 546). **Political champions** are similar to policy entrepreneurs who work to elevate energy infrastructure solutions onto "the political agenda, enroll other councilors from across the political spectrum, create an advocacy coalition, and help to de-risk large scale investments by displaying a commitment to long-term infrastructure development" (p. 546).

Sustainability professionals including those from intermediary organizations can work with both types of champions to devise *strategies and instruments* to accelerate the shift from the stagnation and inertia phase to the transition and renewal phase (Bolton and Foxon, 2015). Strategies include incentives for research and development (R&D) to overcome risk adverse business cultures, and instruments include changes to the regulatory regime to allow more competition as a means of driving innovation in technology and infrastructure. Sustainability professionals can help develop *strategies and instruments* to accelerate the shift from the system building and establishment phase to the expansion and momentum phase. Strategies include increasing government intervention to support niche experiments of new energy technologies, and instruments include regulatory changes to provide a more stable investment environment for green energy supply and transmission infrastructure and for demand management technologies. Acceleration Point: Sustainability professionals can use their **normative**

competence to guide transitions to energy infrastructure in a direction that is anticipated to improve the resource maintenance and efficiency and the intra- and intergenerational equity sustainability principles.

Greening the energy return–on–energy–investment equation

One way to assess the sustainability of energy socio-technical systems is to focus on the *energy-return-on-energy-investment* (EROEI). This is the amount of energy output (net energy) that is available from a given amount of energy input associated with mining, extraction, and transformation. The amount of energy consumed in the process of delivering energy to end uses can also be added to EROEI analyses (Feng et al., 2018). The EROEI is important for sustainability because economic development is related to the amount of net energy available to society after subtracting the energy required for mining, extraction, transformation, and delivery (Feng et al., 2018). The EROEI differs by type of energy and by the level of technology available at a given time. For example, the EROEI ratio ranges from less than 0.8:1 for biofuels to 6.8:1 for solar photovoltaic to 11:1 for oil and gas to 18:1 for wind turbines and finally to greater than 100:1 for hydropower (Murphy and Hall, 2010). This means that 18 units of energy are gained for every 1 unit of energy input required to produce wind turbines. As the authors point out, these numbers are subject to numerous assumptions and limitations, for example, the need for backup energy for intermittent energy options (e.g., solar, wind), which would greatly decrease the EROEI ratio. The ratio for oil and gas has fallen over time from over 100:1 in 1930 to single digits (2–5:1) for current marginal sources like oil sands and shale. The coal ratio has remained relatively unchanged at 80:1 (Murphy and Hall, 2010). Acceleration Point: Sustainability professionals can use the EROEI to compare renewable energy options as well as to measure progress in those energy technologies over time. Caution should be used however when comparing renewable to non-renewable energy sources, as the EROEI does not incorporate environmental impacts associated with the energy systems.

The EROEI ratio give us insight into which energy sources may not be sustainable given the huge amount of energy input required like in the case of biofuels. Biofuels are being studied as part of technological innovation system transitions (Suurs and Hekkert, 2009) and innovation is leading to new types of biofuels using waste as inputs. Take for example a partnership between Bio-bean, Shell, and Argent Energy to develop a biofuel made in part from coffee beans. This new biofuel may soon be used to power London, England's double-decker buses. The company estimates that for every tonne of coffee beans recycled 6.8 tonnes of CO_2 emissions will be eliminated (ABC, 2017). A series of process and technology innovations are also making biofuels from biomass more sustainable by improving efficiencies and therefore the EROEI (Herron et al., 2017).

The scale and locked-in nature of fossil fuel and nuclear energy systems compared to the growing but still relatively small-scale use of renewable energy options (Murphy and Hall, 2010) poses a bottleneck for sustainability professionals. Sustainable technology niche experiments must stay ahead of fossil fuel technology niche experiments conducted by regime actors who are constantly working to improve the EROEI ratios of oil sands, coal, and natural gas. Improving the EROEI may allow for reducing the costs of extraction and transformation (e.g., removing the oil from the sand), serving to reinforce the regime by extending the life of technologies and infrastructures that depend on fossil fuels. Raugei et al. (2012) addressed limitations of previous studies examining the EROEI ratio for solar PV systems. They concluded that over the 30 years of operations (the lifetime of the technology) the ratios for solar PV and oil and gas are comparable. While coal has a higher EROEI ratio, the lifecycle greenhouse gas (GHG) emissions are significantly higher and therefore reduce the sustainability of coal as an energy option in the context of climate change (Kuramochi et al., 2017). The other advantage of solar is that the fuel is free, unlimited, and not controllable by large market incumbent companies. In contrast, fossil fuel supply options fluctuate in price, decline in availability, and are controllable by a few large public and private companies. The shift to marginal sources (e.g., oil sands, shale, methyl hydrates) will likely reduce the EROEI ratio over time as both the financial and energy costs to extract and transform these sources increases.

The challenge for society is that as the global EROEI declines, the proportion of total actors in the economy (industries, businesses, governments) that are devoted to finding, extracting, refining, transporting, and transforming energy will increase. At some point, say if the global EROEI falls to 10–1 or 5–1, society will become so concentrated on energy production that social and political subsystems may breakdown, economic subsystems may slow and contract, and the fabric of society may unravel as it becomes more challenging to maintain gross domestic product (GDP) growth rates and Human Development Index (HDI) performance levels. This is the idea of the net energy cliff, which suggests that the proportion of net energy as a percentage of total energy that is made available by actors and processes in the economy may begin to decline more rapidly over time as conventional fossil fuel sources become scarce and are substituted for with renewables and unconventional fossil fuel options, both of which have lower EROEI ratios (Brandt, 2017). Sustainability professionals can focus on making green energy more competitive by improving the EROEI ratio either through technological upgrades to decrease the energy input required or to increase the energy output possible from technologies that are based on renewable fuel sources (e.g., solar systems).

What strategies and instruments should sustainability professionals use to instigate *sustainable niche experiments* and infrastructure changes when considering ongoing and future changes to EROEI ratios? For example, increasing the EROEI ratio for urban transportation systems represents an *incremental* improvement but does not address the reliance on fossil fuels and the carbon content of these systems. Rather, urban planning instruments that increase density and reduce the distance between where people live and work will reduce the demand for energy of any type and create public good benefits for society including cheaper and lower carbon intensity transportation systems (Nichols and Kockelman, 2014; Shammin et al., 2010). Acceleration Point: Strategies and instruments should address the entire socio-technical energy system including the interconnections between supply and demand practices, and technology and infrastructure changes, in order to identify and implement solutions that generate the most sustainability value by minimizing tradeoffs between human capital, human made capital, and natural capital.

From carbon reduction (CR) to carbon product production (CPP)

Many studies, frameworks, and theories have focused on how to reduce CO_2 emissions through technology, behavior, practices, policies, and infrastructure system change. Net-zero buildings delivered at little to no economic cost premium (Torcellini et al., 2015) is one example of technology and design practices that were once considered radical but are now becoming mainstream. The challenge for sustainability professionals is that even if we create strategies and instruments to retrofit all existing buildings to net-zero energy or carbon status, the transition would not occur quickly enough to mitigate climate change

(Kuramochi et al., 2017). As a result, many actors and especially those in the fossil fuel regime have pushed carbon capture and storage technologies as a means of climate change mitigation while allowing the continued production and consumption of coal, oil, and natural gas. But early conceptions of this type of system had a serious flaw: who would voluntarily choose to pay to pump CO_2 emissions underground? What was the business case to be made to invest in this technology?

Sustainability professionals are helping develop a market for CO_2 as an input to products and processes in order to compliment efforts at reducing CO_2 emissions. New technology breakthroughs are changing the equation but require a complimentary language that views CO_2 as a resource by closing the loop and building a circular economy for carbon (McDonough, 2016). Researchers are discovering ways of sucking CO_2 out of the air and using it as an input to produce carbon fiber that can be used in buildings, transportation systems, and other infrastructure (Lau et al., 2016; Licht et al., 2010; Ren et al., 2015). This would allow a market to be created for the capture and use of carbon not only at the smokestack where high ambient concentrations occur, but anywhere that low concentrations of CO_2 occur (e.g., near highways, in urban areas). In 2017, the first commercial factory went online to remove CO_2 from the air and use it to accelerate the rates of growth for vegetables in a greenhouse (Nguyen, 2017). Other potential secondary markets for this technology include fertilizer, fuel, and even carbonated soft drinks. As part of the process, waste heat from a nearby water incinerator plant is used to heat up the filters and release the CO_2. This adds a third dimension to the industrial ecology system: carbon is sucked from the air, waste heat is used as a way to remove the carbon from filters, and the carbon is then used to grow vegetables or create products. The CO_2 is expected to increase growth rates of vegetables by 30 percent (Climeworks, 2017), which could provide a solution to food shortages due to drought or other natural or socio-political disruptions to food systems. Acceleration Point: Sustainability professionals can focus on sustainable niche experiments that combine food, energy, and water systems to garner political support and financial investment from three industries rather than just one. This also diversifies the risk associated with these experiments among many actors who then share responsibly for success.

Lifecycle sustainability assessment

A popular method for measuring the potential sustainability value of projects, products, technologies, and infrastructure is a lifecycle assessment (LCA). Onat et al. (2017) reviewed studies focusing on integrated frameworks that combine LCA with other models. They identified limitations of standard LCA models, which do not incorporate social and economic factors and often focus at the product or building level (process models) rather than the socio-economic system level (federal, state, city). *Lifecycle sustainability assessment frameworks* are modified versions of the LCA that can better handle uncertainties, incorporate stakeholder feedback to enhance decision-making, and improve the ability of these integrated models to capture the relationships between the social, economic, and environmental dimensions of sustainability (Onat et al., 2017). Onat et al. (2017) outlined an integrated model that combines four sub-models: (1) the system of interest (e.g., transportation, energy, water), (2) the social system, (3) the economic system, and (4) the environmental system. The goal is to show and measure the interrelationships and feedback effects between the sub-models as well as between their constituent parts (e.g., public welfare, human health, employment, GDP, vehicle ownership cost, GHG emissions, air pollution, population change, fuel economy of vehicles). Sustainability assessments based on these integrated models can be used to inform triple-bottom-line economic development strategies, policy mixes focused on niche creation and regime change, and infrastructure investment strategies. Sustainability professionals can use these integrated models to understand feedbacks and interactions in order to manage tradeoffs that can result from changes to complex socio-technical energy systems.

Renewables, micro-grids, and electric mobility

As societies continue to electrify, opportunities for new types of systems increase given that more technologies are now available that can act as generators, storage, or users of energy. In particular, distributed energy systems are becoming more popular both in developing and developed countries as a means of democratizing energy systems. Developing distributed energy systems has faced many bottlenecks including incumbent regime actors blocking grassroots innovations (Hess, 2013). How can small solar actors respond when faced with barriers from the existing regime actors who do not want to open the electricity system to on-site generation, micro-grids, and other forms of distributed generation options? Additionally, how do grassroots (small-scale and local) renewable energy producers (e.g., community-based organizations, local governments, new businesses) avoid being enveloped by large-scale, well-funded renewable energy entrants that are either owned or partnering with incumbent energy actors?

Hess (2013) outlined and compared four models of funding distributed energy systems that can overcome some of the limitations of traditional financing models like home-equity loans:

1   Public ownership and local solarization

  - Public ownership of profits allows for reinvesting in distributed energy systems.
  - Some cities offer feed-in tariffs for distributed energy systems (e.g., Los Angeles).
  - Other cities support community solar projects (e.g., Seattle).
  - Cities like Austin, Texas, also support residential and commercial rebates and incentives for solar PV.
  - These municipal programs helped to shift ownership of energy supply from national/state/private investor-owned to the local and community level.
  - Challenges: high transaction costs due to municipalities having to pay investor owned utilities for use of their power lines; had to develop expertise to manage the distributed energy systems, legal battles in courts, and political challenges in elections.

  - Case study: San Francisco:

    o   Tried to pass propositions in 2001 and 2002 to localize the electricity system, both were defeated due to strong opposition from large investor owned utilities.
    o   Passed propositions in 2001 that allowed San Francisco to finance green energy through municipal bonds.
    o   In 2004, the California Public Utilities Commission adopted a plan to allow cities and counties across California to adopt community choice aggregation strategies.
    o   San Francisco adopted a community choice aggregation strategy, which involved grouping customers in the same geographic area to gain power for negotiating prices in a public–private partnership with investor owned

utilities. The new contract negotiations allowed the city to negotiate for a greener energy mix.

- o   In 2011, San Francisco purchased bulk green electricity to sell to 75,000 customers at a $10 per month premium price.
- o   The investor owned utilities resisted by introducing a state ballot proposition in 2010 that attempted to require a two-thirds vote in any district that wanted to adopt a community choice aggregation agreement. They spent nearly $50 million but lost the vote, and additionally, California passed a senate bill to allow for public funds to community choice aggregation programs, as well as ban investor owned utilities from negative marketing targeting these programs.
- o   Summary: the regime actors attempting to slow the transition to distributed energy systems were counteracted by the state government, which provided niche protection for distributed energy experiments.

2   Property Assessed Clean Energy (PACE) financing

- •   Cities issue bonds to fund costs of solar; homeowner's payback the upfront loan as part of their property taxes in proportion to the annual energy savings.
- •   The owner of the property owns the solar system; it transfers to the new owner if the property is sold.
- •   States started to pass enabling legislation in 2009.
- •   In 2010, the United States Housing Finance Agency said that PACE loans had a senior lien status to the local governments, which meant that mortgages resold to the federal agency would not be able to recoup their investment before local governments could. Because of this status, the residential PACE program was ended in the United States.
- •   In 2011, commercial PACE programs were growing especially in California with hundreds of millions of dollars invested from private capital firms.
- •   Summary: PACE models challenged the incumbent residential property financing regime and the federal government blocked the program. States and local governments acted as countervailing powers to support the program and helped scale-up the commercial PACE.

3   Share-based models

- •   Cooperative models where investors purchase shares and partially own the solar energy generation technology.
- •   Solar gardens like SunShare in Colorado allow residents to purchase shares and received credits on their energy bills.
- •   Summary: Organizations like SunShare faced a bottleneck from investor owned utilities and state governments aiming to slow these community distributed generation systems by influencing laws that make it harder (red tape) and costlier to install solar.

4   Third-party financing

- •   In this case, homeowners do not own the solar technology system installed on their property, but they instead purchase the energy from another organization that owns and maintains the solar system.

All four models have drawbacks and require new technologies to fully democratize micro-grids. A technology known as *blockchains* is allowing micro-grids to become truly distributed for the first time. Social practices utilizing blockchains allow individuals or organizations to generate solar energy on-site and sell it directly to their neighbors using digital currency exchanges like Bitcoin, which eliminates the need for a bank, a centralized utility, and a centralized energy transmission system. This socio-technical solution combines energy and software technology innovation, governance innovation, and changes to practices that co-evolve with changes to technologies. In Brooklyn, a company called LO3 Energy (2017) is using blockchain technology to allow residents to install solar panels on their roof and sell that energy to their neighbors through an auction market (Deaton, 2017). This differs from previous micro-grids, which were either wholly off-grid or allowed homeowners to generate and sell back to the grid. A similar sustainable niche experiment is underway in Australia (Diss, 2017). While regime actors will likely fight against this new model as a competitive threat to their business, there are advantages for centralized grid producers. For example, during peak times, utilities could shut down coal and natural gas and instead offer to purchase the distributed solar for a higher price than those blockchain-enabled producers were selling to their neighbors. This would create a competitive market of many small producers and a few large producers, further driving innovation in technology, infrastructure, institutions, and social practices. Sustainability professionals can help test and learn from distributed blockchain-solar markets and can work to build coalitions of powerful actors to protect these sustainable niche experiments from attempts to undermine or slow their development.

Berlin's electricity grid transition

Germany has undergone an energy transition in part to address climate change (significant GHG emission reduction targets of 80 percent below 1990 by 2050) and in part to modernize the energy supply and transmission system to become more resilient and less reliant on nuclear power (Rocholl and Bolton, 2016). One of the challenges of this rapid transition was the need to upgrade transmission grids to be able to handle the increase in renewable energy supply from large and small suppliers. Rocholl and Bolton (2016) examined the relationship between local energy governance and ownership preferences and national regulations aiming to transform the German electricity system. They focused on the role of cities like Berlin as both a place where energy innovation can occur and also as a driver of that innovation through its policies and network connections to other places and other types of actors. A process called *re-municipalization of the electricity grid* is occurring in Berlin, where decentralized, small-scale cooperatives and private individuals are owning and generating electricity for sale back to the grid (Rocholl and Bolton, 2016). This move from the national to the local created a number of political and governance challenges: who owns and operates the transmission and distribution grids? Is electricity a public good, or is electricity a private good that can be managed and controlled by actors wishing to increase profits?

Food and water systems in the Anthropocene

The Anthropocene has been defined as "the time when human impacts are widespread on earth" (Barnosky et al., 2014, p. 78), including climate change, species extinctions, loss of biodiversity, air, water, and land pollution, and human population and material consumption levels. Similar to energy systems, food and water systems require changes in response to human and ecological pressures in order to move towards a strong sustainability pathway. How can sustainability professionals help design and modify food and water systems given that human demands have led to large-scale environmental and social impacts that are either irreversible or costly to mitigate?

The new water cycle: R3 principles (reduce, reuse, recycle)

The water cycle in the Anthropocene considers human uses as a portion whereby actors can increase/decrease their water demand or increase/decrease the pollution contribution based on how the water is used. Water conservation programs are a common type of organized environmental management focusing on sustainable behavior (CBSM, 2017) that can help to **reduce** water use rates. The Anthropocene theory suggests that human systems must consider radical changes to the water cycle if society wishes to continue large scale irrigated agriculture as well as meeting increasing potable (e.g., for residential consumption) and non-potable (e.g., for energy and industrial use) water demands for growing cities. Polycentric governance approaches and adaptive co-management as described in Chapter 3 is one way that water system sustainability can be enhanced by managing supply and enforcing quality constraints. Water system innovation focusing on improving water supply and demand technologies and practices as described in Chapter 4 is another way that sustainability value can be created within water systems. Perhaps the most radical socio-technical innovation for water systems that combines changes to technologies with changes to user practices and perceptions is water recycling and reuse.

Water **recycling** technologies are continually improving with filtration plants and biological filtration options becoming more common in developed and developing countries. Water recycling and reuse offers tremendous potential, but can citizens be convinced that reused water is safe and healthy? Harris–Lovett et al. (2015) found that using a portfolio of strategies rather than a single strategy helped build public *legitimacy* for water **reuse**. These strategies included public outreach campaigns, incorporating users into the planning and management processes, transparent information policies, publicizing data about high water quality performance, adopting stringent monitoring procedures, investing in advanced water treatment technology, having water managers including engineers communicate directly with water users, organizing water tastings, and relating potable water reuse to other practices that most people have already adopted like recycling. Harris–Lovett et al. (2015, pp. 7558– 7559) concluded that many different but complimentary types of legitimacy needed to be enhanced by these strategies for water reuse to be acceptable to users:

> potable water reuse projects must demonstrate how they will benefit the end users of the water (exchange legitimacy), strengthen public involvement in planning and decision-making (influence legitimacy), incorporate transparent communication procedures and develop an organizational reputation for high quality (dispositional legitimacy), and have reliable risk management procedures and emergency intervention procedures in place (procedural legitimacy). The legitimacy portfolio also requires involvement of experienced utility managers in public outreach (personal legitimacy) and relation of potable reuse to established social practices (taken-for-grantedness legitimacy).

Acceleration Point: Sustainability professionals can accelerate sustainability transitions by using a portfolio of strategies and instruments to target different types of people with different combinations of interventions that will enhance the legitimacy of the sustainable innovation or practice and therefore increase the adoption rates by water users.

Desalination as an economic development strategy

Another socio-technical innovation that requires changes to technologies and user practices is desalination, which is the process of removing salt from ocean water or soils. This process is energy intensive and was therefore only used initially in water-constrained regions like the Middle East, Australia, and California where the costs were justifiable with early levels of technology. Fast forward to 2015 and thousands of desalination plants exist in 150 countries filtering water for more than 300 million people (International Desalination Association, 2017). The challenges for desalination are to reduce the energy and costs per unit of drinkable or agricultural water produced, to switch from fossil fuel to sustainable energy sources, and to develop marketable uses for the salt that is left behind by the process. Desalination systems have improved efficiencies and reduced energy requirements by switching technology options from reverse osmosis to multi-stage flash and multiple-effect distillation, then finally to vapor compression distillation and electrodialysis (Ghaffour et al., 2015). Integrated desalination systems can be combined with bubble greenhouses to filter the salt from the water while increasing the growing rates for crops in water constrained regions (Schmack et al., 2015). These systems can also be coupled with solar and geothermal energy to improve sustainability and allow for off-grid applications. This type of food, energy, and water system can contribute to triple-bottom-line economic development strategies.

Sgouridis et al. (2016) assessed potential renewable energy and policy transitions for the United Arab Emirates (UAE), which is seventh in the world in primary energy demand per capita partly due to energy to run water desalination plants. The UAE is the eighth largest producer of oil and the third largest exporter of oil. Demand for both water and energy is expected to increase and new sources of supply will be needed to expand the desalination capacity well above the 7.2 million cubic meters per day in 2012. A scenario analysis revealed that solar is expected to form the core of the future energy strategy because natural gas prices are increasing and solar prices are falling (Sgouridis et al., 2016). Large increases in utility-scale solar PV, rooftop solar PV systems, and concentrated solar power plants with storage are anticipated to make up the gap between projected energy demand and current levels of supply without having to increase coal or natural gas production capacity by 2030. A cost curve analysis showed that some technologies would save in excess of US$20 per gigajoule, including landfill gas for electricity, solar water heating, solar PV at the utility scale, and solar PV at the rooftop scale. Marginal technology options would lead to a net increase in costs per gigajoule including concentrating solar with storage and solar thermal for cooling buildings (Sgouridis et al., 2016). Taking all technologies into account, the average cost to substitute renewable energy for fossil fuel options is expected to be negative, leading to a savings of $6.3 per gigajoule equating to $1.9 billion in annual savings by 2030 (Sgouridis et al., 2016). The energy system changes will therefore enable additional desalination capacity at lower costs and environmental impacts as part of UAE's triple-bottom-line economic development strategy. Acceleration Point: In countries where fossil fuels are abundant and formed the core of export revenues for many decades, sustainability professionals can help guide a transition to renewables as a means of avoiding the *natural resource curse* and diversifying energy systems to build resilience into the economy.

Food systems and sustainability

Urban agriculture is one option for reducing energy and water demands and environmental impacts from resource use and pollution associated with growing food. Martin et al. (2016) found that the main sustainability benefits of urban agriculture were social rather than ecological. This was due to small yields relative to the size of the population, and an increase in ecological knowledge about the health benefits of organic food. Social benefits were also derived from social capital networks, social innovation, and new forms of organizations like food hubs in urban areas. *Food hubs* are "urban facilities that engage in aggregation (which can include growing), preparation, distribution, and marketing of food" (Martin et al., 2016, p. 13). They can be social enterprises that supply food to restaurants, small grocery stores, and food services for schools (Martin et al., 2016). Food hubs focus on sustainability (local food, healthy food, affordable food) and provide economic development opportunities for urban areas.

Food hubs and urban agriculture represent new frameworks of sustainability emphasizing social components in a more central way. One such framework outlined by Eizenberg and Jabareen (2017) included four components: safety, equity, eco-prosumption, and sustainable urban forms. **Safety** is based on managing uncertainties and focuses on adaptation and vulnerability of an urban area. **Equity** aims to reduce disparities between access to resources and is similar to environmental justice approaches. It addresses inequalities, redistribution of opportunities, and participation of vulnerable groups. ***Eco-prosumption*** is framed as a societal responsibility to reduce social risks posed by global and local threats. It focuses on mitigation efforts and co-producing economic and environmental value through reorganizing modes of consumption, production, and value creation. **Sustainable urban forms** suggests that the principles of *green new urbanism* should be followed: compactness (e.g., increasing connectivity), mixed land-use (e.g., residential, commercial, industrial, institutional, transportation), diversity (e.g., building types, demographics, employment options), clean energy and passive solar design (e.g., low-impact technologies), greening (e.g., bringing nature back into the city), sustainable transport (e.g., reducing demand for traffic, trip times), and renewal and utilization (e.g., brownfield redevelopment). Acceleration Point: Sustainability professionals can incorporate and highlight social elements into strategies and instruments to gain support from regime actors who may not prioritize sustainability or climate change mitigation. The principles of green new urbanism also align with a pragmatic approach to sustainability and a triple-bottom-line economic development strategy.

The food–energy–water nexus

The food–energy–water (FEW) nexus offers sustainability professionals a framework for analyzing the complex interactions and feedbacks between these systems and their economic, social, and environmental characteristics. The framework outlined by Smajgl et al. (2016) in Figure 10.1 emphasizes three areas to improve the sustainability of a FEW system: (1) food security, (2) water access, and (3) energy security. Framing strategies and instruments based on these areas may be more politically feasible than focusing on sustainability in some jurisdictions. By analyzing the FEW as a nexus of interactions,

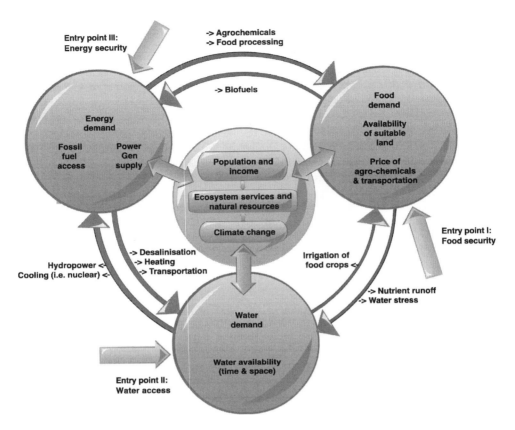

Figure 10.1 The food–energy–water nexus
Source: Smajgl et al. (2016, p. 535).

sustainability professionals can work to increase energy and water availability and flows between the systems, encourage the creation of integrated technology-infrastructure solutions, and reduce the impacts on natural capital and ecosystem services that underpin FEW systems. Integrated FEW analyses identify points in a FEW system where large amounts of water are needed to produce energy or food, or where energy with a high carbon intensity is used to produce food or water. These intervention points allow sustainability professionals to introduce strategies and instruments to encourage technology innovation and sustainable behavior. Acceleration Point: Sustainability professionals can use their **interpersonal relations competence** to help actors from the food, energy, and water sectors and industries understand the connections between their systems and collaborate to pursue sustainability pathways based on integrated FEW solutions that create sustainability value.

Buildings and infrastructure as living systems

Childers et al. (2015) compared two models of urban infrastructure development. The first follows a linear pathway from planners designing project needs, to engineers and designers creating and constructing the infrastructure, to scientists and researchers examining the performance of the infrastructure over time relative to the service delivered to society. The second model represents an integrated approach where infrastructure is co-produced and re-produced based on multiple learning and feedback loops. Actors including social and ecological scientists are part of the infrastructure development process, and the goal is to design infrastructure systems that deliver multiple services to help address sustainability and climate change. This approach is similar to adaptive co-management and the co-production of knowledge theories in Chapter 3, but with a specific focus on transforming urban infrastructure. Sustainability professionals are concerned with infrastructure solutions that hold promise for encouraging new building designs and new technologies.

Circular economy and vertical systems

The circular economy aims to close the loop of materials and energy flows through a system (e.g., an organization, a city, a country). It is based on the concepts of lifecycle analysis, cradle-to-cradle systems, and upcycling (McDonough and Braungart, 2013). The goal of the circular economy is to "keep valuable materials in circulation through a series of systemic feedback loops between lifecycle stages, powered through resource-efficient industrial processes" (Hobson, 2016, pp. 88–89). Ghisellini et al. (2016) highlighted the importance of mobilizing key actors and developing the capacity to foster effective collaboration between them in cases where circular economy transitions occurred. They found that success depended on demonstrating an economic return-on-investment to build support from additional actors wishing to invest in circular economy development. The circular economy can represent a business model and an economic development strategy rather than simply an industrial ecology system to reduce waste.

A circular economy approach aims to redesign products and production processes to add value to resources and to decouple economic benefits from resource consumption costs (UTS, 2015, in Ghisellini et al., 2016). The circular economy is similar to the steady state economy described by ecological economists because materials and energy throughput levels must be maintained at or below a sustainable scale prior to addressing the social justness of access to resources and opportunities and the efficient allocation of resources (Daly and Farley, 2011). While much of the focus of the circular economy has been at the organization or industrial park scales (Giurco et al., 2014), the concept can be applied to understand infrastructure change at the city or regional scales. Energy, waste, and water demands can be reduced as part of eco-city initiatives including regulations on polluting sectors, incentives to improve energy and water efficiency, and requiring companies to adopt and comply with ISO total quality management, energy management, and zero waste programs (Ghisellini et al., 2016). The FEW nexus also provides a useful framework for understanding the circular economy at the urban scale.

Hobson (2016) argued that creating a circular economy requires changes to design, production, and consumption, but also to *practices* of material and energy use and reuse. Social practices (Chapter 2) are shaped by history, norms, and preferences, which enable learning and adapting to new technologies. Hobson (2016) defined *prosumption* as a process where citizens (consumers) and organizations (producers) aim to co-create value through social practices. One example of prosumption is the do-it-yourself installation seminars offered by hardware stores, which train individuals how to install their own insulation or appliances. The goal is to engage citizens in the process to reduce their installation costs while increasing demand for the products sold by the store. The role of citizens within the circular economy and prosumption processes shifts from consumer to user and from owning to renting goods (e.g., ladders and power washers, car sharing, solar systems on roofs owned by other organizations with payments transferred through a blockchain system). *Product service systems* are frameworks for viewing the product lifecycle as a circular economy where producers and consumers are engaged in the process of "reworking the ways products and services are calibrated to meet human needs" (Hobson, 2016, p. 97). Business models centered on product service systems could increase the likelihood of reuse and repair instead of disposal as businesses can continue receiving revenues as long as they maintain the technologies/products over time. Acceleration Point: Sustainability professionals can help companies understand the triple-bottom-line benefits of practicing *extended producer responsibility* through product service systems. This will increase the chances that they will participate in such programs, and create sustainability value by reducing material and energy waste associated with high product disposal rates.

Smart, adaptive, and renewable building systems

Smart energy monitors have been used to track and display energy, cost, and environmental impacts to residential and commercial occupants. But how effective are these monitors at changing behavior, and more importantly, at reducing energy demand overall and during peak times? Hargreaves et al. (2013) found mixed results in a study of homeowners in the United Kingdom. While homeowners became more confident in understanding their energy use levels, that confidence did not consistently translate to a reduction in energy use. In fact, energy monitors may make it harder to change household energy use practices because homeowners become accustomed to their own personal limits for energy saving. Some homeowners may increase energy use due to the *rebound effect* (Greening et al., 2000), where energy savings from technology or behavioral conservation are spent on other energy consuming things like hot tubs or vacations via airplane travel. If presented with information about how their personal consumption compares to that of their neighbors, a *boomerang effect* (Chapter 2) may occur whereby residents discover that their energy use levels are lower than their neighbors and consequently use more energy (Schultz et al., 2008). The *comfort effect* is when homeowners do not want to reduce energy use even if presented with data on the energy monitor that showed high use times or potential savings because they are accustomed to a certain level of benefits from the energy services (Hargreaves et al., 2013). This could apply to air temperature, water temperature, shower duration, opening windows for fresh air, or excessively using ventilation fans in the kitchen or bathroom. Can smart buildings that automate energy and water systems (Balta-Ozkan et al., 2013) guide user decisions to help address the rebound, boomerang, and comfort effects? Acceleration Point: Combining technology and real-time messaging with financial incentives for technology upgrades and price increases in response to peak energy use could improve the effectiveness of these programs.

Innovation in building materials is critical to sustainability transitions. Many companies are creating adaptive and renewable building materials that can both sense occupant preferences and reduce environmental impacts. These include dynamic windows that can tint to balance heat gain throughout the day (Suntuitive, 2017), and animated metal surfaces that can shift automatically to manage light, solar energy, and airflow while providing privacy and aesthetic appeal for building occupants (Tessellate, 2017). Another product in development is a spray on SolarWindow coating, which could provide shorter payback periods than conventional solar PV when applied to a 50-story office building (SolarWindow, 2017). The advantage of this technology is that no new land is needed for its installation, as it would be applied to glass on existing buildings. If such a technology were adopted by several major cities, it would have low lifecycle costs while generating high sustainability value. A company called SolarGaps created window blinds that are also solar panels, which track the sun during the day and balance light and energy generation demands (SolarGaps, 2017). Another area that holds potential for sustainability is thin film materials. Researchers at the University of Minnesota, for example, have created a nano-scale thin film material that is expected to help produce more efficient solar panels and other electronics with business applications that can lead to sustainability benefits (Prakash et al., 2017).

While advanced materials are being developed by public and private sector innovators around the world, building to low energy and water standards is already possible with currently available and affordable technologies. The Residential Energy Efficiency Project in Ontario, Canada, retrofitted a century old home to Leadership in Energy and Environmental Design (LEED) Platinum standards to demonstrate sustainable technology and affordable living practices. The house uses 86 percent less energy, costs 85 percent less to power, and has reduced CO_2 emissions by 54 percent (REEP, 2017). The house is for public and school tours to show the water, energy efficiency, energy generation, insulation, lighting, appliances, green materials, and automation features that were installed using existing technologies available on the market. Certified energy advisors who have conducted more than 14,000 energy audits of homes in the region (Hoicka et al., 2014; Parker et al., 2003, 2005) run the tours, ensuring that the public learns from engineers and contractors with years of experience engaging homeowners with energy and sustainability practices. Harvard University is conducting a similar project called HouseZero to retrofit a century-old home into a sustainable, low energy, and zero carbon emissions home (Sisson, 2017). This is a particularly impressive project given that they are not only aiming for zero emissions from the energy system but also from the embodied energy in the materials used to construct the home (HouseZero, 2017). Sustainable niche experiments designed to improve the performance of buildings and infrastructure contribute cumulatively to sustainable cities.

Sustainable cities and communities

By some measures, all cities are unsustainable because of the scale of materials and energy throughput that is drawn from resource hinterlands and transported to the city to meet growing populations, lifestyle, and economic demands. But by other measures, cities are the definition of sustainability due to lower per capita resource use than sprawling subdivisions and rural areas. Efficiencies gained from density and public transportation systems, brownfield redevelopment, reurbanization, and other green new urbanism initiatives combined with a modern building stock allow more people to live at higher standards of living with fewer environmental impacts (Ramaswami et al., 2016). How can sustainability professionals help to further improve the sustainability of cities?

Hawkins et al. (2016) examined factors that influence local governments to address sustainability as measured by the level of human and financial resources allocated to sustainability commitments. They found that local priorities (e.g., a higher priority on social goals), participation in regional governance (e.g., regional collaborations like watershed management or economic development programs), and membership in climate protection networks (e.g., Local Governments for Sustainability and the Cities for Climate Protection programs of the International Council for Local Environmental Initiatives: ICLEI, 2017) were related to the amount of resources allocated to sustainability goals. Other factors including the level of interest group support or opposition (e.g., chamber of commerce, environmental groups) and the fiscal capacity of the local government provided mixed results. Environmental groups and chambers of commerce did not have a significant impact on resources allocated to sustainability, but neighborhood organizations (e.g., home owners associations that work to improve quality of life and property values) did have a moderate impact. Acceleration Point: Sustainability professionals can use their **interpersonal relations competence** to encourage the city to participate in regional governance and international networks to build commitment and instigate the allocation of additional resources to sustainability solutions.

Sustainability professionals are starting to envision and plan for post-carbon cities and communities (Chatterton, 2013). As part of this transition, sustainability professionals are placing a greater focus on engaging and empowering actors in the decision-making and political processes. Viewing sustainability as a process rather than as achieving a set of outcomes (Chatterton, 2013) is important to increase actor acceptance due to the social and economic benefits of greater employment and livelihood opportunities. Chatterton (2013) described a low-impact and affordable cohousing community in the United Kingdom designed for a "world where carbon is used more responsibly and equitably by our economies and societies" (p. 1655). This type of community aims to incorporate economic, social, and environmental aspects of sustainability. For example, straw and timber were used as key building materials to increase environmental performance (e.g., straw bale walls have high *R-values* and also act as a form of carbon storage because the plant materials are now locked into the walls and do not release their carbon back into the atmosphere), generate social benefits of participation and engagement (e.g., can be built largely by community members participating in the construction process), and create local economic development benefits in the form of indirect and induced jobs for the community (e.g., materials were purchased from local producers) (Chatterton, 2013). A company that makes individual straw and timber panels was used to create the panels, which were assembled near the site and then installed by workers and community members in a modern form of barn raising.

Measuring progress towards strong sustainability

Sustainability initiatives including strategies and instruments are being implemented all over the world in organizations, communities, cities, states/provinces, and countries. Numerous examples in this book have shown that sustainable value can be created in different sectors, industries, and systems. Sustainability professionals have to find new ways of measuring progress towards sustainability that takes into account the interactions and feedbacks between different socio-technical systems. The comprehensive indicator for measuring socio-technical system change towards a sustainability transition (Chapter 8) provides a way to learn and adjust strategies and instruments aimed at niche and regime changes at the micro scale of a single socio-technical system. Additional metrics are needed to measure progress towards strong sustainability at the meso (state/province or national/federal) and macro (global) scale including the interactions and feedbacks between multiple socio-technical systems.

Genuine Progress Indicator: a strong sustainability metric for the meso scale

Kubiszewski et al. (2015) calculated the Genuine Progress Indicator (GPI) for Oregon between 1960 and 2010 and compared it to the gross state product (GSP), which is defined as the total value of goods and services produced in Oregon per year. They found that the GPI began to diverge from the GSP in 2000 due among other things to increasing inequality and a reduction in the amount of farmland. The GPI includes economic (e.g., personal consumption expenditures) and social (e.g., income inequality) indicators. It then incorporates many factors that detract from the GPI, including costs of underemployment; changes to the built capital stock; costs of water, air, and noise pollution; net changes to wetlands, farmland, and forest cover; costs of climate change, ozone depletion, non-renewable resource depletion; and costs of commuting. It then adds value for housework, volunteer work, and higher education. The goal of the GPI is to reward things that provide economic, social, and environmental value to society while subtracting things that decrease economic, social, and environmental performance. A summary of the components of the GPI is outlined in Table 10.1.

Table 10.1 Summary of methodology used to calculate the Genuine Progress Indicator for Oregon

Indicator number and name	+/−	Brief description	Calculation method
1 Personal consumption expenditures (PCE)	+, base value	Component of GDP which represents money spent on goods and services for personal use and consumption	National ratio of consumption expenditure to income times Per capita income
2 Income inequality	+ or −	Measure of the difference between actual distribution and equal distribution by income quintiles, ranging from 0 (all households have same income) to 1 (one household has all income)	Gini coefficient in a given year divided by Gini coefficient at lowest value times 100
3 Adjusted personal consumption expenditures	+ or −	Consumption adjusted for income inequality becomes the base number from which all other indicators are then either added or subtracted	Indicator 1 (PCE) divided by Indicator 2 (income inequality)
4 Services of consumer durables	+	Adding in value of annual services provided by household appliances and equipment	Indicator 5 (cost of consumer durables) times depreciation rate
5 Cost of consumer durables	−	Actual expenditures on consumer durables are subtracted from GPI to avoid double counting the value of their services (Indicator 4)	National percentage of spending on consumer durables times per capita PCE (Indicator 1)

(continued)

Table 10.1 (continued)

Indicator number and name	+/−	Brief description	Calculation method
6 Costs of underemployment	−	Subtracting for the decrease in community welfare due to wages not provided to constrained or unemployed workers	Number of underemployed persons times hours not provided per constrained worker, times average hourly rate
7 Net capital investment	+ or −	Estimating the changes in stock of built capital available per worker	National figures scaled to Oregon's population
8 Cost of water pollution	−	Subtracting for the value of lost benefits of water quality due to impairment. Accounts for value of recreational fishing, boating, swimming, drinking water, as well as non–use benefits (ecology, esthetics, property value)	Percentage of river miles of impaired quality times benefits of unimpaired waters
9 Cost of air pollution	−	Subtracting for the damage cost estimates associated with air pollution to households, infrastructure, and the environment, excluding health or mortality costs	Pollution data times cost per unit of air pollution damage
10 Cost of noise pollution	−	Subtracting for estimated costs of noise pollution	Urbanization index values times World Health Organization estimate of noise pollution costs
11 Net wetlands change	−	Subtracting for loss of purified water, wildlife habitat, and other ecosystem services provided by wetlands	Total ha wetland lost times estimated wetland value per ha
12 Net farmland change	−	Subtracting for losses in sustainable local food supply, esthetic, scenic, and historic values, decreases in water quality and flood control as well as degraded wildlife habitat associated with net loss of farmland	Farmland ha lost to urbanization times estimated farmland value per ha
13 Net forest cover change	−	Subtracting for loss of forests and associated goods and services provided by them including: flood control, air and water purification, biodiversity, habitat, medicinal products, as well as esthetic and recreational value	Forest ecosystem service value per ha times area of ha of forest cover lost

14 Cost of climate change	−	Subtracting for costs associated with long-term environmental degradation as a result of climate disruption	Marginal social cost of CO_2 emissions in a given year times energy consumption
15 Cost of ozone depletion	−	Subtracting for costs associated with loss of ozone including both health and economic costs of this long-term environmental problem	Measure of ozone depleting chemicals released times cost per kg
16 Cost of non-renewable resource depletion	−	Subtracting for costs associated with depletion of non-renewable resources by estimating renewable energy replacement costs	Consumption level of non-renewable resources times renewable resource replacement cost
17 Value of housework	+	Adding in the positive value contribution of household labor including meal preparation, cleaning, repairs, and parenting, all of which are not included in calculation of GSP and GDP	Net opportunity cost method = total hours of housework performed times wage paid to hire outside help to perform equivalent tasks
18 Family changes	−	Subtracting for the negative economic costs on society associated with divorce and excessive amounts of time spent watching television	Cost of divorce added to cost of excessive television viewing
19 Cost of crime	−	Subtracting for the direct costs from crime such as medical expenses and lost property, as well as the indirect costs of preventing or avoiding crime	Defensive expenditures to avoid crime + direct costs of property crimes
20 Personal pollution abatement	−	Subtracting for expenditures made to compensate for pollution-related externalities imposed by economic activity, such as spending on air filter equipment, waste treatment, and other compensatory costs	Cost of solid waste disposal added to cost of sewage and septic systems added to cost of automotive air filters and catalytic converters
21 Value of volunteer work	+	Adding in the positive value provided by volunteer work	Total hours of volunteer work performed times average hourly wage rate
22 Value of leisure time	−	Subtracting for loss of leisure time corresponding with increased economic output	Employment level times lost leisure hours times average hourly rate

(continued)

Table 10.1 (continued)

Indicator number and name	+/−	Brief description	Calculation method
23 Value of a higher education	+	Adding in the positive value contribution of higher education to society in the form of increased productivity, civic participation, charitable giving, savings rates, health, etc.	Number of people at least 25 years old with four years minimum of college completed times estimated value contribution of $16,000 per year
24 Services of highways and streets	+	Adding in the positive value contribution of government-provided services associated with functioning highway and street infrastructure	Net stock of highways and streets times 7.5% annual value
25 Cost of commuting	−	Subtracting for direct costs associated with spending on personal vehicle or public transit, plus the indirect costs of potentially productive time lost during transit	Cost of vehicle times percent vehicle use for commuting plus cost of public transit plus cost of commuting time using local wage rate
26 Cost of motor vehicle crashes	−	Subtracting for direct costs of motor vehicle crashes on property damage and healthcare expenditures, as well as indirect costs in the form of lost wages	Number of accidents times cost per accident

Source: Kubiszewski et al. (2015, p. 3).

The GPI is considered a metric of strong sustainability, which if universally adopted, would influence different types of strategies and instruments. The challenge for sustainability professionals is to convince decision-makers to adopt the GPI as a standard or legally binding metric. What states/provinces/cities would you want to partner with in your country to build support for the GPI? How would you convince businesses to support the GPI? What strategies and instruments could help support a transition from GSP/GDP to GPI as a standard measure of progress? Maryland and Vermont have officially adopted GPI in practice, and Maryland has tracked changes in GPI relative to GSP (Maryland, 2017). How will this affect the development pathways in these states? See Daly and Mcelwee (2014) for a discussion of the experiences and outcomes of using GPI thus far. Evidence suggests that both states have successfully reduced CO_2 emissions while experiencing continued economic development and population growth. Table 10.2 shows the *KAYA Identity* for Maryland and Vermont. Both states reduced CO_2 emissions per year between 1997 and 2014. Substantial annual reduction rates were achieved between 2005 and 2014 for Maryland averaging 3 percent per year from 2007–2011. Significant improvements in both energy and carbon intensity were achieved for Maryland. Vermont had similar improvements in energy intensity but did not achieve as large of carbon intensity improvements. Using the GPI to guide triple-bottom-line economic development strategies can therefore potentially yield positive results.

Table 10.2 KAYA Identity for Maryland and Vermont, U.S.: average annual percent change

Maryland	1997–1999	1999–2001	2001–2003	2003–2005	2005–2007	2007–2009	2009–2011	2011–2014	1997–2014
CO_2 emissions	2.5	0.1	1.2	1.2	-2.4	-3.0	-2.9	-1.5	-0.9
Population	0.6	0.8	0.8	0.6	0.4	0.5	0.7	0.7	0.9
GDP/capita	2.0	1.7	1.2	2.4	0.4	-0.1	1.1	-0.1	1.7
Energy intensity (energy/GDP)	-1.5	-1.7	1.1	-2.6	-2.3	-1.5	-2.7	-0.8	-1.8
Carbon intensity (carbon/energy)	1.5	-0.6	-1.8	1.0	-0.9	-2.0	-1.9	-1.2	-1.0

Vermont	1997–1999	1999–2001	2001–2003	2003–2005	2005–2007	2007–2009	2009–2011	2011–2014	1997–2014
CO_2 emissions	0.0	0.5	0.0	1.0	-1.5	-1.5	-2.2	0.6	-0.5
Population	0.4	0.4	0.3	0.2	0.1	0.1	0.1	0.0	0.3
GDP/capita	2.4	2.4	2.0	1.4	-0.1	-0.5	1.8	-0.1	1.9
Energy intensity (energy/GDP)	-4.8	0.4	-1.5	0.3	-1.0	0.8	-3.2	-2.3	-1.8
Carbon intensity (carbon/energy)	2.5	-2.5	-0.7	-0.8	-0.5	-1.9	-0.8	3.1	-0.4

Source: EIA (2017a, 2017d). Calculations by authors.

Sustainable development progress indicators: strong sustainability metrics for the macro scale

Griggs et al. (2013) reframed the Brundtland Commission definition of sustainable development to add additional importance to natural capital and ecosystem functions and services as the foundation for the socio-economic system: "development that meets the needs of the present while safeguarding Earth's life-support system, on which the welfare of current and future generations depends" (p. 306). Six specific sustainable development goals are outlined by Griggs et al. (2013): thriving lives and livelihoods, sustainable food security, sustainable water security, universal clean energy, healthy and productive ecosystems, and governance for sustainable societies. These goals are similar to the sustainability principles in Chapter 1, with the exception of specifically framing food and water systems as security, and placing a special emphasis on maintaining ecosystem functions and services rather than using resources more efficiently. But is progress being made to global sustainable development goals?

The United Nations Sustainable Development Goals include no poverty, zero hunger, good health and well-being, quality education, gender equality, clean water and sanitation, affordable and clean energy, decent work and economic growth, industry, innovation and infrastructure investments, reduced inequalities, sustainable cities and communities, responsible consumption and production, climate action, peace, justice and strong institutions, and partnerships for the goals. The UN Progress Report (2017) suggests that while improvement has been made on many of the sustainable development goals including extreme poverty reduction and a reduction in the number of undernourished people, indicators suggest that the benefits have been uneven and in many cases too slow. An acceleration is needed to address the hundreds of millions who are still living below the poverty line, without access to clean water, in cities with extreme air pollution, in rural areas without access to the benefits of electricity systems, and who are starting to feel the impacts of climate change.

Achieving the goal of universal clean energy would of course make the other goals easier in the long term, but in the short term it could pose challenges in many parts of the world for thriving lives and livelihoods. A question that has been debated since the Brundtland Commission report in 1987: is sustainable development a human right, a normative goal set by elites to guide the direction of resource decisions, or an economic strategy to promote (or allow) more growth? Food, energy, and water security can be achieved at local levels in regions, communities, and places independent of whether global goals of healthy and productive ecosystems and governance for sustainable societies are met. The one common denominator that connects the local and global goals is thriving lives and livelihoods. Having the opportunity to earn a living wage that allows for improving quality of life is a pragmatic and impactful goal of sustainability. It also includes access to education and information, better health and housing, and reduced inequality.

One positive sign is found by examining the scope of sustainability instruments and how they changed in different countries (Sommerer and Lim, 2016). While Western countries had a wider policy scope, averaging 21.5 policies per country, compared to non-Western countries averaging 18 policies per country in 2005, the gap between these groups of countries has narrowed. When disaggregated into individual policies, the differences between Western and non-Western nations in some cases disappear completely. For example, in the case of regulating lead in gasoline, vehicle emissions, power plant emissions, industrial discharges, soil protection, construction waste, refrigerator energy use, endangered species, and environmental impact assessments, non-Western countries were as likely to adopt these policies. Non-Western countries were as likely to adopt a sustainability plan as were Western countries in 2010. Non-Western countries were more likely to have policies to regulate water efficiency in households. Western countries were more likely to have sulphur regulations for gasoline, regulations for detergents, regulations for cleaning up contaminated sites, feed-in tariffs and carbon taxes, and regulations to prohibit DDT in pesticides. Overall, non-Western countries have rapidly closed the gap in the scope of environmental regulations and, in some cases, have become leaders relative to Western countries.

Challenges including huge disparities in sustainability outcomes between regions remain. For example, if half of the world achieves food, energy, and water security by 2050, while hundreds of millions still do not have the opportunity for thriving lives and livelihoods, can we really say by any objective measure that sustainability has been achieved? How can sustainability professionals help close these gaps? Should sustainability professionals focus on strategies and instruments to encourage convergence by raising the poor or by encouraging innovation and economic development among the rich and hoping for a trickledown effect?

Check on learning

- Read Rocholl and Bolton (2016) and attempt to answer these questions in the context of the Berlin case study. How are the local–national dynamics playing out? Who are the key actors involved, and how do they differ in their goals for the energy system? Thinking of your own city/town, who would be the key actors in a multi-level energy transition? What type of ownership of the electricity system occurs in your city/town? How does ownership and power accelerate or inhibit attempts to transform the regime towards the sustainability principles outlined in Chapter 1?

- Read Harris-Lovett et al. (2015). Thinking of your town or city, create a plan for increasing public acceptance of water reuse that includes at least one strategy or component from each dimension of legitimacy outlined on page 7554. As a sustainability professional, how would you coordinate each of these strategies in order to deliver a water reuse program at the lowest possible cost?

- How does the Eizenberg and Jabareen (2017) framework differ from the frameworks of sustainability in Figure 1.1 and the Gibson sustainability principles in Chapter 1?

- How does the circular economy differ from ecological modernization theory? Does the circular economy fit with weak or strong sustainability? How can social and cultural factors guide development of the circular economy? And finally, how do *sufficiency* goals based on meeting normative criteria for sustainability relate to the *efficiency* goals of the circular economy?

- When reading Hobson (2016), what is the Fairphone and how is it an example of prosumption? Can you think of another example of a technology and practice that could be considered a prosumption?

- How does the concept of *extended producer responsibility* through product service systems relate to *environmental stewardship*? Find a website or online document from an organization that practices *extended producer responsibility*. What type of products are involved? How does the organization generate revenues using extended producer responsibility?

- The smart grid holds promise for managing peak energy demand and improving the sustainability performance of electricity supply and demand. Review the Mah et al. (2012a, 2012b) studies on the smart grids in South Korea and Hong Kong. What are the key lessons learned from these studies that could help sustainability professionals better design a smart grid to increase producer and consumer acceptance? Who were the key actors in each case and how were barriers overcome? What are some of the economic, social, technical, and policy factors that limited smart grid development? Identify some of the regime and niche level factors in the South Korea and Hong Kong cases that differ from your city or country.

- Do some research into blockchains and rooftop solar systems. How would you describe a blockchain system to your friends? Identify three technology innovations that were necessary for blockchain solar markets to be possible? How could you as a sustainability professional design a community-based social marketing program to explain blockchain-solar markets and encourage homeowners and commercial property owners to install solar or buy solar from their neighbors?

- Read the articles on desalination citied in this chapter. Identify the type of desalination technology that you believe will fit best with the sustainability principles outlined in Chapter 1 as part of a strong sustainability pathway. What technologies would you include within an integrated energy-water system for a coastal country that has an increasing population and constrained water sources? As a sustainability professional, how would you optimize the use of desalination as part of a food–energy–water nexus? Think about the ways that food systems, energy systems, and water systems overlap and integrate. What actors manage these systems? At what societal and governance levels are decisions made about food, energy, and water, and how would you influence changes at those levels based on understanding of the interrelationship between these systems? How would your answers differ for developing countries in North Africa or the Middle East?

- When comparing GPI and GDP growth rates, many countries see the GDP/capita increase while the GPI/capita flattens or even declines – what explains these differences? Read Kuramochi et al. (2017) and make an argument as to which short-term sectoral benchmarks, if achieved, would contribute most to the GPI in your country.

Assignments

- Writing a national water policy that includes a water quality trading mechanism and a provision for food-energy-water system innovation
- Developing alternative global scenarios to achieve sustainability by 2050, 2100, and 2200

References

ABC. (2017). London buses to be powered by waste coffee grounds. ABC news. Available at: www.abc.net.au/news/2017-11-21/london-buses-to-be-powered-by-waste-coffee-grounds/9174660

Balta-Ozkan, N., Davidson, R., Bicket, M., & Whitmarsh, L. (2013). Social barriers to the adoption of smart homes. *Energy Policy*, 63, 363–374.

Barnosky, A. D., Brown, J. H., Daily, G. C., Dirzo, R., Ehrlich, A. H., Ehrlich, P. R., . . . & Wake, M. H. (2014). Introducing the scientific consensus on maintaining humanity's life support systems in the 21st century: Information for policy makers. *The Anthropocene Review*, 1(1), 78–109.

Bolton, R., & Foxon, T. J. (2015). Infrastructure transformation as a socio-technical process: Implications for the governance of energy distribution networks in the UK. *Technological Forecasting and Social Change*, 90, 538–550.

Brandt, A. R. (2017). How does energy resource depletion affect prosperity? Mathematics of a minimum energy return on investment (EROI). *BioPhysical Economics and Resource Quality*, 2(1), 2.

Busch, J., Dawson, D., & Roelich, K. (2017). Closing the low-carbon material loop using a dynamic whole system approach. *Journal of Cleaner Production*, 149, 751–761.

CBSM. (2017). Fostering sustainable behavior: community base social marketing. Created by McKenzie-Mohr, D. Available at: www.cbsm.com/pages/guide/preface/

Chatterton, P. (2013). Towards an agenda for post-carbon cities: Lessons from Lilac, the UK's first ecological, affordable cohousing community. *International Journal of Urban and Regional Research*, 37(5), 1654–1674.

Childers, D. L., Cadenasso, M. L., Grove, J. M., Marshall, V., McGrath, B., & Pickett, S. T. (2015). An ecology for cities: A transformational nexus of design and ecology to advance climate change resilience and urban sustainability. *Sustainability*, 7(4), 3774–3791.

Climeworks. (2017). CO_2 fertilization in greenhouses. Available at: www.climeworks.com/greenhouse.html

Daly, H. E., & Farley, J. (2011). *Ecological Economics: Principles and Applications*. 2nd Edition. Island Press, Washington DC.

Daly, L., & Mcelwee, S. (2014). Forget the GDP. Some states have found a better way to measure our progress. *New Republic*. Available at: https://newrepublic.com/article/116461/gpi-better-gdp-measuring-united-states-progress.

Deaton, J. (2017). In Brooklyn, you can now sell solar power to your neighbors. *Grist*. Available at: http://grist.org/article/in-brooklyn-you-can-now-sell-solar-power-to-your-neighbors/

Diss, K. (2017). Blockchain technology fuels peer-to-peer solar energy trading in Perth start-up. Available at: www.abc.net.au/news/2017-10-11/blockchain-technology-fuels-peer-to-peer-energy-trading-start-up/9035616

EIA. (2017a). CO_2 emissions data. U.S. *Energy Information Administration*. Available at: www.eia.gov/environment/emissions/state/

EIA. (2017b). Population, energy demand, and GDP data. State Energy Data System. U.S. *Energy Information Administration*. Available at: www.eia.gov/state/seds/seds-data-complete.php?sid=US

Eizenberg, E., & Jabareen, Y. (2017). Social sustainability: A new conceptual framework. *Sustainability*, 9(1), 68.

Feng, J., Feng, L., Wang, J., & King, C. W. (2018). Modeling the point of use EROI and its implications for economic growth in China. *Energy*, 144, 232–242.

Ghaffour, N., Bundschuh, J., Mahmoudi, H., & Goosen, M. F. (2015). Renewable energy-driven desalination technologies: A comprehensive review on challenges and potential applications of integrated systems. *Desalination*, 356, 94–114.

Ghisellini, P., Cialani, C., & Ulgiati, S. (2016). A review on circular economy: The expected transition to a balanced interplay of environmental and economic systems. *Journal of Cleaner Production*, 114, 11–32.

Giurco, D., Prior, J., & Boydell, S. (2014). Industrial ecology and carbon property rights. *Journal of Cleaner Production*, 80, 211–223.

Greening, L. A., Greene, D. L., & Difiglio, C. (2000). Energy efficiency and consumption – the rebound effect – a survey. *Energy Policy*, 28(6), 389–401.

Griggs, D., Stafford-Smith, M., Gaffney, O., Rockström, J., Öhman, M. C., Shyamsundar, P., . . . & Noble, I. (2013). Policy: Sustainable development goals for people and planet. *Nature*, 495(7441), 305–307.

Hargreaves, T., Nye, M., & Burgess, J. (2013). Keeping energy visible? Exploring how householders interact with feedback from smart energy monitors in the longer term. *Energy Policy*, 52, 126–134.

Harris-Lovett, S. R., Binz, C., Sedlak, D. L., Kiparsky, M., & Truffer, B. (2015). Beyond user acceptance: A legitimacy framework for potable water reuse in California. *Environmental Science & Technology*, 49(13), 7552–7561.

Hawkins, C. V., Krause, R. M., Feiock, R. C., & Curley, C. (2016). Making meaningful commitments: Accounting for variation in cities' investments of staff and fiscal resources to sustainability. *Urban Studies*, 53(9), 1902–1924.

Herron, J. A., Vann, T., Duong, N., Resasco, D. E., Crossley, S., Lobban, L. L., & Maravelias, C. T. (2017). A systems-level roadmap for biomass thermal fractionation and catalytic upgrading strategies. *Energy Technology*, 5(1), 130–150.

Hess, D. J. (2013). Industrial fields and countervailing power: The transformation of distributed solar energy in the United States. *Global Environmental Change*, 23(5), 847–855.

Hobson, K. (2016). Closing the loop or squaring the circle? Locating generative spaces for the circular economy. *Progress in Human Geography*, 40(1), 88–104.

Hoicka, C. E., Parker, P., & Andrey, J. (2014). Residential energy efficiency retrofits: How program design affects participation and outcomes. *Energy Policy*, 65, 594–607.

HouseZero. (2017). Future home: HouseZero. Harvard Center for Green Buildings and Cities. Available at: http://harvardcgbc.org/research/housezero/

ICLEI. (2017). Local Governments for Sustainability USA. Available at: http://icleiusa.org/

International Desalination Association. (2017). Desalination by the numbers. Available at: http://idadesal.org/desalination-101/desalination-by-the-numbers/

Kubiszewski, I., Costanza, R., Gorko, N. E., Weisdorf, M. A., Carnes, A. W., Collins, C. E., . . . & Schoepfer, J. D. (2015). Estimates of the Genuine Progress Indicator (GPI) for Oregon from 1960–2010 and recommendations for a comprehensive shareholder's report. *Ecological Economics*, 119, 1–7.

Kuramochi, T., Höhne, N., Schaeffer, M., Cantzler, J., Hare, B., Deng, Y., . . . & Mir, G. U. R. (2017). Ten key short-term sectoral benchmarks to limit warming to 1.5° C. *Climate Policy*, 18(3), 287–305.

Lau, J., Dey, G., & Licht, S. (2016). Thermodynamic assessment of CO_2 to carbon nanofiber transformation for carbon sequestration in a combined cycle gas or a coal power plant. *Energy Conversion and Management*, 122, 400–410.

Licht, S., Wang, B., Ghosh, S., Ayub, H., Jiang, D., & Ganley, J. (2010). A new solar carbon capture process: Solar thermal electrochemical photo (STEP) carbon capture. *The Journal of Physical Chemistry Letters*, 1(15), 2363–2368.

LO3 Energy. (2017). Brooklyn microgrid. Available at: http://lo3energy.com/projects/

Mah, D. N. Y., van der Vleuten, J. M., Hills, P., & Tao, J. (2012a). Consumer perceptions of smart grid development: Results of a Hong Kong survey and policy implications. *Energy Policy*, 49, 204–216.

Mah, D. N. Y., van der Vleuten, J. M., Ip, J. C. M., & Hills, P. R. (2012b). Governing the transition of socio-technical systems: A case study of the development of smart grids in Korea. *Energy Policy*, 45, 133–141.

Martin, G., Clift, R., & Christie, I. (2016). Urban cultivation and its contributions to sustainability: Nibbles of food but oodles of social capital. *Sustainability*, 8(5), 409.

Maryland. (2017). Maryland Genuine Progress indicator. Department of Natural Resources. Available at: http://dnr.maryland.gov/mdgpi/Pages/default.aspx

McDonough, W. (2016). Carbon is not the enemy. *Nature*, 539, 349–351.

McDonough, W., & Braungart, M. (2013). *The Upcycle: Beyond Sustainability – Designing for Abundance*. North Point Press, New York, NY.

Moreau, V., Sahakian, M., Griethuysen, P., & Vuille, F. (2017). Coming full circle: Why social and institutional dimensions matter for the circular economy. *Journal of Industrial Ecology*, 21(3), 497–506.

Murphy, D. J., & Hall, C. A. (2010). Year in review: EROI or energy return on (energy) invested. *Annals of the New York Academy of Sciences*, 1185(1), 102–118.

Nguyen, T. (2017). Going negative: This factory will be the first to suck up carbon dioxide and feed it to vegetables. Vice News. Available at: https://news.vice.com/story/this-factory-will-suck-carbon-out-of-the-air-and-feed-it-to-plants

Nichols, B. G., & Kockelman, K. M. (2014). Life-cycle energy implications of different residential settings: Recognizing buildings, travel, and public infrastructure. *Energy Policy*, 68, 232–242.

Onat, N. C., Kucukvar, M., Halog, A., & Cloutier, S. (2017). Systems thinking for Life Cycle Sustainability Assessment: A review of recent developments, applications, and future perspectives. *Sustainability*, 9(5), 706.

Parker, P., Rowlands, I. H., & Scott, D. (2003). Innovations to reduce residential energy use and carbon emissions: An integrated approach. *The Canadian Geographer/Le Géographe Canadien*, 47(2), 169–184.

Parker, P., Rowlands, I. H., & Scott, D. (2005). Who changes consumption following residential energy evaluations? Local programs need all income groups to achieve Kyoto targets. *Local Environment*, 10(2), 173–187.

Prakash, A., Xu, P., Faghaninia, A., Shukla, S., Ager, J.W., Lo, C.S., & Jalan, B. (2017). Wide bandgap $BaSnO_3$ films with room temperature conductivity exceeding 10^4 S cm^{-1}. *Nature Communications*, 8, 15167.

Ramaswami, A., Russell, A. G., Culligan, P. J., Sharma, K. R., & Kumar, E. (2016). Meta-principles for developing smart, sustainable, and healthy cities. *Science*, 352(6288), 940–943.

Raugei, M., Fullana-i-Palmer, P., & Fthenakis, V. (2012). The energy return on energy investment (EROI) of photovoltaics: Methodology and comparisons with fossil fuel life cycles. *Energy Policy*, 45, 576–582.

REEP. (2017). REEP house for sustainable living. The Residential Energy Efficiency Project and REEP Green Solutions. Available at: https://reepgreen.ca/what_we_offer/community-action/reep-house/

Ren, J., Li, F. F., Lau, J., González-Urbina, L., & Licht, S. (2015). One-pot synthesis of carbon nanofibers from CO_2. *Nano letters*, 15(9), 6142–6148.

Rocholl, N., & Bolton, R. (2016). Berlin's electricity distribution grid: An urban energy transition in a national regulatory context. *Technology Analysis & Strategic Management*, 28(10), 1182–1194.

Schultz, W. P., Khazian, A. M., & Zaleski, A. C. (2008). Using normative social influence to promote conservation among hotel guests. *Social Influence*, 3(1), 4–23.

Schmack, M., Ho, G., & Anda, M. (2015). The bubble-greenhouse: A holistic sustainable approach to small-scale water desalination in remote regions. *Desalination*, 365, 250–260.

Schmidt-Bleek, F. (2008). Factor 10: The future of stuff. *Sustainability: Science, Practice & Policy*, 4(1), 1–4.

Sgouridis, S., Abdullah, A., Griffiths, S., Saygin, D., Wagner, N., Gielen, D., . . . & McQueen, D. (2016). RE-mapping the UAE's energy transition: An economy-wide assessment of renewable energy options and their policy implications. *Renewable and Sustainable Energy Reviews*, 55, 1166–1180.

Shammin, M. R., Herendeen, R. A., Hanson, M. J., & Wilson, E. J. (2010). A multivariate analysis of the energy intensity of sprawl versus compact living in the US for 2003. *Ecological Economics*, 69(12), 2363–2373.

Sisson, P. (2017). Harvard's building a model for energy efficiency by renovating a decades-old home. The HouseZero project will turn a wooden home from the '20s into a model for efficient, affordable green design. Green Design. Curbed. Available at: www.curbed.com/2017/5/25/15690208/harvard-renovation-green-building-sustainable-housezeroharvard-r

Smajgl, A., Ward, J., & Pluschke, L. (2016). The water–food–energy Nexus: Realising a new paradigm. *Journal of Hydrology*, 533, 533–540.

SolarGaps. (2017). SolarGaps: World's first solar smart blinds. Available at: https://solargaps.com/

SolarWindow. (2017). SolarWindow Technologies Inc. Available at: https://solarwindow.com/technology/

Sommerer, T., & Lim, S. (2016). The environmental state as a model for the world? An analysis of policy repertoires in 37 countries. *Environmental Politics*, 25(1), 92–115.

Suurs, R. A., & Hekkert, M. P. (2009). Cumulative causation in the formation of a technological innovation system: The case of biofuels in the Netherlands. *Technological Forecasting and Social Change*, 76(8), 1003–1020.

Suntuitive. (2017). Self-tinting glass. Suntuitive dynamic glass. Available at: www.suntuitive.com/

Tessellate. (2017). Tessellate animated metal surfaces. Available at: http://stage.azahner.com/tessellate.cfm

Torcellini, P., Pless, S., & Leach, M. (2015). A pathway for net-zero energy buildings: Creating a case for zero cost increase. *Building Research & Information*, 43(1), 25–33.

UN Progress Report. (2017). The Sustainable Development Goals Report. Available at: https://unstats.un.org/sdgs/report/2017

UTS. (2015). What will a circular economy look like in Australia. Available at: www.uts.edu.au/research-and-teaching/our-research/institute-sustainable-futures/news/what-will-circular-economy

von Weizsäcker, E. U., Lovins, A. B., & Lovins, L. H. (1998). *Factor Four: Doubling Wealth-Halving Resource Use: The New Report to the Club of Rome*. Earthscan, London, UK.

11 Conclusion

Learning objectives

- Summarize how strategies and instruments can help improve the Gibson sustainability principles
- Discuss how intermediaries can align sustainable niche experiments with institutional and infrastructure changes during a window of opportunity when regime subsystems converge
- Describe how sustainability competencies can help sustainability professionals pursue pathways to strong sustainability
- Identify the skills, training, characteristics, and career options of sustainability professionals

Pathways to strong sustainability via socio-technical system change

This book provides a roadmap to help sustainability professionals initiate or support socio-technical system changes by creating solutions that are proactive, pragmatic, and appealing to a broad set of actors. To contribute to strong sustainability pathways, solutions must generate *sustainability value*, which implies that economic, social, *and* environmental value should be increased or maintained relative to a business-as-usual scenario. The level of sustainability value can be assessed based on anticipated improvements to the Gibson principles of sustainability that result from interventions (strategies and instruments). *Strategies and instruments* contribute to sustainability value creation by, for example, increasing the number of better paying green jobs (livelihood sufficiency and opportunity), improving health and education system outcomes (intra-generational equity), reducing greenhouse gas (GHG) emissions per capita by switching to renewable energy sources (inter-generational equity), implementing protections for ecosystem services as part of conservation corridors (socio-ecological system integrity), enhancing water supply systems with automated technologies (resource maintenance and efficiency), encouraging sustainability-minded young adults to vote and run for office with community-based social marketing programs (civility and democratic governance), incorporating adaptive co-management, knowledge co-production, and polycentric frameworks as transition arenas (precaution and adaption), and normalizing the Genuine Progress Indicator and other sustainability-focused metrics for measuring progress in society (immediate and long-term integration). The challenge for sustainability professionals is to design, support, and implement strategies and instruments that create value based on all of the principles simultaneously to support a transition.

The solutions-oriented sustainability transition framework (Chapter 1) was used to identify and understand important interconnections between the individual and organizational levels, and the policy making and governance levels, which drive sustainability transitions in a socio-technical system. These interconnections occur from the niche to the regime level and from the regime to the niche level, and can be facilitated by sustainability professionals including environmental champions, community activists, non-profit organizations, green technology entrepreneurs, triple-bottom-line economic development agents, intermediary organizations, and policy entrepreneurs. Each chapter contained numerous strategies and instruments that can be used by sustainability professionals, in combination with other important niche and regime actors, to encourage sustainability transitions to technology, infrastructure, and institutions. The strategies and instruments included education and engagement campaigns, sustainable behavior change programs, organizational strategic sustainability initiatives, green innovation partnerships, green city planning, appliance and building labelling and certification systems, infrastructure investment, circular economy and industrial ecology systems, feed-in tariffs and other innovation-focused energy policies, environmental movements, and triple-bottom-line economic development strategies. The ultimate goal of sustainability professionals is to unlock the regime and allow technology, infrastructure, and institutions to change along a strong sustainable pathway that leads to an environmental state (Figure 1.10). An environmental state would signify that the subsystems of the regime have been disrupted, modified, realigned, and restructured based on sustainability principles.

When initiating a transition along a pathway to strong sustainability (Figure 1.10), the first step is to develop *sustainability competencies* within individuals associated with the transition. These competencies can help sustainability professionals work with stakeholders to link short-, medium-, and long-term goals to the sustainability principles (Chapter 1) with the help of an ends–means diagram (Chapter 8). In order to achieve these goals, changes to behavior and practices of individuals and communities are fostered by community-based social marketing and other engagement techniques (Chapter 2). This will help to increase demand for greener products and services (Chapter 3) that are created by green entrepreneurs and supported by champions as part of niche creation and protection processes (Chapter 7). Organizations can implement sustainability strategies as a means of gaining green competitive advantages through the development and marketing of greener products (Chapter 3). Sustainability-oriented innovation intermediaries (Chapter 6) aid entrepreneurs and champions within green businesses, government agencies, and non-profits in guiding the development of new technology innovation in combination with infrastructure investments (Chapter 4). Sustainability professionals within intermediary organizations work with policy entrepreneurs (Chapter 6) to influence changes to the regime subsystems that will allow niche experiments to scale-up and expand throughout the socio-technical system. A set of integrated metrics (Chapter 8) can inform sustainability professionals of important and ongoing adjustments needed to accelerate and amplify niche and regime changes, as well as the strategies and instruments necessary for overcoming bottlenecks and supporting seedbeds (Chapter 9). Triple-bottom-line economic development strategies (Chapter 5) can create jobs, which encourages a broader base of support from the political subsystem of the regime. This broad support will make it more likely that elements of an environmental state (Chapter 9) can take shape and persist over time. Acceleration Point: Sustainability professionals can monitor and evaluate the outcomes of these changes against the sustainability principles and adjust strategies accordingly as technology, infrastructure, and institutions change.

Sustainability professionals can use **normative** and **strategic competence** to design a set of integrated metrics that link each level of the solutions-oriented sustainability transitions framework (Figure 1.9). For example, metrics can be used as checkpoints to guide a sustainability transition by measuring interactions between sustainable behavior and organizational green strategies, between green innovation and triple-bottom-line economic development, and finally between sustainability-oriented intermediaries and institutional and policy change at the regime level. One metric could be the number of green jobs created per number of green technology innovations. This would tell sustainability professionals something about the scale of green job creation relative to green technology development. Another metric could be the number of green technology patents or innovations created per number of organizations implementing sustainability strategies. This would allow sustainability professionals to measure the impact of strategies on the creation of technologies. Strategies can then be adjusted over time in response to data collection and analysis. The number of green organizational strategies per number of community-based education and engagement programs could be an effective metric for tracking change from sustainable behavior to the organization level. The number or mix of sustainability policies per sustainability-oriented intermediary organization could help track change from intermediaries to the regime subsystems, which are displayed on Figure 11.1. Acceleration Point: Sustainability professionals can develop integrated metrics that measure interactions between the levels in the solutions-oriented sustainability transitions framework as a means of understanding how efficient and effective niche actors, regime actors, and intermediary organizations are at accelerating changes within the socio-technical system.

Integrating a panarchy with the MLP sustainability transitions framework

Modifying and realigning the subsystems of the regime requires a diversity of sustainable niche experiments that focus on improving technologies that have the potential to contribute to climate change mitigation and strong sustainability pathways. Sustainable niche experiments are part of socio-technical systems that link the strategies of entrepreneurs (technology creators) and the functions of manufacturers (technology producers) to changes in the practices of actors within infrastructure systems (technology adopters) and the preferences of actors within institutions (technology enablers). Different types of technologies co-evolve and have the potential to influence and/or compliment changes to institutions and infrastructure. In particular, six key interrelated technology areas were outlined throughout the book that are part of an energy socio-technical system: renewable energy, energy efficiency, energy storage, CO_2 removal and product creation, green buildings, and sustainable transportation and mobility systems. These technology innovation processes at the niche level are co-evolving with institutions and infrastructures at the regime level while constantly progressing through different phases that are represented as *complex adaptive cycles* (Figure 11.1).

Sustainability professionals can use **systems thinking** and **anticipatory competence** to understand the timing of these phases. Knowing the timing is important for aligning technology, infrastructure, and institutional changes during key windows of opportunity when the regime subsystems are converging. Sustainability professionals can use **strategic competence** to design and implement strategies and instruments during these windows of opportunity. Policy entrepreneurs as sustainability professionals can implement policy mixes including financial support instruments and research and development (R&D) strategies that encourage incremental innovations to institutions and infrastructure during their exploitation (**r**) and conservation (**K**) phases (Figure 11.1). This type of policy mix also supports a pragmatic triple-bottom-line economic development strategy. The resulting incremental innovations further encourage niche experiments via the *regime-to-niche* remember interactions.

Alternatively, policy entrepreneurs as sustainability professionals can implement policy mixes that include a feed-in tariff or a carbon tax with a revenue redistribution function to accelerate radical changes to institutions and infrastructure by igniting *niche-to-regime* revolt interactions during the release (Ω) and reorganization (α) phases of the technology complex adaptive cycles (Figure 11.1). Sustainability-oriented innovation intermediaries can amplify these radical changes by connecting technology entrepreneurs who are creating complimentary sustainable niche experiments within incubator and accelerator centers in different clusters. Green champions and grassroots entrepreneurs can also support these radical changes with the help of their **interpersonal relations competence** by encouraging organizations to adopt sustainability strategies and by engaging potential technology adopters with community-based social marketing programs.

Integrating a *panarchy* with the MLP sustainability transitions framework **allows sustainability professionals to view sustainability as an ongoing and continuous process** while identifying Acceleration Points when strategies and instruments could amplify or accelerate sustainable behavior and practices into radical changes that can restructure and realign the regime subsystems. It also provides insight into **how change is created as part of sustainability transitions and resilience is maintained as part of adaptive governance** within the same socio-technical system. Figure 11.1 represents an energy socio-technical system and highlights institutions and infrastructure as the two most critical regime subsystems for sustainability transitions. Each regime subsystem (institutions, infrastructure, economic, industry, political, policy, social, culture, science) is constantly progressing through phases of a complex adaptive cycle. Taken together, the regime subsystems are pulsating, converging or diverging depending on landscape pressures, the stage at which each subsystem's cycle is at, the preferences of regime and niche actors, and the timing of sustainable niche experiments.

The role of sustainability intermediaries is highlighted in Figure 11.1 as a connecting agent that can identify, accelerate, and coordinate sustainable niche experiments during a window of opportunity for institutional and infrastructure change when the regime subsystems are converging. While it is unlikely that all subsystems would converge and align at the same time, sustainability professionals can use their **integrated sustainability research and problem-solving competence** to anticipate trends in the subsystems and adjust strategies and instruments accordingly to capitalize on, and in some cases, create windows of opportunity. Conceiving a sustainability transition as a panarchy implies that success relates as much to the perseverance of the actors involved as it does to the level of technology development or the policy and economic trends at any particular time. **Systems thinking** and **anticipatory competences** can help to develop a new generation of strong sustainability pathways with permutations related to the roles and functions of sustainability professionals as intermediaries, who are trained to intervene, guide, and accelerate change based on their **normative competence** towards sustainability principles.

The complexity of sustainability problems becomes even more evident when considering that Figure 11.1 represents an **energy** socio-technical system. This system is connected to ongoing changes in other socio-technical systems including **food** and **water**. Numerous *niche-to-niche* and *regime-to-regime* interactions exist between agriculture and food production, energy technology and infrastructure, and water governance and

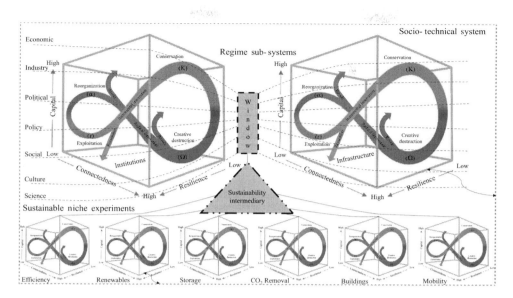

Figure 11.1 Sustainability as an ongoing process of change to institutions, infrastructure, and technologies

Source: Authors' rendition – complex adaptive cycle three-dimensional figure adapted from Holling and Gunderson (2002, p. 41).

conservation practices, which are represented by the two black arrows that leave and enter Figure 11.1. Sustainability professionals can identify and monitor those interactions as part of a food–energy–water nexus. By focusing on complementarities in objectives, capabilities, and socio-technical system processes, sustainability professionals can build a broad and formidable coalition for driving and supporting changes to institutions, infra-structure, and technologies that includes actors from multiple industries and places.

Example cases from around the world were used throughout the book to show how sustainability value has been created as part of transition efforts led by sustainability profes-sionals from different sectors, industries, and groups in society. Challenges to sustainability were discussed as regime bottlenecks, which have slowed down or stopped efforts to mini-mize environmental harms and maximize sustainability value in many countries, states/provinces, cities, and communities. Overcoming bottlenecks can be accomplished with the help of seedbeds, integrated metrics, acceleration points, and sustainability-oriented intermediaries. Seedbeds offer hope that sustainability principles can be improved and that strong sustainability pathways can be followed. Adopting integrated metrics for measuring progress towards a sustainability transition between each stage in the solutions-oriented sustainability transitions framework can change the incentive structure by which individu-als and organizations make decisions, leading to sustainable behavior and social practices, as well as new strategies and different types of investments. Tips to jump-start a transi-tion described as Acceleration Points show sustainability professionals where to focus their efforts to help move society towards a strong sustainability pathway. Sustainability-oriented intermediaries provide a mechanism for sustainability professionals to encourage changes from the niche to the regime, as well as from regime subsystems to niche experiments.

Sustainability professionals

Sustainability professionals exist in every country. They can work or volunteer for organizations from any field or sector in society, and can range from concerned citizens to planners, lawyers, and CEOs. Sustainability professionals share a common goal to reduce environmental harms while establishing a just and thriving society. They share a vision for creating change and developing solutions to environment and resource problems. Their background and experiences allow them to create transitions in socio-technical systems. Examining the profiles of board members of the International Society of Sustainability Professionals (ISSP, 2018) highlights the tremendous diversity among sustainability professionals who are researchers, educators, writers, consultants, managers, coordinators, community organizers, scientists, engineers, planners, economic developers, business strategists, and politicians. They have worked for governments, non-profit organizations, businesses, and universities. The common elements are leadership, communication, collaboration, and a passion for change.

Sustainability professionals use different approaches to develop sustainability solutions, which are shaped by unique sets of training and experiences. Take for example Patrick, who is the farm operations director for World Hunger Relief, a 40-acre training farm in Waco, Texas. Patrick combined formal training from degrees in English, horticulture, and international agricultural development, with practical experiences working on farms in Massachusetts, Australia, and New Zealand, as well as serving as an educational program specialist at Purdue University focusing on an international organic weed management project. He currently serves as the vice president of the Texas Organic Farmers and Gardeners Association (TOFGA), and is a representative for non-profit organizations on the Southern Sustainable Agriculture Research and Education (SARE) administrative council. The goal of the SARE program is "to support farmers, researchers, and educators as they explore practices that improve stewardship, profitability, and the social and economic health of farm communities" (SARE, 2018). Patrick had an 'agricultural conversion' after earning his English literature degree when he began volunteering at Heifer International's educational farm in Massachusetts. Patrick was amazed by their farming techniques that integrated multiple elements to create a thriving system of livestock, plants, and humans. As the farm director at World Hunger Relief, Patrick helps prepare individuals for practicing sustainable agriculture both in developed and developing countries. As Patrick points out, one unique aspect of teaching sustainable agriculture is the importance of the social element because we are all part of these systems. The goal of World Hunger Relief is to refine agricultural systems as part of a learning laboratory for sustainability where new practices represent sustainability experiments.

Figure 11.2 shows other careers of sustainability professionals from **civil society** including non-profit organizations, **government and governance institutions**, small and large **businesses**, **integrated organizations** focused on innovation and technology development processes, and **transdisciplinary researchers** focused on sustainability. The outermost sub-categories of sustainability professionals require different combinations of sustainability skills, training, and competencies. The innermost main categories necessitate sustainability competencies in addition to being highly capable communicators, coalition builders, network navigators, and support mobilizers. These sustainability professionals have a special responsibility for enabling connections between other sustainability professionals within each category as well as between the sub-categories.

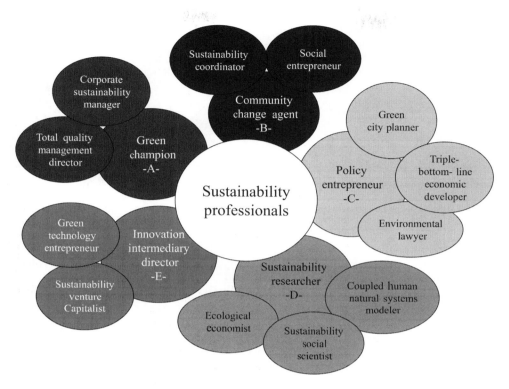

Figure 11.2 Sustainability professionals

Source: Authors' rendition.

Legend: A = small and large businesses; B = civil society including non-profit organizations; C = government and governance institutions; D = transdisciplinary research focused on sustainability; E = integrated organizations focusing on innovation and technology development processes.

Each sub-category of sustainability professionals can benefit from formal and/or informal training and experience. For example, total quality managers can complete courses to become certified in environmental management programs such as Six Sigma, ISO 9001 quality management, ISO 26000 social responsibility, or ISO 50001 energy management. Green technology entrepreneurs may have formal engineering degrees, or they could invent a new product by accident within their garage. Sustainability venture capitalists may have an interdisciplinary green MBA degree, or they may simply see sustainability as an opportunity for achieving a return-on-investment outside of their traditional industry. Coupled human-natural systems modelers may have formal computer science degrees, or they may use ethnography and mental maps to develop a sense of the connections between environmental change and diverse communities. Triple-bottom-line economic developers may have a formal degree in economic development, sustainable development, or economic geography, or they may be community elders working to encourage a more sustainable use of local resources to provide an income for current and future generations. Social entrepreneurs may have a formal business degree, or they may have practice-based experience developing a non-profit organization to help low-income families reduce their energy bills. Although more sustainability degrees and programs are being added at colleges and universities every year, **sustainability professionals are continually reinventing the field and developing solutions to problems as part of their everyday lives. They take initiative and do not wait for others to propose solutions.**

What behaviors and skills characterize a sustainability professional? Knight (2016) conducted a survey of sustainability professionals to create a behavioral competency model for sustainability leaders. Effective sustainability leaders were characterized as **results driven** (action-based with a passion for learning), **visionary thinkers** (inter-disciplinary understanding and strategic outlook), **ethically oriented** (act with integrity and build trust-based relationships), **change agents** (willing to challenge established views), and **inclusive operators** (understands the motivations of others) (Knight, 2016). Specific behavioral competencies that were important to effective sustainability leaders included developing expertise, establishing rapport, articulating information, interacting with people, exploring possibilities, generating ideas, challenging ideas, and understanding people. Two new behavioral competencies were also found to be important for sustainability leaders: impressing people and valuing individuals. Many of these behavioral competencies broaden the conception of the **interpersonal relations competence** described in Chapter 1, including establishing rapport, articulating information, interacting with people, impressing people, understanding people, and valuing individuals. Generating ideas relates to the **normative, anticipatory, and strategic competences**. Developing expertise relates to the **anticipatory, strategic, and systems thinking competencies**. Exploring possibilities and challenging ideas are carried out by the **integrated sustainability research and problem-solving competence**.

The mission of the International Society of Sustainability Professionals includes working to (1) "make sustainability standard practice through empowering professionals to advance sustainability in organizations and communities around the globe" and (2) "improve the skills of sustainability practitioners through ISSP Sustainability Professional Certification, education, knowledge sharing, research, and professional credentials" (ISSP, 2018). The International Society of Sustainability Professionals provides resources and capabilities to support professional development, sustainability professional certification, and the creation of new partnerships and policies to help amplify sustainability value creation. Both individuals and organizations can join the ISSP. It may be tempting to emulate these certified professionals as archetypes for sustainability careers. However, **viewing sustainability as a process that is continually adjusting to new challenges** implies that archetypes for sustainability professionals must also constantly change. The defining characteristic of sustainability professionals is that **they make and remake their profession and careers in the process of devising solutions to new and yet unforeseen problems**.

Universities are perhaps the best-known intermediaries for instigating changes in society. They act as knowledge creators and disseminators. They are able to mobilize tremendous resources to focus on solving problems that could have private economic benefits (e.g., new spin-off technologies that are patented and become entrepreneurial ventures) or public benefits (e.g., medicines, engineering solutions to water problems, cheaper solar technologies that reduce emissions). The roles of universities include teaching, research, technology transfer, and more recently **generating solutions to major societal problems** (Trencher et al., 2013). This shift in role of traditional university functions is important because of the transdisciplinary nature of sustainability, but also challenging because stakeholders in the community have to be convinced of the importance of partnering with students and professors on these projects (Bullock and Wilder, 2016; Frisk and Larson, 2011; Hesselbarth and Schaltegger, 2014; Sonetti et al., 2016;

Urbanski and Leal Filho, 2015). The goal is to find the most effective models for turning sustainability teaching into research, and research into technology transfer and sustainability solutions (Soini et al., 2018). This could involve integrating sustainability into existing departments, or creating new colleges or departments that focus on sustainability from an inter- or trans-disciplinary perspective (Tziganuk and Gliedt, 2017).

After reading this textbook, **you are now able to understand and execute sustainability transitions theory and practice**. As you continue the journey to becoming a change maker, remember the following points:

1   There is no single, universal method or approach for encouraging sustainability transitions;
2   Strong sustainability pathways are part of an ongoing process;
3   Overcoming bottlenecks and creating seedbeds is context specific;
4   Timing is a critical element for achieving change in socio-technical systems;
5   Sustainability transitions are accelerated by competition and/or collaboration between many niche and regime actors;
6   Different strategies, instruments, and metrics can be more effective at some scales than others;
7   Sustainability competencies are important for understanding complex problems and developing and implementing sustainability solutions;
8   The principles and sub-principles as indicators of sustainability need to be tailored to specific regions and places.

As a sustainability professional, you have the opportunity and the responsibility to select and implement changes that you believe are most important to *sustainability principles*. The problem- and project-based learning assignments fostered participation in sustainability solutions by connecting each stage in the solutions-oriented sustainability transitions framework. The assignments allowed you to develop and apply *sustainability competencies* in real world settings. You now have the skills, knowledge, and competencies to encourage sustainable behavior and practices, organizational strategies, technology innovation, triple-bottom-line economic development, and policy and institutional changes that can move society towards *strong sustainability*.

Check on learning

- What characteristics make an effective sustainability leader?
- What skills or training should sustainability professionals have?
- How could a sustainability-oriented intermediary identify a window of opportunity for initiating a transition?
- Do some searching within job databases on the internet and find three jobs that you would categorize as sustainability-oriented. What education, skills, or competencies are required for these jobs?
- Describe in one or two paragraphs why it is important to use problem- and project-based research to address and solve sustainability problems.
- As a sustainability professional, what strategies can you use to maintain objectivity when doing problem- and project-based research that is aiming to make changes in society? Is maintaining objectivity important? Why or why not?

References

Bullock, G., & Wilder, N. (2016). The comprehensiveness of competing higher education sustainability assessments. *International Journal of Sustainability in Higher Education*, 17(3), 282–304.

Frisk, E., & Larson. K. L. (2011). Educating for sustainability: Principles & practices for transformative action. *Journal of Sustainability Education*, 2, 1–20.

Hesselbarth, C., & Schaltegger, S. (2014). Educating change agents for sustainability: Learnings from the first sustainability management master of business administration. *Journal of Cleaner Production*, 62, 24–36.

Holling, C. S., & Gunderson, L. H. (2002). Resilience and adaptive cycles. In: Gunderson, L. H., & Holling, C. S. (Eds). *Panarchy: Understanding Transformations in Human and Natural Systems.* pp. 25–62. Island Press, Washington DC.

ISSP. (2018). A future where sustainability is standard practice. International Society of Sustainability Professionals. Available at: www.sustainabilityprofessionals.org/about-issp

Knight, B. (2016). A behavioral competency model for sustainability leaders. University of Cambridge. Available at: www.sustainabilityprofessionals.org/sites/default/files/ERN003_Full_160208.pdf

SARE. (2018). Southern Sustainable Agriculture Research and Education Program. Available at: www.southernsare.org/About-Us

Soini, K., Jurgilevich, A., Pietikäinen, J., & Korhonen-Kurki, K. (2018). Universities responding to the call for sustainability: A typology of sustainability centers. *Journal of Cleaner Production*, 170, 1423–1432.

Sonetti, G., Lombardi, P., & Chelleri, L. (2016). True green and sustainable university campuses? Toward a clusters approach. *Sustainability*, 8(1), 83.

Trencher, G., Yarime, M., McCormick, K. B., Doll, C. N., & Kraines, S. B. (2013). Beyond the third mission: Exploring the emerging university function of co-creation for sustainability. *Science and Public Policy*, 41(2), 151–179.

Tziganuk, A., & Gliedt, T. (2017). Comparing faculty perceptions of sustainability teaching at two US universities. *International Journal of Sustainability in Higher Education*, 18(7), 1191–1211.

Urbanski, M., & Leal Filho, W. (2015). Measuring sustainability at universities by means of the Sustainability Tracking, Assessment and Rating System (STARS): Early findings from STARS data. *Environment, Development and Sustainability*, 17(2), 209–220.

World Hunger Relief. (2018). Nourishing people, communities, and the land. World Hunger Relief. Available at: www.worldhungerrelief.org/#home

Index